David P. Werlich

PERU

A Short History

Southern Illinois University Press

CARBONDALE AND EDWARDSVILLE

Feffer & Simons, Inc.

LONDON AND AMSTERDAM

Library of Congress Cataloging in Publication Data

Werlich, David P 1941-
  Peru: a short history.

  Bibliography: p.
  Includes index.
  1. Peru—History—1829-   I. Title.
F3446.5.W47   985'.06   77-17107
ISBN 0-8093-0830-4

For Don Beatty

❧ CONTENTS ❧

❦ List of Maps ❧

❧ PREFACE ☙

A CYNICAL but serviceable definition characterizes the historian as a person who complicates the simple and simplifies the complex. To help ourselves and others better understand the past, and perhaps the present, we employ details to challenge faulty generalizations that distort the complicated interactions of persons, ideas, and things we call "events." Conversely, historians "interpret" the past—create new generalizations—to make it more meaningful. The results of our efforts are always imperfect.

Some of the imperfections in this volume result from my decision to stress the republican period, especially the twentieth century. The early history of Peru has been compressed to emphasize those developments that I believe are more important to an understanding of the contemporary era. In simplifying the complex some fascinating stories were eliminated and a few significant topics, especially those adequately treated elsewhere, were reduced to their essentials. I have complicated the simple primarily to question generalizations about modern Peru. The academic graveyard is strewn with the reputations of historians who strayed too close to the present, thus losing their objectivity. Nevertheless, I have devoted a long chapter to the important developments that occurred after 1968. My conclusions about the very fluid "Peruvian Revolution," of course, are tentative.

This book is intended primarily as an introduction to Peru for the student and general reader. However, it also may be useful in providing historical background for Peruvian specialists in other disciplines and as a reference for historians whose major interests lie outside of Peru. Specialists in Peruvian history will take exception to some of my observations. I welcome opportunities to be corrected in my errors of fact and interpretation.

Authors of historical surveys owe a special debt to scholars who supplied the monographs from which their syntheses are fashioned and to those writers whose earlier general histories stimulated further analysis. Space limitations restricted my use of footnotes. Therefore, it is hoped that many of the scholars whose works I have employed will find their names in the bibliographical essay and recognize, without too much consternation, the uses I have made of their research in the text. Many other persons directly assisted me in the preparation of this volume and have my sincere gratitude. Professor Robert L. Gold read the entire manuscript and made many valuable suggestions. Several other colleagues, too numerous to mention, along with students in my Andean history course served as sounding boards for my ideas. William Tuggle, Steven Reichert, and L. David Norris aided in research work. Lorie Zaleskas helped with the typing. Barbara Long prepared the maps. The librarians of the Social Science Division of the Morris Library at Southern Illinois University were most generous with their time and expertise. The Office of Research and Projects at Southern Illinois University at Carbondale provided financial assistance. David, Thomas, and Susan Werlich suffered their father's preoccupation with this project. Finally, this book could not have been completed without the cooperation and encouragement of my wife, Sandra.

David P. Werlich

Carbondale, Illinois
January 1, 1977

PERU

1

Peru: A Portrait

✿ The Land

THE REPUBLIC OF PERU, on South America's Pacific coast, has suffered major territorial loses at the hands of cartographers. To show the dominant northern hemisphere in greater detail, maps commonly drawn for European and North American audiences reduce the relative size of nations lying south of the equator. Although it is only the fourth largest country of Latin America (ranking after Brazil, Argentina and Mexico), Peru's half-million square miles are equivalent to the combined area of France, Spain, and the United Kingdom. Superimposed upon the heartland of the United States, Peru would cover almost all of Minnesota, Wisconsin, Iowa, Illinois, Ohio, Indiana, and Missouri. Nature used Peru to exhibit its flair for extravagance. Great extremes in physiography and climate provide a wide range of environments for a tremendous variety of living things. Unfortunately, the land that has given a wealth of information to natural scientists and delight to the eyes of foreign tourists yields only a meager subsistence to most of its sixteen million inhabitants.

Peru has three major regions—the Sierra, the Montaña, and the Costa. The Sierra, or Andean highlands, is the mountainous backbone of the nation. This rugged area includes about a quar-

1

ter of the country's territory and has more than half of Peru's population. Only about 60 miles wide at its narrowest point, near the northern border with Ecuador, the mountainous zone broadens to about 200 miles at the Bolivian frontier in the south. The Andes have a complex geomorphology. In general, three parallel ranges form a northwest to southeast axis in line with the coast. The Western Cordillera, an unbroken wall, faces the Pacific. The so-called Central and Eastern cordilleras are actually disconnected chains. Some ranges defy this north-south pattern and intersect the other cordilleras to form mountain "knots." From the standpoint of scarce agricultural land, the most important surfaces within the Sierra are the high plains and gentler slopes usually located between 9,000 and 15,000 feet. Called *punas* or *altiplanos,* these areas normally have thin, stony soils that sometime give way to barren rock or even sterile salt flats. Deep canyons, some plunging to less than 3,000 feet above sea level, dissect the highlands. The rivers found in these valleys frequently have cut narrow terraces that are cultivated intensively. Massive, awe-inspiring mountains tower above the *puna.* Many of their snow-capped peaks stand 18,000 feet above the Pacific and a dozen surpass 21,000 feet in elevation.

The climate of the Sierra matches the complexity of its landforms, but can be characterized as cool and dry. Because of its location near the equator, the region has little variation in average monthly temperature—only seven degrees between the warmest and coldest months. At the high elevation of the Andes, however, great fluctuations in temperature occur almost every day. Warmed by the sun to over seventy degrees, the air can cool to below freezing at night. The rainfall pattern of the Sierra also is extremely variable and unpredictable. The northern portion of the area generally receives the most moisture, with the north- and east-facing slopes being the wettest. Small irrigation systems provide water in some districts, but most Andean farmers are precariously dependent upon rainfall. Periodic droughts, sometimes continuing for several years, parch areas that normally have adequate precipitation. Conversely, cloudbursts wash away crops and bring disastrous mudslides and flash floods. Although forests covered large portions of the highlands in prehistoric times, today significant woodlands are found only where the Amazon jungle ascends the slopes of the easternmost ranges. For most of the region the characteristic vegetation is widely spaced bunches of coarse grass and cactus.

2

Because of the great diversity of elevation and climate, the Sierra produces a wide range of crops. Farmers cultivate bananas, citrus fruits, sugarcane, and other tropical plants in the deep valleys. Maize, wheat, barley, and a few hardy cereals found only in the Andes can be grown at heights of up to 13,000 feet. The potato originated in the Andean area and countless varieties are produced in fields lying as high as 14,000 feet, the upper limit for agriculture. Between this point and the permanent snow line (15,000 to 17,000 feet), the land supports livestock. In addition to the common domesticated animals of the Old World, Peru has its native llama and alpaca.

Most Serranos, as the common people of the highlands are called, gain their livelihood from agriculture and stock raising. The region's mining industry, however, plays a far more important role in the national economy. Peru's mountains contain vast amounts of copper and significant quantities of lead, zinc, silver, gold, vanadium, and bismuth. Under Peruvian law the state owns all subsoil minerals, but foreign companies have worked most of the mines through concessions obtained from the government. Semi-isolated enclaves, these operations have had limited effect on the surrounding regional economies. The workers often live in company towns and shop at company stores for goods produced outside of the area. The minerals themselves are extracted primarily for export. For centuries the Cerro de Pasco district, in the central highlands, accounted for the bulk of the nation's mineral production. But after 1960, this zone lost its preeminence to the region around Toquepala, on the western edge of the southern Sierra, which boasts the world's largest open-pit copper mines.

Transportation always has been a major problem in the Sierra. Rugged terrain makes the construction of modern roads and railroads very difficult and expensive. Once built, these arteries often are blocked by avalanches and washouts, or destroyed by Peru's frequent earthquakes. Traveling can be hazardous even when the roads are in good repair. Most of the passes through the cordilleras are over 14,000 feet high and unacclimatized persons often succumb to *soroche*. This "mountain sickness"—actually, the effects of insufficient oxygen and rapidly reduced air pressure—produces severe headaches, vomiting, and has been fatal on a few occasions. Today, wealthier travelers carry bottled oxygen in their cars or, better, make use of the country's relatively good system of air transportation.

3

Fortunately, the Andean natives are physiologically adapted to the rarified atmosphere; the enlarged lungs within their thick chests make efficient use of the limited supply of oxygen. They continue to carry much of their produce to market on their own backs or those of surefooted llamas over crude mountain trails.

Because of the broken topography and the limited amount of arable land, most residents of the Sierra live in dispersed farmsteads or small isolated hamlets. Nevertheless, large concentrations of rural population are clustered in some of the broader valleys and intermontane basins. The most notable of these is the Lake Titicaca Basin, in the far south, where the cordilleras bifurcate to enclose an extensive *altiplano*. The lake itself, which Peru shares with Bolivia, stands at 12,500 feet and covers nearly 3,500 square miles. Unfortunately, this beautiful body of water has become badly polluted in recent years and its once abundant fish have declined greatly in number. Although the Sierra is overwhelmingly rural, the region has three large cities. The southern commercial center of Arequipa has about 200,000 residents and for many years was the second largest city in Peru. The ancient Inca capital of Cuzco, northeast of Arequipa, today has some 100,000 inhabitants as does the rapidly growing city of Huancayo in the central Sierra. A half-dozen other urban centers in the highlands have populations of about 25,000 persons.

Almost two-thirds of Peru's land surface lies east of the Andes in the Amazon Basin, a region called the Montaña. This vast area has two main subregions: the forested oriental slopes of the easternmost cordilleras, known as the Ceja de la Montaña (literally, the "eyebrow of the forest") and the lowland Montaña Baja, with its dense tropical rain forest and broad, winding rivers. The Montaña provides a home for slightly more than one-tenth of Peru's population, including perhaps 150,000 tribal Indians. In recent decades the land-hungry nation has made increased efforts to colonize and develop this relatively empty region. Amazonian Peru, however, presents many serious obstacles to human settlement. First, the area is isolated from the rest of the country by the rugged Ceja de la Montaña, where mountain walls, torrential rains, raging rivers, and exuberant vegetation combine to form the nation's most formidable barrier to transportation. Furthermore, high temperatures and humidity, insects and other pests, and the diseases which thrive under these conditions make many parts of the area unattractive. Finally, the

4

COLOMBIA

ECUADOR

R. Napo

R. Putumayo

R. Pastaza

R. Iquitos

R. Amazon

Tigre

R. Marañón

BRAZIL

Ucayali

Cajamarca

Trujillo

R.

Cerro de
Pasco

Lima

Madre de Dios

Puerto
Maldonado

Chincha
Islands

Cuzco

BOLIVIA

Peru:
Physical
Features

L. Titicaca

Arequipa

Pacific

Ocean

0   100   200   300

CHILE

5

lush vegetation of the jungle belies the fact that the soils of most of the region cannot support permanent cultivation, at least at present levels of technology. A few zones within the Montaña, particularly some of the sheltered western valleys, do have considerable potential for agriculture, but their successful development will require substantial investment.

Settlement within the Montaña is concentrated along the few roads that penetrate the region from the west and on the banks of the rivers which are the principal avenues of transportation in the lowlands. Of the countless streams that traverse the Montaña, the Marañón is the most important, draining the northern two-thirds of eastern Peru. Rising high in the central Andes, this river flows northward through a deep valley until it nears the Ecuadorian border. Then it turns abruptly eastward, bursts through the last mountain barrier to the plains below and continues its journey to the Atlantic Ocean. The Río Huallaga gathers the waters of a long valley at the eastern base of the Andes and joins the Marañón from the south, as does the Ucayali River farther to the east. According to Peruvian usage, the Marañón becomes the mighty Amazon after receiving the flow of the Ucayali. Downstream from this point, the city of Iquitos stands upon the north bank of the river. With nearly 100,000 people, it is the political capital and commercial center of the huge Department of Loreto which encompasses the northern two-thirds of the lowlands. Although it is 2,300 miles from the mouth of the Amazon, Iquitos regularly receives visits from large ocean-going ships. Smaller steamers ply the thousands of miles of other navigable waterways in eastern Peru. Pucallpa, the second largest city of the Montaña with more than 50,000 residents, is located on the west bank of the navigable Ucayali, at the terminus of a highway from Lima.

The economy of eastern Peru traditionally has rested upon subsistence agriculture and the gathering of forest products, most notably wild rubber which brought a brief economic boom to the region around the turn of the twentieth century. In more recent times, the construction of motor roads linking the Montaña with the markets to the west has given impetus to some commerical agriculture and lumbering. This last industry is not so lucrative as it might seem. Only a few of the hundreds of species of trees found in the forest have established markets. These do not grow in large stands, but are scattered throughout the jungle. For a half century geologists have known that petroleum underlies much of the Montaña and a few producing wells were opened as early as 1938. But the Amazon had a limited market for oil and the deposits did not seem large enough to warrant the high cost of transporting the petroleum outside of the region. In the late 1960s, a gigantic oil field was discovered in eastern Ecuador and geologists soon determined that this rich deposit extended southward into northeastern Peru. While a score of companies drilled exploratory wells, the government began construction of a pipeline to carry the petroleum from the Amazon over the Andes to the Pacific coast.

One-third of Peru's population occupies only 11 percent of the national territory—the Costa or coastal lowland that fronts the Pacific Ocean for 1,200 miles from Ecuador southward to Chile. About 125 miles across at its broadest point in the far north, this zone rapidly narrows toward the south. Mountain spurs interrupt the lowland at several points and reach the sea in some places. Most of the region is not a true plain. Broken terrain separates the relatively small areas of flatland and sand dunes move relentlessly across many level surfaces. Along the southern third of the coast a string of hills borders the Pacific, enclosing a trough of largely barren rock between the Andes and the ocean.

Peru's coastal farmers, unlike those in the Sierra, do not worry about rain—it almost never falls. Lima receives an average of slightly more than one inch of precipitation per year. Some other coastal towns do not record moisture for several years at a time. Deserts cover the west coasts of all continents between about 10 and 30 degrees latitude and Peru is no exception. But the extreme aridity of its coast is due to the presence of the Humboldt Current offshore. This 200-mile wide oceanic stream is very cold. When warm, moisture-laden winds from the central Pacific cross this frigid water, the air becomes stabilized. Heavy clouds block the sunlight and make average temperatures on the Peruvian coast about 10 degrees cooler than comparable points along the Atlantic shore of the continent. Dense fogs develop, but it does not rain. The little moisture begrudgingly yielded by the atmosphere comes in the form of dew, called *garua*. On coastal hills and the lower Andean slopes, where condensation is heaviest, a low vegetation of bright green leaves and colorful flowers appears intermittently. Except for these isolated patches of verdure, almost the entire Peruvian coast would be a lifeless wilderness if it were not for the rivers that cross the region.

7

Some fifty streams carry water from the Andes to the Costa. Only about a dozen of these flow throughout the year, but the rivers and thousands of supplementary wells provide water to irrigate 1.7 million acres of land distributed among forty oases. Large plantations—many of them very modern, heavily capitalized "factories in the field"—produce foodstuffs and fiber for the domestic market and large surpluses for export. The northern oases, Peru's biggest and richest, specialize in the production of sugarcane and long-staple cotton, two of the nation's leading exports. The bulk of the country's large rice crop, most of which is consumed domestically, also comes from the north. Near Lima, on the central coast, much of the land is devoted to dairy and truck farming. The smaller southern oases specialize in cotton, olive, and grape cultivation.

Marine life abounds in the cold water of the Humboldt Current. Although tuna, bonita, and other large fish are plentiful, the humble anchovy is most important to Peru. These tiny fish feed millions of aquatic birds whose excrement, guano, is an excellent fertilizer. Exports of this material made Peru the most important trading nation of South America during the middle decades of the nineteenth century. Since 1950, however, the republic has exploited its ocean resources in a more direct manner. Harvesting anchovies to make high-protein fish meal, Peru quickly became the world's foremost fishing nation. The republic vigorously enforces a 200-mile fisheries limit to conserve its valuable marine resources.

The Humboldt Current, like other elements of the Peruvian environment, is not always reliable. At irregular intervals a warm oceanic stream from the north invades the cold water off Peru. Called "El Niño" (literally, "the child") because this phenomenon occurs around Christmas, it wreaks ecological havoc. The anchovies die or seek cooler water. Millions of sea birds starve to death and their decaying bodies foul the air. And only Noah saw such rain! The north coast city of Trujillo received a total of 1.4 inches of precipitation between 1918 and 1925. Then El Niño visited, bringing nine inches of rain in three days and more than twenty-five inches in a month. Houses built to give minimum shelter in this normally mild and arid climate crumbled. Roads and bridges washed away. Floods destroyed crops and irrigation systems and left the fields covered with stones. The recent development of the fishing industry has made El Niño, which last occurred in 1972, an even more costly event.

The Costa has eight of Peru's thirteen cities of more than 50,000 people, including Lima, the capital, with about three million residents. Many of these urban centers stand a few miles back from the ocean and are connected by road and railroad to smaller port cities. The Peruvian coast has few natural harbors. Until well into the twentieth century, most ports were merely shallow, open roadsteads. Deep-draft vessels could not discharge cargo directly onto piers, but were loaded and unloaded by lighters. In recent decades several major ports have been provided with concrete breakwaters and basins, but many small maritime terminals still employ the inefficient lighterage system. Callao, Lima's contiguous port, is the nation's busiest harbor, handling more than half of Peru's foreign commerce.

The small manufacturing sector of Peru's economy is concentrated on the coast, especially in the Lima-Callao area. Businessmen favor this region because of its large urban market, its proximity to supplies of raw materials, and its superior transportation facilities for both internal and foreign commerce. Although Peru has some heavy industry, most of its factories produce light consumer goods—especially processed foods and textiles—for sale within the country, or prepare primary products for export. In addition to its preeminence in commercial agriculture, manufacturing, and fishing, the Costa also is a very important source of minerals. Most of Peru's petroleum comes from the north coast and adjacent offshore fields. The Marcona Mine, the nation's largest iron deposit, is located near the southern port of Ilo. Although some of the ore supplies the government's steel mill at Chimbote, on the coast north of the capital, Peru exports the bulk of this mineral to Japan.

The People and Their Problems

Peru's population of sixteen million persons (1976) has increased dramatically since World War II, primarily because of a sharp drop in the death rate. Average life expectancy jumped from less than thirty-seven to more than fifty-eight years between 1940 and 1970. Meanwhile, the birthrate climbed steadily until the early 1960s, when it began a gradual decline. But this decrease has not been sufficient to offset the continued rapid fall in mortality, particularly among infants. By 1972, almost half of all Peruvians were younger than seventeen years of age. At its

9

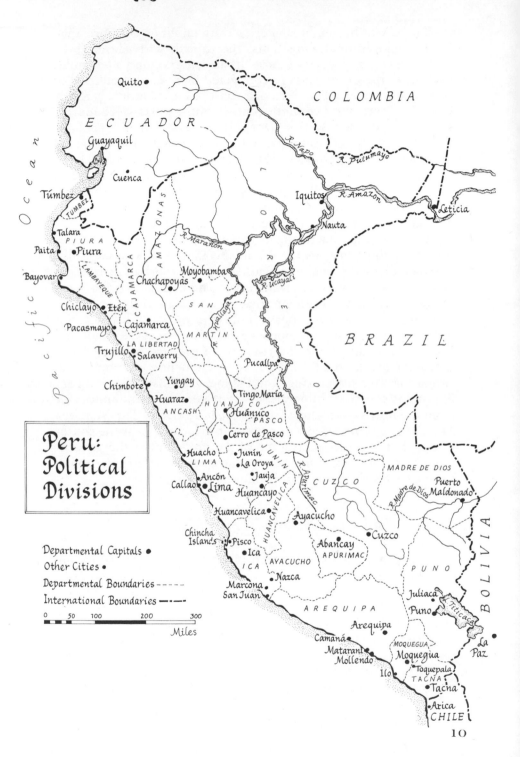

Peru: Political Divisions

Departmental Capitals •
Other Cities •
Departmental Boundaries - - - - -
International Boundaries — · — · —

0   50   100   200   300

Miles

present rate of growth, 2.9 percent annually, Peru's population will nearly double in two decades. The census of 1972 reported that almost 60 percent of the population lived in "urban" areas. However, many of these towns were very small.* Less than one-third of the nation's citizens resided in centers of 20,000 persons or more. Regardless of how it is defined, urban Peru has grown phenomenally in recent years. Between 1940 and 1972, the population of the republic's dozen largest cities quadrupled, a rate of increase four times greater than that for the country as a whole.

Four major groups of the human family have contributed to Peru's population: Amerindians, whites, blacks, and Orientals. The government traditionally described all mixtures of these stocks as "mestizo," although in everyday speech this term usually denoted the European-Indian amalgam most common in the country. Up until a century ago, Negroes were quite numerous, especially in Lima and other coastal areas. Intermixing, however, has nearly eliminated this group as a significant, visible component of the population. Today, blacks and Asiatics (primarily Chinese and Japanese) together account for less than 1 percent of the nation's inhabitants. Except for these two ethnic elements, racial labels are as much social and cultural designations as categories based upon physical features. Boundaries between the groups are imprecise; white merges into mestizo and mestizo into Indian. Ultimately, the racial term applied to an individual depends upon how the person perceives himself and is viewed by others. Peruvian perceptions of race, like beauty, are in the mind of the beholder.

Geography texts used in Peruvian schools sometimes estimated that 10 to 15 percent of the country's inhabitants were "white"—lighter-complexioned members of the upper and middle classes. But in Peru, as in most of Latin America, "money whitens." Many whites have some non-European forebearers and are biological mestizos. Similarly, mestizos and Indians, who comprise at least 85 percent of the population, cannot be differentiated by appearance alone. Some "Indians" have white ancestors; many "mestizos" do not. The criteria defining these two groups are cultural and, increasingly, socioeconomic. In general, mestizos are persons of varying degrees of Indian ancestry who

*The census defined as "urban" towns with more than 100 houses along with all district capitals, no matter how small.

11

are accepted as participants in the dominant, Hispanic culture of the nation. Indians adhere to a different way of life or, at least, are considered by society to have a non-Western view of the world. The Hispanic cultural element—the whites and mestizos—has assigned the indigenous population a subordinate position in society and speaks of Peru's "Indian problem." This vague concept primarily refers to the presence of a large mass of aboriginal people who are not assimilated into the national life. To a lesser extent, it also includes the social and economic backwardness of the natives and the obstacles which this presents to the modernization of the country along Western lines.

Peru's national censuses of 1876 and 1940 recognized the difficulty of identifying persons by physical race. Except for the blacks and Orientals, the population was grouped into two cultural categories—Indian or "white and mestizo." In the 1961 and 1972 censuses, the government did not ask respondents to indicate their race. This omission partially reflected a desire to reduce social distinctions based upon ethnic background. But also, rapid changes in society since 1940 had blurred the cultural line between Indians and mestizos almost beyond recognition.

A number of elements traditionally comprised the native culture complex. All of these did not have to be present to identify the Indian. However, some characteristics, most notably language, were thought to be sure indicators of aboriginal culture. Indians did not speak Spanish. A majority of the natives used Quechua, the official tongue of the Inca Empire. A significant minority, concentrated around Lake Titicaca, spoke Aymará and tribes in the Montaña employed several Amazonian languages and dialects. Spanish was the language of instruction in the public schools. Therefore, Indians by definition were illiterate, a condition that barred them from voting. Indians also were farmers. They usually lived as tenants on haciendas or in their own "indigenous communities." A popular stereotype of the latter, born of both admiration and prejudice, contained several misconceptions and exaggerations. Indian *comunidades* were thought to be largely unchanged since the pre-Columbian era, examples of "timeless Inca socialism." Their laws and customs protected the community from the encroachment of outsiders and supposedly maintained the native culture undisturbed by the influx of new ideas. Members held the lands in common, assisted each other in various tasks, and contributed their labor to public works for the commonweal. Social rank within the community

12

was determined through the participation of its members in a series of civil and religious offices. Individuals acquired great prestige by financing the major religious festival of the village. According to the stereotype, this charge impoverished the sponsor, reduced social distinctions based upon wealth, and dissipated the surplus capital needed for economic development.

Although the Indian most commonly was described by reference to language, occupation, and place of residence, a constellation of other traits completed the picture of native culture. Indians could be recognized by their distinctive clothing, house types, music, medical practices, agricultural methods, religious rituals, and dietary habits, including the use of the narcotic coca. The last item is the delicate leaf of a bush grown in limited areas of optimum soil and climatic conditions in the Andes. Addicts chew the dried leaf with a little lime which releases the alkaloid cocaine. Coca depressess feelings of hunger, fatigue, and frustration—common sensations for many natives. Less tangible elements characterized the Indian ethos and helped distinguish it from the world view of the mestizo. The native had a deeper attachment to his land and animals; placed a higher value on hard, physical labor; had more democratic family relationships than those found in the male-dominated mestizo households; and was more fatalistic. Overawed by the massive mountains and austere plains of the Sierra, the Indian adjusted himself to the environment and did not attempt to conquer it.

Contrary to popular belief, native culture in Peru has changed significantly since the Spanish conquest. Many of the quaint, "distinctively Indian" traditions, in fact, are archaic survivals of European implants that make the native way of life a "cultural museum." By studying the Indians of today, much can be learned about the music, clothing styles, technology, religious rituals, and other practices of sixteenth-, seventeenth-, and eighteenth-century Spain. Many adopted features of native culture are more recent in origin. However, the natives often have blended borrowed elements of Western culture with their own aboriginal practices. The "indigenous communities" also have undergone great transformation since the days of the Incas. Sizable variations in wealth exist in most *comunidades* along with fairly complex social structures based upon wealth. Aboriginal culture, then, has not been immutable. The natives have changed, but often they have done so as Indians—in a manner that continues to set them apart from the rest of society.

While Indian culture, as a whole, retains some distinct

characterisitcs, it has become increasingly difficult to differentiate individual natives from some of their non-Indian neighbors. Many mestizos exhibit, in varying degrees, elements of both Indian material culture and its underlying ethos. In some parts of Peru a man who lives in town, pursues an urban trade, speaks Spanish, and in other ways conforms primarily to the Western pattern of life may be considered an Indian by those around him. In different areas Quechua-speaking farmers who live in legally registered "indigenous communities" and possess many Indian cultural traits may be described as mestizo. The problems of classifying individuals according to culture were illustrated in the 1940 census, the last to provide data on both language and "race." That enumeration placed almost 46 percent of the population within the Indian culture group. About 53 percent of the people were "whites and mestizos." Of the persons responding to questions concerning both "race" and language, about two-thirds of the Indians spoke only a native tongue. Seventeen percent used Spanish as well as a native dialect and an equal number spoke *only* Spanish. Among the whites and mestizos, more than 72 percent were monolingual in the national language. But almost 17 percent also used an Indian tongue and 9 percent spoke *only* an indigenous language. The non-Spanish-speaking "whites and mestizos" were most numerous in the southern highlands, while the phenomenon of the non-Indian-speaking "Indian" long had been observed in the northern Sierra. Today, culture remains the major criterion for distinguishing between Peru's Indians and mestizos as groups. But clearly, the line separating some Indians from some mestizos is highly subjective, more social than cultural.

In many areas of Peru, especially in the Sierra, the nucleus of the white and mestizo classes had been formed early in the colonial period. Immigrants from other parts of the country and abroad augmented these two groups, but local Indians had difficulty acquiring mestizo social status. The dominant classes erected caste barriers to reinforce the cultural wall that originally separated Indian from mestizo. For racially ambiguous mestizos the differences between themselves and the natives, real or imagined, helped to justify the exploitation of their humble neighbors. In some regions the term "Indian" became half of a word: The whites and mestizos invariably referred to the natives as *indiosbrutos*—brute Indians. Highland farmers who periodically worked on the coast frequently lived as mestizos in the lowlands only to revert to Indian social status when they returned home. Natives who persisted in their adopted Western ways often were not accepted by either the Indians or mestizos. Social scientists have described these marginal people as *cholos,* a term that is very old in Peru. In the eighteenth and nineteenth centuries it was a highly derogatory label for a rustic mestizo, a barely Hispanicized Indian. In the twentieth century, however, *cholo* lost some of its pejorative connotations. It became nearly synonymous with mestizo in the common speech of several coastal and some highland districts.

The *cholo* type, in the old sense of transitional mestizo, appeared very early in Peru as individual Indians left agriculture and became town artisans, muleteers, peddlers, and wage laborers. They often learned Spanish and made other adjustments to Western culture. With the economic development of the coast, especially in the second half of the nineteenth century, entire native villages in that region were "cholified." Isolation slowed the process of acculturation in the highlands. But after 1920, the construction of motor roads brought a communications revolution to many Sierra districts. Whole communities, like those on the coast before them, became increasingly Westernized. Mestizo clothing often replaced native garb. Many Indians learned to speak Spanish. Some became literate in the national language and voted. Others continued to use Quechua, but acquired a greater awareness of regional and even national politics. Language became an increasingly unreliable indicator of world view. The tempo of cultural change quickened after 1940. Attempting to atone for past neglect, the government built many schools in the highlands. Additional roads and a bicycle boom further reduced geographical isolation. Organizers from political parties and labor unions, civic action groups, government agents of various kinds, and the inexpensive transistor radio carried the message of modernization to the remotest of villages. The core of the "Indian problem"—the culturally isolated, unassimilated native mass—began to shrink more rapidly.

Language statistics from the last three censuses partially indicate the changes that have occurred in recent decades. In 1940, monolingual Indians comprised 35 percent of the population over four years of age. By 1961, this group's share of the population had fallen to 19 percent; an equal number of Peruvians aged five years and older were bilingual. In 1972, 30 percent of the population over four years old reported a native language as their "mother tongue" (that is, "that spoken in childhood"). However, 61 percent of these people also spoke Spanish and almost half of the native speakers were literate in Spanish. The share of monolingual Indians had declined to 11.7 percent of the total population. In absolute terms, however, the decrease in Indian monolingualism has not been so dramatic. In 1940, about 1,830,000 Peruvians over four years of age spoke only an indigenous language. Thirty-two years later, Peru continued to have 1,383,000 monolingual Indians. As in the past, these people were concentrated in the southern Sierra and isolated enclaves of the central highlands.

Peru has a great territorial expanse and a relatively small number of inhabitants. Nevertheless, the country is badly overcrowded. Almost 40 percent of the population gains its livelihood from agriculture, but less than 3 percent of the nation's surface is suitable for cultivation. Peru's ratio of over 500 rural persons per square mile of arable land is nearly the highest in Latin America and exceeds those for such heralded overpopulated countries as India and China. Although agriculture employs the largest portion of the Peruvian labor force, it contributes less than 15 percent to the national income. Moreover, the country's farms do not adequately supply the population, so scarce foreign exchange must be used to import increasing amounts of foodstuffs. It has been estimated that three-quarters of Peru's farmland is exploited inefficiently, sometimes using a technology that dates back to pre-Columbian times. The adoption of new methods could close the gap between production and population growth, but until 1969, modernization was hampered by tenure and labor systems that in some ways resembled European feudalism of five centuries ago. Not only did this adversely effect the nation's economy, but it also retarded the social development necessary for Peru to achieve a modern, democratic society.

Peru's land-tenure problem could be summarized in two words: latifundia and minifundia. Latifundia were huge estates requiring the labor of many persons. Minifundia were parcels of land that were too small to feed a farmer and his family, or occupy them productively throughout the year. These two phenomena have existed side by side and one within the other in a maze of tenure systems. Peru's agricultural census of 1961 dramatically illustrated the great disparity in land distribution. More than 83 percent of the nation's farms occupied only 5.5

percent of the land and in parcels of less than 12.5 acres. Almost 300,000 farms—about one-third of the total—were smaller than 2.5 acres. At the other extreme, four-tenths of one percent of the agricultural units controlled more than three-quarters of the land and in holdings larger than 1,250 acres. More than 60 percent of the land was held by some 1,100 estates which exceeded 42,000 acres in size. Less than one-eighth of the units, occupying less than 5 percent of the land, were considered "family-sized" farms.

The latifundia-minifundia dichotomy was common throughout Peru in 1961, but great regional variations existed in the use of the land and the socioeconomic status of the labor force. The Sierra, where the vast majority of the farmers lived, was the most backward zone. Here, more than four-fifths of the land was held in units averaging over 11,000 acres. The twenty largest estates averaged over 250,000 acres and five of these exceeded an average of 750,000 acres. Most of the Sierra latifundia were traditional haciendas, where the land was worked much as it was centuries ago and a servile master-and-man relationship characterized labor relations. These archaic operations had very small capital investments and held all cash outlays to a bare minimum. The area planted in crops was very limited, much of the land remained fallow for excessive periods and potential cropland often was used for pasture. Although productivity was quite low, the great size of the traditional haciendas provided sufficient income to permit their owners to live comfortably in the departmental capital or Lima, while managers directed day-to-day operations.

Colonos ("colonists") performed most of the labor on the traditional haciendas. In return for the use of a small parcel of marginal land where they built their crude houses and rasied their own food, the *colonos* worked two, three, or even four days each week for the landowner. This labor service included tending hacienda fields and livestock and, especially for the women, periodic stints as domestic servants in the house of the owner or overseer. Because the law required that all workers be paid a cash wage, *colonos* received a token sum. Less than four cents per day was common. These humble farmers often had lived on the same estate generation after generation. Although debt peonage had long been illegal, some workers still were tied to the haciendas by cash advances. Traditionally, *colonos* had been considered part of the estate and bills of sale sometimes listed the number of "hacienda Indians" included when the property changed hands.

No contract protected the very limited benefits provided the *colonos* under this system. They could be evicted from their plots at any time.

Some Sierra estates, especially in regions with easy access to large urban markets, had begun to modernize prior to 1961. These "transitional haciendas" were differentiated from the archaic properties by their greater capital investments and productivity and the employment of larger numbers of wage laborers rather than *colonos*. Most of these were temporary workers, often farmers who owned small plots nearby. Wages were low and these workers did not receive the benefits of national labor legislation. Yet, their social and economic condition was superior to that of the *colonos*. Many transitional haciendas and some traditional estates leased part of their lands to *yanaconas*, renters who compensated the landowner in cash or with a share of the crop. Parcels worked under this system normally were large enough to provide only a subsistence income. But some *yanaconas* rented sufficient land to hire workers, or provide plots to their own *colonos*.

Large haciendas controlled most of the Sierra countryside in 1961. Nevertheless, a sizable majority of the farmers had some form of title to their own lands as small freeholders or members of about 4,500 "indigenous communities." Of the latter, about one-third were registered with the government and received special protection and privileges under the law. Many registered communities, in fact, were mestizo in culture, while true Indian *comunidades* often were unregistered and unprotected. Landholding patterns varied considerably within both kinds of communities. Most often the members *(comuneros)* used the pastures in common, but croplands usually were divided into private parcels. Under national law in the registered communities and by tradition in the others, lands could not be sold to outsiders. However, property frequently changed hands within the community and considerable disparities in landownership existed. Because of these internal transfers and the division of property through inheritance, the typical *comunero* owned several widely separated parcels which often were measured in square yards. The farmer could spend much of his day walking from one minuscule plot to another. Most *comunidades* did not own enough land. A majority probably had less than 2.5 acres of cropland per capita. Frequently the communities rented additional land, especially pasture, from nearby haciendas in exchange for cash, produce and, most commonly, labor service.

18

For many years Peruvian governments resisted pressure for agrarian reform, claiming that the Montaña contained enough vacant land to satisfy the needs of the nation's poor farmers. Ironically, the 1961 census demonstrated that the same pattern of latifundia and minifundia found in the settled portions of the country existed in the eastern forests as well. Vast stretches were relatively empty, but the best farmlands—those with superior soils and adequate transportation links with the outside—already were owned in large blocks. Land use and labor systems resembled those of the traditional hacienda in the southern Montaña, while the more modern, transitional form was common in the central and northern sections of this region.

The archaic, traditional hacienda has not existed on the coast for many years. In 1961, a quarter of the farmlands here were controlled by "modern haciendas," producing sugar and cotton for export. Highly integrated operations, these plantations invested large sums in irrigation systems, farm machinery, fertilizers, processing plants, and sometimes even their own railroad and port facilities. Foreign companies usually owned the largest agro-industrial complexes. Frequently they purchased cotton and sugar from neighboring small farmers and less modern haciendas, or processed and marketed their crops under contract. Permanent wage-workers provided most of the labor on the modern agricultural enterprises. The elite of Peruvian farm workers, they were strongly unionized, protected by labor laws and enjoyed relatively high wages and many fringe benefits. They often lived in company towns which in recent years usually provided modern housing, recreational facilities, good schools, and many other social services. The modern company towns, in fact, often were criticized for a paternalism that retarded the development of a healthy, independent citizenry. Temporary workers, often from the highlands, supplemented the permanent labor force. Although these people were not compensated so well as the regular employees, their wages were three times higher than the prevailing rate in the Sierra.

A majority of the large units of the Costa were transitional haciendas owned primarily by Peruvian nationals. These estates had significant capital investments but not so great as those of the modern properties. In addition to producing sugar and cotton for export, they supplied the domestic market with vegetables, meat, dairy products, rice, and other cereals. Important differences existed between the modern and transitional haciendas of the coast in the realm of labor relations. The latter employed a much larger proportion of temporary workers. The permanent labor force usually was not unionized and labor legislation frequently was evaded. Wages and working conditions were considerably inferior to those of the modern estates but still superior to the standards for the Sierra. The great estates controlled four-fifths of the coastal farmland and employed a significant portion of the agricultural labor force. Yet, a large majority of the region's farmers owned small plots, or rented surplus hacienda land. Over 80 percent of the farm units of the Costa were too small to support a family at an acceptable standard of living.

The uneven distribution of land conformed to a general pattern of inequity that divided Peruvian society into two sectors. One was modern, predominantly urban, and relatively prosperous; the other was archaic, largely rural, and desperately poor. Because of this dichotomy, standard indices of social and economic development using national "averages" actually described a level of living characteristic of very few persons. For example, the average personal income for the entire Peruvian labor force in 1963 was about 650 dollars per year, a meager sum on which to support a family. But 85 percent of the workers did not receive so much as 650 dollars. Sharing slightly more than one-fourth of the national income, the average earnings for this group was about 200 dollars per year. At the other end of the scale, one-fourth of one percent of the economically active population—some 8,760 persons—received 35 percent of the national income, an annual average of more than 82,000 dollars. Between these two extremes was a "middle-income" sector comprising about 14 percent of the population, with salaries spanning the wide gap from about 650 dollars to 7,500 dollars. Sharing 38 percent of the national income, this group had an average annual income of about 1,580 dollars.

Great disparities in wealth and well-being existed in each of Peru's twenty-three departments and in the cities as well as the countryside. The dual structure of society was demonstrated most effectively, however, through statistical comparisons of different regions. As the table illustrates, modern Peru was concentrated in the predominantly urban Department of Lima and the adjacent Constitutional Province of Callao. Archaic Peru was typified by five rural departments in the southern highlands—Apurímac, Ayacucho, Cuzco, Huancavelica, and Puno—where over half of the population still spoke only an

Peru: A Portrait

Indian language. Both of these regions had approximately an equal share of the nation's population in 1961.

A STATISTICAL DESCRIPTION OF TWO PERUS IN THE EARLY 1960s

	LIMA-CALLAO	FIVE INDIAN DEPARTMENTS	TOTAL PERU
Share of national population in percent	22.1	23.2	
Share of national income in percent	42.5	12.6	
Literacy rate in percent	91.8	29.2	60.1
Share of total registered voters in percent	43.3	9.6	
Infant deaths per 1,000 births	68.3	143.5	93.2
Number of doctors	1,754.0	103.0	2,775.0
Percent of houses with electricity	70.7	5.9	26.1
Number of workers included in the social security system	474,245.0	30,414.0	782,897.0

In the last three decades and especially since 1950, many Peruvians have abandoned the backward Sierra to seek a better life in the urban centers of the Costa. The industrial city of Chimbote grew from 4,200 inhabitants in 1940, to 60,000 in 1960, and reached an estimated 210,000 persons a decade later. Other important coastal cities—Ica, Chiclayo, Trujillo and Piura—quadrupled in size during the same period. More than half of the nation's internal migrants went to Lima, which increased from about 500,000 persons in 1940 to 3 million in 1972. At that time two-thirds of the adult residents of the capital were natives of the provinces. For the most part, these newcomers were not the wretched, poorest element of Sierra society, forced from their homes by the scarcity of land. The majority of these migrants were amitious, often literate young adults from provincial towns searching for better jobs for themselves and schools for their children.

This brain-and-brawn drain caused problems for some Sierra communities, but the cities had even greater difficulty absorbing these new urbanites. The government's efforts to provide low-income housing were woefully inadequate, leaving the migrants along with the poor, native city-dwellers to fend for themselves. Their practical solution to the problem of shelter was the *barriadas,* squatter shantytowns that girded all important coastal cities and many regional centers in the Sierra and Montaña. By 1970, *barriadas* housed over 80 percent of Chimbote's swollen population and nearly half of the residents of Greater Lima.

The founding fathers of these marginal neighborhoods exhibited a degree of initiative and efficiency rarely matched in Peru. Typically, a group of inner-city renters organized for the undertaking. After selecting their target, usually a vacant area on the outskirts of town owned by the government or a private real-estate speculator, they prefabricated their houses. Initially, they needed only woven straw mats for the walls and poles to support them; roofs could be added later in the dry climate of the coast. On the appointed night, hired transportation carried the urban pioneers and their materials to the site. By sunrise a settlement of a score to more than one hundred makeshift shelters confronted the landowners. The shanties frequently were topped by little Peruvian flags to make any attempt to remove them seem unpatriotic. In the early days of the *barriada* phenomenon—the first ones appeared around Lima after a destructive earthquake in 1940—the police often evicted the squatters. Later governments, however, accepted these instant urbanizations as unpleasant facts of life.

"Cancerous growths," "open sores" and other unpleasant medical metaphors have been employed to describe the *barriadas.* Indeed, these marginal settlements are crowded, unsanitary, and very ugly. The residents are poor, frequently rather rustic provincials who have difficulty adjusting to life in the big city. But their houses often are no worse than the back-alley hovels that these people have abandoned in the central city. Most importantly, no rent collector appears. For Serranos, life on the whole is at least as good as it was in the highlands and the city provides much more hope for the future. Most *barriadas* are not true "slums"—areas of physical, spiritual, and social deterioration. The government prefers to call them "young towns" *(pueblos jóvenes),* a not entirely euphemistic term. Many residents are upwardly mobile. With the money saved on rent they often improve their houses, slowly transforming the flimsy shacks into more substantial dwellings of wood and adobe. Some have purchased title to their lots. Citizens of the *barriadas* elect their own governing councils which also represent them before the municipal and national authorities. These bodies have had considerable success in obtaining schools and even water and electricity. A few of Lima's older *barriadas* have become stable, working-class neighborhoods with normal city services, including paved streets and sewers.

The *barriadas* brought the problems of underdevelopment literally into the backyard of the modern sector of society. The privileged classes no longer could ignore them. Frequently viewing the sprawling shantytowns as "hotbeds of revolution," governments after 1960 not only attempted to placate the *barriada* residents, but also were spurred to begin long-overdue reform and development programs for the provinces. While the great inequity in socioeconomic rewards persisted between the city and the countryside, the Costa and Sierra, the flood of internal migrants threatened to inundate Lima and other urban centers. It was feared that if these newcomers did not find the better life they sought, the *pueblos jóvenes* would become "quarters of despair" and foci of political unrest.

The rush to the cities of Europe and the United States, which began about a century ago, was accompanied by rapid industrialization. This has not occurred in Peru and most other nations of the contemporary Third World which are becoming urbanized at an even quicker pace. Although the manufacturing sector of the Peruvian economy has expanded notably since World War II, it does not provide nearly enough jobs for the more than 150,000 persons who enter the labor force each year. These people cannot be absorbed productively by agriculture, an activity already beyond the point of saturation. Until recently, unemployment statistics for Peru were not alarming; the official rate of joblessness for the Lima-Callao area was under 4 percent during the early 1970s. But over one-fourth of the workers in the capital and more than a third of the labor force in other major cities were underemployed. These people earned a precarious living by menial, relatively unproductive activities in the swollen "service" sector of the economy.

Many of Peru's workers lacked the basic skills needed by modern industry. The census of 1961 reported that 60 percent of the population could read and write, but the quality of literacy was very poor. Fewer than 43 percent of all Peruvians older than four years of age had completed a year or more of primary school. Less than 8 percent of the population had attended a secondary school and only 1.5 percent received some higher education. In the late 1960s, more than 85 percent of the nation's children enrolled in the first grade, but almost half of these did not return for the second year. Although most children had access to some public education, the schools in many small towns did not provide instruction beyond the third grade. As late as the mid 1960s, more than half of the primary-school teachers had no formal pedagogical training; barely one-third had graduated from accredited normal schools. The education system responded poorly to the needs of most Peruvians and the country's requirements for economic development. The schools stressed the traditional, humanistic curriculum rather than vocational instruction. Training at the nation's public trade schools was notoriously deficient. The universities produced a superfluity of lawyers and men of letters but few engineers and business managers.

For many years Peruvians have complained that their country does not control·its own destiny, that the nation suffers from "economic imperialism." The modern sector of the economy, the hope for the future, has been highly dependent upon foreign markets, capital, and technology. International commerce provides about a quarter of the republic's gross national product and is the dynamic force in the economy as a whole. Nevertheless, Peru has been more fortunate than some of its neighbors who rely precariously upon a single product for the bulk of their export earnings. A sharp drop in the price of Chile's copper, Bolivia's tin, or Colombia's coffee produces severe economic problems in those countries. Because of the remarkable growth of Peru's fishing and copper industries, those two sectors combined earned 50 to 60 percent of the country's foreign exchange during the 1960s. But iron ore, silver, sugar, cotton, zinc, coffee, and lead continued to play important roles in Peru's international trade. Although their country does not have a classic "one-crop economy," at the mercy of international supply and demand, many Peruvians believe that they have a fundamental disadvantage in their commercial relations with the more developed world. Experience seems to indicate that over the long run, the prices of primary products—the agricultural and mineral raw materials traditionally exported by Latin America—do not keep pace with the cost of the finished goods supplied by the industrialized nations. Although challenged by many economists, this theory of Latin America's "unfavorable terms of trade" can be appreciated by North American farmers. It is analogous to the "cost-price squeeze" of which they complain when demanding "parity" of prices between agricultural and manufactured products.

Prior to 1968, foreign companies produced or marketed most of Peru's trade items. Giant North American firms mined nearly all of the nation's metalic minerals, processed and exported the bulk of its cotton, and marketed much of Peru's surplus sugar. Even the relatively new fish products industry, initially developed by native entrepreneurs, became increasingly penetrated by foreigners. Hoping to achieve greater self-sufficiency, ease the problem of unfavorable terms of trade, and provide jobs for the expanding labor force, the Peruvian government encouraged the growth of manufacturing. But here too, imported capital and technology played a key role. Most of the larger, modern factories were subsidiaries of non-Peruvian companies. Outside of manufacturing and the export industries, the list of activities controlled from abroad included most of the nation's railroads, more than 80 percent of the petroleum industry, the major telephone companies, and the largest suppliers of electricity. Foreign capital also held a powerful position in Peru's banking system. Estimates of the degree of foreign control over the economy varied widely—from 5 to 80 percent depending upon the source and the definitions employed. Whatever the correct figure, outside investment was very conspicuous in the country's most dynamic enterprises. Adding the words *del Perú* to IBM, Toyota, and Volkswagen did not conceal this fact.

Peruvian nationalists made several accusations against foreign companies. The mining firms, they asserted, removed exhaustible resources from the country without adequate compensation to Peru. They charged that alien enterprises often reaped excessive profits which were remitted to stockholders overseas and that these outflows actually exceeded the amount of new investment from abroad. Thus, the country was being "decapitalized." Many foreign companies were parts of giant multinational conglomerates. Some of these had annual sales throughout the world that exceeded Peru's gross national product. This great economic power, according to the critics, had been used to corrupt Peruvian politics and undermine the nation's sovereignty.

The preponderance of North American investment compounded the threat to Peru's independence. In 1970, more than 300 United States firms operated in Peru. With a book value of 700 million dollars, these holdings accounted for about two-thirds of the direct foreign investment in the country. North American companies had received considerable support from Washington during their disputes with the Peruvian government. As Peru's principal commercial partner, the United States could significantly effect that nation's economy through its tariffs, import quotas, and other trade controls. Moreover, grants and loans from the United States government and international agencies controlled by Washington provided much of the capital required for the development programs of the Peruvian government. The United States employed this leverage to assist its investors and exerted economic pressure to influence other aspects of Peru's national policy.

During the 1960s many of the earlier, largely disconnected observations concerning the economic relationship of Latin America to the outside world were brought together in a coherent, general schema known as the "dependency theory." Although highly controversial, this concept has been adopted in different degrees by many scholars of both Marxist and non-Marxist orientation. Dependency analysis became very influential in the formulation of government policy in Peru and some other countries of Latin America. Simply stated, dependency theorists believe that the developed and underdeveloped nations are linked in mutually dependent economic relationships. But the wealthier countries—the "center" or "metropoles"—have great advantages in their dealings with the poorer nations, the "periphery." Development and underdevelopment, furthermore, are not two distinct phenomena, but are different ends of the same continuum. The center has been enriched by impoverishing the periphery.

According to the dependency interpretation, Peru entered the Western, capitalist world as the "periphery" of the Spanish "center." The nation then became subject to British economic domination and finally to that of the United States. The chain of dependency that began in Madrid, London, or Washington did end in the Peruvian capital. The elites in Lima assisted in the foreign exploitation of their country and themselves profited from it. Their ties to the overseas metropoles reinforced the dominant, exploitative position which Lima enjoyed with its own periphery in the provinces. This pattern was repeated at the local level, ensnaring all Peruvians in the web of dependency. Thus, Peru's dependent relationship with the center shaped the basic structure of its economy. For many dependency theorists, it also helps to explain the evolution of the country's politics, society, culture and, ultimately, its entire history. Advocates of the dependency concept disagree about whether the center-periphery relationship "influences," "conditions," or "determines" the course of events and what governments can and should do about it.

Peru officially has embraced republican government for a century and a half, but political democracy has not worked well in this undemocratic society. The nation's sixteen constitutions have been honored most often in the breach. Revolutions have been more common than elections and few of the latter have been free of fraud or coercion. Because illiteracy long barred the majority of adults from the electoral process, republican institutions, when operative, meant unrepresentative government at best. Liberties cherished in modern democracies have had little meaning for the Peruvian masses. Freedom of the press has not seemed important to those who cannot read or afford a newspaper. Free speech has not been valued by Indians who do not understand the national language and are unaware of important public issues. For most Peruvians economic freedom has meant the liberty to live a life of poverty. Understandably, many of the nation's people have been willing to foresake republican government for authoritarian regimes that promise social justice rather than political liberty. But more often than not, dictatorship has benefited the few at the expense of the many.

2

A Heritage of Conquest: First Incas, Then Spaniards

THE SPANISH INVADERS WHO TOPPLED the Inca Empire in the third decade of the sixteenth century marveled at the advanced civilization of the Andean peoples. Centered on the city of Cuzco in the southern highlands of Peru, the Inca state encompassed more than 300,000 square miles. It extended along the Andes from northern Ecuador to central Chile and from the Pacific Ocean on the west to the fringes of the Amazon Basin and northwestern Argentina on the east. The number of persons governed by the Incas has been a topic of lively debate. Modern estimates range from three to more than thirty million. The author's liberal estimate is eighteen million people with perhaps half of these living within the present boundaries of Peru. Whatever the true number of inhabitants, scholars do agree that the central Andean area was one of the more densely populated regions of pre-Columbian America.

This large population supported itself by an intensive system of agriculture employing a relatively sophisticated technology.

The natives cultivated scores of plants in irrigated fields, some of which were terraces cut in steep mountain slopes, and understood the principles of crop rotation and fertilization. The inventory of domestic animals included the dog, a food item as well as a pet; the guinea pig and Muscovy duck, important sources of meat; and the wool-producing alpaca and its cantankerous cameloid relative the llama, the only beast of burden used by aboriginal Americans. The surplus produced by this economy maintained a sumptuous royal court, a large aristocracy, a sizable religious establishment and thousands of craftsmen and soldiers. Native metallurgists worked with gold, silver, copper, lead, and tin and made the alloys bronze (copper and tin) and *tumbaga* (a gold-copper combination). Indian weavers employed almost every technique known in contemporary Europe plus a few unique to Andean textiles. Knowledge of mathematics, astronomy, and even surgery was quite advanced, and the massive stone structures of Peru reminded the Spaniards of ancient Egypt. For the early European observers, however, the most impressive feature of Andean civilization was the Inca Empire itself. The intellectual achievements of the Maya and the artistic genius of the Aztec surpassed those of the Inca. But of all the Amerindian peoples, the "Lords of Cuzco" were the unrivaled masters of statecraft.

From the time of the first Spanish chroniclers until well into the present century it was generally believed that the Incas had established their empire early in the thirteenth century and that the high civilization that amazed the followers of Pizarro resulted from 300 years of tutelage by the Cuzco imperialists. Indeed, the official court historians of the Incas, the *amautas,* promoted this interpretation to enhance the reputation of their sovereigns. According to these wise men, who were important sources of information for later Spanish historians, the Indians of Peru lived in primitive barbarism prior to the coming of the Incas. The men from Cuzco supposedly taught their backward neighbors the art of agriculture and the other skills admired by the conquistadors. Today we know that these legends exaggerated the antiquity and achievements of the Inca Empire. Peruvian civilization of the sixteenth century, in fact, evolved over thousands of years. The Incas had occupied the Valley of Cuzco at least since the thirteenth century. Until the early fifteenth century, however, their dominion probably did not extend much beyond the immediate environs of their capital. At that time the Incas were only one of hundreds of groups living in the Andean area who shared a common material culture and whose basic social, economic, and political organization was very similar. The languages spoken by these peoples, though linguistically related, were mutually unintelligible. The Incas later gained control over this "co-tradition area," but the different groups within the region already had developed the basic social and economic infrastructure upon which the empire was built.

◆◢ The First Conquerors: Peru Before the Incas

Man has lived in Peru for at least 12,000 years and perhaps for 10,000 years more. A stone-age people, the first Peruvians roamed the country in small bands pursuing game and gathering other foods found in their environment. They were contemporaries of several animals that long have been extinct, including hairy mammoths which were hunted in the river valleys of the north coast. About 4000 B.C., agriculture began on the Peruvian littoral. The idea of cultivating useful plants probably reached Peru from Mexico, but many of the first crops—gourds, beans, squash, peanuts, and cotton—were of local origin. The pace of development quickened with the onset of farming. By 1800 B.C., when pottery made its appearance, the coastal peoples had reached a degree of sophistication that properly can be called "civilization." Maize had become the principal crop of the coast dwellers who also had use of the major domestic animals of the region. Much less is known about the highlands during these early years. Because the climate of this region is not conducive to the preservation of organic matter, the Sierra has attracted less attention from archaeologists than the arid coast. Nevertheless, available information indicates that advancements similar to those on the littoral were being made in the mountains. The Serranos first cultivated the potato, their great staple, probably in the period between 2500 B.C. and 1500 B.C.

Substantial evidence of human settlement in the very humid Montaña dates only from the introduction of durable pottery about 1000 B.C. However, man certainly occupied these forests long before that time. Peruvians living beyond the Andes differed markedly from their neighbors to the west, sharing a culture pattern common to the Amazon Basin. Some groups

were very primitive. Organized in small bands, they lived in
isolated areas between the major streams and sustained themselves solely by hunting and gathering. But along the banks of
the large rivers with their broad floodplains, the land yielded
plentiful crops of manioc (the starchy tuber that was the staff-of-
life in the Amazon) and fish and game were abundant. These
areas supported relatively permanent settlements with hundreds
of persons.

Hunting, fishing, and gathering wild foods continued to be
important components of the highland and coastal economies
after 1800 B.C. But the technological advances of the years that
followed permitted a great increase in population, larger settlements, refinements in the arts, and a more complex social
organization. Metallurgy, the last of the major innovations, appeared between 900 B.C. and 200 B.C. During the next eight
centuries the Peruvians perfected their irrigation technology and
by A.D. 600, handicrafts, engineering and many features of social
organization reached their zeniths. Thus, the more notable
achievements of Andean civilization were present long before
the rise of the Incas and a millennium prior to the Spanish
conquest.

Warfare became very common in Peru after about 200 B.C.,
perhaps as a result of population growth and the need for more
land. The peoples of the coast and southern Sierra built many
large fortified cities. Some of these were capitals of sizable states,
and two may have been centers of vast empires. Between A.D.
600 and A.D. 1000 the ceramic styles and perhaps the political
dominion of Tiahuanaco and Wari spread over large areas. Located on the south shore of Lake Titicaca in modern Bolivia,
Tiahuanaco's sphere of influence encompassed the entire
Titicaca Basin and the coastal region to the west. The city of
Wari, near present-day Ayacucho in the Peruvian Sierra, dominated the Costa and the highlands from the Tiahuanaco zone
northward to near the Ecuadorian border. Following the decline
of these two great centers, regional states again flourished. Several of these existed well into the Incaic period and knowledge of
a few can be found in the written historical record.

The most famous of the pre-Incaic states was the Kingdom of
Chimor or Chimu which included the coastal area from the
Ecuadorian boundary southward for 600 miles. Chanchan, the
Chimu capital whose ruins are near the modern city of Trujillo,
was the largest urban center of ancient Peru. Covering six square

miles, it had a population of at least 50,000 persons and perhaps twice that number. Other powerful kingdoms controlled the coastal region to the south. In the southern highlands the Incas of Cuzco vied for supremacy with the nearby Chancas, while the kingdoms of the Collas and Lupacas dominated the Lake Titicaca area. Archaeologists have described the northern Sierra as the most "democratic" region of ancient Peru because governmental units were smaller and less complicated in their organization. With relatively small and isolated areas of good land, it was difficult to concentrate large numbers of people there. Furthermore, the northern highlands receive more rain than the coast and southern Sierra and had less need for the large irrigation systems associated with considerable state control in other regions of Peru.

The salient characteristics of Andean society existed long before the Inca conquest. Although some large cities existed, the vast majority of Peruvians lived in small agricultural villages. Beyond the nuclear family, the *ayllu* was the basic social unit. Considerable difference of opinion exists concerning the exact nature of the *ayllu;* it seems to have varied from place to place. Nevertheless, it can be defined as a localized group that possessed a common territory called a *marca.* Most pre-Columbian communities consisted of a single *ayllu* and the two terms often have been used synonymously. *Ayllu* members frequently were blood relatives or at least believed that they descended from a common ancestor, usually a mythical demigod. All of the married men of the community held the *marca* in common, but use rights to particular plots could change hands within the *ayllu.* Members usually chose their mates from within the community to avoid foreign encroachment on *marca* lands.

A headman, called a *curaca,* governed the small simple Andean village. In some *ayllus* he may have been the patriarch of a large extended family which comprised the community. The people "elected" their chiefs in a few areas. By the beginning of the Incaic period, however, most *curacas* were hereditary rulers and many were petty tyrants. In most communities no intermediate social classes separated the headman from the common folk. A formal military elite did not exist. All able-bodied males formed a village militia in time of war. Nor was there a class of full-time religious specialists. The shaman was an occasional religious practitioner who devoted most of his time to farming. Slaves and other landless, servile workers were rare in the small communities. The adult males (married men with land rights) were *hatun runa,* "big men" who participated fully in the *ayllu* organization. Through them the women and children were tied to the community.

Each family had rights to some portion of the *marca*—ideally, enough land to support itself. In some *ayllus* an annual redistribution of land took place. Those families that had increased in size got more land; those with decreases received less. In other places the yearly division of the *marca* became only symbolic and each family was assigned the same parcel year after year regardless of changes in its composition. Persons who left the community forfeited their claim to the *marca.* Thus land rights, to some extent, were related to the actual use of the soil. The *ayllu* as a whole possessed all woodlands and pastures in common and regulated the distribution of precious water for irrigation. The community often held in common fields used to grow coca and those planted in maize for making *chicha* beer, two items essential for religious festivals. Llamas and alpacas were owned both privately and communally.

Some agricultural tasks such as planting and harvesting were done communally, but each family usually received the produce of its assigned fields. The lands of widows, orphans, and invalids were worked for their benefit by the other *ayllu* members. The Andean peoples employed a system of reciprocal labor for the construction of houses and similar tasks for the benefit of private parties. The beneficiary provided the workers with food and drink and agreed to assist them in future projects of their own. *Ayllu* members also labored on "public works" for the commonweal. They built terraces and irrigation systems and tended communal fields and flocks. This labor service, called *minka,* was assigned to each household. The lands used by the *curacas* may have been part of the communal *marca,* but frequently they were considered the private property of the headman. In the larger communities the cultivation of these fields became part of the *minka* obligation and the common people often performed other tasks for their chief. They worked as servants in his household, minded his flocks, and made clothing and utensils for him.

Political, economic, and social organization was more complex in the regional states, kingdoms, and empires. Nevertheless, the *ayllu* was the basic building block of these larger structures. An emperor, king, or "super-*curaca*" had dominion over many *ayllus* in these entities. Often an intermediate level of

33

provincial governors existed within the bureaucracy. Village *curacas,* whether the original headmen or chiefs imposed from the outside, administered the *ayllus* at the local level. The larger states, with their much greater populations, had more occupational specialization and rather complicated social structures. Created by conquest, these entities had a military elite and frequently a priestly class. The bigger political units employed artisans to make luxury goods for the aristocracy, and polygamy was the rule at the higher levels of society. All of the privileged groups in the larger states owned or were assigned lands usurped from subject *ayllus.* Chimu nobles owned entire valleys which were cultivated by sharecroppers and slaves. Most frequently, however, the villagers tilled the fields of these intruders under the *minka* system. For the peasants of ancient Peru, whether they were part of an independent community or a great empire, labor service was the most common form of taxation.

The Cuzco Imperialists

In the 1430s, during the reign of Viracocha Inca, the eighth recorded ruler of Cuzco, the Chanca tribe attacked the Inca capital and almost overwhelmed its defenders. But Viracocha's son and successor, Pachacuti, rallied his father's army and led it to victory. The Incas incorporated the vanquished Chancas into their state and Pachacuti directed the enlarged imperial forces in a rampage of conquest. By 1493, when Pachacuti's son Topa Inca Yupanqui died, the empire almost had reached its maximum extent, ruling more than seventy different states.

This amazing success in a period of little more than a half century was achieved by a combination of military might and skillful diplomacy. Peoples who readily submitted to the Cuzco imperialists received conciliatory treatment. They retained much of their land and the Incas respected local traditions if these were compatible with the objectives of the state. The rulers of newly acquired territories often kept their posts as part of the Inca bureaucracy. Nominal supremacy had to be given to the sun god, Inti, the principal diety of the empire. But devotion to local gods continued. Those groups who chose to resist Inca designs were overwhelmed by the large, well-organized, and expertly led imperial armies. States that tenaciously defended their independence could expect no mercy. The Incas frequently moved newly conquered peoples from the fringes of the empire to more secure zones and replaced them with *mitmaes,* colonists from older dominions.

Like other conquerors who preceded them, the Incas usurped lands from their subjects. Rebels lost all of their property, but most communities were left enough land for subsistence. In densely populated regions with little surplus land, the Incas often appropriated unproductive areas which they then made arable through terracing or irrigation. Sometimes population pressure was relieved by relocating people in more sparsely inhabited zones. A three-part division of the land took place in most communities. One portion belonged to the state and its produce fed the army and other groups removed from agriculture for government service. The emperor frequently granted royal lands to victorious generals and other favorites. Herds and pastures often were expropriated by the government and mining and coca production became royal monopolies. The Incas, like the Chimu, restricted hunting to the nobility. A second portion of the *marca* was devoted to the support of the "church"—both local cults, where these were important, and the state religion with its large priesthood and many "virgins of the sun." At least in the early days of the empire, the common people probably retained the largest segment of the *marca* for their own use. These fields continued to be worked according to local tradition.

Labor service remained the primary form of taxation under the Cuzco regime, and Inca administrative machinery seems to have been geared primarily to achieve maximum efficiency from various systems of forced labor. The common people worked the lands of the state, the "church," and those of their own *curacas* as part of their local *minka* obligation. To this the Incas added an imperial labor tax called the *mita* (literally, a "turn") based upon the ancient traditions of *minka* and reciprocal labor. Through the *curacas* each community supplied a quota of workers to the state for a fixed period of time. Perhaps three months was the most common stint. Persons took their "turn" in a variety of ways. Some performed personal service in the households of the elites. Others worked in the mines and isolated coca plantations. The Incas employed corvée gangs numbering hundreds of men on major projects such as terraces, irrigation systems, road construction, and the erection of large buildings. During the *mita* period workers were fed by the government and their fields were tended by *ayllu* members who remained at home.

35

Some groups were in the permanent employ of the state and the aristocracy. The most numerous of these were the *yanaconas*—landless persons who may have lost their fields because of rebellion and other crimes or individuals whose *ayllus* no longer had sufficient land to support their population. Some members of this class served as valets or administrative assistants to members of the nobility and enjoyed a privileged status. Most *yanaconas,* however, were common agricultural workers whose condition was similar to slavery. In addition, large numbers of master craftsmen made luxury goods for the aristocracy and a corps of state engineers directed the work of *mita* laborers on public projects. There was, of course, a sizable professional army and many beautiful women were selected to serve as concubines for the elite.

For administrative purposes, the Incas divided their empire into four *suyu,* or quarters, and the whole was called Tahuantinsuyu, the "Land of the Four Quarters." The Sapa Inca, or emperor, possessed absolute temporal power over these realms. His authority was buttressed by a belief that the monarch descended from the sun god and was himself divine. A council of state drawn primarily from the royal *ayllu* advised the emperor and his will was enforced by a bureaucracy of eight levels: "viceroys" for each of the four *suyu,* provincial governors, and *curacas* of six ranks. A remarkable system of roads radiated from Cuzco to the distant corners of the state. Couriers stationed at intervals along this network quickly relayed information to royal officials. At strategic points along these arteries the Incas constructed granaries to supply the army and *mita* workers and maintained inns called *tambos* to serve travelers. Although the Andean peoples were accomplished mathematicians, employing the decimal system, they had no written language. To maintain records of the labor supply, the amount of foodstuffs and other products in state warehouses, and to manage other resources efficiently, the Incas employed a corps of statisticians. These men recorded quantitative data on *quipus,* bunches of knotted cords, a complicated device borrowed from the Chimu.

In the years that followed the destruction of the Inca Empire, critics of Spanish rule and that of later republican regimes often pointed to "lessons of the past," to a supposedly golden age of wise and benevolent government under the Cuzco dynasty. During the twentieth century the empire frequently has been viewed as a socialist welfare state. Conversely, apologists for post-

Columbian administrations in Peru have denounced the Incas as usurpers and tyrants. One scholar even compared Tahuantin-suyu with the totalitarian dictatorships of twentiety-century Europe. Although such analogies are strained and have little utility, evidence can be found to support both interpretations. Inca rule was tyrannical, but in some ways still may have been more wise and benevolent than that of subsequent regimes. The Inca state was not a "socialist empire," however, especially if it is judged by Bertrand Russell's concept of socialism: the common ownership of land and capital within a democratic system; production for use rathern than for profit; and the distribution of the product in an equitable manner or at least with only those inequities justified by the public interest.

The Inca Empire definitely was not democratic. The emperor was the state. Society was rigidly stratified with a small aristocracy and a large mass of commoners. With very limited social mobility, status was determined largely by birth. Nor was equality even an ideal of society. The elite appropriated the surplus production of the economy while the ordinary people became poorer. The government distributed food from state granaries to the masses during periods of famine, but this was not entirely altruistic. The Incas valued people for their labor and the privileged classes wanted to preserve the human resources that supported their high standard of living. In the later years of the empire, when plunder was not so plentiful, newly incorporated subjects surrendered increasingly larger portions of their lands to the Incas. These people welcomed the Spaniards as deliverers from oppression. Features of Andean life which suggest socialism—communal ownership of land, the *minka,* and doles to the needy—were ancient pre-Incaic practices of the *ayllus* and they continued to be primarily local institutions. The Incas merely exploited some of these traditions for their own benefit. Even at the community level an increasing tendency toward private property developed and few villagers viewed their *curacas* as democrats.

The Incas were not imaginative inventors but clever adapters and effective disseminators of ideas. Theirs was a practical genius, a talent for organization and implementation. Utilizing the contributions of others, the men from Cuzco left a profound imprint upon Peruvian history which remained long after the destruction of their principal monument, the empire. The Incas weakened parochial traditions and achieved a greater stan-

37

dardization of local political organization and religious beliefs. Uprooting and transplanting the populations of entire districts, they significantly altered the ethnic map of the central Andes. Quechua, the imperial language, began to supplant the myriad of dialects spoken in the region. Spanish missionaries later would continue this linguistic unification by employing the *lengua general* of Cuzco in their work. Valuable tools and techniques, often of non-Incaic origin, were diffused throughout the empire. The knowledge of metallurgy and the use of metal tools increased greatly. The Andean foot-plow became the standard agricultural implement of the empire. State-sponsored irrigation and terracing projects brought more land under cultivation and some crops were introduced into new areas. The technique of mortarless masonry became widespread and an Incaic ceramic style—rather bland, utilitarian vessels that were mass produced—generally replaced the distinctive and usually more attractive regional potteries. The Incas brought greater cultural homogeneity to the Andean peoples, but in doing so deprived the region of some of the richness that comes from diversity.

Under the Inca Empire several important, enduring themes in Peruvian history became manifest. A small elite dominated the state and demanded almost absolute submission of the masses to its authority. The development of social castes quickened as did the concentration of land in private estates worked by tenants or forced labor. As with many later regimes, political centralization was the ideal. But local rulers maintained considerable autonomy. Descriptions of the Inca administrative apparatus as a finely tuned machine controlled from the capital are "bureaucratic fictions," the world as it was viewed from Cuzco and not from the countryside. Today, mountainous terrain makes communications very slow in Peru; floods and landslides often block roads for many weeks at a time. So it must have been under the Incas. The small, dispersed communities always have been isolated and local power structures tenacious in protecting their independence from meddling central governments. In modern Peru, as under the Incas, petty political bosses sometimes are called *curacas* and their methods of control have remained largely unchanged.

Huayna Capac, the eleventh Inca emperor, conquered Ecuador and established his residence at Quito. His death there around 1525 produced a disastrous schism within the empire. Huayna Capac's son and presumed heir, Huascar, claimed the throne from his palace in Cuzco. However, his title was challenged by Atahualpa, another of the emperor's sons, who lived with his father at Quito. In a bloody civil war that lasted until 1531, Atahualpa defeated the armies of Huascar, whom he imprisoned, and installed himself as sovereign of the reunited empire. But the new monarch's reign was short.

ஜ The European Usurpers

Francisco Pizarro, a veteran conquistador of modest origins, landed in northern Peru with some 180 followers early in 1532. After establishing a base on the coast, Pizarro led his men to the highland city of Cajamarca where the emperor was enjoying nearby mineral baths. Atahualpa's armies could have annihilated the small force of Europeans as they marched through the narrow mountain passes, but the monarch could not comprehend that these few strangers posed a threat to his exhalted person. On Novemeber 16, 1532, the emperor accepted an invitation to dine with Pizarro within the confines of the city. Entering the central plaza with a retinue of 5,000 lightly armed men, Atahualpa was boldly attacked and captured by Pizarro and a team of 20 assailants. Perhaps drawing upon the experiences of his kinsman Hernán Cortés, the conqueror of Mexico, Pizarro had decapitated the Inca state with a single stroke. While the all-powerful monarch remained in the hands of the Europeans, the emperor's subordinates offered little resistance.

Atahualpa proposed to buy his freedom with enough gold and silver to fill two rooms. The Spaniards accepted this seemingly impossible ransom agreement. It seemed an efficient way to gather up the imperial treasure. When the emperor complied with his part of the bargain, however, his captors faced a dilemma. Once free from the grasp of the Europeans, Atahualpa probably would have commanded his armies to destroy the invaders. Yet, if he remained a prisoner of the Spaniards, it seemed likely that his people would attempt a rescue of their god-king. In July 1533, after receiving dubious information that a large Inca force was preparing to attack Cajamarca, the Spaniards accused Atahualpa of treacherously ordering the assault and hastily executed him.

While still a prisoner of the Europeans, Atahualpa had ordered the execution of his half-brother Huascar and several other claimants to the Inca throne so that they could not profit from the monarch's distress. At the same time, Atahualpa's Ecuadorian armies continued to ravage many towns that had supported Huascar in he recent civil war. The Spaniards exploited this internal strife. Posing as champions of the vanquished Cuzco faction, they installed the first in a series of puppet emperors drawn from the southern branch of the royal family and received the support of many districts. But Atahualpa's generals, who controlled the major cities, attacked the Spaniards as they marched southward along the highlands from Cajamarca to Cuzco. The massive armies of the Incas proved to be no match for the vastly superior tactics and arms of the Europeans, especially their steel swords and horses. These initial victories, clever diplomacy, and the continued discord among the Indians gave the Spaniards time to consolidate their Andean foothold.

The Europeans quickly despoiled the treasure of royal palaces and temples and distributed this booty without major controversy. But Pizarro feuded with his partner Diego de Almagro, the organizing genius of the expedition, over the division of the newly acquired territories. In 1538, the forces of the two men met in combat at Las Salinas and Pizarro's followers carried the field. The victors executed Almagro and stripped his partisans of many prerogatives. Three years later the Almagristas revolted and assassinated Francisco Pizarro. Unhappy with this strife and anxious to assert its control over the new colony, the Spanish crown dispatched Cristóbal Vaca de Castro to Peru as its new royal governor. Vaca de Castro sided with the Pizarro camp and crushed the rebellion of the Almagro party. Blasco Núñez Vela, Peru's first viceroy, replaced Vaca de Castro in 1544. His high-handed treatment of the conquistadors and determination to end their control over the Indian population brought a rebellion by Francisco Pizarro's brother Gonzalo. The rebels killed the viceroy on a battlefield near Quito in 1545, and Gonzalo Pizarro ruled Peru for the next three years. Then the forces of a new royal official, the statesman-priest Pedro de la Gasca, crushed the rebellion and executed its leader. Although a few minor Spanish uprisings occurred during the next decade, the conquistadors had been tamed.

By 1536, the schism within the ranks of the Indians had healed sufficiently to permit a rebellion against the Spaniards. Under the leadership of Manco Inca, a one-time puppet emperor of the Europeans, the natives laid siege to Cuzco for many months and overwhelmed several smaller Spanish garrisons. Manco allied himself with the various factions in the civil wars of the conquistadors and in 1539, he established a neo-Inca state in the mountain-and-jungle wilderness of the Vilcabamba region, north of Cuzco. From isolated strongholds, Manco and his successors fomented rebellion among the natives, raided Spanish settlements, and constantly threatened communications between Cuzco and Lima, the European capital founded in 1535. Finally, following more than three decades of resistance, Viceroy Francisco de Toledo resolved to crush this dangerous state and its monarch who challenged Spain's legal title to Peru. In 1572, a large colonial army defeated the forces of the Inca. Túpac Amaru, a lineal descendant of Huayna Capac and the fourth of the Vilcabamba emperors, was brought to Cuzco and executed. Peru was quiet.

The Spanish crown felt genuine concern for the welfare of its new Indian subjects. The king had an obligation to instruct them in the Catholic faith and to protect their persons and property from the greed of his European vassals in America. But Spain's New World dominions had been won by soldiers of fortune with little material assistance from the government and the conquistadors expected rewards for their sacrifices. Furthermore, the Spanish monarchy hoped that the vast American empire would become a great source of wealth and power and this could be achieved only by tapping the native labor supply. In this conflict between the royal conscience and the imperial cashbox, the Spanish sovereigns attempted compromise. The Indians would have to labor for the king and his European subjects. However, this exploitation was to be restricted and the rights of the natives—who were considered legal minors and wards of the crown—were to be protected. Thousands of well-intentioned laws were decreed in Spain only to be emasculated, ignored, or perverted in the Andean countryside. The lot of the Indian was truly miserable under Spanish rule. Of course, the Incas also had exploited the masses, but European control brought a new element of oppression: an entirely alien people relegated the natives and their culture to an inferior position within society, sowing the seeds of the "Indian problem."

A decline of catastrophic proportions in the native population of America shaped Spain's Indian policy. Within the first century of European contact, the aboriginal inhabitants of the

New World may have decreased by 90 percent. In some lowland areas, the natives entirely disappeared. By 1620, the Indian population of what is now Peru had fallen to about 825,000 persons, and it continued to decline until at least the second half of the seventeenth century. Contemporary critics of Spanish policy, such as Bishop Bartolomé de las Casas, and later Hispanophobic historians often charged that the Spaniards cruelly exterminated the natives. Willful abuse by the Europeans, however, was only a small part of this sad story. In Peru the civil war between Huascar and Atahualpa cost many lives and the Spanish conquerors continued the bloodshed. The battle casualties in these struggles probably were much less than the indirect losses from starvation, as production and distribution systems were disrupted and armies confiscated crops and livestock. Under the Spaniards, many Indians died from overwork and mistreatment. But the greatest conquistadors of them all were Old World diseases—smallpox, measles, plague, influenza, and typhus—for which the New World peoples had no natural immunity. A smallpox epidemic preceded Pizarro to Peru from Panama and may have halved the population of the Inca Empire, claiming Huayna Capac among its victims. Epidemics struck repeatedly throughout the sixteenth and into the seventeenth century assisted, unwittingly, by the Spanish policy of concentrating the Indians into larger communities.

The Spaniards, like the Incas before them, redirected native institutions to serve their own purposes. The Indians continued to live under their ancient laws and traditions so long as these did not conflict with the crown's objectives. The substance of native religion survived under a veneer of Catholic ritual. Several members of the Inca royal family were co-opted into the Spanish nobility. *Curacas* enjoyed the legal status of hidalgos, lesser nobles, and retained much of their authority within the colonial bureaucracy. The evolution of land and labor systems followed a logical, though perhaps more rapid, progression from one empire to the next. In many ways the Spanish colonial period in Peru was an extension of the Cuzco imperium rather than an abrupt break with the past.

In the first half of the sixteenth century, when Spain first acquired its American dominions, the *encomienda* system was the principal device for both rewarding the conquistadors and consolidating the empire. In lieu of the tribute the Indians owed their new sovereign, the natives of specified districts provided goods and services to individual Spaniards. These grantees, the *encomenderos,* were surrogates of the king and assumed his obligation to Christianize and protect their wards. But many *encomenderos* neglected their duties and exploited their charges and the king soon became wary of creating a new class of feudal lords in America such as that which he was trying to weaken in Spain. In 1542, after a long and bitter controversy, the crown issued the New Laws "for the good treatment and preservation of the Indians." These regulations prohibited the granting of additional *encomiendas* and the inheritance of those already given, restricted the obligations that the Indians owed their *encomenderos* to money payments, and in other ways attempted to limit the exploitation of the natives. Few of the New Laws could be enforced. In Peru, the attempt to implement them produced Gonzalo Pizarro's revolt against Viceroy Núñez Vela. During the next decade the New Laws were amended considerably to permit the exaction of tribute in goods and allow the *encomenderos* to demand labor from their Indians in return for a token wage. The crown compromised on the critical issue of inheritance. After "three lives"—those of the original grantee, his son, and grandson—the tribute obligation of the Indians reverted to the king.

The *encomienda* had proven to be an inadequate source of labor even before this sentence of gradual death was imposed upon the institution. Peru had fewer than 500 *encomenderos* in the mid-sixteenth century, but many more Spaniards desired Indian workers. To satisfy this need the crown resurrected and refined the *mita* draft of the Incas. All adult male Indians, excluding the *curacas,* were to spend a portion of their time engaged in labor deemed beneficial to the king and the general welfare. By law the *mitayos,* or draftees, were to be paid a "just wage" that would provide for the necessities of life and leave sufficient surplus to pay the tribute tax. *Mitayos* worked in a variety of industries, the most dreaded of which was mining.

The *mita* provided several mines with labor, but the largest employer was Potosí, the source of 85 percent of the silver extracted from the central Andean region. This "mountain of silver," located in present-day Bolivia, drew upon the labor supply of the Lake Titicaca Basin. The Indians traveled there in large caravans, often accompanied by their families. In the early days the *mitayos* worked twelve hours per day, five days each week. After two weeks of mining, they received a rest period of equal length. But as the shafts became deeper, the lodes poorer, and labor less abundant, more and more work was exacted from the Indians. They entered the mines on Monday morning and remained underground, working alternate shifts, until Saturday. Production quotas were onerous. Each *mitayo* was expected to mine 2,500 pounds of ore per day, load it into 100-pound bags and carry this material up ladders to the surface, sometimes a climb of 750 feet.

Mita Indians incurred considerable expense while serving their king at Potosí. They were supposed to be paid travel expenses for their journey to the mines, but usually were not. Although many natives brought food from home, this rarely sufficed and they had to purchase additional supplies at inflated, mining-town prices. Many *mitayos* hired assistants to avoid fines for failing to meet their quotas and often they had to buy candles to light the dark shafts. The *mita* officials extorted "gifts" and, finally, the king exacted his tribute tax. The Indians received a wage, but in the eighteenth century this was only about half the amount needed to support a family. To cover this deficit, *mitayos* worked overtime on Sundays, found jobs for their wives and children and sometimes continued working at the mines as wage laborers after their *mita* service had ended.

The Potosí *mita,* as originally organized, required one year of service in seven for taxable males. In actual operation, however, they labored almost one year in four. Including travel to and from the mines, the *mitayo* often spent eighteen months away from home. When the draftee returned to his village he frequently had to depend upon charity until he could harvest his own crops. Because the *mita* was assessed against the *ayllu* as a unit, many Indians refused to return to their communities. They gave up their land rights and moved to new districts where they often worked on Spanish estates, safe from the *mita* officials. Others became permanent workers at the mines, earning wages three times higher than those of the draft laborers. Some, of course, died at Potosí. As the population of the communities declined, their *mita* quotas were supposed to be reduced. However, the census takers appeared much less frequently than the *mita* officials and the burden of labor service became heavier for those villagers who remained.

The Patio Process, utilizing mercury to refine silver, was introduced to Peru in 1571, and permitted the profitable exploitation of lower-grade ore. Thereafter, the government-owned mercury mines at Huancavelica, near Ayacucho, became as vital to the economy as Potosí itself. In fact, the Mexican mining industry also depended upon the liquid metal from Peru. An extremely hazardous occupation, wage laborers did not volunteer for mercury mining. Shafts frequently collapsed and many miners died from mercury or carbon monoxide poisoning. Alternate exposure to the tremendous heat of the subterranean galleries and the cold mountain air at the surface produced a very high incidence of pneumonia among the workers. Indians from the surrounding province were pressed into service at the mercury mines. After 1609, only Potosí and Huancavelica received regular *mita* drafts, but other mining operations frequently were granted special allotments of Indians.

Only about one-quarter of the taxable natives in Peru were subject to the mining *mita,* but 90 percent could be drafted for agricultural service or other work. These Indians were called *plazeros* because they assembled in town plazas for assignment to various employers. Typically, *mitayos de plaza* worked two-week "turns" three or four times each year. Workshops *(obrajes)* producing textiles and other goods also participated in the draft. Conditions in these establishments were so appalling that the courts commonly sentenced criminals to labor in them. Debt peonage among wage workers was widespread, though illegal, in the *obrajes.* They frequently employed children of nine or ten because the minimum wage for minors was lower than for adults. *Mita* officials also allotted Indians for public works projects, including the construction of churches and government buildings and road maintenance. Other *mitayos* carried mail and served in the *tambos* as they had under the Incas. One student of the *mita* has estimated that half of the Indians' time could have been spent fulfilling this obligation. In addition to the exactions of the *encomienda* and *mita,* the natives had to provide goods and services to Spanish provincial officials, to the local priest, and to their own *curacas.*

The despoliation of Indian lands and the formation of Spanish haciendas are topics that did not receive serious study until recent years. In the past it often was assumed that *encomienda* grants included the natives' land as well as rights to their labor. This was not the case. Officially, the crown sought to protect the holdings of the Indians, but achieved only limited success. Many *encomenderos* used their wealth, political influence, and control over their wards to usurp communal lands. The largest estates frequently belonged to members of this privileged class. But Peru had relatively few *encomenderos,* so most of the haciendas were acquired by others. The king empowered Pizarro and his lieutenants to distribute vacant lands, fields belonging to rebellious Inca nobles, and those devoted to the support of native religious cults to deserving conquistadors. The *cabildos,* town councils established by the Spaniards, also assumed this authority in the early years of the colony. Private parties were not the only recipients of land grants. The Church, especially its religious orders, acquired huge tracts, as did the crown and various municipal governments. The incomes from many haciendas endowed schools, hospitals, and other institutions.

Viceroy Francisco de Toledo uprooted many Indians from their villages during the 1570s and concentrated them in larger communities of several *ayllus* called *reducciones.* Instituted to facilitate the supervision and religious conversion of the natives, this program regrouped about 1.5 million Indians of Peru and Bolivia into some 600 *reducciones.* Although the natives received new fields, some communal holdings became "vacant" and subject to sale. Indians were not permitted to dispose of their lands without government approval, but sales did occur illegally or with the connivance of royal officials. Because cash payments could be made in lieu of *mita* service, *ayllus* sometimes sold surplus land. Some Spaniards forced sales of Indian lands by gaining control over vital water resources, or exploited the natives' ignorance of the law to obtain their property.

The financially pressed Spanish crown began the first *composición de tierras* in 1591. For a regularization fee, the *composición,* individuals presenting some evidence of valid ownership received legal titles to their estates. At the same time, the government encouraged the sale of "vacant" lands. A second general *composición* began four decades later. This time landholders with very dubious claims to their haciendas were permitted to buy bona fide titles. These transactions produced a chorus of petitions from Indian communities and their Spanish friends and the government sent judges to investigate charges of fraud. Even in the most obvious cases of chicanery, however, the *ayllus* recovered only enough land to support their current populations at the subsistence level. In the eighteenth century a special court functioned in Lima to handle individual *composiciones* and adjudicate land disputes. But justice was slow, expensive, and rarely impartial, and the Indians were preyed upon by a class of petty lawyers who thrived under this system.

The decrease in the aboriginal population of Peru, the decline of the *encomienda,* and the growing demand for *mitayos* among employers of Indian workers encouraged the development of new labor systems. Meanwhile, the land hunger of the natives and the flight of individuals to avoid the *mita* worked toward the same end. By the eighteenth century various forms of tenancy—some of which survived into the twentieth century—became the most important arrangements regulating agricultural labor. The conquistadors rapidly gained control over the landless *yanaconas* of the Incas. Other Indians were invited to "colonize" Spanish estates, receiving the use of small plots in exchange for labor service. Rapacious men merely usurped communal lands and permitted the dispossessed farmers to remain in return for their work. Although illegal even under colonial law, debt peonage often tied tenants to the haciendas.

After the local *curaca,* the royal official most concerned with Indian affairs was the *corregidor de indios,* a post established in 1565 to assume the functions originally assigned to the *encomenderos.* The crown divided the present-day area of Peru into 54 *corregimientos,* provinces governed by *corregidores.* The chief administrator and judge within his district, the *corregidor* was charged specifically to protect the natives, collect the tribute tax, and assist the *mita* officials. The provincial governors usually served only a single short term (one to five years) and rarely received promotions to higher positions. Their salaries were small and after the sixteenth century they had to pay for their appointments. All of these circumstances encouraged corruption on a grand scale. The *corregidores* viewed their posts as highly speculative business enterprises and they engaged in many economic activities utilizing Indian labor. The provincial governors often were the principal merchants in their districts. Purchasing Indian produce at depressed prices, they charged the natives exhorbitant amounts for merchandise, sometimes useless items which the Indians were forced to buy. The crown at first prohibited all of these practices, but later attempted to check only the worst abuses. This proved to be impossible so long as the king refused to pay adequate salaries.

In the early decades of the colonial period, *curacas* sometimes complained about the erosion of their power and status under Spanish rule, but few chiefs raised their voices in defense of their humble countrymen. The headmen also benefited from the exploitation of the common Indians and most *curacas* became

47

willing allies of the *corregidores*. Often educated at special schools for the sons of chiefs, many of these hereditary village leaders were rich, highly literate, and "Indians" only by legal definition. The collective memory of these native elites concerning preconquest Peru had become badly blurred by 1607, when Garcilaso de la Vega published his *Royal Commentaries of the Incas*. Born in Cuzco to one of Pizarro's captains and a niece of Huayna Capac, Garcilaso (called "El Inca") spent most of his adult life in Spain, where his tales of his mother's people made him a favorite at the royal court. The Peruvian's charming though distorted account of a model government under the Cuzco rulers was the only widely available treatment of the topic until the nineteenth century and promoted unfavorable comparisons of the Spanish Empire with that of the Incas.

For the *curacas* the Inca state was the source of their privileged status and they readily accepted this Garcilasan view of a glorious past. Some native leaders, strongly influenced by the *Comentarios reales,* developed a new sense of noblesse oblige toward their unfortunate brothers. Under the leadership of these Indian elites, an Inca nationalist movement began in the second half of the seventeenth century. A renaissance occurred in some ancient decorative arts and new plays treating Incaic themes were performed during village fiestas. On ceremonial occasions, at least, *curacas* often abandoned Western garb for the traditional dress of Inca nobles. The most significant manifestation of Inca nationalism, however, was a growing demand by native chieftains for a reform of Spain's Indian policy.

Notwithstanding an aborted, *curaca*-led conspiracy of 1666–67, the Indian leaders initially attempted to gain redress of their grievances through the courts and peaceful petition. They had little success. Then, in the 1730s, a series of Indian uprisings began under the direction of *curacas* who frequently assumed the names of former Inca emperors. This unrest culminated in 1780 with a massive rebellion led by José Gabriel Condorcanqui, the headman of a village in the southern highlands who claimed noble Inca lineage. Adopting the name Túpac Amaru II, after the last of the Vilcabamba monarchs, he directed his people in an uprising that engulfed the Sierra from Cuzco to La Paz, Bolivia, and threatened to spread even farther. In this crisis, the government was able to exploit the mistrust and factionalism within Indian society, while uniting the frightened privileged classes in defense of their position. After two years and much bloodshed, the rebellion was suppressed. The royal government executed the Inca leader and many of his followers. Reforms followed the uprising, but these proved to be ineffectual. Some historians have described Túpac Amaru II as a precursor of Peruvian independence from Spain. Like most of the king's American subjects, however, the Indian leader viewed the distant and mysterious Spanish monarch as a good and just ruler whose laws were distorted by evil subordinates. Túpac Amaru II wanted reforms within the empire and protection from all groups who exploited the Indians—both the Spaniards and the Peruvian-born elites.

Other ethnic groups partially replaced the declining Indian population of Peru. A census taken in the early 1790s reported that the area of the modern republic had almost 1,100,000 inhabitants. Indians comprised over 58 percent of this number; whites, 12 percent; Negroes, 7 percent; and "half-castes," 22 percent. The criteria differentiating Indians from non-Indians were legal as well as cultural during the colonial period. Because the natives did not share European values, they were considered *gente sin razón,* "irrational people" who had to be protected by the crown. Under the law, their status was second only to the whites. But in many ways, especially in the esteem of their non-Indian neighbors, the natives were at the bottom of the social ladder.

Blacks accompanied the conquistadors to Peru, assisted in the subjugation of the Indians, and later participated in the civil wars of the Spaniards. By the middle of the sixteenth century, the colony had about as many Negroes as whites, a fact that frightened the government and encouraged discriminatory legislation. The Spaniards imported an estimated 95,000 black bondsmen into Peru during the course of the colonial epoch. Large numbers of these slaves labored on the coastal estates where their exploitation was as rigorous as in other plantation areas of the New World. A majority, however, lived in Lima and other urban centers, where the physical demands upon them generally were much less severe. They labored as domestic servants, artisans, and performed many other tasks. Although some slaves worked in the highlands, they were a relatively expensive source of labor in that region. Indian muscle always supported the economy of the Sierra. Unlike the natives, blacks—both free and slave—were "rational people" who adopted Western ways. They sometimes served as overseers of

49

Indian laborers. About half of the 80,000 Negroes enumerated in the census of the 1790s were slaves.

The 22 percent of the Peruvian population described as "half-castes" in the census were various mixtures of Indian, European, and African stock. Most Peruvian *castas* were mestizos, persons of Indian and European descent. The "society of castes" also included the Negro and white combination (mulatto) and persons of Indian and black ancestry. This last mixture, usually referred to as *zambo* in most of Spanish America, was called *chino* (Chinese) in Peru, a term that later caused much confusion when true Chinese came to the country. Finally, there were triple crosses of Indian, European, and African. The *castas* along with the free blacks occupied the intermediate socioeconomic strata spanning the wide gap between the Indians and the whites. They were the skilled workers, petty traders, and the common labor force of Lima and other major cities. On the coastal estates their occupations ranged from manager and overseer to mechanic and field hand. Mestizos comprised a provincial aristocracy in many areas of the highlands, dominating local commerce and owning large haciendas. Half-castes held some minor Church and government posts and provided the rank and file of the colonial militia.

The white population of Peru concentrated in the urban areas. More than 40 percent lived in three cities—Lima, Cuzco, and Arequipa—and most of the remainder were distributed in a half-dozen other regional centers. Even those whites who owned rural property frequently maintained urban residences. Lima was the focal point of upper-class Peruvian society. Called the "City of Kings" because of its founding on the Feast of the Epiphany, many *limeños* believed that their city also deserved this title by virtue of its regal splendor. Lima was the capital of the Viceroyalty of Peru, a geographical unit that included all of Spanish South America until the eighteenth century. It was the most important political, commercial, and ecclesiastical center of the American empire. In addition to many substantial government buildings and magnificent churches, Lima in the mid-eighteenth century supported twelve hospitals, eighteen nunneries, and more than a score of monasteries. It had several secondary schools and San Marcos University. Chartered in 1551, San Marcos claimed to be the oldest institution of higher education in the New World.

Peru's white inhabitants monopolized the upper and

middle-level posts in the government bureaucracy and the choice religious offices. They controlled the most lucrative business enterprises, including large-scale commerce, mining, and many of the great haciendas, especially those along the coast. The more prestigious liberal professions, notably law, and even some trades were reserved for the light-skinned elite. This dominant class included European-born Spaniards, or *peninsulares,* and whites born in America, the creoles. Although marriage and business relationships united these two groups, a strong undercurrent of hostility existed between them. The Europeans viewed the Americans as provincial yokels and sometimes questioned their "purity of blood." In the American "white," there was always the possibility of mixed racial ancestry, which also implied illegitimacy. In fact, wealthy Peruvians with darker-skinned ancestors could purchase "certificates of whiteness" which removed the legal disabilities placed upon mestizos. But even the acquisition of titles of nobility often did not give the Americans social equality with the European aristocrats.

Creoles and *peninsulares* were equal under the law. The crown referred to both groups as "Spaniards." Yet, creoles complained of royal partiality toward Europeans in the appointment of civil and religious officials. *Peninsulares* retorted that the Americans were less deserving of important posts: their educations usually were inferior to those of the Europeans, while they demonstrated greater venality in office. In operation, royal patronage policy did place creoles at a disadvantage. Councils in Spain filled key imperial offices overseas. Job-seekers who applied in person—most often native Spaniards—had an edge over distant petitioners. Furthermore, the law sought to guard against conflicts of interest by prohibiting the appointment of persons to sensitive positions in their native colony, a practice which also handicapped the creole. In spite of these policies, however, American complaints of systematic exclusion from high office were exaggerated until the late colonial period. Peruvians did not hold the post of viceroy and most archbishops were Europeans. But many creoles became bishops and abbots or held important civil posts. Americans came to control the *audiencia* of Lima in the eighteenth century. This high court possessed executive and legislative functions as well as judicial authority and shared power with the viceroy. Creoles had dominated provincial and municipal government since the sixteenth century.

Until well into the eighteenth century, the Spanish crown

grouped all of its New World possessions into two geographical
entities. The Viceroyalty of New Spain, with its capital at Mexico
City, included the dominions north of Panama. The Viceroyalty
of Peru encompassed all of South American except for Pro-
tuguese Brazil. As the empire grew, peripheral regions received
their own *audiencias* and increasing autonomy from the viceroy
at Lima. In theory, colonial government in Peru and its sister
colonies in America was a model of royal absolutism and administrative centralization. The king, through his councils in
Spain, sent laws to Lima. From there the royal will was to be
enforced by the viceroy and *audiencia* who supervised the administration of the *corregidores* in the provinces. The city *cabildos,*
composed primarily of wealthy creoles who had purchased their
positions, had little power under the law. Royal control over the
Catholic Church in America reinforced the monarch's authority
in civil affairs. Under the *patronato real,* a papal grant to the
crown of Castile, the king "nominated"—in practice, named—all
ecclesiastic officials and supervised the finances and temporal
administration of the Church.

In reality the colonial administrative system was crippled by
red tape and the great distance between the metropolis and the
isolated outposts of the empire. Royal suspicion stifled healthy
initiative by crown officials and corruption pervaded the entire
bureaucracy. Wealthy individuals and powerful interest groups
greatly influenced law enforcement at all levels of government.
The weakest link in the bureaucratic chain was the *corregidor* who
often gave free rein to local elites such as those represented by
the legally anemic city councils. For the Indian tenant on a large
estate, the will of the *hacendado,* not the king, was law. Even the
Church had its own institutional interests which often conflicted
with those of the crown, and individual clerics were far removed
from royal supervision. In fact, the high degree of local independence enjoyed by the dominant classes in America helps to
explain the remarkable longevity of Spain's New World empire.

Spain maintained a legal monopoly of trade with its American colonies and for more than two centuries closely regulated
commercial intercourse within the empire. To protect against
foreign encroachment and facilitate the collection of taxes,
trans-Atlantic trade was restricted to a single port in southern
Spain (first Seville and later Cádiz) and two primary terminals in
America—Veracruz in Mexico, and Lima's port city, Callao.
Each year two fleets sailed for the New World protected by a
naval escort. The convoy destined for Peru unloaded at Panama,

where the cargoes were transported across the isthmus by river and road. A Pacific fleet then carried these goods to Lima. Powerful merchant guilds *(consulados)* in Spain and the Peruvian capital controlled this trade for their own benefit. After adding handsome commissions, the Peruvian traders forwarded European merchandise to Ecuador, Chile, Bolivia, and even far-off Argentina. Shipments from South America to Spain reversed this route.

Peru sent vast amounts of silver to Spain during the sixteenth century and imported manufactures and even basic commodities such as flour, wine, and olive oil from the mother country. As the colonial economy developed, however, it became less and less dependent upon Spain. By the seventeenth century, plantations on the coast and haciendas in the Sierra brought near self-sufficiency in foodstuffs. The south cost produced excellent wine grapes and olives; the northern oases contributed sugar and rice. Wheat, preferred by the whites to the maize of the Indians, was grown in both the highland and coastal zones. Livestock was abundant and estates near Lima kept this market well supplied with fresh fruits and vegetables. Using cotton from the coast and wool from the Sierra, *obrajes* met the demand for common textiles. Peruvian artisans fashioned many other simple manufactures. A brisk intercolonial trade within the viceroyalty supplemented the domestic economy. After the late sixteenth century, the mining industry declined sharply. More and more of the silver that was extracted remained in Peru to purchase local produce and defray the increasing costs of government.

As the American colonies matured, Spain's internal economy declined. The mother country became unable to absorb American treasure and agricultural exports, or adequately supply the growing colonial demand for high-grade manufactures and luxury goods. The metropolis eventually was reduced to the status of an entrepôt for trade between America and the countries of northern Europe. The small, closed group of merchants at Cádiz acted as middlemen in this exchange, receiving large fees for placing foreign goods on the convoys bound for the New World. The crown had to be content with revenues obtained from heavy taxes on this trade. The increasingly exploitative economic relationship between Spain and America encouraged the growth of a vigorous contraband trade. Foreign merchants often dealt directly with their American customers, bypassing middlemen and tax collectors in both Cádiz and Lima.

In 1700 the Spanish Bourbons, a branch of the French royal

family, replaced the ossified Hapsburg dynasty on the Iberian throne. During the next century an influx of new ideas, a series of global wars, and many important reforms would shake the Spanish Empire to its foundation. Spain's Bourbon monarchs allied themselves with their French relatives, a compact that gained them the persistent enmity of Great Britain, the world's foremost naval power. For long periods of time communications were disrupted between the mother country and its overseas dominions. Necessity as well as a desire to develop the economies of heretofore neglected portions of the empire brought a liberalization of imperial trade policy. The fleet system ended and the crown opened several ports in Spain and America to direct, trans-Atlantic commerce. The colonies received permission to trade with Spain's allies and later with neutral nations. Many of the king's American subjects benefited from these changes. Those in the Río de la Plata region now traded through the newly opened port of Buenos Aires, while ships sailed directly to Chile around Cape Horn. Even in Peru, some new economic interests profited. But the reforms hurt the favored merchants who had prospered under the old restrictive system, especially members of the Lima *consulado.*

To increase the king's control over the colonies and secure more revenues for the prosecution of expensive wars, the Bourbons attempted to put substance into the hollow theory of royal absolutism. In South America the crown carved two new viceroyalties from the largely titular jurisdiction of the Peruvian viceroy. The Viceroyalty of New Granada, with its capital at Bogotá, included the modern republics of Venezuela, Colombia, Panama, and Ecuador. This last district had been rather closely supervised from Lima. The second new viceroyalty, headquartered at Buenos Aires, comprised present-day Argentina, Uruguay, Paraguay, and Bolivia. The latter region, known as Upper Peru during the colonial period, had close ties with Peru proper. Under the new regime, however, much of its silver flowed into the treasury at Buenos Aires, to the detriment of the Peruvian economy.

For greater efficiency at the provincial level, the Bourbons abolished the *corregimientos* and consolidated these districts to form intendancies. In Peru, seven (later, eight) intendants replaced the fifty-four *corregidores.* Usually men of superior quality, the intendants received adequate salaries and had broad powers to implement royal policy. At the same time, the *cabildos* were given increased responsibility for municipal affairs. These changes eroded the real, though extralegal, influence which local interest groups long had enjoyed and strengthened royal control. The intendants encouraged material progress, especially the development of agriculture, but they also enforced unpopular laws with greater vigor. Taxes were increased and, worse, more efficiently collected.

The crown hoped that the intendant system would end the abuses that had produced the rebellion of Túpac Amaru II. Other reforms also were instituted to achieve this objective. The government prohibited forced sales of goods to the Indians and established a new *audiencia* at Cuzco. Unfortunately, these measures did not bring significant relief to the natives. Subdelegates, district officials responsible to the intendants, assumed the functions of the old *corregidores* and continued to exploit the Indians as their predecessors had done. The *audiencia* of Cuzco initially aroused great hope for improved government in the southern Sierra. But this high court accomplished little and became an incubator of even greater discontent in that region. Royal inspectors sent to investigate the Indian uprising in Peru persuaded the crown that the cupidity and ineptitude of creole officials had sparked the rebellion. Now, the government began a conscious policy of replacing American-born bureaucrats with peninsular Spaniards. Europeans staffed most of the intendancies and the *audiencia* of Lima, where the creoles had enjoyed a majority of posts, became an almost exclusive preserve of the *peninsulares*. Old American protests against royal discrimination now intensified.

Reforms designed to curb the power and independence of the Church also disturbed colonial tranquillity. Although the religious establishment performed many useful educational and social services today provided by the secular state, the crown questioned the cost of these benefits. In the late colonial period, clerics comprised almost 10 percent of Lima's population. The Church owned nearly one-third of the buildings in the capital and many estates, *obrajes,* and other enterprises in the provinces. Unlike the holdings of individuals, which often were divided upon the death of their owners, the Church and its component parts were continuing corporations. Once within its grasp, properties rarely seemed to escape from the "dead hand of the Church." To check the growing wealth and power of this institution, the Bourbons placed new restrictions on its acquisition of property and sought to limit the number of persons entering the monasteries and convents of the religious orders.

The crown had political as well as economic reasons for reducing the influence of the regular clergy, members of the religious orders. In the early colonial era Dominicans, Franciscans, Jesuits, and other groups were granted considerable independence as they worked in the isolated Indian communities. They received instructions from abbots appointed by royal officials, but the religious orders also had superiors in Rome who influenced policy. After the success of these missionary activities, the government sought to replace the regulars with secular clergy, priests directly supervised by bishops who reported only to Madrid. Furthermore, the Bourbon monarchs claimed the power to control the Church because of their sovereignty rather than by virtue of the papal donation. This theory, called "regalism," received its most rigorous challenge from the Society of Jesus. The Jesuits were the most powerful and effective religious order in America. Drawing members from many nations, this highly disciplined organization was directed by a general of the order in Rome and individual Jesuits took an oath of personal obedience to the Pope. With lightning quickness in 1767, the Spanish crown expelled all Jesuits from the empire and confiscated the society's property. Other religious orders increasingly were placed under the episcopal authority of secular bishops.

The composition of the imperial bureaucracy in the eighteenth century also reflected a decline in clerical influence. Because many of the better educated individuals in the New World were churchmen, clerics frequently filled high civil offices—some simultaneously held the posts of archbishop and viceroy. The "Bourbon Century" witnessed a great influx of military men into key positions and a relative decrease in clerical representation. The unstable international situation and growing unrest in the colonies themselves encouraged this militarization of the government and prompted the king to send the first significant contingents of Spanish troops to America. Still, Spain continued to rely primarily upon colonial forces to defend its overseas possessions. Local militias, commanded by creole officers, were increased in size and effectiveness. The crown unwittingly trained the military leaders of the independence movements.

The ideas of the French Enlightenment which inspired many of the Bourbon reforms also influenced the thought of the creole elite. With a few notable exceptions, the antireligious sentiment and political radicalism of this intellectual current did not appeal to the Americans. But the creoles were infected with the idea of progress and they enthusiastically joined in the search for "useful knowledge." With increased frequency the colonials scrutinized the Spanish imperial system. Often they found it wanting. The crown's anticlerical tendencies, especially its treatment of the Jesuits, offended many Americans. The new commercial policy satisfied few creoles. Those who favored liberalized trade called for an end to the remaining restrictions; old, well-entrenched interests wanted a return to the monopolistic system. The political reforms of the Bourbons and the high taxes they collected to fight their European wars angered most Americans.

Bonds of tradition, language, and religion tied the Americans to the mother country, and they had great loyalty to the king—a distant, almost mystical father-figure. By the eighteenth century, however, the creoles had developed their own self-consciousness, a proto-national identity. They no longer thought of themselves as expatriate Spaniards, but as Americans or even Argentines, Chileans, and Peruvians. The North American revolution against Britain caused some creoles to think the unthinkable. But most Latin Americans believed that the social and economic conditions that augured well for an independent republic in the English colonies did not exist in the Spanish New World. The excesses of the French Revolution, then the Haitian slave uprising and other servile insurrections of the late eighteenth and early nineteenth centuries sobered the conservative creoles. Yet, they believed that the king should have been more solicitous of the needs of his American subjects. If the creoles often could not agree upon a common course of action, especially in economic matters, they believed that greater autonomy would benefit them. They wanted an American policy geared to American interests administered by American officials. Still, reform within the empire rather than independence was their desire. Then suddenly and seductively the creoles were confronted with opportunities for change. They grasped at these only to be frustrated by royal intransigence.

57

3

Independence and Anarchy

[1808–1845]

NAPOLEON BONAPARTE PROVIDED THE SHOCK that jolted Latin America from its colonial inertia. In 1808, he treacherously imprisoned his Spanish ally, King Ferdinand VII, and forced him to abdicate the Iberian throne in favor of Joseph Bonaparte, the French emperor's brother. The Spanish masses rose in rebellion against the usurper and installed their own local governments to rule in behalf of Ferdinand. Under the protection of a British army, these loyalists established a Junta of Regency at Cádiz, in southern Spain. This body attempted to gain the allegiance of the American colonies, but the creoles spurned these overtures. The Spanish officials present in America at the time of Napoleon's coup tried to retain power. With their sovereign held captive, however, they lacked legitimacy. In 1809 and 1810, the creole-dominated *cabildos* of several colonial capitals established their own governments to rule in Ferdinand's name. Some American leaders desired outright independence, but a majority only wanted reforms and greater autonomy within the empire.

After its initial rebuff by the colonies, the regency in Cádiz sought support by summoning a *cortes,* or congress, with representatives from both Spain and America. Dominated by an unrepresentative group of rather progressive Spaniards, the *cortes* adopted a liberal constitution in 1812, which relegated the autocratic Ferdinand to the status of a feeble constitutional monarch. The regency promised reforms for the colonies, but its liberalism was specious. The government's lofty ideals of equality among all Americans—whites, Indians and *castas*—and its anticlericalism found little support among the creole elite. At the same time, the *cortes* rejected American demands for complete political equality with Spaniards and refused to grant the colonies meaningful autonomy. The defeat of Napoleon in 1814 restored King Ferdinand to power and he quickly destroyed the handiwork of the *cortes*. Even talk of reform now ended and the monarch launched a campaign to crush the autonomous governments in America. In the face of reaction, the creoles opted for complete independence.

◆ℯ *The Reluctant Revolutionaries, 1808–1826*

Peru's role in the drama of Latin American independence was largely that of an interested spectator until the final act. The wars of independence in all of the Spanish colonies were civil struggles: American patriots found American royalists. And nowhere was royalist sentiment stronger than in Peru. In spite of the disadvantages of colonial status, a disproportionate share of the benefits that still existed within the old regime were concentrated in Lima. Peru had more than 100 titled nobles and many imperial bureaucrats. Furthermore, the rebellion of Túpac Amaru II had frightened the creole upper class and discouraged any new dissension among the white elites that might have prompted the oppressed classes to strike again for their freedom. Finally, Peru was the bastion of Spanish military power in South America. Unlike most of the other colonies, where inept royal officials meekly submitted to creole demands, Peru's viceroy during the critical years 1806–16 was José de Abascal, a strong-willed executive and a skillful politician. The viceroy's army suppressed autonomous governments established in 1809 at Quito, Ecuador, and the Bolivian cities of Chuquisaca and La Paz. Three years later, viceregal forces restored royal control in Chile. A series of revolts in Peru—beginning at Tacna in 1811, and culminating in the uprising of Mateo Pumacahua which swept through the southern highlands in 1814—also were crushed with brutal efficiency. Individual Peruvians enlisted in the cause of independence in other colonies, but caution was the watchword in Peru itself. There, outside assistance would be needed to sever the bonds of empire.

In 1814, an Argentine army commanded by Gen. José de San Martín in northwestern Argentina was deadlocked in a struggle with royalist forces supplied from Bolivia and Peru. San Martín became convinced that the independence of his homeland and all of South America would be insecure until the Spaniards were driven from Peru. Logistical problems, especially the rugged Andes protecting Peru's southwestern flank, required that Chile first be liberated to serve as a base for a seaborne invasion of the royalist stronghold. San Martín skillfully prepared for his ambitious undertaking and in 1817, he led a force of Argentines, Chilean exiles, and European adventurers over the Andes from Argentina into Chile. Within a year this Army of the Andes routed the royalists and San Martín installed an independent Chilean regime under Bernardo O'Higgins. The new government enlisted the services of Lord Thomas Cochrane, a brash, former British naval officer, who organized the Chilean navy. With an improvised fleet, Cochrane quickly terrorized Spanish shipping in the Pacific and forced the royalist navy to seek safety under the guns at Callao harbor. The vital sea lanes to Peru had been secured.

In late August 1820, Cochrane's fleet sailed for Peru carrying 1,600 sailors and marines and San Martín's 4,500-man army. The patriot forces faced overwhelming odds—the viceroy of Peru commanded 23,000 troops. But with the aid of a printing press, San Martín hoped to revolutionize the Peruvians and he brought weapons to equip 15,000 new recruits. Landing at the southern port of Pisco on September 8, San Martín informed the Peruvians that their hour of deliverance was at hand and proclaimed freedom for all slaves who would join his army. During the next several months, San Martín raided isolated royalist garrisons, but avoided major engagements with his numerically superior foes. Time seemed to be on the patriots' side as hundreds of Peruvians enlisted in San Martín's army. On December 24, 1820, the Marquis de Torre Tagle, the Peruvian-born intendant of Trujillo, joined the cause of independence.

Meanwhile, the royalists' grip on the viceregal capital steadily weakened. Fevers racked the army of the viceroy, Gen. José de la Serna. Cochrane's blockade of Callao caused a shortage of supplies and the citizens of Lima became increasingly hostile. In June 1821, La Serna sent half of his army into the fortress at Callao and marched to the Sierra with his remaining forces. San Martín entered Lima two weeks later. Before a public meeting of the *cabildo* on July 28, San Martín proclaimed Peru "free and independent by the will of the people and for the justice of their cause which God defends." Unfortunately, Peru's independence was incomplete and God's defense of it halfhearted at best. Once in control of the capital, San Martín lost the initiative against the Spaniards and his own popularity suffered a notable decline.

Like many creoles and especially Argentines of that period, San Martín was a monarchist. He believed that the infant nations of Latin America needed the strong, guiding hands of their own kings. Constitutional monarchies, patterned after the British government, would protect basic liberties while maintaining the established social order. San Martín urged the adoption of the monarchical system in Peru and secretly sent agents to Europe in search of a suitable prince. The Argentine's conservatism initially won him the support of Peruvian monarchists such as the Marquis de Torre Tagle. But many creoles equated monarchism with the despotism of Ferdinand VII. They believed that republicanism promised greater freedom. San Martín was unable to placate the republicans and he was unwilling to suppress them, as some of his advisers recommended. At the same time, the general alienated much of his conservative following.

A week after San Martín's declaration of independence, an assembly of prominent citizens named him Protector of Peru with dictatorial powers to prosecute the war. The new government adopted harsh measures against the Spanish civilians who had elected to remain in Lima and instituted several anticlerical reforms. When eighty-year-old Archbishop Las Heras protested against these measures, San Martín ordered him to leave the country within forty-eight hours. Pressed for money, the regime levied heavy taxes and exacted forced loans from wealthy individuals. Several merchants purchased exclusive rights to import various products which they sold at monopoly prices. Many of these favored businessmen were foreigners, as were two of the Protector's three cabinet ministers and most of his top military commanders. The Peruvians soon feared that they had exchanged Spanish rule for domination by other outsiders. Increasingly dictatorial in his manner, San Martín also displayed a love for pomp and luxury. He was accused of personal monarchical

61

ambitions and his friends and enemies alike dubbed him "King
José."

In the more healthful highlands, General La Serna rebuilt his
army with Indian conscripts and silver from the mines. The
viceroy's forces seemed capable of holding out indefinitely in
their mountain strongholds. Furthermore, a daring attempt by
royalist Gen. Joseph Canterac to break San Martín's siege of
Callao in September 1821 demonstrated the vulnerability of
Lima to attack. The starving royalist garrison at Callao surrendered a few days later, but the patriots had few other victories to
savor. San Martín's refusal to carry the war boldly to the
Spaniards and his failure to pay the navy caused a breach with
Lord Cochrane. The British officer seized the Peruvian treasury,
which had been entrusted to the navy during Canterac's raid, and
sailed away to Chile. The Protector's Argentine and Chilean
troops, whose pay also was in arrears, demanded to be sent
home. In October 1821 their officers attempted to overthrow
the government. With Lima freed from Spanish control and San
Martín's growing unpopularity, Peruvian enlistments declined.
Disease and desertion greatly reduced the patriot army. The final
defeat of the royalists required military and political strength
which San Martín did not possess. He appealed to Argentina and
Chile for reinforcements, but they refused him further aid. The
Protector now looked northward.

Gen. Simón Bolívar had driven the Spaniards from Colombia
in 1819, and secured the independence of his native Venezuela
two years later. In May 1822, his army scored a decisive victory
over the royalists near Quito. San Martín met with the Venezuelan leader at the Ecuadorian port of Guayaquil for three days
in July 1822. The main topic of this famous and very controversial conference was the use of Bolívar's troops in Peru, but the
two men also discussed other matters during their private talks.
San Martín wanted to incorporate Guayaquil into Peru, but
Bolívar desired this fine harbor for his Confederation of Gran
Colombia, an entity comprising the old Viceroyalty of New
Granada. Colombian troops already controlled the coveted port
when San Martín arrived and the "Liberator"—as Bolívar was
called—welcomed the Protector to "Colombian soil." The patriot leaders expressed their views concerning the proper form of
government for the new nations of Latin America. San Martín, of
course, favored monarchy. Bolívar professed republicanism, although his ideal republic had many attributes of a monarchy. The
principal issue—that of troops for Peru—could not be resolved.

Bolívar had not yet quieted all royalist opposition in Ecuador, and he refused to send large numbers of his soldiers southward until his position was secured. Moreover, the Liberator harbored grave though unexpressed doubts about the military competence and political designs of the Argentine general. Agustín Iturbide, the Mexican independence leader, recently had installed himself as emperor, and Bolívar wanted no part in placing San Martín on a Peruvian throne. The Venezuelan also believed that a campaign which the Protector proposed to lead against La Serna was faulty. Bolívar's monumental vanity already was legend. And when the Liberator refused San Martín's generous offer to serve as Bolívar's subordinate, the Argentine became convinced that only his abandonment of the Peruvian stage to the Venezuelan would bring the necessary aid. San Martín returned to Lima and on September 20, 1822, he resigned his authority to a recently assembled Peruvian congress. Accepting the title "Founder of the Liberty of Peru," he departed for Chile and eventual exile and death in Europe.

The Peruvian congress now entrusted executive power to a three-man junta. After a decisive royalist victory in the south, however, prominent military leaders demanded the installation of a single chief of state. Congress complied in February 1823, naming the aristocrat José de la Riva Agüero Peru's first president. The new executive demonstrated great vigor in organizing another expedition against the Spaniards, but his commanders failed him in the field. Congress impeached and removed Riva Agüero from office in June, and placed the Marquis de Torre Tagle in power. Challenging the legitimacy of the new regime, the deposed president went to Trujillo where he reestablished his own government in opposition to that in Lima. Riva Agüero received the support of the northern region, much of the army, and the newly created Peruvian navy.

Gen. Antonio José de Sucre, Bolívar's protégé, arrived at Lima in May 1823 with 3,000 Colombian troops. On September 1, the Liberator himself received a triumphant welcome to the Peruvian capital. Torre Tagle continued to be the nominal president, but Bolívar controlled the army and, therefore, was the actual ruler of the country. The Liberator attempted to end the feud between the Lima and Trujillo governments but without success. Riva Agüero was determined to regain control over his nation which he feared would become completely dominated by Bolívar and his Colombian forces. Late in 1823, Riva Agüero wrote to La Serna proposing a Spanish-Peruvian alliance to drive the Colombians from the country and the establishment of an independent monarchy in Peru under a Spanish prince. The Lima government intercepted this letter and denounced Riva Agüero as a traitor. A short time later, two of his aides (Gen. Antonio de la Fuente and Maj. Ramón Castilla) delivered their chief to the Bolívar camp. A court martial condemned Riva Agüero to death, but Bolívar commuted this sentence to banishment from the country.

President Torre Tagle shared Riva Agüero's suspicions of Bolívar. He also resented his subordinate position within the regime and the more liberal tone of the independence movement under the republican Liberator. The old monarchist secretly offered to surrender Lima, Callao, and the troops under his immediate command to La Serna. But before he could act, the dissatisfied Argentine and Chilean soldiers that garrisoned the Callao fortress released their Spanish prisoners and raised the imperial flag. Torre Tagle joined the royalist uprising, and a Spanish force from the highlands occupied the capital on February 21, 1824.

That same day, congress formally conferred dictatorial powers on Bolívar and he established an openly authoritarian regime at Trujillo. The patriots' situation was extremely precarious. La Serna commanded an army of 17,000 men and controlled most of the country. The Liberator's much smaller force held little more than the north coast of Peru. Worse, tuberculosis struck the Venezuelan leader, rendering him delirious for two months. But he escaped death and in the days that followed, the still-weakened Liberator demonstrated that his determination matched his tremendous ego. While General Sucre acted as his legs, scouting the country and securing supplies, Bolívar trained his army for a final campaign against the royalists.

By April 1824, the patriot forces numbered 6,000 Colombians and 4,000 Peruvians. Bolívar wanted more time to prepare his army, but in July, La Serna's commander in Upper Peru rebelled, depriving the viceroy of 4,000 troops. The Liberator seized the opportunity afforded by this dissension within the imperial ranks and marched his men into the Sierra. On August 6, the two armies clashed on the 9,000-foot high Plains of Junín, near the central highland city of Jauja. Not a shot was fired during this ninety-minute battle, as both sides used only sabers and lances. The patriots carried the field and, although they did not inflict large losses on the royalists, Bolívar gained the initiative. At this critical moment the Liberator received word from his government in Bogotá that he, as president of Gran Colombia, could not lead a Peruvian army. Infuriated, the Venezuelan entrusted supreme command to thirty-one-year-old General Sucre.

For the next three months, Sucre and the royalists marched back and forth along the Sierra, maneuvering for strategic advantage. On December 9, 1824, the two armies faced each other at the hacienda of Ayacucho, near Huamanga (a city later renamed Ayacucho in honor of the battle). Both sides sensed that the ensuing combat would determine the fate of Peru. In the morning darkness before the attack, friends and relatives in the opposing camps met between the lines to bid farewell. The royalists outnumbered the patriots by nearly two-to-one. They also possessed superior artillery and held a good position on a hill overlooking the plain where Sucre had encamped his army. At nine in the morning the royalists, with General La Serna in the lead, marched down the hill. Gaining momentum, they threatened to drive the patriots from the field. But a desperate cavalry charge turned back the viceroy's columns and the patriot infantry pursued them up the heights. In about an hour's time, the battle ended in complete victory for Sucre. The royalists suffered 1,400 dead and 700 wounded compared with 900 total casualties for the patriots. La Serna was wounded and captured. That evening, General Canterac surrendered the remanents of the imperial army in the Sierra and Lima capitulated a few days later. Jubilant with the news of Sucre's triumph, Bolívar bestowed the title "Grand Marshal of Ayacucho" on his lieutenant.

The battle of Ayacucho delivered a death blow to the Spanish Empire in South America, but a few die-hard royalists continued the struggle. It required an additional six months to suppress the Spaniards in Bolivia. The royalists in the fortress at Callao, under General Rodil, refused to surrender until January 1826. By that date two-thirds of these besieged stalwarts, including the unfortunate Marquis de Torre Tagle, had starved to death.

◖ Caudillos and Chaos, 1826–1845

A new Peruvian congress assembled two months after the victory at Ayacucho. Bolívar submitted his *pro forma* resignation to that body, but it required very little effort by the legislators to persuade him to continue as chief of state. During the next year the Liberator devoted most of his attention to Bolivia, or Upper Peru as it was then known. Although this region enjoyed a separate administration within the Spanish Empire, it had been a geographical component of the Viceroyalty of Peru until the late eighteenth century. At that time the viceroy at Buenos Aires received titular authority over Upper Peru, but the area continued to have strong commercial ties with Peru proper. Both Argentina and Peru claimed this territory in 1825, and each of these contenders had some support within Upper Peru. But many Bolivians desired their own independent nation and Bolívar encouraged this group. The Liberator thought it wise to have a buffer state between Peru and Argentina and he probably feared the presence of a strong, unified Peru-Bolivian nation on the southern border of his Confederation of Gran Colombia. Bolívar also hoped to create and control a federation of the Andes comprising the three units of Gran Colombia together with Peru and Bolivia. The unification of the last two countries would have upset the balance required for harmonious federalism.

In the spring of 1825, Bolívar began a triumphal, ten-month tour of southern Peru and Bolivia. In August, he addressed a Bolivian assembly called to decide the fate of that country and declared Upper Peru independent. The assembly directed that the new state be named Bolivia in honor of the Liberator. They also asked Bolívar to write a constitution for the republic and serve as its first president. The charter drafted by the Venezuelan was a strange document. Although republican in name, it provided for a life-term president empowered to name his successor. Bolívar declined the post himself, but his friend Marshal Sucre agreed to a trial presidency of two years. As Peruvian chief executive, the Liberator sought to strengthen the independence of his namesake by concluding a treaty between the two nations which fixed Bolivia's boundaries, including a corridor to the sea.

Bolivar's grand design faced considerable opposition in Peru. The Peruvians did not want an independent Bolivia and they were hostile to the Liberator's plan for an Andean federation, especially if Bolívar dominated this union. Nationalists disliked the continued foreign control over their country and the presence of thousands of Colombian soldiers in Peru. Peruvian military leaders resented the preference Bolívar gave to foreign officers. Liberals disliked the Venezuelan's authoritarian rule and they accused him of emulating the political career of his admitted military hero, Napoleon Bonaparte. After a heated debate, the Peruvian congress adopted Bolívar's life-term constitution in August 1826 and elected him president under the system. Ironically, the Liberator's tenure lasted less than one month. A serious quarrel between Bolívar's lieutenants in Gran Colombia required his personal attention. Turning over his executive powers to a government council headed by Gen. Andrés Santa Cruz, a Bolivian, the Liberator left Peru on September 3, 1826. He never returned.

The two decades following Bolívar's departure from Lima were the stormiest in Peru's history. The nation was torn by civil strife and plagued with international conflicts. While men of thought debated fundamental questions of polity and drafted six constitutions between 1823 and 1839, men of action seized power with little concern for these abstractions. Although formal political parties did not exist, the labels "liberal" and "conservative" were applied rather loosely to individuals and their ideas. Few Peruvians of the period subscribed to the basic tenets of liberalism or conservatism in their purest form. Practical considerations tempered their ideas. But certain concepts molded their views of the state and its proper organization. Faith in the innate goodness and ultimate perfectibility of man— qualities that implied the fundamental equality of all human beings—underlay the liberal ideology. Men of this persuasion had confidence in Peru's capacity for self-government. They sought to protect the individual from the abuse of power which citizens entrusted to the state. Conservatives distrusted man and feared the triumph of passion over reason. They believed that society was composed of inferiors and superiors and that the latter group should ensure its control over the state. Government needed ample power to protect the established social order and preserve traditional institutions, especially the Church. Peru's liberals emerged victorious from the ideological conflicts of San Martín's conservative protectorship. Led by Francisco Javier de Luna Pizarro, a brilliant priest from Arequipa, they controlled congress for more than a dozen years and their ideas prevailed in the constitutions of 1823, 1828, and 1834. The conservative position found expression in the Bolivarian constitution of 1826 and in charters drafted in 1837 and 1839. Nevertheless, most of these documents exhibited a considerable amount of compromise.

Frustrated in their early attempts to secure a monarchy, Peru's conservatives hoped to establish an aristocratic republic with a very strong president. They wanted literacy and property qualifications for voting and election to public office. The liberals favored nearly universal manhood suffrage and relatively unrestricted access to government office. Fearing presidential power, they made congress the dominant branch of government. The issue of centralism versus federalism—a hallmark of the liberal-conservative dispute in most of Latin America—was less prominent in Peru. In many of the new republics the liberals tried to check the power of the central government by creating a federal system with considerable authority vested in elected provincial officials. Conservatives usually favored a highly centralized state with power concentrated in the national capital. Peru's liberals and conservatives generally agreed that the unitary system best suited the needs of their country. However, liberals favored the election of departmental juntas that would share administrative authority with executive officers appointed by the central government and greater home rule for the municipalities.

Peru's liberals and conservatives reached a basic agreement on the proper relationship between Church and state, another issue that caused bloody conflicts in several Latin American countries. From San Martín's time onward, Peru asserted that the republic had inherited the powers of ecclesiastical patronage from the Spanish crown. All of the early constitutions proclaimed Roman Catholicism the religion of the state, obligated the government to protect it, and prohibited the practice of all other sects. Surprisingly, the many churchmen who participated in the constituent assemblies usually displayed greater religious toleration than did their secular counterparts. Another compromise was reached on the liberal ideal of the equality of all citizens before the law. Churchmen and military officers retained the special privileges, or *fueros,* that they had enjoyed during the colonial period, most notably certain tax exemptions and separate courts. But the government removed the old legal distinctions between Indians, mestizos, and whites. The early charters protected the property rights of slaveholders by prohibiting emancipation without compensation to the owners, but these constitutions also provided for the eventual death of the institution: the international slave trade was banned and children born of slaves under the republic were declared free.

Outside of the congressional chambers in the world of practical politics, regional interests, family ties, and especially personal loyalties and enmities reigned supreme over constitutions and ideologies. By one count Peru had more than thirty chief executives between 1826 and 1845. The more significant of these men were caudillos—audacious leaders who commanded the loyalty of their largely illiterate armies by the force of their personalities and the promise of spoils. The caudillos were of diverse origins. Highborn white aristocrats vied for power with mestizos from rather humble backgrounds. But most of these leaders had achieved high military rank during the struggle for independence. Some of the caudillos were sincere patriots who believed that their rule would benefit the nation; others sought only personal aggrandizement or economic gain.

Soon after Bolívar returned to Colombia, the Peruvians began to undo his accomplishments. Early in 1827, the Colombian troops left behind by the Liberator mutinied and demanded that they be paid and sent home. The Peruvians gladly complied with their wishes and by March the country was free of foreign soldiers. In June, a liberal-dominated congress restored the Constitution of 1823. Two months later, congress elected Gen. José de la Mar to the presidency, replacing the caretaker regime of Santa Cruz. The new government abrogated Bolívar's treaty with Bolivia and demanded that its southern neighbor oust President Sucre, repatriate his Colombian forces and renounce the Bolivarian constitution. When the hero of Ayacucho rejected these demands, Peru invaded Bolivia. Instead of meeting this attack, Sucre's troops in La Paz revolted and the beleaguered president resigned. With its southern flank secured, Peru turned its attention toward Ecuador. The Peruvians had not accepted the inclusion of Guayaquil into Gran Colombia and in 1828, President La Mar led his army across the northern border. Guayaquil soon fell to the attackers, and La Mar's forces marched almost to the important highland city of Cuenca before suffering defeat at Portete de Tarquí. The victory was especially sweet for the Colombian commander—the embittered Marshal Sucre.

While directing the campaign in Ecuador, President La Mar was arrested and exiled by Gen. Agustín Gamarra, who had brought reinforcements to the front. Simultaneously, Gamarra's co-conspirator, Gen. Antonio de la Fuente, overthrew La Mar's vice-president in Lima. The new regime hastily concluded a peace with Gran Colombia, relinquishing Peru's claim to

Guayaquil. In August 1829, congress yielded to pressure and elected Gamarra president and La Fuente vice-president. The authoritarian Gamarra was unique among the caudillos of the period: he survived a full, four-year term. Nevertheless, to accomplish this feat, he had to crush seventeen rebellions, including one led by Vice-President La Fuente. Legally barred from a second successive term, Gamarra attempted to obtain the election of his henchmen Gen. Pedro Pablo Bermúdez in 1833. Weary of arbitrary government, congress rejected the dictator's candidate and elected Gen. Luis de Orbegoso, a mild-mannered man who promised to respect the constitution. Gamarra and Bermúdez, however, did not accept the decision of the legislature. They ousted the new chief executive one month later. But Orbegoso and constitutionalism had strong support among the civilian population and a four-month civil war restored the deposed president to power. Unfortunately, the luckless Orbegoso had only a few months to enjoy his office. In February 1835 he was overthrown by Gen. Felipe Salaverry, the young army commandant at Callao.

After his replacement by La Mar as Peruvian chief of state, Gen. Andrés Santa Cruz had returned to his native Bolivia, where he secured the presidency in 1829. The general was a shrewd politician and a capable administrator. Within a few years he greatly strengthened the Bolivian government. Santa Cruz was a mestizo and claimed royal Inca ancestry. Enlisting the past glories of the ancient Indian empire and, more directly, borrowing Bolivar's idea of an Andean federation, he labored to unite Peru and Bolivia under his leadership. Defeated by the forces of Orbegoso, General Gamarra agreed to help Santa Cruz accomplish his ambition in return for a high post within the new federation. But shortly after the conclusion of this pact, Gamarra's implacable enemy Orbegoso was deposed by Salaverry. He also offered his services to Santa Cruz. Because Orbegoso still held legal claim to the Peruvian presidency, Santa Cruz deemed him to be a more valuable ally than Gamarra, who now was eliminated from the alliance. Thus betrayed, Gamarra offered his support to President Salaverry, the man he recently had plotted against. Santa Cruz first defeated an army commanded by Gamarra and then smashed a second force led by Salaverry, who was captured. This dashing caudillo fell before a firing squad in February 1836, one year after he had seized power.

Santa Cruz quickly organized the Peru-Bolivia Confederation which was formally proclaimed in October 1836. The new entity consisted of three states—Bolivia, Southern Peru, and Northern Peru. The bisection of Peru pleased many people in the south who resented the dominance of Lima and increased the relative strength of Santa Cruz's Bolivian power base. Each of the three units had its own capital, president, and legislature. But Santa Cruz, who styled himself "Protector of the Confederation," controlled the union's armed forces, finances, and foreign policy as well as the Bolivian presidency. The marriage of Peru and Bolivia had much to recommend it: geographical unity, a common culture, close historical ties, and strong economic bonds. But many groups within the confederation were unhappy. Lima resented the debilitating division of Peru and domination by a Bolivian. Southern Peru would have preferred a union of only itself and Bolivia, a weaker confederation that might have been controlled from Arequipa, the capital of the south. La Paz opposed the selection of Lima as the seat of the general government of the confederation and citizens in both Peru and Bolivia objected to the impairment of their nations' independence. Liberals disliked the authoritarian Protector and partisans of the unfortunate Salaverry awaited an opportunity to avenge the death of their leader.

Chile nervously watched the formation of this new power on its northern frontier. This nation had a number of grievances, old and new, against Peru and Santa Cruz. The Chileans had harbored animosity for Peruvians since the colonial period when the haughty *limeños* controlled the trade of the Pacific coast and deprecated their more rustic southern neighbors. Relations between the two countries were strained badly during the wars of independence. Royalist Peruvian forces crushed Chile's First Republic. And after Chile had contributed mightily to Peru's independence, Lima refused to repay a loan which the O'Higgins government had obtained in Britain to finance San Martín's liberating expedition. More recently, the two nations engaged in a bitter trade war and in 1836, Santa Cruz had permitted an exiled Chilean caudillo to organize an expedition in Peru against the government in Santiago. But of greatest concern to Chile, the Peru-Bolivia Confederation—if allowed to consolidate— would have upset the balance of power which the Chileans hoped to maintain in the Pacific.

In August 1836, two Chilean vessels slipped into Callao harbor under the cover of darkness and captured three Peruvian warships, virtually the entire navy of the confederation. Possessing naval supremacy, Chile presented Santa Cruz with several demands, including the dissolution of the Peru-Bolivia union. The Protector rejected this ultimatum and Chile declared war on November 11. Argentina also felt discomfort concerning the new confederation and dictator Juan Manuel de Rosas needed a foreign adventure to enhance his prestige and divert attention from his unpopular domestic policies. Buenos Aires declared war, but contributed little to the military effort.

A Chilean force of 3,500 men commanded by Adm. Manuel Blanco Encalada sailed for Peru in mid-September 1837. Landing on the south coast, the invaders marched to Arequipa and into a trap. Blanco Encalada signed a peace treaty and was permitted to return home with his embarrassed army. The Chilean government renounced this agreement and in July 1838 Gen. Manuel Bulnes led a second expedition against the confederation. Among its 6,000 men was a large contingent of Peruvian exiles commanded by generals Gamarra, La Fuente, and Ramón Castilla, who proclaimed their intention of restoring Peru's independence from Bolivia. In February 1839, the Chileans decisively defeated the forces of Santa Cruz at Yungay, in the highlands north of Lima. The confederation disintegrated and its Protector fled to Ecuador.

The Chilean forces left Lima in October 1840, after placing their ally General Gamarra in power under a new conservative constitution. This wily caudillo crushed one dangerous rebellion and he might have completed another term in the Peruvian presidency. But Gamarra, who had just assisted the Chileans in smashing Santa Cruz's confederation, now attempted to resurrect the union under his own protectorship. Accusing the Bolivian government of a plot to restore Santa Cruz to power, Gamarra led his army across the southern border. At the battle of Ingaví, on November 18, 1841, the Bolivians routed the Peruvians and killed Gamarra. A period of almost incomprehensible confusion ensued. The Bolivians invaded Peru from the south and the Ecuadorians, inspired by Santa Cruz, prepared to do the same from the north. The commanders of the two armies sent to resist these invasions denounced the government in Lima and each other, only to be betrayed themselves by their subordinates. In the multi-sided civil war that followed, a flurry of revolutionary proclamations emanated from the provinces, while the people of Lima witnessed a veritable parade of caudillos. Manuel Menéndez, Gamarra's constitutional successor, was ousted by General Torrico. General Vidal replaced him, but he soon was deposed by General Vivanco. In July 1844, Gen. Ramón Castilla defeated Vivanco at Carmén Alto, near Arequipa, and Lima nervously awaited the arrival of the new "supreme chief."

The War of Independence and the political chaos of the years that followed brought economic decline and social disruption. The unattended mines of the Sierra flooded and their equipment deteriorated. The coastal estates suffered from an ever-contracting labor supply as peons were conscripted and slaves freed to fill the ranks of revolutionary armies. Military leaders confiscated crops, livestock, and other property. The nation's inadequate road system fell into even greater disrepair. Peru lacked the capital to restore the economy and political turmoil discouraged foreign investment. The long wars of indepdence in America disrupted Peru's trade with its neighbors and European customers. The country lost many of these old markets. What remained of the republic's foreign commerce fell almost exclusively under the control of British, French, and North American merchants. Tariffs designed solely to produce revenue often subjected small artisan industries to ruinous foreign competition, while discouraging imports of equipment needed to develop the nation's mining and agriculture. The country financed a foreign trade deficit with outflows of gold and silver. This resulted in a shortage of specie which hampered internal commerce. Lima, the once proud and affluent "City of the Kings," became shabby and its population declined sharply.

The lot of the Indians probably worsened. Soon after his arrival in Peru, San Martín decreed that the aborigines no longer be called "Indians" or "natives," but that they be addressed simply as "Peruvians." He also abolished the discriminatory *mita* and tribute tax. But these brotherly sentiments quickly waned and both exactions reappeared under new euphemisms. The tribute tax became the "indigenous contribution"; forced labor on roads and other public works was called "republican service." While the substance of colonial discrimination remained, the official egalitarianism of the republic stripped the Indians of the limited protection they had received under Spanish law.

The leaders of the new nation adopted a hostile policy toward the indigenous communities, which they viewed as incubators of ignorance and obstacles to national unification. The remanents of the old *curaca* class, greatly reduced since the rebellion of Túpac Amaru II, were divested of their political authority. This

73

freed some villages from their native oppressors, but others lost their leaders and protectors at a time when they were needed badly. Corporate landholding seemed an anachronism in Adam Smith's world of economic individualism. Expressing a desire to create a class of yeomen farmers, Bolívar decreed the inclusion of communal lands into the public domain in 1823. The Indians received small parcels as private property. "Surplus" village lands were sold by the impecunious government, or distributed to its supporters. The Indians generally were illiterate and ignorant of Spanish and often did not understand the Western concept of private land ownership. *Gamonales,* ruthless rural bosses who used armed force as well as the law to amass land, easily despoiled the natives' holdings. Alarmed by the rapid transfer of Indian property to whites and mestizos, the government prohibited the sale of land by illiterate natives in 1828, but this law could not be enforced. Whether they were called "Indians" or "Peruvians," the natives continued to be exploited by the republican successors of the colonial elites.

Public administration in Peru suffered from the expulsion of many capable and experienced Spanish officials. The national treasury was usually empty and the government lived from hand-to-mouth. Military expenditures regularly consumed more than 60 percent of the state's revenues. Yet soldiers as well as bureaucrats went unpaid for months, a situation that encouraged mutiny and graft. The government could not provide basic services such as schools and police protection for the nation's citizens. Highwaymen infested the six-mile road between Lima and Callao. Informed by spies in the two cities about the movements of travelers, especially wealthy foreigners, these bandits robbed and then good-naturedly stripped their victims. Other gangs of outlaws roamed the countryside extorting "protection money" from property owners. The government often was reluctant to suppress these brigands: in times of revolution the bandits became *montoneros,* irregular cavalry units.

The weakness of Peru's early governments frustrated the nation's territorial ambitions in Ecuador and Bolivia and threatened its possession of the vast Montaña, a region with very tenuous bonds to the rest of the country. Most of the missions established there during the colonial period along with several secular towns were abandoned and Indian marauders boldly attacked those that remained. Trails connecting the eastern lowlands with the Sierra rapidly deteriorated and Brazilian merchants monopolized the commerce of most of the region, which

74

now utilized the Amazon River to reach foreign markets. Brazil, Ecuador, Colombia, and Bolivia claimed ownership of vast portions of this vaguely delimited territory and Peru was unable to protect its interests.

Peru's external debt, contracted during the struggle with Spain, mounted rapidly as even the interest on these obligations fell into arrears. The republic lost its credit abroad. Foreigners who suffered losses of life and property during the frequent political upheavals often appealed to their own governments for assistance. These nations sometimes employed insulting language and heavy-handed tactics in pressing the claims of their nationals. Humiliated in war and unable to govern itself in peace, the greatest of Spain's former colonies in South America became an object of international ridicule. The law and governmental institutions did not earn the respect of the people and the nation lost faith in itself.

After almost a decade in Lima, United States Chargé d'Affaires James C. Pickett gave a most unflattering description of Peru in 1845.

> I doubt much whether the Spanish Americans have gained anything by their independence, except freedom of commerce, and that they would have had probably before now, even had they continued in a state of colonial dependence.—I doubt too their fitness, in general, for a democratic form of government and for democratic institutions; but still they ought to have and might have, something better than the despicable and detestable military depostisms by which they have been so long dishonored and oppressed.

> The officers of the [Peruvian] army . . . number from two to three thousand, being about *one* to every *two* soldiers. Of these not less than forty I believe, are general officers, and colonels and other field-officers are almost inumerable: And the worst of it is, that with few exceptions, there is not one of this official mob that would not be ready at any moment to plunge the country into a civil war, if he thought he would be personally benefitted by doing so. The political changes in Peru called *revolutions,* are nothing more than military treacheries and mutinies, the people having nothing to do with them, unless when compelled at the point of the bayonet.*

---

*J. C. Pickett to Secretary of State John C. Calhoun, Despatch No. 110, Lima, February 8, 1845; and Pickett to Calhoun, Despatch No. 111, Lima, March 3, 1845, Record Group 59, "General Records of the Department of State, Despatches from United States Ministers to Peru, 1826–1906" (Washington, D.C.: National Archives, Microcopy T-52, Reel 6).

75

Peru's political instability was not entirely the product of the personal ambition of the caudillos, as Pickett implied. Caudillism was only one symptom of a more profound social malady. The ideal of political democracy, far from universal in Peru, was contradicted by a distinctly undemocratic society. Seedling republican institutions had difficulty surviving in the thicket of authoritarian traditions deeply rooted in both the Indian and Iberian cultures. Spain had not prepared its colonies for democracy. The nation did not have it to give. But every *hacendado* had a long apprenticeship in dictatorial rule. The authority of the Spanish monarchs and the Inca emperors before them had been sanctioned by divine right, strengthened with the passage of time and guarded by an aura of mystery and omnipotence. Independence produced both a crisis of political legitimacy and a power vacuum. Lacking strong national political institutions and with few well-known civilian leaders, Peruvians naturally turned to the heroes of the independence movement in these years of crisis. Unfortunately, Peru had an overabundance of ambitious officers with equally valid revolutionary credentials. The country's poor degree of physical and social integration impeded the establishment of even stable dictatorships.

Peru's twenty-year plague of caudillism may not have been an unmitigated curse. Indeed, there was much death and destruction and the period produced scant material progress. But the chaos of the era weakened the nation's undemocratic social and economic structure. The old colonial aristocracy nearly disappeared, giving new importance to the small middle strata of society. Racial barriers were breached as caudillos, including mestizo leaders, seized power and dispensed rewards to their half-caste followers. The freeing of slaves hurt the plantation economy, but it was another step toward a more democratic society. Notwithstanding laws designed to give legal equality to the Indians, the natives continued to be second-class citizens in their own country. But driven from the protective shells of their communities by *gamonales* and army press gangs, increasing numbers of Indians confronted the outside world and adapted to their new circumstances. The slow process of their assimilation into the dominant national culture was quickened. Old entrenched economic interests that could not withstand the test of adversity gave way to new and sometimes more modern groups. Many of the great estates of the Church and the old elite were confiscated or sold and often divided into smaller units. But a continuation of this brutal leveling process threatened to bring social dissolution. By 1845, most Peruvians of all classes desired peace.

4

Stability, Reform, and a

Precarious Prosperity

[1845–1879]

GEN. RAMÓN CASTILLA BECAME PRESIDENT of Peru in 1845, and inaugurated a thirty-year epoch of increased political stability, significant reform, and economic growth. For the first time since independence, the country enjoyed extended periods of constitutional government. Castilla made serious efforts to improve the administration of the state and provide basic services for its people. Peru's international reputation recovered from the embarrassment of the early years. Under Castilla, in fact, the republic aspired to a leadership role among the nations of Latin America. Because this strongman was the dominant personality in Peruvian politics until his death in 1867, the middle decades of the nineteenth century have been called the "Age of Castilla."

Ramón Castilla deserves his place in Peru's pantheon of national heroes. Nevertheless, he must share credit for the progress of his era with millions of birds which for centuries deposited their guano on rocky promontories along the coast and several offshore islands. Between 1840 and 1880, Peru exported nearly eleven million tons of this highly nitrogenous fertilizer valued at 600 million dollars. Bird manure provided the government with a fabulous income that supported the public programs of the period and generated capital for the development of new industries. Economically, the years of Castilla's tenure and beyond were the "Age of Guano." Unfortunately, Castilla and his successors mismanaged the nation's guano revenues. Peru's highly visible prosperity rested upon an unsound base and crumbled in bankruptcy at the end of the era.

Catilla and Guano, 1845–1868

Ramón Castilla was born in 1797 to a middle-class miner in Tarapacá, the southernmost coastal department that Peru later lost to Chile. Of Spanish, Italian, and Indian ancestry, he has been attractive to modern Peruvians as a symbol of the nation's mestizo heritage. Castilla's formal education ended at a secondary school in Santiago, where his long military career began. In 1812, the fourteen-year-old student enlisted in the royalist army that suppressed Chile's first independence movement. A decade later, however, he joined San Martín in the struggle to liberate Peru and fought with distinction at Junín and Ayacucho. Castilla actively participated in the political struggles of the early republic and held a number of government posts, culminating with a short but notable tenure as treasury minister during the last Gamarra administration. Although primarily associated with conservative regimes in his early years, Castilla was a political pragmatist skilled in the art of compromise. He appointed men of diverse ideologies to public office. Vigorous in quelling rebellions against his authority, Castilla initiated a long tradition of magnanimity toward defeated foes. No political opponent faced a firing squad during his rule. Castilla tolerated peaceful criticism of his regime. The nation's highly partisan press enjoyed considerable freedom. Congress met regularly and openly debated the issues of the day.

Because Castilla gave Peru its first taste of constitutional government, he has been called the "soldier of the Law." But in moments of crisis, the soldier in his personality prevailed over the defender of strict constitutionalism. After suppressing several conspiracies against his regime and exiling their leaders, Castilla explained his actions to congress in June 1849.

> The first of my constitutional functions is the preservation of internal order; but the same constitution obliges me to respect the rights of the citizen. In my own conscience . . . the simultaneous fulfillment of both duties would be impossible. The former—the preservation of internal order—could not be accomplished by the existing authority [under the constitution], without some measures to check the enemies of that order in a manner more stringent than was provided for by the laws. Ought I to have sacrificed the domestic quiet of the country to the constitutional rights of a few individuals?*

Although Castilla valued order and stability above freedom and reform, he did not abandon these secondary objectives to achieve his primary goals. His fame rests upon significant contributions in both of these areas.

Castilla had less success in financial matters, but he was not so imprudent with the nation's wealth as some historians have thought. Near the end of his service as treasury minister in November 1840, Castilla approved the first of many arrangements for the export of guano. Francisco Quiroz, a prominent Peruvian businessman with European financial backers, obtained a six-year license for the exclusive sale of this product overseas. Quiroz agreed to pay the government 10,000 *pesos* per year for this privilege and immediately advance the treasury 40,000 *pesos* of the total license fee. The sale of similar monopoly rights long had been employed by Peru's penurious governments to raise ready cash and Quiroz approached the regime at a propitious moment: Gamarra's war with Bolivia was about to begin and the treasury was empty.

The first guano venture prospered beyond the expectations of both the entrepreneurs and the government. Although employed in Peruvian agriculture since pre-Incaic times, the value of this fertilizer was practically unknown outside of the country. Curious British farmers rapidly purchased the first guano shipments. Soon, other business groups approached Peruvian officials and offered to improve upon the contract with Quiroz. After only one year, the administration canceled the original

*Translated text enclosed with J. Randolph Clay to Secretary of State John M. Clayton, Despatch No. 29, Lima, July 12, 1849, Record Group 59, "General Records of the Department of State, Despatches from United States Ministers to Peru, 1826–1906" (Washington, D.C.: National Archives, Microcopy T-52, Reel 8).

license. The Quiroz organization, anxious to maintain its monopoly, outbid its competitors and was awarded a new one-year contract. They agreed to pay the state 64 percent of their net receipts and loan the government 287,000 *pesos* against its share of the anticipated proceeds. Three months later, the regime received further overtures from a different firm and again terminated its arrangement with Quiroz. Now, a consortium combining the Quiroz group and several European companies secured a five-year monopoly on guano exports. The treasury received advances totaling nearly a half-million *pesos,* and the state's account was to be credited with the first 30 dollars per ton obtained from the sale of guano plus 75 percent of any remaining profits. The guano market quickly slumped and the treasury received nearly all the proceeds of this venture. In these early dealings the government clearly bested the businessmen.

After the third guano contract expired in 1847, the Castilla administration negotiated new one-year agreements with the Montané Company of Paris for a monopoly of guano sales in France and with the Anthony Gibbs Company for exclusive rights to market the fertilizer in Britain and most other regions of the world. These contracts provided for the consignment system that would characterize the guano trade for the next two decades. Consignment was a common practice in international commerce, especially for countries like Peru that were far removed from the major markets of the North Atlantic. Poor communications and slow transportation made long-distance trade highly speculative, particularly dealings in primary products subject to rapid and profound fluctuations in price. Desiring profits commensurate with their risks, merchants made low bids to producers of commodities. If the producer wanted the high, risk-taking gains for himself, he would retain ownership of his goods, but market them through a consignee who acted as the owner's sales agent. Under the 1847 contracts, the Peruvian government hired Montané and Gibbs to load, transport, and market the state's guano. The treasury reimbursed these firms for their marketing costs and paid them a commission based on these expenses plus a share of the gross proceeds from sales of the manure. As in earlier agreements, the consignees made large interest-bearing advances to the government.

The consignment contracts negotiated by the Castilla administration and later regimes had many critics, then and now. Because the consignees earned commissions partially based on their expenses, they were encouraged to decrease their efficiency in loading and transporting guano. Furthermore, the state could have obtained the greatest total return over the long run by asking a high price for each ton of this exhaustible resource. However, the consignees often preferred to maximize their short-term profits by reducing the unit price of the fertilizer and increasing the volume of their sales. The government recognized these shortcomings and later inserted restrictions in the contracts to protect its interests. But the state had difficulty enforcing these measures and charges of fraud frequently were made against the consignees. Some Peruvians suggested that the government market the manure itself, or sell it outright to bidders at the guano deposits. However, the state lacked the resources to develop its own distribution system and experiments with guano auctions did not demonstrate the superiority of this alternative to consignment. Eventually, as the treasury became increasingly indebted to the consignees, impoverished regimes found it easier to extend existing agreements, with further advances, than to experiment with new systems for selling the fertilizer.

By demanding substantial cash advances from contractors, the state effectively limited the trade to persons with access to plentiful supplies of money—in practice, foreigners. Native businessmen loudly protested against this feature of the system, and in 1849 the Castilla regime ruled that Peruvians and resident aliens would receive preference in the award of future contracts. During the next few years, national businessmen did become consignees. But most of these ventures soon failed because of a shortage of capital and entrepreneurial skills, scarce resources in Peru at that time. In the 1860s, however, Peruvians succeeded in the trade and a large share of the industry's profits flowed directly to native capitalists. The principal financial errors of Peru's Guano-Age regimes were neither the consignment system nor the prominent role of foreigners in the trade. Problems arose because of the government's growing dependence on advances and its failure to employ guano revenues more productively.

Most of Peru's guano came from the Chincha Islands, in the Bay of Pisco, where some manure deposits were 100 feet deep. In the 1850s and 1860s, the heydey of the industry, scores of ships simultaneously loaded guano at the Chinchas. One of these islands had a narrow-gauge railroad and a town of about 1,000 residents. Wage workers shunned the guano pits, so slaves, army deserters, convicts, and Chinese indentured servants comprised most of the labor force. These unfortunates dug the dry, gypsum-like substance with spades and used wheelbarrows to load it into carts or railroad cars that carried the guano to the sea cliffs. Here they chuted the manure through canvas hoses of about two feet in diameter into open lighters below. The shallow-draft boats took the fertilizer to deeper water where basket winches transferred it into larger vessels, often the oldest ships afloat. A thick, ammonia-smelling cloud enveloped the ships during the loading process and workers wore gauze bandages over their noses and mouths to reduce the inhalation of the choking fumes. On many days, the stench across the bay at Pisco was almost unbearable.

Restricted to a single term by the constitution, Castilla surrendered his office to Gen. José Rufino Echenique in 1851. The new president was a well-intentioned but naïve man. Although apparently honest himself, Echenique surrounded himself with self-serving friends and too readily accepted their advice. The relative tranquillity and freedom of expression under Castilla had afforded Peru the luxury of a brisk liberal-conservative dialogue that intensified in the aftermath of the liberal-nationalist Revolutions of 1848 in Europe. Flexible in his attitudes, Castilla charted a middle course in these controversies. Echenique, however, allowed himself to be ensnared by the conservatives. The increasingly rightward drift of the administration and its authoritarian tenor evoked sharp criticism from liberals, while the regime's corruption produced a national chorus of protest.

Most of Echenique's problems stemmed from his handling of the country's public debt. In an attempt to restore the nation's credit, Castilla had used part of the guano receipts to begin service on Peru's foreign bonds. Many Peruvians also had old claims against the treasury for goods confiscated, slaves liberated, and loans exacted during the struggle for independence and its aftermath. They demanded that their government be as mindful of these obligations as it was to the claims of European creditors. A law of 1850 provided that all instruments of domestic indebtedness—from official bonds to the scrawled notes of military chieftains—could be presented to a special tribunal for validation and coversion to new 6 percent government securities. The Echenique regime grossly maladministered this program, accepting many fraudulent claims. Peru's internal debt quickly soared from four to twenty-three million *pesos*. The beneficiaries of this largess feared that a later administration might repudiate this debt. Therefore, the government was persuaded to convert thirteen million *pesos'* worth of bonds held by well-connected individuals into cash and more-secure foreign obligations through secret sales of new bonds in London. Echenique justified this transaction as an economy measure. The foreign bonds carried a lower rate of interest than the domestic issues. But the public rejected this explanation.

Several liberal leaders began an uprising in early 1854, and they persuaded Castilla to take charge of the movement. Rapidly gaining broad popular support, the revolution ousted Echenique after a bloody, year-long struggle. Castilla began his second presidency in July 1855, and he would retain that office until 1862. The restiveness of the vanquished conservatives forced the president to rely heavily upon liberal support during the first three years of his new term, and the regime's programs reflected this influence. In fact, Castilla decreed his most notable reforms while leading the movement against Echenique. One of these ended the tribute tax paid by the Indians. The other completely abolished slavery. This last act, which emancipated more than 25,000 black bondsmen, was accomplished by compensating the slaveholders with 300-*peso* manumission bonds. Both of these reforms had gained considerable support among liberals in recent years and even had some conservative adherents. But military expedience also influenced the timing of these decrees. Castilla hoped that Indians and blacks would join him in the revolution to make these laws effective.

Castilla's countrymen honored him with the title "Liberator" for his role in these reforms. Ironically, the measures that freed the slaves and eased the burdens of the Indians contributed to the most reprehensible aspect of Castilla's rule—the beginning of a sordid commerce in Chinese coolies. Since the sixteenth century, Peruvian employers had complained of a "labor shortage"—men were unwilling to sell their services under the prevailing wage and working conditions. Increased economic activity after 1840 intensified this problem and the shortage became acute following emancipation and the abolition of tribute. The head tax on Indians often had forced the natives to work for cash wages. To meet the increased demand for labor an immigration law of 1849 offered contractors thirty *pesos* for each male aged ten to forty brought to Peru in groups of at least fifty persons. The government hoped to encourage an influx of European farmers and craftsmen. But Peru—where manual labor was

84

disdained and rewarded accordingly—could not compete successfully with other New World nations for Europe's surplus population. Therefore, unscrupulous contractors brought about 100,000 Chinese into the country between 1850 and 1880.

The commerce in coolies had many of the worst features of the African slave trade. The entrepreneurs often lured the Chinese to Peru through misrepresentation. Some were kidnapped. On an average voyage across the wide Pacific about 10 percent of the coolies died in the overcrowded and poorly provisioned ships. More than half of the human cargo perished during some journeys. The Chinese signed contracts of indenture obligating them to work for eight years. Because these documents were transferable, the coolies could be bought and sold. The indentured workers were supposed to receive a small wage, but employers illegally deducted most of this for food and clothing. Debt peonage ensnared many of these Orientals after their legal period of service had expired. About 90 percent of the Chinese labored on the plantations of the coast and some 5,000 were employed in railroad construction. But the most unfortunate coolies worked under the lash in the hot, stinking hell of the guano pits. Those Asiatics who survived these rigors eventually gained their freedom. However, their strange customs and the industriousness that brought them economic success inspired an ugly nativist reaction among Peruvians. The Chinese and, later, Japanese immigrants became victims of "yellow peril" madness that periodically infected the country.

After months of acrimonious debate, Peru's victorious liberals secured a new constitution in 1856. Like previous liberal charters, this document substantially reduced the power of the executive in favor of the legislature. It eliminated the president's emergency powers, authority often invoked in the past to establish dictatorial rule. The cabinet became an independent unit of the executive branch, sharing power with the president and checking his actions. The new fundamental law limited the chief of state's control over local affairs by reestablishing departmental juntas with greater autonomy than ever before. Congress received the power to approve military promotions, remove cabinet ministers, and declare the office of president vacant for violations of the constitution. For the first time, the 1856 charter called for the direct popular election of the chief executive.

The constituent assembly voted unanimously to continue the union of Church and state and overwhelmingly defeated a proposal to permit the private practice of religions other than Catholicism. Yet, the liberals of 1856 exhibited a much greater degree of anticlericalism and antimilitarism than had their predecessors. The new constitution abolished the religious and military *fueros* and barred both churchmen and soldiers from election to congress. The tithe, a tax collected by the government for the support of the Church, was ended and the state assumed almost complete control over the finances of the institution. Congress was empowered to limit the size of the armed forces and create a civilian national guard to offset the influence of the regular military establishment. The Constitution of 1856 reiterated the abolition of slavery and Indian tribute. It provided for free primary education in the public schools. Finally, the charter banned military impressment, prohibited exile without due process of law, and eliminated the death penalty.

Castilla took an oath to support the new constitution, but he also expressed grave reservations concerning several of its features. He questioned the timing of the anticlerical provisions of the charter, fearing that these would bring a violent reaction by Peru's already agitated conservatives. He was especially dismayed by the president's loss of power to maintain internal order. The anticipated rightist rebellion began soon after the promulgation of the new document and required more than a year to extinguish. Thereafter, Castilla acted to put the nation on a more moderate course. He forcibly dissolved the liberal-controlled congress in 1858, and supervised the election of a more conservative constituent assembly. This body adopted a new constitution in 1860 that better reflected the nation's ideological milieu and more closely conformed to Castilla's own views.

The Constitution of 1860 reestablished the executive as the dominant branch of the government. The president was to be elected indirectly for a four-year term and could not immediately succeed himself. His control over the cabinet was restored as were his emergency powers. National authorities again assumed rigid control over local governments. Still, the new charter provided greater safeguards against the abuse of executive power than had the conservative Constitution of 1839. Although softened in some details, the fundamental law retained most of the anticlerical and antimilitary provisions of the previous charter. Essentially a compromise between the ideals of the liberals and Peruvian political realities, the Constitution of 1860 would pass the test of time. Save for two brief interruptions, it remained the basic law of the nation until 1920.

The thirteen years of Castilla's two presidencies, bridged by the troubled tenure of Echenique, witnessed notable improvements in public administration. In 1845, Castilla's finance minister submitted Peru's first national budget to congress, initiating more modern management practices in the republic's fiscal affairs. The regime also established a government accounting agency, complete with a statistics bureau. This office undertook the nation's first true census in 1862, an enumeration that revealed a population of almost 2.5 million persons. Several new legal codes were drafted and Peru's civil servants became the first in Latin America to receive state pensions. The government brought the great Italian naturalist Antonio Raimondi to Peru and he began a long career surveying the country's mineral resources. Mariano Felipe Paz-Soldán was commissioned to reform the republic's penal system. After studying many prisons in the United States and Europe, he planned a model penitentiary in Lima where all inmates received instruction in useful trades.

The Castilla administration issued an Ordinance of Instruction in 1855, Peru's first significant attempt to organize a public school system. A General Bureau of Studies in Lima prescribed the curriculum, set educational standards, and provided funds for school construction. Local communities, however, bore the expenses of operation. Although tuition was charged, the law established scholarships for poor children. The government opened many new educational facilities, including secondary schools in most departmental capitals and a Central Normal School in Lima to train teachers. Ancient San Marcos University was reorganized and revitalized. It absorbed several private colleges in Lima and acquired a school of medicine. These measures, though impressive, only began to attack the problems that beset Peruvian education after decades of neglect. Less that 16,000 students were enrolled in the nation's public primary schools in 1859.

A new Bureau of Public Works supervised a large number of government construction projects, especially in Lima. The state paved the principal streets, built new promenades, erected statues, and installed gas lighting in the central district. The capital acquired a new central market, a public slaughterhouse, a mint, and Paz-Soldán's mammoth penitentiary. To check the epidemics that periodically panicked the city, the regime improved the primitive water and sewer systems. The administration also provided potable water for Arequipa, Islay (near present-day Matarani), Callao, and the Lima suburbs of Chorrillos and Bellavista. Many churches, orphanages, asylums, and hospitals were constructed throughout the country.

Castilla's public works program gave top priority to improving the nation's grossly inadequate transporation facilities. While serving as Gamarra's treasury minister in 1840, Castilla signed a contract with the Valparaíso-based Pacific Steam Navigation Company which soon initiated service to Peru. Thereafter, the rapid expansion of the republic's foreign trade placed a severe strain on the country's antiquated port facilities. The government provided Callao with a new lighthouse and modern docks, complete with a tramway. A half-mile-long iron pier was constructed at Pisco and other port improvements were made at Paita and Arica. After studies by several teams of explorers and engineers, the regime issued the republic's first national road plan. Several bridges and roads were built and many old ones were repaired.

In 1851, President Castilla inaugurated one of Latin America's earliest railroads, an eight-mile line connecting Lima with the docks at Callao. This new facility provided service for about 1,000 passengers during its first year of operation. However, violent protests by mule drivers elicited a government ban on freight service by the railway. The administration built another railroad to link the capital with Chorrillos, nine miles away, and a line of thirty-nine miles between the southern coastal towns of Tacna and Arica. Castilla also introduced the telegraph to Peru, installing the first wires between Lima and Callao in 1857.

General Castilla believed that the republic needed a strong, professional military establishment to preserve internal order and protect the country's interests in foreign affairs. Therefore, he gave special attention to the army and navy. The armed forces were reorganized and promptly paid. The national military academy, closed soon after its establishment by San Martín, was reopened. Other training facilities and armories were constructed. Castilla equipped the army with modern rifles and artillery. The navy acquired several new vessels, including the first steam-powered warships in South America. This program of military preparedness soon brought dividends. In 1857, Ecuador granted a huge area claimed by Peru in the Amazon Basin to a group of British creditors. Castilla personally directed a naval and land campaign that seized Guayaquil and forced the cancellation of the offending agreement. After many humiliating defeats, Peru finally had won a war.

Motivated by a desire to protect Peru's vast Amazonian territory from its neighbors and develop the region's economic potential, Ramón Castilla took the first important steps to bring the Montaña under the effective control of the national government. His regime, along with that of Echenique, repaired old trails and built new ones penetrating the region. The government strengthened its military outposts in the eastern lowlands and supported the reestablishment of missions among the jungle Indians. A few colonies of Europeans and native Peruvians were settled east of the Andes. These pioneers received lands, agricultural supplies, and cash subsidies from the state. Most significantly, the Peruvian government introduced steam navigation to the rivers of the northeastern lowlands. A commercial treaty negotiated with Brazil in 1851 permitted Peru to import and export goods duty free by way of the Brazilian portion of the Amazon River. Two years later, a Brazilian steamship company, with a subsidy from the Lima treasury, began service to the Peruvian river port of Nauta. The government's own fleet of steamers plied the waterways beyond that point. The national administration provided other public services for the region, including schools and mail delivery. In 1861, the northern portion of the Montaña became the huge new Department of Loreto.

President Castilla greatly enhanced Peru's international prestige. A reorganized diplomatic service established permanent legations in important foreign capitals and staffed these posts with distinguished representatives. The resumption of service on the nation's external debt restored the republic's credit abroad. Castilla's large expenditures on defense placed Peru among the leading military powers of South America. Finally, the mestizo statesman revived the ideal of Latin American solidarity, a goal nearly forgotten after 1826, when Simón Bolívar presided over the first inter-American meeting at Panama. Peru hosted a gathering of representatives from four Pacific coast republics at Lima in late 1847 and early 1848. The conference was called to discuss the activities of former Ecuadorian dictator Juan José Flores, who was attempting to obtain European support for the establishment of a monarchy in his country. But the diplomats also expressed concern about the ambitions of the

United States, at that time concluding its war of conquest against Mexico.

During the next dozen years, Latin American governments became more and more apprehensive of the Yankees. Private North American armies, the filibusters, invaded several countries to the south. In 1856, a Tennessean named William Walker seized control of Nicaragua and attempted to create a Central American empire. Washington denied complicity in the activities of these adventurers, but the increasingly bellicose tone of North American diplomacy weakened these disclaimers. Peru helped organize and actively participated in a conference of seven Latin American nations at Santiago, Chile, in 1856. Here, the diplomats signed a Continental Treaty, pledging to assist each other in defense of their sovereignty against outside aggressors. Castilla kept his nation's promise. Peru loaned Costa Rica 100,000 *pesos* to finance that republic's war against William Walker. Lima also offered to help the Costa Ricans build and defend an interoceanic canal through their territory.

Relations between Lima and Washington already were strained. North American farmers bitterly protested against the Peruvian guano monopoly and Yankee diplomats labored in vain to lower the price of the fertilizer. At the same time, the United States vigorously pressed the claims of its nationals who had incurred damages during revolutions in Peru. Although never seriously considered by the State Department, Peru viewed with alarm suggestions that the United States might seize several Peruvian islands to break the guano monopoly and force payment of North American claims. An attempt by former President Echenique to organize a Yankee filibustering expedition against the Castilla government further exacerbated tensions between the two countries. Primarily because of the claims issue, Washington severed diplomatic relations with Lima in 1860. But as the North American Civil War approached, the United States mended its diplomatic fences and reached a compromise with the Castilla administration. Largely because of his opposition to United States policy, Yankee diplomats were almost universally unkind in their assessments of Ramón Castilla. However, under his leadership Peru had gained considerable prestige among the other nations of Latin America.

Peru experienced another period of internal unrest and foreign conflict following Castilla's departure from office in 1862. Gen. Miguel San Román, the old caudillo who succeeded him, died after only a few months in office. Gen. Juan Antonio Pezet, the vice-president, assumed the post of chief executive at a most troublesome time. During the 1860s the government of Spain attempted to enhance its prestige in Latin America and, perhaps, reestablish control over some of its former colonies in the region. The murder of two Spanish colonists on an estate in northern Peru in 1863 afforded Madrid a pretext for intervention. Spain demanded an apology and a large indemnity from Peru and seized the guano-rich Chincha Islands to force compliance. Many prominent citizens, including ex-President Castilla, called for a declaration of war to uphold the nation's honor. But Pezet believed that his navy was not strong enough to challenge a powerful Spanish fleet cruising off the coast.

In January 1865, the Spaniards threatened Callao with a naval bombardment and the Pezet regime capitulated to the aggressor's demands. Spain relinquished its control over the Chincha Islands, but only after it had removed large amounts of guano. Pezet's humiliating submission outraged the public. Col. Mariano Ignacio Prado launched a revolution that ousted the president in November 1865. The new regime quickly repudiated the settlement with Spain and signed a defensive alliance with Chile, Ecuador, and Bolivia. The Spanish navy bombarded defenseless Valparaíso, Chile, and then steamed northward to attack Callao. On May 2, 1866, the 50-gun shore batteries protecting the Peruvian port fought the 275-gun Spanish fleet to a draw. The Spaniards withdrew from the Pacific coast and Peru claimed a victory.

President Prado received the laurels of a national hero, but his popularity had waned by early 1867. Drawn under the influence of Peru's liberals, Prado permitted them to proclaim a new constitution similar to the short-lived liberal charter of 1856. From his home in Tarapacá, Ramón Castilla proclaimed a revolution to restore his constitution. But it was one campaign too many for the nearly seventy-year-old warrior. On May 30, 1867, the former president slumped in his saddle and died a few minutes later. Gen. Pedro Diez Canseco, Castilla's brother-in-law, assumed leadership of the movement which succeeded early in the following year. The victors reestablished the Constitution of 1860 as the nation's fundamental law and in July 1868 placed Col. José Balta in the presidency.

Balta, Civilismo, and Economic Collapse, 1868–1879

The Peruvian treasury became dangerously dependent upon guano money after 1850. In the previous decade the government's annual income had been approximately 3 million *pesos*. Customs receipts contributed about 1.6 million *pesos* to this total and the Indian tribute about 1.2 million. Sales of stamped paper, license fees, fines, and taxes on businesses, property, gifts, and inheritances provided the rest of the money. Customs collections nearly doubled during the 1850s, but the government reduced or abolished many unpopular direct taxes. The revenues from all of these old imposts had increased to only about 4 million *pesos* by 1860. Meanwhile, expenditures had soared to some 20 million *pesos*. Guano receipts covered most of this deficit. The civil struggles and especially the war with Spain in the mid 1860s badly strained the state's finances. The seizure of the Chincha Islands deprived Peru of its main source of income and the government borrowed large sums of money in Europe to meet the normal costs of administration as well as extraordinary military expenses.

At the time of Balta's inauguration in 1868, the national budget anticipated a deficit of seventeen million *soles**. The government already had received advances of sixteen million *soles* on its share of future guano sales. To manage this fiscal crisis, Balta entrusted the treasury portfolio to young Nicolás de Piérola, the scion of an aristocratic Arequipa family and the son of Echenique's finance minister. Most Peruvian "men of affairs" advised a policy of retrenchment. But Piérola believed that the country could achieve solvency and greater economic stability through even heavier borrowing. He argued that massive expenditures on public works would enable Peru to exploit vast, untapped mineral and agricultural resources and end guano's stranglehold on the treasury. Furthermore, the development of new sources of income seemed imperative because the quantity and quality of the nation's guano reserves were declining rapidly. A bluff, career soldier inexperienced in finance, Balta did not want to be a "hard-times president." He readily embraced his minister's sanguine policy.

*The *sol*, like the *peso* it replaced in the mid-1860s, was worth about one United States dollar until 1870. Thereafter, it declined in value until it was stabilized at about U.S. $0.50 in 1897.

Piérola canceled all guano consignment contracts in 1869 and signed a comprehensive financial agreement with the Dreyfus Company of Paris. The French firm purchased outright two million tons of the natural fertilizer and secured a monopoly for the European guano trade. Peru's compensation was to be determined by the retail price of guano and the quantity sold. Dreyfus immediately advanced the government 2.4 million *soles* and promised to make further remittances of 700,000 *soles* per month for the succeeding twenty months. The financial house also assumed the treasury's 16-million *sol* obligation to the old guano consignees and agreed to service Peru's foreign debt, a burden of about 5 million *soles* per year. The government paid 5 percent interest on the money borrowed from the firm. In addition, Dreyfus became Peru's exclusive financial agent in France, where Piérola hoped to secure new loans.

The Dreyfus Contract had many critics in Peru, especially among the old guano consignees, who charged that Piérola had been too generous with the foreign company. But the arrangement had much to recommend it in 1869. The contract with Dreyfus eased the treasury's immediate fiscal crisis, provided it with a steady income, and gave the debt-encumbered government an opportunity to escape from the financial clutches of the consignees. Peru's finances might have been stabilized if the Balta regime had lived within its new income and borrowed additional money only for productive projects that would have rapidly paid for themselves. Unfortunately, two new bond issues arranged by Dreyfus increased the foreign debt tenfold, and Balta began a spending program so extravagant that even Piérola resigned in disgust. By 1872, service on Peru's external obligations consumed all of the income from guano, but the budget for that year provided for expenditures twice as large as the state's other revenues.

The Balta administration lavished money on salaries and pensions for soldiers and civil servants. Two million *soles* were squandered on a National Exhibition Palace in the capital and considerable sums were lost through graft. One of the more destructive earthquakes in the nation's history devastated southern Peru in 1868, and the new president began the expensive task of reconstruction. The government improved the water and sewer systems of Lima, built several schools, and extended the telegraph network. Callao harbor was deepened and provided with a concrete breakwater and new docks. But Balta's consuming passion was the iron horse. He declared that the theme of his

93

administration would be "turning guano into railroads." Between 1868 and 1872, the government signed contracts for the construction of nine lines at a cost of more than 140 million *soles*. Henry Meiggs, an indefatigable promoter-engineer from New York, built most of these.

Meiggs connected the southern port of Mollendo with Arequipa and then extended the line to Puno, on Lake Titicaca. About 325 miles in length and reaching heights of over 14,600 feet, the Southern Railway was the longest and highest railroad in South America at that time. To supply more than 400,000 gallons of water per day for the steam locomotives, the Yankee engineer built an 85-mile iron pipeline from Arequipa to rainless Mollendo. As a compliment to the Southern, Meiggs transported two steamboats over the Andes in pieces and reassembled them on Lake Titicaca. He also began work on a railroad between Puno and Cuzco. An even more spectacular engineering achievement was the Central Railway, an extension of the Lima-Callao line to La Oroya, in the central highlands. Climbing more than 15,000 feet in only 78 miles, Meiggs used multiple, V-shaped switchbacks to keep the maximum grade at 4 percent. The Central had 65 tunnels, totaling 30,000 feet in length, and 61 bridges, including an iron span of 580 feet. The contractor simultaneously employed 8,000 men—Peruvians, Chileans, Bolivians, and Chinese—and 600 mules on this herculean project. Accidents and disease took the lives of an estimated 7,000 workers.

Meiggs also built a 93-mile railroad from the harbor at Pacasmayo inland toward the Sierra city of Cajamarca, another one of 50 miles from the coastal town of Chimbote up the Santa River Valley and a 60-mile line connecting Moquegua with its port, Ilo. Other engineers contructed state-owned railways linking Trujillo and the port of Salaverry and Piura with its outlet, Paita. In addition, private capital financed railroads between Pisco and Ica, Lima and Ancón and a line extending from the northern port of Etén to nearby sugar plantations. Including both state and private projects, Peru acquired about 2,000 miles of railroad at a cost of more than 185 million *soles*.

In a world increasingly obsessed with materialism, it was not unusual for Balta and many other Peruvians to have placed such blind faith in the railroad, that period's symbol of economic progress. The shorter lines in the the coastal zone did contribute significantly to the development of that region's economy. But the longer roads penetrating the Sierra would not become financially viable for many years. Because they rank among the engineering wonders of the world, Henry Meiggs had been called the "Yankee Pizarro." Unfortunately, the Central and Southern railways also were among the world's most expensive to build, maintain, and operate. They traversed long stretches of desert and mountain wasteland that produced little freight to haul. In the end, the railroads frequently could not compete with the llama and mule, slower though often more economical modes of transport in the Andes.

Antimilitarist sentiment had existed in Peru since the 1820s. It reached a climax, however, during the regime of Colonel Balta, which many citizens viewed as the epitome of inept, prodigal, and corrupt military rule. From San Martín's time onward, soldiers had maintained a near monopoly on the presidency. The few civilians who exercised supreme power did so briefly and only because the uniformed president was absent from the capital, had died, or been overthrown. None had been elected. Soldier-presidents seemed desirable during Peru's many decades of extreme internal disorder and frequent foreign perils. But, by the 1870s, the need for sound fiscal management appeared far more pressing than that for strong, military leadership. The criticisms of the antimilitarists were echoed by the guano merchants adversely affected by the Dreyfus Contract and by the nation's political outs, most notably persons associated with the previous liberal regime.

A year before the election of 1872, many of Balta's opponents coalesced in Peru's first political party, the Civilista ("Civilianist") party. Their candidate, thirty-seven-year old Manuel Pardo, embodied the Civilista ideal of managerial competence and conscientious public service. While still in his twenties, Pardo had earned a fortune in banking, insurance, and international commerce. He then performed efficiently as Mariano Prado's finance minister and was concluding a very successful term as mayor of Lima when he entered the presidential race. Ideologically, Pardo also was a good choice to lead the Civilistas, who as individuals often had been on opposite sides in the old liberal-conservative debates. Although conservative in background, the Civilista candidate had adopted many liberal ideas, though in moderate form. Pardo espoused governmental respect for republican institutions and civil liberties. He called for more local autonomy, a reduction of clerical influence in

95

government, a much greater commitment to public education, and well-planned programs for economic development. Finally, Pardo stressed the need to reduce military expenditures and replace soldiers in government with technically proficient civilians.

Rankled by Civilista criticism, President Balta hoped to secure the election of a successor less hostile toward the armed forces. But the electoral college preferred the very popular Pardo, and Balta decided not to interfere with his installation. Unfortunately, Col. Tomás Gutiérrez, the minister of war, did not share the president's resignation to the will of the electorate. On July 22, 1872, one week before the scheduled inauguration, the unhappy minister imprisoned Balta and proclaimed himself president. The coup immediately received opposition from the army and navy garrisons at Callao and the outraged citizens of the capital. Gutiérrez and his brothers Silvestre, Marceliano, and Marcelino—also army colonels—attempted to crush this resistence. Their actions ended in personal disaster. After Silvestre fired his pistol into a jeering crowd at the Lima railway station, an armed civilian shot and killed him. A short time later, Balta's guards murdered the helpless president in his cell. News of the crime quickly spread through the capital and the fury of the civilian population became uncontrollable. An enraged mob killed Tomás Gutiérrez and hung his mutilated body from the steeple of the cathedral, where it was soon joined by the headless cadaver of Silvestre. Marceliano Gutiérrez died in combat at Callao and only Marcelino escaped the carnage. With militarism thoroughly discredited, Manuel Pardo received the presidential sash on August 2, 1872.

Peru approached the brink of bankruptcy when Manuel Pardo took office and the nation's finances became even more precarious with the onset of a worldwide economic recession in 1873. Within a program of severe austerity, the new president attempted a reorder the country's priorities. Pardo pared the bureaucracy, reduced the size of the army by three-fourths, and halted a naval procurement program. To meet its ordinary expenses the government increased taxes and issued inconvertible paper money. While Pardo sharply reduced defense and administrative expenditures, he gave great impetus to public education which he believed held the ultimate solution to Peru's problems. His administration opened seven normal schools to train teachers, founded national colleges of mining and engineering, and established several vocational schools, including one for Indians. Honoring his campaign promises, the Civilista president gave more autonomy to local governments and created a civilian national guard to counterbalance the professional army.

Although Pardo had been highly critical of his predecessor's more extravagant railroad programs, he believed that the nation had to protect its already huge investment in the new transportation system. Therefore, the appropriations for Meiggs's projects continued. The government negotiated new, more favorable contracts with the Dreyfus Company. In 1875, however, the administration ended its ties with the French firm and began selling guano through competitive bidding. Pardo attempted to refinance the nation's external debt but without success. Peru suspended service on its foreign obligations January 1, 1876.

Internal political strife plagued the Pardo administration. After the flush years of the free-spending Balta, austerity was very unpopular. The Church questioned the value of mass education and bitterly opposed secularized instruction by the state in public schools. The armed forces disliked the regime's antimilitarism, especially its effects upon their budget. In August 1874, Pardo barely escaped assassination by an officer who had lost his commission because of the president's reductions in army personnel. A number of military revolts occurred, several of these inspired by Nicolás de Piérola. A devout Catholic, Piérola objected to the mild anticlericalism of the administration and angrily responded to Civilista criticism of his management of the nation's finances during the Balta regime.

The Civilistas elected a military chief executive, former President Mariano Ignacio Prado, in 1876. Manuel Pardo believed that new international problems and domestic political unrest, especially within the armed forces, required a military president. Furthermore, the Civilistas counted General Prado as one of their own and assumed that he would be receptive to the counsel of civilian advisers. Soon after his inauguration, however, the new executive lost the support of his original backers and failed in his efforts to woo the followers of Piérola. Revolts by both the Civilistas and Piérolistas were crushed with difficulty. Ex-President Manuel Pardo was assassinated in November 1878 by an army sergeant who blamed his failure to gain a promotion on the Civilista leader. The slain statesman's partisans charged that Piérola, through his intemperate anti-Pardo speeches, was at least indirectly responsible for the murder. The already bitter quarrel between the Civilistas and the supporters of Piérola reached a peak from which it would not recede for many years. At a time when Peru desperately needed unity, President Prado had a badly divided nation on his hands. The treasury was bankrupt and, worse, a war with Chile loomed over the horizon.

◆ℰ Economic and Social Change in the Guano Age

Peru's coastal region assumed a position of unchallenged dominance within the economy during the Guano Age, a supremacy that it has never lost. At the same time, the prosperity of this zone and that of the nation as a whole increasingly became subject to the vicissitudes of world trade. Subsistence farming and the production of food crops for the domestic market began to give way to new mining enterprises and commercial agriculture for export. A few factories, notably textile mills, appeared in Lima after the middle of the century. But because of the general poverty of the population, the internal market was too small to support large-scale manufacturing. Shipping raw materials overseas in exchange for finished goods and growing amounts of foodstuffs, Peru exhibited a greater degree of economic dependence than it had under Spanish rule. Although the nation received benefits from its participation in the global economy, a drop in the price of a key export commodity in the markets of London, Paris, or New York could bring severe economic hardship to this Andean republic.

Peru experienced a tremendous expansion in the supply of capital during the mid-nineteenth century. Although native businessmen complained that foreigners received too much of the income from guano, the government retained more than half of the proceeds from this industry and injected considerable sums into the economy through salaries, public works, and graft. More and more Peruvian nationals shared directly in the guano bonanza after 1850. The manumission bonds that freed the Negro slaves also liberated the capital invested in human property. These securities and the debt consolidation bonds circulated freely, adding to the money supply. A significant influx of foreign capital took place as European entrepreneurs began to engage in mining and commercial agriculture. British, French, and North American trading companies advanced larger amounts of money to Peruvian producers of export commodities. Without a single bank before 1860, Lima boasted nine lending institutions a decade later. Individual citizens and the government squandered much of this new wealth, but considerable sums were channeled into productive enterprises.

Railroads, new port facilities, and especially steam navigation brought a transportation revolution to the coast and put Peru more securely within the international trading community. The Pacific Steam Navigation Company, which began service to Peru in 1840, had 70 steamers in operation by 1873. These vessels primarily serviced the trade among the Pacific coast republics. The number of ships arriving at Callao from Europe and the United States increased dramatically. Between 1841 and 1860, an average of 186 vessels from the northern hemisphere called at Peru's main port each year. The annual average reached 936 ships during the 1870s. The two decades following 1840 also brought prosperity to the northern ports of Paita and Túmbez. In many years more than 100 whalers—almost all of these from the United States—called there to purchase supplies and raise hell after six months at sea.

Peru's trade statistics reflected its growing participation in world commerce. From less than six million *pesos* in 1840, the nation's exports increased to almost thirty-two million *pesos* in value by 1875. Imports surged from under four million *pesos* to more than twenty-four million during the same period. Guano, of course, provided the bulk of the republic's exports, but the country recorded large gains in the international sale of other products. Peruvians had cultivated cotton in the coastal valleys since pre-Columbian times, but only small amounts of this fiber were exported prior to 1861. Then, the United States Civil War and the increased availability of capital for irrigation gave new impetus to this ancient industry. Valued at less than 100,000 dollars in 1862, Peru's cotton exports approached one million dollars in 1867. As the cotton-producing region of the United States recovered from the war and prices dropped, Peruvian planters shifted their efforts to sugarcane. About 125,000 dollars worth of sugar was exported in 1868. One decade later, foreign sales of this product reached almost 10 million dollars and sugar replaced guano as the republic's leading export. The premier position of sugar in Peru's foreign trade would not be challenged until the first decade of the twentieth century.

Sugar and cotton were the most dramatic examples of the changing agricultural economy of the coast, but advances also occurred in the production of other crops. Rice cultivation became more commercialized and the introduction of new presses modernized the olive oil industry of the south coast. Cochineal and indigo, two dyestuffs, enjoyed a brisk demand before their replacement by coal-tar dyes. Domingo Elías, a liberal politician and the nation's most innovative planter, expanded his vineyards in the Ica Valley and adopted new varieties of grapes. In 1860, he produced 10,000 barrels of wine and 70,000 large earthen jugs of a distinctive brandy marketed under the name *pisco,* after its point of export.

The extraction of minerals along the coast increased notably after 1850. Stimulated by high prices and a new railroad, old copper mines in the Ica-Nazca district reopened. Henry Meiggs and other businessmen drilled the first oil wells on the north coast in the 1860s and established primitive refineries to distill kerosene from the crude petroleum. But the most important extractive industry developed in Tarapacá, Peru's extremely arid, southernmost province. There, Peruvian and foreign entrepreneurs made fortunes from *caliche,* a hard, white strata of mineral salt found four or five feet below the surface of the ground. Varying from a few inches to more than two feet in thickness, this substance was the remanent of ancient saline lakes that once occupied the depression between the Andes and the coastal hills. *Caliche* was a scientific curiosity without commercial value until the third decade of the nineteenth century. William Ruschenberger, a Yankee sailor who visited the region in the early 1830s, could not understand why the local miners had begun to work these beds. The salt was "contaminated" with several elements that rendered it unfit for human consumption. Indeed, the principal component of *caliche* was not sodium chloride (table salt) but sodium nitrate, or saltpeter.

By the time of Ruschenberger's journey, scientists had discovered that nitrate of soda manufactured from *caliche* made excellent fertilizer. As progressive farmers throughout the world became aware of this new product, saltpeter exports climbed from less than 1,000 tons in 1830, to 80,000 tons, worth more than three million dollars by 1860. Then, the invention of powerful explosives made from the high-grade nitrates of Tarapacá, an epidemic of wars in the 1860s, and ever-heightening arms races thereafter brought great prosperity to this desert industry. Peru produced 3.5 million tons of nitrates between 1860 and 1879. In the latter part of this period, the value of saltpeter exports reached ten million dollars per year.

Nitrate mining and the processing of this mineral for export required vast amounts of capital. Nevertheless, the Peruvian government's very generous concession policy encouraged investment and, by 1875, native businessmen and foreign firms had established more than 400 large nitrate works in Tarapacá. These operations exported their product duty free until 1868, when a small impost was levied to help repair earthquake damage in southern Peru. As the nation's fiscal crisis deepened, however, the government began looking toward this burgeoning industry to replace its vanishing guano revenues. The state raised export taxes, but this action produced unexpected results. To maintain their profits, the companies sharply increased production. This glutted the market and drove prices downward. As a fertilizer, nitrates competed with guano and adversely affected its market. Therefore, the Peruvian government undertook the establishment of a national nitrate monopoly in 1876. The state hoped to control the volume of exports and the price of saltpeter and maximize the treasury's income from both guano and nitrates. The government combined three-quarters of the nitrate operations to form the Peruvian Nitrate Company. The state shared in the profits of the venture. Companies that refused to cooperate—primarily large foreign-owned firms—were expropriated and received government bonds for their properties. By 1878, income from the nitrate monopoly accounted for more than one-quarter of the treasury's revenues. Unfortunately, the Peruvian industry still had competition from the lightly taxed nitrate producers in neighboring Bolivia.

The Guano Age was a period of transition for the Sierra economy. Important changes occurred, but these were not so apparent as those along the coast. The old mining centers continued to decline as the production of silver and gold followed a downward trend. At the same time, however, the foundation was being laid for a more modern extractive industry exploiting industrial metals, especially copper and lead. The National School of Mines, established in 1876, began training Peruvian technicians for the future. The adoption of a liberalized mining code the following year and increased government stability attracted new foreign capital. Most important, the railroads that were so unsuited to the transportation needs of the region in the 1870s would be indispensable to the development of the new mining industry three decades later.

Highland agriculture, in contrast with mining, enjoyed relative prosperity. As the plantations of the coast began to specialize in export crops, food prices rose sharply. Sierra farmers with access to coastal markets responded to this opportunity and regional fairs flourished in several highland centers. Southern Peru's trade with Bolivia and even northwestern Argentina, destroyed during the late colonial and early republican periods, experienced a rebirth. Alpaca wool was the major item in this commerce. Produced primarily in the Lake Titicaca Basin of Peru and Bolivia, merchants at Arequipa purchased the fleece for export to Britain. Peru's overseas sales of this item climbed from a value of 500,000 dollars in 1845 to more than 2.5 million dollars three decades later. The prosperity of highland agriculture and stockraising provided new incentives for the acquisition of Indian lands. These became easier to obtain under the Civil Code of 1852, which ended all restrictions on the sale of property by natives.

Sierra merchants also controlled the trade in cinchona bark cut from trees found along the rim of the Amazon Basin in Peru and Bolivia. The source of quinine, "Peruvian bark" began curing malaria in Europe during the second half of the seventeenth century. Exports of this antimalarial drug averaged over 500,000 dollars per year during the third quarter of the nineteenth century. Then, depletion of the "fever trees" and the development of cinchona plantations in the East Indies destroyed this industry.

Like the coastal region, the northern portion of the Peruvian Montaña underwent a profound transformation during the Guano Age. The steady expansion of steam navigation and government services after 1853 produced an economic revolution. The sparse population of the region grew rapidly. The foreign trade of the eastern lowlands by way of the Amazon River increased fifteenfold between 1854 and 1870, surpassing one million dollars by the latter year. Many communities along the major waterways almost entirely abandoned subsistence agriculture to concentrate on the production of salt fish and tobacco, the manufacture of straw hats and hammocks, and the gathering of several forest products, all for export to Brazil and beyond. The region no longer was able to feed itself and imported the most basic foodstuffs from points as distant as the United States and Europe. The sleepy, former mission village of Iquitos became the commercial center of the region after its selection as the base for the government-owned steamer fleet in 1864. Three years later, Peru's Hydrographic Commission of the Amazon, created to chart the rivers of the Montaña, established its headquarters there. The town also acquired a large facility for repairing river craft and a steam-powered sawmill and brick factory. By 1876, Iquitos had 1,500 permanent residents, a much larger transient population, and several mercantile establishments.

Peruvian society also changed during the Guano Age, although not so significantly as the nation's economy. Unfortunately, the crude census and tax records of the period provide only a hazy picture of these developments. Peru's census of 1876 reported a population of 2.7 million persons, double the number at the time of independence. The regional distribution of the country's people had not shifted appreciably in the previous half century. The Sierra continued to be the demographic heart of the nation with 73 percent of Peru's inhabitants. The coast claimed 23 percent of the population and the Montaña about 4 percent. Lima had 100,000 people and nearby Callao counted 35,000.

The Indian element of society comprised more than 57 percent of the total population in 1876, a slight decrease in its relative share since the late eighteenth century. Due to assimilation with other ethnic groups, the proportion of black Peruvians declined sharply. Negroes together with the newly arrived Chinese accounted for less than 4 percent of the nation's inhabitants. While Indians and blacks experienced a drop in their share of the population, the "white and mestizo" category enjoyed a relative increase, numbering nearly 39 percent of the republic's citizens. The ethnic map of Peru showed a large block of Indian population in the southern and central highlands dotted by a few enclaves of mestizos and whites. Non-Indians already comprised a majority in much of the northern Sierra and in most of the coastal and Amazonian provinces. In general, mestizos and whites had made the greatest proportional gains at the expense of the Indian element in zones of increased economic activity. Many of the most prosperous districts, especially along the coast, appear to have received significant numbers of migrants from other provinces. Nevertheless, changes in the ethnic composition of these regions probably did not reflect a sharp decline in the percentage of biological Indians but the acculturation of natives and their acquisition of mestizo social status.

Peru's old colonial aristocracy, nearly destroyed by 1845, had been replaced along the coast by a new wealthy class born of the commercial economy and government largess. The nation's intermediate socioeconomic strata was small, but it had grown appreciably during the Guano Age. The traditional liberal professions increased their membership and the number of small-scale entrepreneurs had expanded. These people were joined by relatively new occupational groups in Peru—managers, engineers, and commercial employees. The rapid growth of the civil bureaucracy and the military officer corps also contributed to the expansion of the middle sector of society. The *hacendados* of the Sierra had widened the economic gap between themselves and their poor peasant neighbors, but the influence of this provincial upper class within the nation as a whole had declined in relation to the new plutocracy of the coastal area. Although slavery and the tribute tax had been abolished, Peru's lower classes probably had not significantly improved their standard of living since the colonial period. In 1870, one observer reported that the republic had 18 "millionaires," 11,587 "rich people," and 22,148 individuals who were "well-off." Some 1,236,000 persons, more than 97 percent of the total, were classified simply as "workers."

Statistics such as these do not permit more than a superficial analysis of Guano-Age society. But the rich texture of life has been recorded in the many travelogues of contemporary European and North American visitors. Although highly opinionated and often bigoted, these accounts are usually informative and almost always delightful to read. Ricardo Palma more favorably recalled the customs of the country in his nostalgic *Tradiciones peruanas* (1883). Finally, a mulatto primitive artist called Pancho Fierro (1803–79) left to posterity hundreds of charming watercolors and charcoal drawings of Lima street scenes. These sources describe a very pietistic society that enjoyed life more than it pursued wealth. The comfortable classes of the capital amused themselves with tea parties, bathing at the nearby resort town of Chorrillos, and mediocre performances of opera watched from flea-infested theater boxes. With the lower classes they shared a passion for flowers, music, and dancing; the diversion of promenades and religious processions; and the excitement of cockfights, the national lottery, and bizarre forms of bull-baiting, including the antics of a dwarf matador who enraged his adversary with fireworks.

Innumerable hawkers of a great variety of goods and services, each proclaiming his function in a distinctive song or shout, animated the narrow streets of Lima. The wealthier citizens enjoyed this scene from the balconies or behind the grated windows of their homes, lightly constructed, pastel-colored row houses that abutted on the dusty walkways. The colorful garb of the peddlers and muleteers contrasted sharply with the somber attire of the upper class, the men in their black suits and their women enshrouded in the traditional, dark-colored *saya y manto*. The *saya* was a long pleated skirt that could be worn full at the hem, or drawn tightly at the bottom, hugging the form of the wearer. The *manto,* a mantle fitted into the back of the skirt, was pulled over the shoulders and head and held shut in front with one hand so that only a single eye remained visible. Many casual visitors suspected that this dress facilitated illicit romances. But more seasoned observers concluded that it merely permitted the late-rising ladies of Lima to leave their homes without arranging their ample coiffures. Much of the innocence of Pancho Fierro's Peru died with the artist in 1879.

5

Disaster and Recovery

[1879–1914]

P ERU AND ITS ALLY BOLIVIA fought Chile in the disastrous
War of the Pacific from 1879 to 1884. The struggle left
Bolivia landlocked and afflicted the country with a national
claustrophobia that would lead to another bloody war with
Paraguay to gain an Atlantic outlet. Peru lost two departments,
vast mineral resources, and its short-lived status as a South
American power of the first rank. Victorious Chile emerged
wealthier, but forces unleashed by the war destroyed that nation's inner tranquillity. Finally, all three belligerents became
locked in an expensive arms race as the dispute continued to
smolder for nearly a half century after the end of the military
conflagration.

The War of the Pacific, 1879–1884

Among the scores of international problems that have
plagued the poorly demarcated republics of Latin America, none
has generated more literature than the very complicated "question of the Pacific." Most of these accounts are highly partisan,
attempting to place all of the blame for the war on one side or the

other. The few relatively objective studies do not adequately treat the subject in its entirety, but they demonstrate that all three combatants share major responsibility for this tragedy. Bolivia, the central arena of the conflict, suffered from a series of inept leaders whose irresponsible actions invited the dispute and then precipitated the crisis. Chile skillfully pursued an aggressive policy of economic and territorial expansion in Bolivia. The Chileans supported their diplomacy with ample military power and ultimately employed force to achieve the nation's objectives. Peru unrealistically countered Chilean expansionism with a diplomacy predicated on a preponderance of armed strength which it did not possess. Worse, Lima permitted Bolivia to make the fateful decisions that thrust Peru into the war. The seeds of the conflict matured within the context of old antagonisms and rivalries, a complex balance-of-power diplomacy involving several other South American states, and the unsettling interference of European and North American interests.

It is very difficult to follow the diplomatic maze that led to the War of the Pacific, but the source of the conflict is easily recognized. The struggle concerned the fabulous natural wealth of Peru's southernmost maritime department, Tarapacá, and more immediately, Bolivia's lone coastal province of Antofagasta. A desert wasteland, ownership of this territory did not inspire competition until the discovery of guano, then silver, and finally nitrates in the region. The international boundary between Bolivia and Chile had been poorly defined at the time of independence. But from the beginning, Bolivia asserted that its southern limit was at about the twenty-fifth parallel. Chile did not challenge this claim. The Chilean Constitution of 1833 vaguely described the republic's northern frontier as "the desert of the Atacama." Nine years later, however, Chile's president declared that his country's sovereignty extended northward to the twenty-third parallel.

The Bolivians, a highland people, showed little interest in their coastal area. Rugged mountains isolated largely empty Antofagasta from the population centers of the Altiplano, and most of the nation's foreign commerce utilized old colonial trade routes through Peru, especially the port of Arica. The discovery of guano and minerals in Antofagasta after 1840 attracted almost no Bolivian capital, but the Chileans avidly exploited these resources. Bolivia hoped merely to retain its sovereignty over the coast and tax the export of raw materials extracted by foreigners.

A series of clashes between Bolivian officials and Chilean miners in Antofagasta nearly produced a war between the two nations. Then, in 1866, Chile induced President Mariano Melgarejo, Bolivia's infamous "Dictator of Dictators," to sign the Treaty of Mutual Benefits which, in fact, unduly favored the Chileans. The agreement established the twenty-fourth parallel as the boundary between the two neighbors. Furthermore, they agreed to adopt a common tax regime for the entire zone between the twenty-third and twenty-fifth parallels and share equally in the revenues from these imposts. In the years that followed, succeeding Bolivian regimes regretted the concessions made by Melgarejo. Rich nitrate beds were discovered in Antofagasta and by the mid 1870s, perhaps 85 percent of the people residing there were Chileans. Conflicts arose almost every day between Bolivian officials and the foreign miners, who armed themselves and organized paramilitary organizations. In 1872, Chilean interests apparently supported a group of Bolivian exiles who momentarily seized Antofagasta. Fear steadily mounted in La Paz that Chile might acquire the province as the United States had wrested Texas from Mexico—a local revolution followed by annexation.

Peru also became increasingly apprehensive of the ambitions of its traditional Chilean rival. At the time of the negotiation of the Treaty of Mutual Benefits in 1866, Chile had suggested that in return for the complete cession of Antofagasta, it would assist Bolivia in conquering portions of southern Peru, including the long-coveted port of Arica. Bolivia rejected this offer and dutifully reported the Chilean initiative to Lima, which increased its dipomatic support for the La Paz government. Following the filibuster expedition against Antofagasta in 1872, Peru dispatched warships to Bolivian waters to dissuade similar adventures. Chile responded by ordering the construction of two ironclad cruisers in Britain. Peru also should have purchased vessels to maintain its naval superiority in the Pacific. But the austerity-minded and antimilitary administration of Manuel Pardo cut defense expenditures, believing that hostilities could be averted through diplomacy. Lima urged La Paz to press for a revision of the troublesome Treaty of Mutual Benefits before the arrival of the new Chilean warships. Bolivia, however, needed reassurance, so in 1873, Peru accepted a Bolivian invitation to enter a defensive alliance aimed implicitly at Chile. To avoid provoking Chilean countermeasures, they agreed to keep the treaty secret. The allies also sought to strengthen the compact by gaining the adherence of Argentina, which had its own vexatious boundary dispute with Chile. The Santiago government discovered the existence of the "secret treaty" before the end of 1873. Chile quickly began discussions with Brazil—Argentina's old rival—and undercut Buenos Aires' initial enthusiasm for an alliance with Peru and Bolivia.

Emboldened by the commitment from Peru and deteriorating relations between Chile and Argentina, aggressive Bolivian diplomats secured the nullification of the Treaty of Mutual Benefits in 1874. A new agreement, the Treaty of Sucre, again fixed the twenty-fourth parallel as the international boundary. But Chile relinquished the revenue-sharing provisions of the previous arrangement. Bolivia promised not to increase existing taxes or impose new ones for twenty-five years on Chilean enterprises operating between the twenty-fourth and twenty-third parallels. Two years later, however, the municipal council of the city of Antofagasta, Bolivia's principal nitrate port, proposed to abolish several old port duties that supported the city government and replace these with a single tax of ten *centavos* per hundredweight of nitrates exported, a small increase over the total of the previous imposts. This evoked a loud protest from the Antofagasta Nitrate and Railway Company, an Anglo-Chilean enterprise that had consolidated most of the Chilean holdings in the region. The firm charged that the proposed tax violated the Treaty of Sucre and its own contract with the Bolivian government, signed in 1872, which exempted the company's exports from all duties for fifteen years. Bolivia retorted that the firm's concession, granted by a previous regime, was invalid because it had not been approved by congress. Thereafter, the legislature in La Paz offered to give its sanction to the company's contract provided that the firm pay a "concession fee" of ten *centavos* for each hundred pounds of nitrate exported. The Chilean government warned that the impost, whatever it was called, would break the treaty of 1874 and compel Chile to "revindicate" the territory it had conceded to Bolivia as far north as the twenty-third parallel.

In December 1878, after a year of haggling, Gen. Hilarión Daza, Bolivia's impetuous president, ordered the Antofagasta Nitrate and Railway Company to pay the tax retroactive to the previous January. When the firm refused, Daza canceled its concession and ordered the company's property auctioned for back taxes on February 15, 1879. One day before the scheduled sale, Chilean troops landed at Antofagasta and quickly occupied the coastal area between the twenty-fourth and twenty-third parallels, about half of Bolivia's littoral region.

Unprepared for war, Peru desperately sought a peaceful solution to the conflict. Lima's minister in La Paz urged Daza to refrain from issuing a declaration of war so that arbitration of the dispute could be arranged. For the same reason, President Prado sent veteran diplomat José Antonio de Lavalle to Santiago. Bolivia's Daza rejected the pleas of his ally, apparently believing that he could force a revision of the treaty with Chile through crisis diplomacy, or oust the Chileans from Antofagasta with the aid of his Peruvian allies. Lavalle encountered equal intransigence in Santiago. Chile now had possession of its two new ironclads and seemed determined to end the problem by force of arms. While Peruvian diplomats sincerely searched for peace in La Paz and Santiago, the government in Lima realistically made hurried preparations for war. Garrisons in Tarapacá were reinforced, the fortifications at Callao were strengthened, and the nation's badly maintained warships were made ready for combat. Meanwhile, Lima's minister in Buenos Aires redoubled his efforts to gain Argentina's adherence to the Peru-Bolivia alliance. But this overture failed as did Peru's efforts to purchase or borrow two Argentine warships.

Bolivia declared war on Chile March 14, 1879, one week after Lavalle began his talks in Santiago. The Chileans informed the beleaguered Peruvian troubleshooter that they knew about the "secret treaty" between his country and Bolivia which Santiago described as both offensive and defensive. Chile accused Peru of perfidiously talking peace while preparing for war. Santiago demanded that Lima cease all military movements and

A. Original Chile-Bolivian boundary; B. Claimed by Chile in 1842; a. Established by treaty in 1866, but in A-B nitrate revenues were divided equally; C. Original Peru-Bolivian boundary; D. Boundary of Chile as a result of the War of the Pacific, 1883, with D-E to be occupied by Chile ten years; d. Chile-Peruvian boundary by settlement of 1929.— Adapted by permission of the publisher from William Jefferson Dennis, *Tacna and Arica: An Account of the Chile-Peru Boundary Dispute and of the Arbitrations of the United States* (New Haven: Yale University Press, 1931)

PERU

Mollendo

Ilo

Moquegua

TACNA

Tacna

Arica

ARICA

Pisagua

TARAPACA

Iquique

Pacific

Ocean

Cobija

Mejillones

Point Angamos

Antofagasta

ANTOFAGASTA

BOLIVIA

Paposo

Taltal

N

Chañaral

ATACAMA

Caldera

Copiapó

CHILE

Cochabamba

Oruro

18°

BOLIVIA

Potosí

Uyuni

Santa
Fe

23°

24°

25°

ARGENTINA

0   50   100
Miles

E

d

D

C

B

a

A

Guide Map to Chilean Expansion

declare its neutrality in the contest between Chile and Bolivia. The alliance of 1873, in fact, permitted the signers to determine for themselves if sufficient cause for war existed. Nevertheless, President Prado believed that should Peru fail to aid its ally after Chile had invaded Bolivian territory, his regime might be overthrown just as he himself had ousted the timid Pezet during the crisis with Spain in 1865. More importantly, Bolivia informed Lima that it had received unofficial invitations from Santiago for an alliance against Peru! The terms were similar to those of the pact proposed in 1866. Bolivia would cede all of Antofagasta to Chile and assist that republic in taking Tarapacá from Peru. In return, Bolivia would acquire Peruvian territory farther to the north, including the port of Arica. Peru's alternatives seemed clear: the nation could support its ally in the fight against Chile, or face the Chileans with Bolivia as an additional enemy. The decision was painful but easy. Lima refused to renounce its treaty obligations and on April 3, 1879, Chile declared war on Peru.

Chile explained its reasons for resorting to war in a circular addressed to the foreign diplomatic corps in Santiago. The Chileans accused Peru of fomenting the dispute between Bolivia and Chile to eliminate the competitors of the Peruvian nitrate monopoly. Agents for Peru, in fact, had acquired Bolivian nitrate concessions to keep them out of the hands of Chilean interests. Furthermore, the Peruvian monopoly had unsuccessfully sought a marketing agreement with the Antofagasta Nitrate and Railway Company to control the supply and price of saltpeter. But no persuasive evidence has ever been presented linking Peru with Bolivia's ten *centavo* tax or La Paz's decision to confiscate Chilean holdings in Antofagasta. If Peru had urged Daza to take these actions, Lima certainly miscalculated Chile's response.

The combined population of Peru and Bolivia was more than double that of Chile at the outbreak of the war, but few objective observers believed that this numerical advantage could offset Chilean superiority in other resources. The central Andean allies were fractured nations. Mountain barriers divided their people physically, while an almost unspannable cultural chasm separated their Indian and non-Indian citizens. This lack of national integration manifested itself in the weakness of their governments, whose vitality had been sapped by frequent revolutions and fiscal mismanagement. In Lima and La Paz, the emergency did not bring greater unity, but only aggravated the feuds between political factions.

Chile, by contrast, was a nation of racially and culturally homogeneous mestizos, most of whom lived in a relatively small region in the central portion of the country. Perhaps no other people of Latin America possessed a greater degree of national identification. The world depression of the 1870s produced severe economic problems in Chile, but the republic's financial position was superior to that of its adversaries and the Chilean government was strong. In the years following 1830, Chile had earned a reputation as the most stable republic of Spanish America. No established regime had been overturned by revolution after that date. Until 1871, moreover, each of Chile's presidents had held power for two consecutive five-year terms. Political stability had fostered considerable continuity in the nation's foreign policy, gaining Chile renown as the master of Latin American realpolitik. "By Reason or Force," as the republic's national motto proclaimed, Chile had been quite successful in disputes with its neighbors. The country was relatively well prepared for war in 1879. In the end, Chilean strength and the weakness of Peru and Bolivia encouraged a military solution to the "question of the Pacific."

The position of the principal belligerents on the Pacific coast with the great, empty expanse of the Atacama Desert separating their vital centers made naval power the crucial factor in the war. Both Peru and Chile had two effective ironclad warships. Peru's *Huascar* and *Independencia* had been built in the mid-1860s, during the conflict with Spain. But rapid advances in military technology had rendered them nearly obsolete. Protected by four- and five-inch iron plates, smoothbore cannon provided most of their firepower. Peru also possessed two wooden warships and a pair of old, unseaworthy ironclad monitors assigned to permanent harbor defense at Callao and Arica. The cruisers *Cochrane* and *Blanco Encalada* were the pride of the Chilean navy. Lauched in 1874 and 1875, they were among the most modern ships afloat. Their nine-inch armor made them almost invulnerable to the Peruvian cannon, while their big rifled guns, shooting armor-piercing projectiles, proved very effective against the enemy ironclads. Superior speed was the only advantage enjoyed by the much smaller and lighter Peruvian vessels. The Chilean fleet also included two small ironclad corvettes, four wooden warships, and ten steam transports. Chile measured its naval superiority not only in ships but also in personnel. Trained in the British tradition (in fact, the country's more prominent commanders were Anglo-Chileans), Chile's mariners had extensive shipboard experience and many Chilean officers had cruised with European navies. By 1879, the Peruvian navy was comprised largely of dockside sailors. Bolivia did not have a navy.

Six weeks after the war began, Peru suffered a catastrophic defeat that nearly sealed its doom. On May 21, the two Peruvian ironclads attempted to break a blockade of the port of Iquique by the Chilean wooden vessels *Esmeralda* and *Covadonga*. A most uneven contest, the *Huascar* rammed and sank the *Esmeralda,* while the *Independencia* gave chase to the *Covadonga*. Hoping to elude the deeper-drafted ironclad, the lighter Chilean ship steamed through rock-studded waters close to shore. The *Independencia* continued its pursuit, however, with a sailor perched on the prow making constant checks for submarine hazards. Then, at a distance of about 200 yards, a Chilean marksman on the *Covadonga* shot the Peruvian lookout. A few seconds later, the *Independencia* struck the rocks and was lost.

With the battle of Iquique Bay, the scale of naval power tipped decisively in favor of Chile. Nevertheless, the Chileans were reluctant to risk a seaborne invasion of Peru while the *Huascar* remained afloat. For the next six months Adm. Miguel Grau, the commander of Peru's remaining ironclad, earned his place as the nation's greatest naval hero. While the *Huascar* avoided confrontation with the enemy cruisers, Grau maneuvered to gain time for Peru to procure new ships. The *Huascar* bombarded Chilean ports, harassed enemy supply lines, and even captured a loaded troop transport. But on October 8, 1879, the formidable Chilean men-of-war trapped the Peruvian vessel off Point Angamos, near the Bolivian port of Mejillones. The world's first major combat between ironclads on the high seas, the battle of Angamos lasted ninety minutes. The *Huascar* scored one hit on the *Cochrane,* but failed in an attempt to ram it. Then, a Chilean shell immobilized the stearing gear of the Peruvian ship, another volley knocked out its main battery, and Admiral Grau was blown to pieces at his post. With his vessel helpless, the *Huascar*'s fourth commander of the engagement—a young lieutenant—gave the order to open the valves and scuttle the crippled warrior. The Chileans, however, boarded and saved the vessel and later used the *Huascar* against Peru.

Now in complete control of the sea lanes, Chile launched an offensive against the allies in Tarapacá, Arica, and Tacna. In battle the defending force normally enjoys the advantage of fighting from fortified positions of its own choosing. But Peru's desert outposts lacked adequate overland transportation to other parts of the country and a Chilean blockade interdicted the flow of supplies by ship. Poorly equipped from the start, the allies quickly depleted their stores of food, water, and munitions. Rather than being starved into submission by the relatively well provisioned Chileans, they often carried the war to the enemy. With the mobility afforded by its navy, Chile could strike at several points along the coast, a threat that kept the defenders dispersed. The new long-range Krupp field guns of the Chilean army and the heavy cannon of its navy pounded Peru's coastal positions, while the fire from the antiquated Peruvian artillery fell short of the enemy. The allies suffered an almost uninterrupted series of bloody defeats. By July 1880, Chile controlled Peru's three southernmost coastal departments and the entire Bolivian littoral.

The already shaky governments of Peru and Bolivia crumbled under the weight of military adversity. From July 1879 until the loss of the *Huascar* four months later, President Prado resided with his troops in the south. Returning to Lima after the disaster at Angamos, the Peruvian leader found his political position equally precarious. A Chilean blockade of Peru's major ports virtually eliminated the treasury's income from tariffs and exports of guano and nitrates. Although some wealthy patriots donated money to the war effort, congress resisted the imposition of heavy new taxes. The government printed reams of inflationary paper *soles,* sold bonds within the country, and attempted to secure loans abroad—a most unlikely prospect in that dark hour. Hoping to silence the caustic criticism of Nicolás de Piérola, Prado offered the finance portfolio and prime ministry to that irascible caudillo. Piérola rejected this appeal, implying that only the presidency itself would satisfy his ambition. For Prado, that office now seemed very unattractive.

In mid-December 1879, President Prado entrusted the executive power to his vice-president and departed for Europe. In a curious letter to his countrymen Prado denied that he was abandoning the ship of state in a gale. His financial expertise and prestige as Peruvian chief executive, wrote the president, would be of great value in securing loans and war materiel on the continent. Peruvians rejected this lame rationalization and a revolution in Lima quickly placed Piérola at the head of the government. That same month, the Daza regime in Bolivia met an equally ignominious end. While personally commanding his army in the desert, Daza failed to relieve a besieged Peruvian force defending the town of Pisagua. His enemies in La Paz charged him with cowardice and seized the government. The fallen dictator fled to Europe.

Chile had militarily occupied the nitrate-rich Atacama by mid-1880 and could claim the region by right of conquest. But Peru refused to sue for peace. Though valued for their mineral wealth, the sparsely populated southern departments were not essential to the functioning of the economy, and the government in Lima would not surrender while it possessed the capacity to resist. To bring the horrors of war to larger numbers of Peruvians and secure booty, a 3,000-man force of Chileans commanded by navy captain Patrick Lynch plundered several northern coastal valleys in September 1880. The raiders held plantations and towns for ransom and destroyed them when the Peruvians proved unwilling or unable to meet their demands. The Chileans carried off agricultural machinery, rails, and port equipment. They fired crops and buildings, cut down fruit trees and shot livestock. Violating the contemporary standards of "civilized warfare," the Lynch expedition only strengthened Peru's resolve to continue the struggle.

At the invitation of the United States government, representatives of the three belligerents met in October 1880 on board the U.S.S. *Lackawanna* at Arica Bay. Seemingly invincible in battle, the Chileans showed no inclination toward magnanimity. In addition to a huge monetary indemnity, Santiago's demands included the cession of Antofagasta by Bolivia and the departments of Tarapacá, Arica, Tacna, and part of Moquegua from Peru. Stunned by the severity of these terms, the allies refused to negotiate. Chile now began to strike at the jugular of the Peruvian state. "On to Lima!" was the battle cry of the 25,000-man invasion force as it moved methodically northward by land and sea. President Piérola prepared the defenses of his capital in the suburbs of San Juan and Miraflores. There, the Chileans overwhelmed the ineptly directed Peruvians, many of them civilian volunteers, in bloody battles on January 13 and 15, 1881. Lima surrendered two days later.

But the war did not end. Piérola retreated to the central highlands and vowed to fight on. Other generals in the interior also continued the struggle. Meanwhile, the Chilean army of occupation in the capital fulfilled the worst expectations of the *limeños.* The conquerors carried off almost all of the books in the National Library. They sent priceless manuscripts and art treasures from the National Archives to Santiago and used the building to stable the mounts of their cavalry. The invaders felled stately trees along the city's boulevards and dynamited ornamental statues and fountains. They crated the animals at the zoo and shipped them to Chile. Raiding parties sent into the interior conducted themselves in a similar manner. Most of the Southern Railway was dismantled and used to extend the Chilean system. Although the worst excesses of the conquerors took place in the early days of their victory and can be attributed to a breakdown in discipline, the Chileans adopted a conscious policy of making continued resistance as painful as possible.

The wealthier people of Lima, forced to contribute large sums of money for the support of the occupation army, soon clamored for peace. On February 22, 1881, a "junta of notables" in the capital declared Civilista lawyer Francisco García Calderón the new president of the republic and authorized him to negotiate with the Chileans. Chile, the United States, and the major European powers recognized the regime in Lima and Piérola renounced his claim to the presidency in November. Chile continued to demand from Peru a money payment and the departments of Tarapacá, Arica, and Tacna as the price for peace. The two latter departments possessed little mineral wealth. Santiago desired them primarily as a buffer zone between Peru and its lost nitrate fields in Tarapacá. Chile also considered providing Bolivia a corridor through captured Peruvian territory to Arica. This would have facilitated a settlement with La Paz, while driving a wedge of hostility between the central Andean allies. With Arica in Bolivian hands, La Paz could be expected to side with Chile in any future war against Peru.

The demands of foreign bondholders and investors, supported by their governments, complicated the peace talks. James G. Blaine, the United States secretary of state, feared that the surrender of the Atacama to Chile would benefit British capital at the expense of Yankee interests. Therefore, he attempted to arrange a settlement on the basis of a monetary indemnity alone. United States diplomats in Lima inspired false hopes that Washington would intervene to forestall Chile's territorial demands, a disservice that embittered United States-Peruvian relations for many years. President García Calderón accepted the loss of Tarapacá as inevitable, but he would not part with Tacna and

Arica. Tired of the president's intractability and fearful that he might place Tacna and Arica under the protection of the United States, the Chileans removed García Calderón from office in November 1881 and imprisoned him in Santiago.

From Arequipa Adm. Lizardo Montero, who had been named vice-president shortly before the arrest of García Calderón, proclaimed himself chief of state. Like his predecessor, Montero expressed a willingness to cede Tarapacá, but he refused to surrender Tacna and Arica. Gen. Andés Cáceres, however, challenged Montero's authority. A grizzled mestizo warrior who had earned a reputation for bravery earlier in the struggle, Cáceres now commanded an army of Indian guerrillas based at Ayacucho. He refused to countenance a settlement that relinquished any national territory, including Tarapacá. With all semblance of unity destroyed in Peru, a powerful Chilean faction spoke openly of establishing a protectorate over the entire country.

The best hope for peace and independence now rested with Gen. Miguel de Iglesias, a planter-turned-soldier, who commanded a small force in the northern highlands. A man who had demonstrated his valor in battle and had lost his eldest son at Miraflores, Iglesias became convinced that Peru would have to surrender more than Tarapacá to purchase peace. Late in 1882, delegates from Peru's northern departments assembled at Cajamarca and elected Iglesias president. The Chileans recognized this new regime and even paid the troops that supported it. But Iglesias was no tool of the enemy. On October 23, 1883, after protracted negotiations, his government signed the Treaty of Ancón, ending the War of the Pacific. The terms obtained by Peru were the best that it could have expected under the circumstances. Chile acquired permanent ownership of Tarapacá. The victor also was to occupy and administer Tacna and Arica for ten years. After that interval, the people of those departments would determine by plebiscite whether they would remain with Chile or revert to Peruvian sovereignty. The nation favored in this vote would pay the loser ten million Chilean *pesos*. Chile agreed to assume part of the responsibility for portions of the Peruvian public debt secured by guano and nitrate deposits which had passed under Chilean control. In realistically admitting defeat and obtaining a painful but necessary peace, Iglesias sacrificed his reputation with his contemporaries and future generations. In later years, Peruvians would celebrate the tenacious resistance of General Cáceres in the service of a lost cause. Many of Iglesias's countrymen have denied him the laurels he deserves for statesmanship, a commodity much dearer than heroism in moments of great crisis.

◖ Reconstruction and Regeneration, 1885–1914

The Chilean army returned home in 1884, leaving Peru with the staggering burden of physical and psychic reconstruction. Thousands of the nation's young men had been killed or maimed. The transportation system was in shambles. Irrigation works and farm equipment on the coastal estates had been destroyed, spoliated, or neglected. The war had uprooted and dispersed the labor force. The mining industry almost ceased to exist and the commercial establishments of Lima lacked the capital to resume their activities. The national treasury remained empty and the towering public debt seemed unbearable with the loss of the nitrate industry. The people had no confidence in their political institutions and the republic's civilian leadership. Many Peruvians believed that the war had been lost behind the lines and not on the battlefield. A deep despair and mortification permeated the country.

President Iglesias symbolized the national humiliation at the hands of Chile. His control of the government became increasingly tenuous, especially after the withdrawal of the Chilean army in August 1884. As his position deteriorated, Iglesias grew more and more dictatorial. Gen. Andrés Cáceres, one of the few surviving heroes of the war, demanded that the president resign and restore constitutional government. His sentiments were echoed by important elements of the armed forces, the Civilistas, and the followers of Nicolás de Piérola, who now organized the Democratic party. Threatened with a massive assault on the capital by Cáceres's army, Iglesias resigned and fled the country in December 1885. His mestizo adversary was awarded the presidency without opposition the following March.

Cáceres owed the unanimity of his election to his military reputation and his professed goal of restoring Peru's republican institutions. But the new regime quickly lost its broad base of support and degenerated into an ironhanded dictatorship that would endure for nearly a decade. As most of the civilians who initially endorsed the president abandoned him, Cáceres's Constitutionalist party became almost entirely an electoral vehicle for the dictator's friends in the armed forces. The irresponsible partisan maneuvers of Peru's regular politicians encouraged the authoritarian drift of the government. However, Cáceres's unpopular austerity program was the underlying cause of this dissension. The administration adopted new taxes to meet its operating expenses and fund the internal debt. Currency reforms designed to stabilize the badly inflated *sol* hurt many influential people, especially the exporters whose products became more expensive on the world market. Most controversial was the regime's program to extinguish the foreign debt and restore the nation's railroad system.

The Cáceres administration negotiated an agreement with Michael R. Grace, who represented a group of Peru's British creditors. These investors formed the Peruvian Corporation and assumed responsibility for the republic's external debt of about 50 million pounds sterling. In return, the Corporation acquired the state-owned railroads for sixty-six years. The Corporation pledged to restore the badly damaged system to efficient operation within two years and extend several of the lines, including the Central Railway to the rich mining district of La Oroya. The new firm also received rights to export as much as three million tons of guano, the free use of seven secondary ports, permission to navigate Lake Titicaca, and a million acres of land in the Montaña. In addition to these concessions, the government agreed to pay the Peruvian Corporation annual installments of 80,000 pounds sterling for thirty-three years. Most Peruvians charged that the Grace Contract was too generous to the foreign creditors and Cáceres extracted congressional approval for it in 1889 only through extreme, extralegal pressure. In retrospect, however, the administration seems to have made an acceptable bargain. Although a source of national pride, the railroads had been a heavy financial burden on the treasury and Peru did not have the funds needed to repair and modernize the system. The Peruvian Corporation put the lines back into operation in less than two years. Thereafter, they played a vital role in the country's economic recovery. The reorganization of the foreign debt, furthermore, liquidated the financial legacy of the Guano Age. Peru's credit abroad was restored and a new era of sound fiscal management began.

General Cáceres obtained the election of his crony Col. Remigio Morales Bermúdez in 1890. Four years later, the administration staged grossly fraudulent elections and Cáceres again claimed the presidency for himself. The prospect of an indefinite military dictatorship sobered Peru's civilian politicians and provided a healing balm for old partisan wounds. Nicolás de Piérola, Peru's eternal plotter, made an alliance with his Civilista enemies to topple the regime. A bloody revolution that cost more than 10,000 lives ousted Cáceres in March 1895. One of the nation's few truly popular revolts, it was the last successful uprising of its kind.

The War of the Pacific dealt a severe blow to the incipient capitalist sector of the Peruvian economy, and recovery proceeded slowly until 1895. After that date, increased political stability, improved fiscal management, the restoration of the country's transportation facilities, programs designed to encourage investment, and favorable markets for Peru's exports all combined to bring a new period of prosperity. By the end of the century the nation's principal agricultural exports—sugar, cotton, and wool—returned to their prewar levels. Still, the income lost with the nitrates of Tarapacá was not replaced until 1912, when the total value of the republic's exports surpassed the figures for the late 1870s.

The most notable economic advances of the postwar period occurred in mining. A law of 1890 exempted this industry from many taxes for a quarter century. A dozen years later, the government promulgated a new, liberalized mineral code and established a National Corps of Mining Engineers which undertook surveys of the republic's subsoil wealth. Stimulated by these measures along with the development of the electronics industry and new technology permitting the efficient exploitation of low-grade ores, the copper-mining industry grew rapidly. This industrial metal quickly replaced silver as Peru's most important mineral. By the turn of the century several independent companies were extracting 800 tons of copper each month from the Cerro de Pasco region in the central highlands. A group of North American businessmen bought several of these properties in 1902 and formed the Cerro de Pasco Corporation. The Central Railroad was extended to their mines a year later and construction began on a large modern smelter. Copper production soared from 9,500 metric tons in 1903 to almost 28,000 tons a decade later. Other branches of the mining industry benefited from copper's success. To meet the huge fuel requirements of the smelters and ore trains, the extraction of coal increased tenfold between 1903 and 1908. As a by-product of the copper refining process, silver production doubled in the decade after 1903.

121

The birth of the modern petroleum industry on the north coast paralleled the development of mining in the Sierra. The petroliferous deposits of this region had been exploited since pre-Incaic times by Indians who used tar from the La Brea pits to make torches and mummify their dead. The first oil wells were drilled in the late 1860s, only to be abandoned during the war with Chile. Faustino Piaggio, an Italo-Peruvian entrepreneur, resuscitated the industry at the end of the conflict and his field at Zorritos had a dozen derricks producing over 2,000 metric tons of crude oil annually by 1890. In that year the acquisition of the nearby La Brea y Pariñas field by the British-owned London and Pacific Petroleum Company signaled the beginning of large-scale capital investment in Peruvian oil. This firm built railroad, port, storage, and refining facilities. In 1913, three major fields were yielding more than 270,000 metric tons of petroleum per year. Peru exported about two-thirds of this production. The remainder was refined at Talara and sold on the domestic market.

The liquid "black gold" yielded by the coastal desert provided important new income for Peru. But exports of crude rubber, the "black gold" from the forests of the Montaña, were ten times more valuable than oil during the early twentieth century. Rubber already had a prominent place among the exports of eastern Peru in the 1850s, when trade statistics for the region first were recorded. After 1880, however, the demand for rubber tires caused by the bicycle fad and then the automobile industry brought a boom to the Amazon Basin. Between that date and 1920, the Montaña produced 80 million dollars worth of wild rubber. From 1902 to 1906, this commodity ranked second among Peru's exports and, the next year, it moved briefly into first place. Then as quickly as it began, the industry collapsed after 1915, when rubber from new Asiatic plantations glutted the market.

While the rubber boom lasted, Iquitos enjoyed fantastic prosperity. Oceangoing steamers as large as 1,000 tons called regularly from New York and Liverpool. The second most active port in Peru, Iquitos had resident consuls from ten foreign countries. The wireless telegraph provided communications with Lima and a cable laid in the Amazon River linked the city with Europe and the United States. The population of Iquitos grew to more than 25,000 persons who were famous for their extravagance. The city imported almost everything, from common foodstuffs, champagne, and caviar to the Malecón Palace, a luxury hotel transported from Paris in pieces and reassembled on the banks of the Amazon. Its ballroom boasted performances by Sarah Bernhardt and the French Grand Opera.

Several commercial houses in Iquitos controlled the rubber industry. For a small fee they obtained concessions from the government to exploit vast tracts of jungle. Most wild rubber was gotten by tapping trees of the genus *Hevea* that grew at widely spaced intervals in the forest. The workers, mainly mestizos drawn from many parts of Peru, cut grooves in the tree trunks and attached cups at their bases to catch the sap which they collected about twice weekly. At camps located on river banks, the tappers coagulated the latex over smoking fires to form large dark-colored balls of crude rubber. Steam launches from Iquitos picked up the harvest and supplied the gatherers with all of their necessities on credit. The merchants paid low prices for the crude rubber and charged exorbitant sums for the items sold to the tappers. Consequently, many men became ensnared in a web of debt peonage.

A fate worse than peonage befell the primitive Indians in some remote areas of the Montaña, most notably those living along the Putumayo River in extreme northeastern Peru. The object of a long-standing territorial dispute between Peru and Colombia, both nations had agreed not to exercise sovereignty within this region until the boundary question could be settled. Julio C. Arana, a Peruvian rubber baron, began large-scale tapping operations in this no-man's-land and established a reign of terror. His private army first drove competitors from the district and then enslaved the Indians. Those who failed to meet their production quotas were beaten and even murdered. News of these atrocities soon reached the outside world and the Putumayo became the subject of an embarrassing international scandal. After the British and United States governments intervened in the affair, Lima took action against Arana. The worst crimes against the natives ended, but their exploitation continued on a lesser scale until the demise of the rubber industry.

Old boundary disputes between Peru and its Amazonian neighbors intensified as rubber prices soared. The danger of territorial loss was most serious in the isolated basin of the Madre de Díos River in the extreme southeastern corner of the nation. The rugged Cordillera de Carabaya made this zone almost impenetrable from the west, while high ground separated the waters of the Madre de Díos system from Peru's navigable waterways to the north. The Madre de Díos, itself navigable only by small steamers along its upper course, flowed eastward through Bolivia and Brazil. Practically unexplored and uninhabited by civilized men, the rubber boom brought many Bolivans and Brazilians into this district, but attracted few Peruvians. To strengthen its control over the Montaña, the Peruvian government constructed new trails into the region and placed flotillas of gunboats on the rivers. The army bolstered its Amazonian garrisons, and paramilitary agricultural colonies subsidized by the state reinforced these units. The Department of Madre de Díos was established to provide more efficient administration for the southeast. Telegraph wires connected Puerto Maldonado, its sleepy riverside capital, with the Sierra. In spite of these measures Peru relinquished its claims to 175,000 square miles of jungle to Brazil and Bolivia through boundary treaties signed in 1909.

The addition of copper, petroleum, and rubber to Peru's list of major exports around the turn of the century was accompanied by dramatic increases in the production of sugar and cotton, the nation's leading commercial crops. Like mining, this sector of the economy benefited from new capital investment, improved technology, favorable market conditions, and government solicitude for its interests, ably represented by the National Society of Agriculture founded in 1896. The National School of Agriculture, opened in 1902, began training the agronomists needed to operate the modern plantations and established experimental farms for the scientific study of agriculture. A new water code, adopted that same year, encouraged private investment in irrigation. In 1904, government engineers began surveying the hydraulic resources of several coastal valleys.

A revolution occurred in the Peruvian sugar industry during the late nineteenth and early twentieth centuries. Even before the War of the Pacific, sugar estates along the north coast had exhibited a trend toward consolidation and mechanization. After 1890, however, huge inputs of capital—much of it foreign—permitted the creation of mammoth agro-industrial enterprises, complete with their own railroads and port facilities. Giant processing plants replaced the small mills of earlier times, greatly increasing the amount and quality of sugar extracted from the cane. Although sugar, in the form of hard, brown cakes, was a staple in the diet of many poor Peruvians, at least three-quarters of the national output was sold abroad. Sugar exports grew from 37,000 metric tons in 1891 to 114,000 tons a decade later and reached 142,000 tons in 1913.

The most dramatic changes in the sugar industry took place in the 300,000-acre Chicama Valley, near Trujillo. During the four decades following the war, most of the sixty-five estates that had occupied this region were absorbed by three giant enterprises. The Cartavio plantation was created by W. R. Grace, an Irishman who made his fortune in Peru before becoming a citizen of the United States. The Italo-Peruvian Larco family owned the neighboring Hacienda Roma until they sold it in the mid 1920s to the Gildemeister interests. The owners of the Casa Grande estate, Peru's largest sugar plantation, the Gildemeisters were Peruvian citizens, but they retained a strong identification with Germany.

The rise of these huge enterprises adversely effected other elements of the region's old economic order. The large plantations obtained the lands of small independent crop farmers by fair means and foul. They evicted tenants to conserve scarce water for the thirsty cane fields. The dispossessed agriculturalists often became laborers, mechanics, and managers for the large operations. The plantations obtained additional workers from the Sierra through the services of labor contractors called *enganchadores*. Besides recruitment, the contractors frequently continued to act as middlemen between the workers and their employers. After subtracting large commissions, the *enganchadores* distributed the payroll to the field hands. They often paid the workers in scrip redeemable only at stores also operated by the contractors. The abuses of the *enganche* system brought periodic outbreaks of violence by the workers. Although most notable on the north coast, large-scale agricultural and mining enterprises in other parts of the country also utilized the services of labor contractors.

A tendency toward larger holdings and greater mechanization was apparent in cotton farming, but it was not nearly so pronounced as in the sugar industry. Small-scale operations, employing ancient methods, continued to exist alongside more extensive, modern plantations. The rapid expansion of cotton cultivation in Peru during the early twentieth century resulted primarily from high prices brought by a decline in the plague-ridden cotton industry of the United States and a major scientific discovery. In 1908, Fermín Tangüis, a planter from Pisco, developed a new variety of cotton which bears his name. A disease-resistant, long-fibered crop, the Tangüis strain yielded 25 percent more lint than other varieties. Within a dozen years, Peruvian planters adopted the new cotton almost to the exclusion of other types in many districts. Even before the generalized use of Tangüis, Peru's cotton production expanded rapidly. Exports of this fiber increased from less than 5,000 metric tons in 1891 to 24,000 tons in 1913.

The intensification of economic activity in the provinces brought new life to several of Peru's regional urban centers, where the electric light symbolized their attempts to enter the modern world. Commercial agriculture generated prosperity for the merchants, artisans, and professional classes of such coastal cities as Piura, Trujillo, Chiclayo, and Ica. The new mining industry revived the stagnant economies of La Oroya and Cerro de Pasco. The extension of the Central Railroad from these mining centers to Huancayo in 1908 strengthened that town's position as the most important agricultural market of the central highlands and encouraged the growth of several small processing industries. Farther to the south, the Southern Railway reached Cuzco in 1908, and the ancient capital of the Incas along with Arequipa acquired a number of new factories, especially woolen mills and leather works.

The greatest advances in commerce and industry occurred in the Lima-Callao area. Between 1895 and 1914, the number of banks increased from three to seven and their deposits grew by more than 600 percent. Peru's first insurance company opened its office in Lima in 1895. Two decades later, nine underwriters were issuing policies. Factories appeared at a rapid rate during the late nineteenth and early twentieth centuries. Most of these processed agricultural raw materials or manufactured textiles and prepared foods. Although small by European and North American standards, a few of these enterprises, like the Vitarte cotton mill, employed more than 500 workers. The businessmen of the capital established the Lima Chamber of Commerce in 1887, and the National Industrial Society in 1896. Two years later, the Lima Stock Exchange opened, listing the securities of some 200 firms. The city itself underwent considerable modernization and beautification, especially during the administration of Mayor Federico Elguera from 1901 to 1908. The government constructed new boulevards, markets, and public baths. Several important streets were paved with asphalt. Telephones and electric street lights were installed and the horse-drawn streetcar system converted to electric power. Yet Lima had few large buildings, most of its streets were narrow, and, with only about 150,000 residents in 1914, it was one of the smaller South American capitals.

Foreigners owned many of Lima's commercial and industrial firms, a fact that disturbed some native Peruvians. Manuel Vicente Villarán reported that in 1896, aliens controlled 451 of the 542 larger enterprises listed in the business registry of the capital. In addition, most of Lima's small grocery stores were owned by non-Peruvians, probably the Chinese who comprised the largest foreign element in the country. After 1898, these Orientals were joined by Japanese brought to Peru under contracts between colonization companies in the mother country and Peruvian employers. By 1923, about 18,000 immigrants from Japan had entered the republic. Even more than the Chinese, the Japanese congregated in the cities where they operated small retail businesses and service enterprises. Most of Peru's European immigrants also preferred urban life, especially in Lima and Callao. The republic had 13,000 resident Italians in the first decade of the twentieth century, about double the number of persons from all other European countries combined. The Italians, primarily from the industrial, northern part of the peninsula, were the most important entrepreneurial group in Peru. Fortunately, they readily identified with their new homeland.

A Progressive, Aristocratic Republic, 1895–1914

Nicolás de Piérola was elected president in July 1895, initiating almost two decades of unusually stable government in Peru. Because the nation's civilian elite dominated the political process and governed more or less according to constitutional norms, historians have called the period the "Aristocratic Republic." This label, however, should not imply a narrowly selfish conservatism. The presidents of the time possessed considerable wealth or high social standing, and literacy requirements limited suffrage to scarcely more than 100,000 persons at the turn of the century. But this era produced important political reforms, advances in public administration, new programs to foster economic development, and even a few cautious attempts to ameliorate some of the country's social problems. Major improvements in the republic's school system, furthermore, would bring a steady expansion of the electorate. In many ways Peru's Aristocratic Republic resembled the contemporary Progessive Era in the United States.

The Civilistas and Piérola's Democrats, the most important political parties of the period, had few important ideological differences. Both groups advocated constitutional government and civilian control over the military. The idea of progress, especially economic development, was central to their programs. Each party had conservative and reformist factions, but neither organization desired fundamental changes in the structure of society. Reflecting Piérola's intense Catholicism, the Democrats favored the continuance of strong Church influence in social affairs. Although the postwar Civilistas retained the mild anticlericalism of their predecessors, they avoided conflict with the Church. Both parties subscribed to the basic tenets of nineteenth-century economic liberalism, but the Democrats were less opposed to government regulation of business and more amenable to the demands of the small urban working class. Personal feuds, economic interests, and regionalist sentiment were of greater import than ideology to the partisan struggles of the period.

The successful businessmen and well-connected members of the liberal professions—men who had "arrived"—together with their clientele most often were found within the ranks of the Civilistas. Their administrations favored the vested interests of the more modern sectors of the economy, including the coastal plantations, the mining industry, the commercial houses of Lima and the urban bankers, manufacturers, and landlords. Viewed as the "rich man's party," leading Civilistas belonged to the most prestigious social clubs and were grouped within the often-mentioned but ill-defined "oligarchy." The Democrats also recruited their top leadership from the ranks of wealthy or socially prominent families, but they relied upon the less affluent portions of the national society for electoral support. The party appealed to the smaller merchants, the less successful professional men, the white-collar employees, artisans, and other skilled workers. The Democrats were popular in the neglected interior, drawing votes from many traditional landowners and provincial businessmen. Piérola's native Arequipa, noted for its religiosity and leadership of regionalist opposition to the dominance of Lima, was the Democratic stronghold.

The Civilistas and Democrats made coalitions of convenience with each other and with the Liberal and Constitutionalist parties. Founded by firebrand Augusto Durand in 1901, the Liberal party combined extreme anticlericalism with the advocacy of unfettered capitalism. The Constitutionalist party, dominated by former President Cáceres, was comprised almost entirely of men with military backgrounds. Their image tarnished by the ten-year, postwar dictatorship, the armed forces preferred to withdraw from public view. The officers continued to be a significant political force, however. The Constitutionalists participated in four of seven administrations after 1895, and 1914 the soldiers would demonstrate that they were still the final arbiters of the nation's politics.

Nicolás de Piérola, fifty-six years old at the time of his inauguration, had been the most colorful and controversial figure in Peruvian politics for more than a quarter century. Historians continue to be puzzled by this paradoxical man. Idolized by the masses, whose cause he championed, Peru has had few leaders with greater charismatic appeal than this bewhiskered, ramrod-straight little petrel. Yet, Piérola was a congenital aristocrat who shunned close contact with the multitude and believed that the nation's social structure was preordained and immutable. Although he had little faith in the ability of the humble classes to rise above their "station in life," Piérola paternalistically sought to ease the suffering of the poor and protect their limited rights. A veteran of countless conspiracies, the "Democratic Caudillo" was Peru's foremost practicioner of revolutionary politics. As president, however, Piérola did much to regenerate his country's moribund republican institutions. His enemies long had castigated Piérola for his handling of Peru's finances during the improvident Balta regime. But his own administration was notable for its honesty and efficiency. Dogmatic, impetuous, and irresponsible when seeking power, Piérola demonstrated considerable talent for pragmatic, constructive leadership during his tenure from 1895 to 1899.

The Democratic-Civilista coalition forged to oust Cáceres continued throughout Piérola's term, giving Peru a much needed recess from partisan strife. The president hoped to preserve this tranquillity and strengthen the democratic process by removing some of the sources of revolution. His regime respected the rights of free expression and the prerogatives of congress and the courts. Elected municipal governments, suppressed under the previous dictatorship, reappeared after 1895. A constitutional amendment provided for the direct election of the president, replacing the electoral college. The administration established an autonomous national board to supervise elections and adjudicate disputed contests. These reforms did not end arbitrary government or electoral fraud. But under Piérola, in the words of one Peruvian scholar, "the republic began to be republican."

The Piérola regime also marked the beginning of a new era in Peru's fiscal history. Several new taxes and the adoption of modern techniques in the administration of the nation's finances brought a substantial increase in the state's revenues and a significant improvement in public services. The government's budgets were nearly balanced, the internal debt was serviced, and exports regularly exceeded imports. To stabilize the *sol* and give the country's currency greater respectability in world markets, Piérola put his government on the gold standard. The regime cooperated with private enterprise to encourage investment and, in 1896, it established the Ministry of Development which undertook an impressive public works program.

Military reform was the most pressing and difficult problem facing the Piérola government. Peru's civilian politicians were determined to prevent another dictatorship of the Cáceres variety, but not at the cost of impairing the armed forces' capacity to defend the nation. The War of the Pacific had demonstrated the imperative of military preparedness and deteriorating relations with Chile underscored the need for an effective army and navy. The Treaty of Ancón had called for a plebiscite in the Chilean occupied departments of Tacna and Arica in 1894 to determine their ultimate nationality. Unfortunately, an agreement to implement this provision could not be reached and a new war threatened between the two countries. To strengthen the armed forces while instilling them with greater respect for constitutional government, Piérola instituted a program of professionalization. A French military mission, contracted by the administration, arrived in 1896. The European officers upgraded instruction at the Chorrillos military academy and reorganized the Peruvian army. The nation's first Military Code of Justice was promulgated in 1898, and more than ever before, merit rather than political considerations became the basis for promotion. Believing that Indians and *cholos* were very susceptible to the wiles of military adventurers, the regime secured a law of universal military service designed to bring members of the educated classes into the ranks of the armed services. Although this last measure was largely ignored after Piérola's term, the other reforms did help develop institutional pride in the military and improve its technical proficiency.

Piérola's alliance of Democrats and Civilistas secured the presidency for Eduardo López de Romaña in 1899, but a revolt of dissident Democrats led by Guillermo Billinghurst marred the election. A man who had fought beside Piérola in the old struggles against the Civilistas, Billinghurst disapproved of the partnership with his old adversaries and chafed at being bypassed as the administration candidate. Piérola had favored López de Romaña, Peru's first minister of development, because he pledged to continue the coalition. As a newcomer to partisan politics, this engineer also was more acceptable to the Civilistas. The new president maintained the progressive tenor of the preceding administration. In 1901, he began a reorganization of the nation's school system that marks the start of modern public education in Peru. Unfortunately, the independence that made López de Romaña an attractive coalition candidate quickly became a liability for him as president. In a spirited contest for the Lima city council in 1900, the Civilista candidates defeated an overly optimistic Democratic slate led by Piérola. Humiliated, the ex-president accused his successor of favoring the Civilistas, and the Democratic chieftain withdrew his support from the regime. As the breach between Piérola and the president widened, López de Romaña was drawn into the Civilista camp. The alliance of Peru's two largest political parties disintegrated.

The Democratic party was split badly as the election of 1903 approached. Some of its members abandoned the organization and joined Augusto Durand's Liberal party. Those remaining within the Democratic fold divided their allegiances between the aging Piérola and Guillermo Billinghurst. The rejuvenated Civilistas, meanwhile, negotiated a new alliance. Ironically, the party of Manuel Pardo—born of antimilitarist sentiment thirty years earlier—now joined forces with the Constitutionalist party, the vehicle of Peru's soldier-politicians. The new coalition nominated Civilista Manuel Candamo, the president of the Lima Chamber of Commerce. With his own party gravely weakened, Piérola endorsed the Civilista candidate, who was an old personal friend. Candamo won the contest without opposition and was inaugurated in November 1903 amid optimism for a revival of the Civilista-Democratic partnership.

Peru suffered a great loss when Manuel Candamo, a man of ability, integrity, and conciliatory moderation, died only eight months after assuming office. Instead of rapprochement between the Civilistas and Democrats, the nation experienced a bitter partisan fight that reopened old political wounds and inflicted new ones. Already enervated by internal feuds, the Democrats now watched the Civilistas wage their "battle of the generations." The older, traditionalist element of the party, uncertain of the course on which the nation was traveling, desired a candidate who would slow the pace of reform. More confident of the future, the younger Civilistas hoped to quicken the process of modernization. The latter wing of the party won the struggle and nominated forty-year-old José Pardo. The son of the first Civilista president, he had demonstrated his own merits as a scholar, businessman, and diplomat. The Civilistas and Constitutionalists maintained their strange alliance of convenience to further Pardo's candidacy. Meanwhile, an equally pragmatic pact linked the Democrats and their anticlerical critics of the Liberal party to elect Piérola. The emotion-charged campaign produced many violent incidents. Then, five days before the start of balloting, Piérola accused the government of rigging the contest and withdrew from the race. Pardo won the election unopposed.

The first administration of José Pardo (1904–8) was the golden age of the Civilista party. Partisan passion quickly subsided after the election and the new regime's respect for the constitution encouraged continued political peace. Pardo appointed a distinguished cabinet and it efficiently managed the government's revenues which increased 50 percent. The Ministry of Development received a threefold boost in its budget, permitting it to undertake many important projects. The Central and Southern railroads were extended to Huancayo and Cuzco and several shorter lines were constructed. The state joined with private capital to create a national steamship company for the republic's coastal trade. The purchase of two new cruisers initiated a long-term naval rearmament program. Like his father, José Pardo believed that education was the key to the nation's future. Therefore, he increased the funds allocated for schools by 250 percent. New legislation, including a utopian provision for free and compulsory primary education, supplemented the reforms of López de Romaña. One of the few failures of an otherwise brilliant administration was the defeat of a comprehensive program of labor legislation. Here, the president proved to be much more progressive than the majority within his party.

At the end of his term in 1908, Pardo obtained his party's endorsement for Augusto B. Leguía, his talented finance minister. The enfeebled Democratic-Liberal coalition provided little electoral challenge to the Civilista-Constitutionalist alliance but staged an unsuccessful revolt on May 1, 1908. The government arrested Liberal party chief Augusto Durand, who had led the uprising, along with several other prominent opposition figures. Leguía was elected without further incident at the end of the month. In many ways the new regime was a continuation of the progressive Pardo administration. Public works, especially railroads, received top priority. Exploiting a loophole in the contract with the Peruvian Corporation that permitted Peru to retain all of the guano needed for its own agriculture, Leguía created the Guano Administrative Company. Through the efforts of this state agency, Peruvian farmers soon consumed the nation's entire production of this fertilizer. An intensification of the Tacna-Arica controversy with Chile and an outbreak of border disputes with Peru's four Amazonian neighbors (Ecuador, Colombia, Brazil, and Bolivia) prompted Leguía to procure several warships, including the navy's first two submarines. In 1911, the president promulgated a law making employers responsible for the job-related accidents of their workers.

Leguía quickly freed the persons arrested after the May 1908 revolt. But an incident the following year produced an authoritarian shift in his regime. In the early morning of May 29, 1909, a brother and two sons of Nicolás de Piérola led a score of men in an attack on the presidential palace. Killing a guard, they stormed through a secondary entrance and seized the president. In a demonstration of his famous iron nerve, Leguía refused to sign a resignation as his captors demanded. Thus thwarted, the conspirators paraded the president through the center of town, hoping to attract public support for their movement. Fortunately for Leguía, a squad of soldiers rescued him and foiled the coup. Because several innocent persons had been killed or wounded in this audacious plot, the public approved the imprisonment of all those implicated in the affair. Leguía, however, used this opportunity to arrest many of his peaceful critics who had no connection with the conspiracy. When students from San Marcos University demonstrated to obtain the release of these political prisoners, soldiers and mounted police attacked the protesters, killing one student and injuring several others.

Leguía's increasingly dictatorial methods caused a split within his own party and an antiadministration bloc of Civilistas in congress united with the small contingent of Democrats and Liberals to combat the president. Leguía responded by purging the National Election Board, rigging the congressional election of 1911, and threatening to dissolve the legislature. Rumors spread that the president planned to cancel the election to choose his successor scheduled for 1912, claiming that pressing domestic and international problems made a change in government "inconvenient." Hoping to avert a presidential coup, the Civilistas nominated Antero Aspíllaga, a compromise candidate, for the presidency. A wealthy, conservative planter, Aspíllaga had remained loyal to Leguía during the intraparty struggle, but he promised to respect the constitution if elected. Although Leguía endorsed the Civilista standard-bearer, his intentions continued to be suspect.

If Leguía planned to retain power, the surprising strength of a resurgent Democratic party rather than Civilista maneuvers upset his scheme. Early in 1912, the president's enemies attempted to unite all of the antiadministration forces behind a common candidate. But Nicolás de Piérola, who would die the following year, refused to participate. It seemed certain that Aspíllaga would win the presidency if Leguía allowed the contest to be held. Then in early May, less than a month before the balloting, Guillermo Billinghurst gained control of the Democratic party and entered the race. A millionaire businessman of English descent, he was noted for his brilliance and, more importantly, his volatility. Billinghurst believed that the survival of republican government and capitalism in Peru depended upon reforms to make these systems benefit the common people as well as the nation's elite. A fiery orator, the new Democratic leader proposed to broaden the electorate, institute an extensive program of labor legislation, and end government favoritism toward the wealthy classes. However, one minor plank in his platform won the allegiance of the masses: he promised to give the poor a larger loaf of bread for five *centavos*. This demagogic populism frightened the upper class, but made "Big Bread Billinghurst" an instant hero to the workers of Lima.

At a rally of 20,000 enthusiastic supporters—an immense crowd for that period—the Democratic leader charged that Leguía would not permit a fair vote and called for the "sovereign people" to demonstrate their power in the streets. And so they did. A general strike in the capital, the nation's first, greeted the start of the election on May 25. At the same time, gangs of

Billinghurst's partisans attacked polling places, intimidating voters and destroying ballots. Their apparent strategy was simple. If fewer than one-third of the registered voters cast ballots, the law required congress to select a president itself, or arrange a new election. Billinghurst probably believed that he could win a vote in the legislature, or gain time to organize a stronger campaign for another popular contest.

Billinghurst's plan received at least the tacit support of the wily Leguía, who abandoned Aspíllaga in this crisis. The president's police did little to maintain order, and the polls, which had remained open for a week in previous elections, were closed by executive decree after only two days. Perhaps Leguía hoped to force a new popular election, retaining power himself until a successor could be chosen, or exact concessions in the event of a congressional election for the presidency. Aspíllaga claimed victory with over one-third of the popular votes. But the legislature nullified the contest, charging that widespread fraud had occurred in the provinces carried by the Civilista candidate. While Billinghurst's supporters continued their street demonstrations and even invaded the halls of congress, the Democratic and Leguiísta legislators reached a compromise. Billinghurst was declared president and Roberto Leguía, the brother of the departing executive, received the vice-presidency.

Soon after his inauguration on September 24, 1912, a series of labor disputes afforded Billinghurst an opportunity to fulfill his campaign promises to the workers. On January 10, 1913, the president ended a four-day strike of the Callao dock workers by decreeing the eight-hour day for this group. Two weeks later, another executive order established Peru's first basic law regulating labor relations. It provided for the democratic organization of unions, legalized peaceful strikes, and made collective bargaining obligatory. With the protection of this law and a sympathetic regime in power, Peru's workers struck again and again, achieving significant gains. Meanwhile, Billinghurst continued to demonstrate his concern for the nation's humble citizens. He amplified the workmen's compensation law, established a bureau of labor statistics, and undertook a pilot project to build houses for the working class. To make public education more responsive to the needs of the common people, the government proposed the addition of courses in manual arts and home economics to the primary-school curriculum. The administration also planned a night school program to combat adult illiteracy.

Following an Indian uprising in the southern highlands, Billing-hurst appointed a pronative army officer to investigate the affair.

At the end of Billinghurst's first year in office, the Civilistas, Constitutionalists, and Liberals had united to block his programs in congress. The president's efforts on behalf of the workers, of course, angered many conservatives. But Billinghurst's reforms—although important early steps in this area—were moderate and conformed to the views of the progressive wing of the Civilista party. President Pardo had proposed a more comprehensive labor program, and a Civilista regime would secure the adoption of several new labor laws a few years later. The executive-legislative conflict had a broader base. Billinghurst proposed to end waste in government by ending several programs favored by special interests. Most controversial, Billing-hurst owned nitrate works in Chilean-held Tarapacá and had close friends in the Santiago government. He thought that the vexatious Tacna-Arica dispute could be resolved by peaceful means. The president slashed the military budget and began personal negotiations with the Chileans. A formula he proposed for a settlement seemed likely to leave the two departments in the hands of Chile.

In his confrontation with the hostile legislature, Billinghurst, like Leguía before him, refused to be bound by the constitutional process. But while Leguía had used the traditional weapons of the executive arsenal—the police, the provincial officials, and the election machinery—Billinghurst employed a much more frightening weapon. Mass demonstrations by workers demanding congressional submission to the presidential will were punctuated by frequent acts of terrorism. A mob smashed the presses of an opposition newspaper. The house of the senate's presiding officer was bombed. A squad of assassins attacked the residence of ex-President Leguía, who barely escaped death. Thereafter, the regime accused Leguía and his brother the vice-president of a conspiracy to kill Billinghurst and assume power. Both men were deported. A self-styled "Committee of Public Health" directed this campaign of intimidation. Their handbills threatened a "terrible war . . . without quarter" against congress and justified the removal of antiadministration legislators "by the dagger or dynamite."

Congress refused to approve the budget for 1914, and Bil-linghurst illegally authorized government expenditures by executive decree. The legislature then began impeachment proceedings against him and the president called for the replacement of congress by an assembly representative of the "real will" of the people. For several months a group of congressmen had been plotting to overthrow the regime. But the armed forces, whose cooperation was essential for a successful coup, were reluctant to strike against their commander in chief. Then they learned that the president planned to open the military arsenal, arm the workers, and dissolve congress by decree. On the morning of February 4, 1914, troops under the command of Col. Oscar R. Benavides stormed the Palace of Pizarro and ousted Billinghurst.

6

The Emergence of Modern Peru

[1914–1930]

⌘ A Nation in Transition

THE YEAR 1914 WAS EVENTFUL FOR PERU. In Europe
the Great War began, driving upward the demand for
Peru's raw materials. These became much more accessible to the
major markets of the North Atlantic with the opening of the
Panama Canal that same year. During the next half decade the
value of the nation's agricultural and mineral exports increased
more than threefold. Meanwhile, the shift from peaceful to
military production by the industrialized world and the disruption of normal shipping patterns severely restricted the flow of
finished goods that Peru traditionally imported. This respite
from foreign competition encouraged entrepreneurs in Peru to
manufacture more items at home. By 1923, when the republic's
first industrial census was compiled, the Lima-Callao area alone
had 224 factories. Peru's industrial labor force, in the urban areas
as well as in the Sierra mines and in the agro-industrial enterprises of the coast, expanded notably as did the number of
white-collar employees. With fixed wages and salaries, both of
these groups were hard-pressed by a spiraling inflation. Manufactures were scarce and expensive. Food prices rose sharply as
lands formerly planted in food crops now were devoted to sugar
and cotton production. An increase of almost 90 percent in the

cost of living between 1913 and 1919 contributed to a wave of strikes, many of them violent.

Peru's organized labor movement was in its infancy in 1914. To be sure, artisan guilds had existed since colonial times, but these consisted primarily of self-employed craftsmen seeking to maintain standards of quality and regulate prices. Mutual aid societies, usually associated with the guilds, provided social services and organized recreational activities for their members. Although these traditional organizations sometimes attempted to influence government policy and even called a few strikes as early as the mid-nineteenth century, they were neither agents of collective bargaining nor political pressure groups. Modern labor unions appeared only with industrialization and new, larger concentrations of wage workers. They were distinct from and often hostile to the basically conservative guilds and mutual aid societies, which declined rapidly after World War I. Only a few unions existed before 1913, when labor's right to organize and bargain collectively first received legal sanction. Nevertheless, Peru's small industrial proletariat was developing a group identity and could be mobilized to achieve specific purposes. True industrial strikes were recorded as early as 1896. Peru's first labor congress met in Lima five years later, and the workers played a crucial role in winning the presidency for Guillermo Billinghurst in 1912.

Peru's labor movement, like that of the rest of Latin America, was born under the influence of anarchism, an ideology introduced by working-class immigrants from Italy and Spain in the late nineteenth century. The principal anarchist workers' doctrine, anarcho-syndicalism, differed markedly from the "business unionism" prevalent in the United States during that period. There, organizations like the American Federation of Labor eschewed radical political programs and concentrated on the attainment of specific economic objectives—"bread-and-butter issues"—through collective bargaining and generally peaceful strikes. In its purest form anarcho-syndicalism viewed the labor movement as a vehicle for political action, the vanguard of social revolution. Beginning with a crippling general strike, this upheaval would climax in a violent burst of mob action that would smash the government. Eventually, through some vague process, a classless society would appear and voluntary cooperation would replace the coercion of all formal institutions. Unlike the Marxian communists who wished to replace the capitalist state with a dictatorship of the proletariat, the anarchists distrusted all concentrations of power. In fact, the extreme individualism of these "voluntary communists" hampered effective organization. The anarchist unions of Peru ascribed to these basic tenets in varying degrees. No central directing body enforced a "party line." Considerable uniformity, however, existed in their tactics. Anarchist unions usually shunned collective bargaining and labor contracts, viewing them as impingements on the freedom of individual workers. They preferred to issue ultimatums to employers. A rejection of their demands often led to "direct action"—violent strikes, sabotage and acts of terrorism.

The anarchists lost influence in the 1920s, but the methods they popularized continued to be employed by new labor organizations. Peru's unions were weak and they had difficulty exacting concessions from management through peaceful strikes. Impoverished workers could not withstand protracted periods without wages, while employers often continued their operations with those men who remained on the job. Most of Peru's early industries were relatively unsophisticated, requiring low levels of skill. Strikers could be replaced readily from the large reservoir of service and agricultural laborers attracted by the higher wages paid in the modern enterprises. Because of this vulnerability, the unions had greater success with "political strikes." They confronted the government with a crisis—a general strike or violent demonstrations—to induce a state-imposed settlement upon management. Peru's unstable regimes often succumbed to these pressures, for failure to maintain order invited overthrow by the armed forces. These tactics also could be used to gain purely political objectives, as the workers demonstrated during the Billinghurst administration. Because of the disruptive potential of the unions, the prominence of radicals within their leadership and, later, their close ties with avowedly revolutionary political parties, many regimes were hostile to labor organizations, if not to the workers themselves. They often bestowed benefits on the laboring classes paternalistically, while suppressing or attempting to control their unions.

The decade following 1914 climaxed thirty years of growing unrest in the rural Sierra, where the War of the Pacific had profoundly disrupted the indigenous communities. Some villages experienced the ravages of battle itself. Many more were invaded by army press gangs searching for conscripts. Peace did not come to the mountains with the Treaty of Ancón. Iglesias, Cáceres, and Piérola struggled for power in the next decade and filled the ranks of their armies with Indians. The end of civil strife in 1895 brought economic recovery and new forces for change. Some highlanders found employment in the rapidly expanding mining industry, while the cash advances of the labor contractors lured an even larger number to the plantations of the coast. Whether pried away from their communities by bayonets or coaxed away by the glimmer of quick *soles,* those villagers who returned home brought with them a greater awareness of the world beyond their mountain retreats and less patience to endure silently the abuses of the past.

Indian uprisings had occurred sporadically in the Sierra prior to the War of the Pacific, but in the following decades these rebellions increased in frequency and ferocity. Very serious outbreaks in the mountains of Ancash in 1885 and in Ayacucho eleven years later were crushed only after months of fighting and hundreds of casualties. Much of the early postwar unrest stemmed from specific acts of oppression by petty officials, especially the customary forced labor on public projects, and the imposition of new taxes. But after the turn of the century a brisk upturn began in the world market for wool which soared to boom proportions during the world war. At the same time, the increased demand for foodstuffs on the coast encouraged greater commercialization of other branches of highland agriculture. Now widespread aggression by *gamonales* on the increasingly valuable Indian lands and the extortions of wool merchants and *hacendados* who acted as middlemen in this trade brought large areas of the Sierra to the brink of civil war.

The growing turmoil in the highlands coincided with and nourished the rise of the *indigenista* ("Indianist") movement among Peru's educated elite. The disastrous defeat at the hands of Chile initiated an agonizing period of national soul-searching by Peruvian intellectuals. Many of these thinkers found the major source of their country's weakness in the poverty, ignorance, and cultural isolation of the indigenous masses. The often-repeated story of the highlanders who thought that the recent war had been a struggle between two obscure caudillos—a General Peru and a General Chile—was a bittersweet illustration of the lack of national integration. During this same period, the educated classes of ethnically similar Latin American republics also addressed themselves to their "Indian problem." Under the

141

intellectual sway of positivism, a materialistic philosophy that gained great popularity in the late nineteenth century, they most often viewed the native Americans as inherently inferior creatures doomed to be trampled under foot in the march of progress. Some Peruvian writers shared this view. But for many intellectuals the struggle for the "survival of the fittest" enacted in the War of the Pacific had not demonstrated the superiority of the nation's white elite. Indeed, the great physical endurance of the Quechua-speaking soldiers in the trenches of the Atacama and the tenacious resistance of Cáceres's Indian guerrillas in Ayacucho were among the few scraps of national pride salvaged from the military humiliation. Many Peruvian social critics concluded that the backwardness of the Indians resulted from the neglect or abuse of Peru's ruling class. By liberating their minds and harnessing their productive energies the indigenous majority could be transformed from a liability to an asset, a vital force for national development.

While social philosophers were making *indigenismo* an important new component of Peruvian nationalism, the country's novelists endowed the movement with a soul. Beginning in 1889, with the publication of Clorinda Matto de Turner's *Aves sin nido* [Birds without a nest], Peruvian fiction increasingly turned away from the dominant romanticism of the period, with its effusive style and "alien" themes, to treat realistically and sympathetically the plight of the Indian and related national problems. Gaining strength from a similar trend that developed in the literature of other Latin American countries, most notably Mexico, Indianism became the major literary current of Peru after World War I. In this friendly atmosphere *indigenismo* pervaded many disciplines. Archaeologists uncovered several important pre-Columbian sites and took steps for their honored preservation. Peruvian historians emphasized the positive aspects of the nation's Indian heritage, while treatises on contemporary problems of the indigenous population filled the pages of a wide range of scholarly journals.

Indianism, although ascendant, did not seduce Peru's entire intellectual community. In their praise of the nation's aboriginal culture, some Indianists scorned Peru's Iberian heritage, condemning it for all of society's ills. These attacks provoked a vigorous response from equally dogmatic Hispanophiles. Often deprecating the natives, the *hispanistas* glorified the Spanish past and found hope for the future almost entirely in the country's white population. The strident voices of extreme *indigenistas* and *hispanistas* filled the classrooms and salons of the elite in a sterile "civil war" that raged for many years. Eventually pragmatic nationalists accepted the fact of Peru's mixed parentage and molded it to create a "useful past." Finding value in the contributions of both the Old and New Worlds, they glorified *mestizaje,* the blending of these traditions to form *peruanidad* ("Peruvianity"), a unique national culture.

Not content merely to write about the exploitation of the Indian, some *indigenistas* worked directly for reform. The Sino-Peruvian Pedro S. Zulen and his common-law wife Dora Mayer de Zulen were outstanding among these early activists. Their Pro-Indian Association, founded in 1909, fought for the natives along several fronts. While the Zulens's newspaper publicized acts of injustice toward this humble class, assocation lawyers defended the natives in court and proposed remedial legislation. As a reform movement, Indianism gradually acquired respectability. By the second decade of the twentieth century, a few committed *indigenistas* had reached positions of influence within the government and many practical politicians embraced the creed in their speeches, if not always in their actions.

For a third of a century following the War of the Pacific, Manuel González Prada (1848–1918) set the pace for Peruvian intellectuals. The product of an old aristocratic family of fading fortune, young Manuel abided by the wishes of his devout mother and entered the seminary. But he soon abandoned study for the priesthood to pursue his own interests in science, philosophy, and literature. González Prada first gained recognition penning beautiful verses, the initial stage in a career that would place him among the literary giants of Latin America. Although he found fault with Peruvian society during these early years, deep disillusionment with the world about him came only in the wake of the war with Chile. A volunteer defender of Lima, the sensitive and shy young writer confined himself to his house and his own anguished thoughts throughout the entire Chilean occupation. When he emerged after months of seclusion, the romantic poet had been transformed into a political polemicist, the role for which he became most famous.

González Prada's philosophy defies neat labeling. During his long life he eclectically borrowed elements from several intellectual movements, adding and rejecting ideas with little regard for consistency. Beginning as a radical reformer, he later proclaimed himself an anarchist, although his ever-deepening pessimism seemed to contradict this fundamentally optimistic ideology. From criticism of Catholicism's temporal power, he moved rapidly toward atheism. But the "Peruvian Cato" became more of a moralist with each step away from formal religion. Although he was the most famous of Peru's Hispanophobic Indianists, these sentiments were secondary to the main thrust of his thought. For him, the wretched condition of the Indian was only one symptom of the ignorance and greed that infected all of Western society. Spain had been merely the agent, albeit a most effective one, that carried the malady to Latin America. The disease had reached the terminal stage in Peru and González Prada proposed to hasten mercifully the death of the victim through social revolution.

Several contemporaries of González Prada shared many of his ideas, but none expressed them so effectively as he. In the hands of the master poet the pen became a rapier slashing out at almost every aspect of society. González Prada directed most of his vitriol at the country's "two great lies: the republic and Christianity." Religion in Peru had not advanced a "step beyond idolatry" and served as a "powerful instrument of servitude," especially for women who were "slaves of the Church." Priests, he declared, were a "force hostile to civilization" and had "no reason to exist." González Prada may have tempered his attacks on the Church out of respect for his mother, but no patroness protected secular institutions from his verbal volleys. The nation's political parties were "syndicates of unhealthy ambition" led by "merchants in political disguise," whose brains were a "prolongation of the digestive tract." Congress was a "great sewer" gathering all the filth of the nation. Peruvian journalism he described as the "purulent secretion" of a putrid society. The policeman was a "mosquito with the pretensions of an elephant." Military leaders? "Toads and ostriches"! González Prada depicted the army promotion list as a "mountain where a man climbs by kissing the ass of the man ahead of him," while being "kissed in the same place by the man that follows." This dishonorable climb terminated at the presidency of the republic, "the ultimate rank in the military career." Nor were the paternalistic *indigenista* reformers spared from the scorn of this iconoclast. "The Indian will be saved," he chided them, "thanks to his own efforts." He only must spend on "rifles and bullets all the money that he wastes on alcohol and fiestas." Peru, summarized González Prada, was an immense "boil." Press down anywhere and "pus runs out."

Unlike the more moderate Indianists and other reformers, González Prada did not find favor with government leaders, although his intellectual stature protected his position as director of the National Library. He first aired his ideas in the Círculo Literario, a writers' club organized in 1886. Five years later, when the circle became the nucleus of the short-lived National Union party, González Prada withdrew from the group and departed for Europe. Returning to Peru seven years later, he devoted his energies to uniting and propagandizing workers and students, the two elements he believed essential for a successful social revolution. González Prada occasionally spoke before labor groups and wrote many articles for their newspapers. He was very influential in the development of the anarchist strain so prominent in the early workers' movement. More lasting, however, was his impact on the nation's students who readily accepted his challenge: "Old men to the tomb; young men to work!" The generation of intellectuals and political leaders emerging from Peruvian universities after World War I would acknowledge many debts to González Prada. From the wide range of his writings they gleaned ideas to support an equally varied assortment of ideologies. But more important than his substantive thought, the old firebrand was the spiritual father of modern Peruvian radicalism. He was the nation's first major proponent of social revolution, and his combative rhetoric became the currency of Peru's radical politics.

The social ferment characteristic of the first decades of the twentieth century was reflected in Peru's universities—San Marcos in Lima and the much smaller national universities at Trujillo, Cuzco, and Arequipa. Enrollment at San Marcos jumped from 789 in 1907, to 1,331 ten years later. This larger student body increasingly included persons of modest, middle-class origins and even some youths from more humble backgrounds. Intensely nationalistic and possessing a deep social consciousness, many students entering the universities at this time hoped to modernize their schools so that these institutions might contribute more significantly to the nation's development. Steeped in the works of their hero González Prada and other social critics, they sympathized with the Indian and industrial worker. The students also exhibited a strong current of anticlericalism and a growing hostility toward the interventionist policies of the United States in Latin America. Many older intellectuals expressed similar sentiments, but each new class at the universities had a greater commitment to action.

Peru's students had reason to complain about their universities. Although the San Marcos faculty had some outstanding scholars, mediocrity was more common, especially in the provincial institutions. The schools comprising the universities were dominated by aged professors, some of whom had obtained their chairs through political influence. They often viewed their pet courses as proprietary fiefs to be protected from the challenge of younger teachers and new ideas. Instructors presented the traditional, humanistic curriculum in published lectures that the students read and then had reread to them in class. A rote regurgitation of this material was expected at examination time. Teachers often considered any questioning of their timeworn theories as deviant behavior. Nevertheless, attendance at class was mandatory for students. The poorly paid professors, however, frequently were absent while they attempted to earn a living at second and third jobs. Although all of the universities suffered from inadequate funding, political meddling, and hardening of the academic arteries, the three "minor universities" in the provinces had an additional handicap. San Marcos, Peru's "major university," used its influence to thwart the development of its step-sister institutions and ensure its hegemony as the nation's premier unit for higher education. Not surprisingly, Peru's first important manifestations of student discontent occurred in the secondary universities.

The student strike—soon to become commonplace in Peruvian academic life—made its debut at the University of Arequipa in 1907, when pupils supported a liberal faction of the faculty in an election for rector. That same year a more significant protest began at the University of Cuzco, where the students petitioned the national director of education for a complete reform of their institution. In March 1909, they established a University Association, Peru's first student organization founded primarily for political action. Demonstrations closed the school six months later. As with most important activities in Peru, however, Lima soon became the focal point of the student movement. In 1908, pupils at San Marcos organized a University Center to sponsor social and cultural events. But after the protests against the Leguía dictatorship in 1911—the first major involvement of students in national politics—discussions at the center rapidly concentrated on university reform. At the suggestion of this organization San Marcos began a modest extension program for the laboring class of Lima, the initiation of significant cooperation between "intellectual and manual workers" advocated by González Prada. San Marcos's first student strike occurred in 1916. The following year, the University Center gave way to a frankly political organization, the Peruvian Student Federation. Although headquartered in Lima and dominated by San Marcos students, the federation also included representatives from the provincial schools. An important new force had been added to Peruvian politics.

The accelerated pace of economic development and the attendant social changes after 1914 placed a severe strain on the Peruvian political system. New entrepreneurs who had amassed their wealth through modern capitalism challenged the power of the older elites. Meanwhile, strategically placed urban groups—students, industrial workers and middle-class managers, technicians, civil servants, and white-collar employees—expanded in numbers and became increasingly politicized. From the right and left of the political spectrum and from the top to the bottom of the socioeconomic pyramid, Peruvians demanded greater governmental concern for their needs and aspirations. Civilian regimes often seemed unequal to the task.

The revolution that ousted President Guillermo Billinghurst in February 1914 differed from earlier military coups and marked an important watershed in Peruvian politics. After almost two decades of increased professionalism and reduced interference in government, the soldiers had been coaxed from their barracks into the center of the political arena by civilian politicians. Acting in the name of the armed forces as a whole, rather than at the bidding of a single ambitious caudillo as in earlier times, the military intervened to rescue the elite-dominated political system from a threat by the urban working class. During the next several decades the Peruvian armed forces continued to identify their own institutional interests with those of the changing upper class.

Col. Oscar R. Benavides assumed the executive power after the overthrow of Billinghurst and installed a mixed military-civilian cabinet. As a career soldier who, as yet, had not developed a taste for politics, it was Benavides's misfortune to hold power at the outbreak of the world war. During the early, uncertain months of the conflict, Peru's foreign commerce briefly came to a standstill. The republic's gold reserves dropped sharply, forcing the government to suspend service on the foreign debt and issue inconvertible paper money. In spite of considerable popular sympathy in favor of the Allies, Benavides put his country on the prudent and profitable path of neutrality. Peru maintained this posture until 1917, when the sinking of a Peruvian steamer by a German submarine caused Lima to sever diplomatic relations with the Central Powers. Benavides was anxious to relinquish the burdens of the provisional presidency, but he wanted to avoid the bitter partisanship that had marred recent elections. At his urging, representatives of the Civilista, Liberal, and Constitutionalist parties met in March 1915 to choose a common candidate for president. The feeble Democratic organization did not participate in this process, but the nomination of former President José Pardo satisfied many of its members. The Civilista leader won the election with only token opposition and was inaugurated in August 1915.

The unusual degree of tranquillity that had characterized Pardo's first term and made him an ideal "candidate of national harmony" in 1915 eluded the Civilista statesman during his second administration. The seven-year interval between his two presidencies had brought an intensification of some old problems and the appearance of new, more troublesome ones. In an emotional atmosphere charged by the hopes and fears of two momentous social upheavals—the Mexican and Russian revolutions—Pardo's brand of mild progressivism seemed inappropriate to both those impatient for change and those who dreaded it.

The always divisive religious issue came to the fore at the very beginning of the new administration. Following mob violence against Protestant missionaries in the southern highlands, congress debated a bill to permit the public practice of religions other than Roman Catholicism. The vast majority of Peruvians were at least nominal Catholics and they favored a privileged status for the church. But the Liberals and many Civilistas believed that Peru's religious exclusivism damaged its reputation in a world increasingly critical of intolerance and discouraged immigration and foreign investment by non-Catholics. After a bitter debate the legislature approved the Law of Religious Toleration and the president unenthusiastically signed the measure. As Pardo feared, he became the target of unmerciful attacks from the pulpit. More controversy erupted in 1916 with the passage of a largely ineffectual law establishing a minimum cash wage of about ten cents (U.S.) per day for agricultural workers. While Pardo alienated traditionalist elements with this legislation, he also gained the hostility of the students and urban workers, who united in opposition to him.

A successful university reform movement at Argentina's University of Córdoba in 1918 reinspired Peruvian students to press for major changes in their schools. Early in 1919, the Peruvian Student Federation presented several demands to the government, including a modernization of the curriculum, the removal of incompetent professors, and an end to political meddling in university affairs. They also asked for more scholarships to permit larger numbers of poor youths to attend college and the abolition of compulsory attendance so that students might work part-time while enrolled at the university. Most importantly, the federation called for *cogobierno* ("co-government"), student participation in college administration. Himself a former rector of San Marcos, President Pardo appreciated some of the students' grievances, but he adamantly opposed student representation in university governance.

While his Civilista party became more conservative in reaction to the social ferment of the period, José Pardo continued to believe that reforms must be made to improve the lot of the working class. His regime secured passage of laws granting paid holidays, extending the benefits of workmen's compensation, and regulating the employment of women and children. But these measures did not satisfy the Peruvian labor movement, which demanded the universal adoption of the eight-hour day in commerce and industry. To achieve this goal, a general strike of Lima's white- and blue-collar workers began on January 1, 1919. The stoppage was organized at the headquarters of the student federation and received the support of this group. The workers, in turn, endorsed student demands for university reform. The first completely effective general strike in the nation's history, all economic activity came to a halt. Although only a few isolated outbursts of violence occurred, these were made more frightening by news telegraphed from Argentina, where enraged mobs of workers terrorized Buenos Aires for several days. On January 15, President Pardo decreed the eight-hour day for all public employees and promised his support for legislation to require the same workday in private enterprise. The agitation subsided only momentarily.

With the end of his term approaching in turbulent 1919, José

149

Pardo hoped to arrange another broad coalition such as that which had elected him four years earlier. Peru's politicians, however, could not agree on a compromise candidate. Meanwhile, the now emboldened and strengthened student-worker alliance exploited the political uncertainty and renewed its onslaught against the lame-duck administration. Demands for university reform were coupled with those for government controls on rents and the rising costs of food and other necessities. Amid protest marches and noisy demonstrations, the election campaign began. Ultraconservative Antero Aspíllaga again received the Civilista nomination and a reluctant endorsement from Pardo. Although he had limited appeal within the broadening spectrum of Peruvian politics, the official candidate expected an easy victory over his challengers from the Democratic and splinter National Democratic parties. Then, another candidate entered the race.

Former President Augusto B. Leguía, returned home from his European exile in February 1919 and announced his willingness to accept "the nation's call" for his leadership, which his lieutenants had carefully orchestrated. Denouncing the Civilista "oligarchy" and promising to create a "New Fatherland" of peace, progress, and social justice for all, Leguía won a broad base of popular support. During the chaotic years of his absence, many Peruvians apparently had forgotten his faults while selectively remembering his virtues. Conservatives recalled the strong hand with which he maintained order. Liberals remembered his progressive economic policies and often attributed the authoritarian abuses of his first term to the international tensions of the period. The armed forces appreciated Leguía's inflexible attitude toward Chile and his ample defense budgets. Students had demonstrated against Leguía in 1911, but the new generation at San Marcos believed that he would support university reform. They proclaimed him "Mentor of Youth," an honor bestowed each year by the students on a prominent benefactor. Leguía reminded labor that the workmen's compensation law, Peru's first piece of modern labor legislation, had been promulgated during his tenure. His slogan "Deeds—not Words!" suggested that he was prepared to do even more for the workers. In the end, politicians scrambled to board Leguía's bandwagon. He received endorsements from the Liberal and Constitutionalist parties, some progressive Civilistas, a small socialist organization, the student federation, and various labor groups.

Peruvians went to the polls on May 18, 1919. Within a week, early returns indicated a decisive victory for Leguía. Believing that the waning Pardo regime was now especially vulnerable, the workers and students called a general strike on May 27, to press their demands for price controls and university reform. Unlike the January work stoppage, widespread violence took place and some demonstrators carried red flags. After a week of tension, Pardo responded forcefully. Troops broke the strike, inflicting many casualties, and arrested 3,000 workers. A presidential decree closed San Marcos University. Leguía watched these events with growing apprehension. Was Pardo merely restoring order, or was he preparing to overturn forcibly the results of the election? No conclusive evidence has been found to prove that a conspiracy existed to deny Leguía the presidency, but he justifiably feared that the government might block his August inauguration. Aspíllaga refused to admit defeat and provincial election officials showed great zeal in scrutinizing pro-Leguía ballots for irregularities. By July, the Supreme Election Tribunal in Lima had invalidated 15,000 votes for Leguía and had agreed to hear a suit for the nullification of the entire contest.

Former President Andrés A. Cáceres organized pro-Leguía elements of the armed forces for a coup. Leguía gave the order to strike on July 3, and early the next morning army and police units seized the presidential palace. They arrested Pardo and proclaimed Leguía provisional president. Immediately after taking the oath of office, Leguía issued a decree dissolving the Civilista-dominated congress, accusing the legislators of conspiring with Pardo to defraud the electorate.

❧ The Oncenio of Leguía, 1919–1930

Augusto Bernardo Leguía y Salcedo autocratically ruled Peru until 1930, an eleven-year dictatorship called the "Oncenio." Including his four-year first term (1908–12), he held power longer than any other president in the republic's history, and no Peruvian chief of state has been more controversial. In 1922, the United States chargé in Lima described the president as a man "whom all discuss, applaud, criticize, and love or despise." Since that time historians also have had difficulty treating Leguía dispassionately. Many of Peru's contemporary problems came into focus during the Oncenio as did conflicting programs for their amelioration. Therefore, Leguía has been viewed as a major actor in a still unfinished drama, but considerable disagreement exists concerning his role. He has been especially bewildering to those who have searched for great ideological significance in the opportunistic meanders of this pragmatic politician. Leguía has been described as a liberal and a conservative; a tool of the rich and a champion of the humble; a man of vision and a fool; a nationalist and a traitor; statesman and scoundrel. Perhaps he was a little of all these things. But one point seems clear. Active intervention by the government in the nation's social and economic life—a major characteristic of the modern state—increased notably during the Oncenio. For better or worse, Leguía was Peru's first modern president.

Leguía's life merits a Horatio Alger biography. Born in the north coast Department of Lambayeque in 1863, he was a sickly child with a chronic bronchial ailment. Augusto attended local schools until he was thirteen. Then his businessman father sent him to more healthful Chile to complete his studies. The young Leguía enrolled in a British commercial school at the bustling port of Valparaíso and acquired a fluency in English that served him well throughout his career. Returning home shortly before the War of the Pacific, eighteen-year-old Sergeant Leguía was among the volunteer defenders of Lima.

Although the president's formal education ended at age sixteen, he was not overawed by the graduates of San Marcos University. Leguía valued more his well-learned lessons in practical business experience. Beginning as an employee of a Lima commercial house, Augusto quickly established his own import-export firm. Largely because of his facility with English, Leguía obtained the Ecuador-Peru-Bolivia agency of the New York Life Insurance Company, a post that later earned him 250,000 dollars per year. In 1895, after new legislation curtailed the operations of foreign underwriters in Peru, Leguía created his own South American Insurance Company and began writing policies throughout the continent. For many years he managed the estates of the British Sugar Company. Leguía also acquired a half-dozen plantations for himself, leased rubber concessions in the Montaña, and was a founding director of the International Bank of Peru. The eminently successful entrepreneur was elected president of the powerful National Agrarian Society, gained admittance to the prestigious National and Union clubs, and he helped organize the Jockey Club.

Leguía showed little interest in politics before 1903, when he became treasury minister in the government of Manuel Candamo. The following year, his successful management of José Pardo's victory in the Civilista "battle of the generations" earned him the post of prime minister as well as the treasury portfolio in that highly productive administration. In 1908, he was the logical choice to follow Pardo in the presidency. During his own first term, Leguía's businesslike approach to government proved effective in economic and foreign affairs, but his authoritarian bent produced a schism within his own Civilista party. Exiled by Billinghurst in 1913, Leguía spent most of the next six years in London, where he served as president of the Latin American Chamber of Commerce and prepared for his return to power.

Fifty-five years old at the time of his 1919 coup, Leguía was well endowed with the qualities necessary for survival in Peruvian politics—a keen mind, cunning, fortitude, a fair amount of oratorical skill, and considerable adaptability. The president was a very small man, but his formal attire, neatly-trimmed white mustache and dignified bearing made him an imposing figure. Although he appeared frail, Leguía's boundless energy was legendary. The "Hundred Pound Dynamo" regularly spent fifteen hours a day in his office and no aspect of government seemed beyond his purview. Widowed two months after becoming president, Leguía simultaneously maintained a pair of mistresses, each of whom bore him two children. Horse racing was one of his few other diversions. Every Sunday the president, who liked to project the image of a "sport," spent the day at the track watching his own champion animals compete.

Leguía apparently did not use the presidency to amass a personal fortune. However, many men around him were corrupt, especially his playboy son Juan, the president's favorite among his six legitimate children. Vanity was the softest spot in the dictator's otherwise thick skin and flattery was most effective when applied by foreigners. Central to Leguía's plans for modernizing his country were massive injections of capital, technology, and "experts" from overseas. The president's critics charged that he was a foreigner at heart, a view frequently shared by outside observers who found him to be Peru's foremost exponent of the Protestant Ethic. But in reality Leguía was a caricature, an exaggerated image, of Peru's new industrial and commercial elite. In proclaiming his "New Fatherland," he christened the attitudes already born of this group.

Soon after he seized power Leguía scheduled an election for a new congress that also served as a constituent assembly. The constitution adopted by this body in January 1920 made several important departures from previous Peruvian charters. Borrowing from the landmark Mexican Constitution of 1917, it included several "social guarantees" and amplified the state's powers within the economic realm to achieve these benefits for the commonweal. The new fundamental law empowered the government to regulate prices, intervene in labor disputes, establish progressive taxation, and expropriate private estates for the purpose of agrarian reform. The document promised Indians the special protection of the government and committed the state to an ambitious program of public education. Catholicism again was declared the religion of the republic and the state was obligated to protect it, but an article prohibiting religious persecution implied freedom of worship.

The constitution also contained the traditional "bill of rights" protecting the civil liberties of individuals. Although the president's term was extended to five years, the ban on a second successive election continued. Both houses of the legislature were to be elected for five-year terms concurrent with that of the president, a feature that sought to ensure greater rapport between the congress and the executive branch. The most curious innovation of the 1920 charter was an attempt to reconcile the desire of the provinces for a greater voice in government with the need for an effective national administration. The new constitution established three regional legislatures, for the northern, central, and southern sections of the country. Each of these assemblies was empowered to legislate for its own region, subject to the approval of the national president. The charter also provided considerable autonomy for municipal governments.

The Constitution of 1920 is noteworthy primarily as an expression of political thought. It bore little relation to the actual operation of the Leguía regime. The system of checks and balances within the government was a sham. Leguía circumvented or ignored the judiciary. Fraudulent elections produced lopsided, proadministration majorities in congress and this body became almost entirely subservient to the president. Relatives of Leguía presided over both legislative chambers in 1929. After an auspicious beginning that produced more than 400 proposed laws, the regional congresses became sterile sinecures for the dictator's cronies. Leguía vetoed most of the measures emanating from these bodies, including petitions for their own dissolution. The autocrat destroyed the autonomy of the municipal governments by imposing "temporary" executives upon them and by depriving the cities of several independent sources of revenue. The regime secured a constitutional amendment in 1923 to permit a second successive term for the president and Leguía was reelected without formal opposition the next year. Another change in the basic law, approved unanimously by the chamber of deputies in 1927, allowed the indefinite reelection of the chief executive. Leguía's continuance in office for a third term was uncontested in 1929.

The dictator also ignored the constitutional guarantees of individual liberties. "In spite of the many constitutional restrictions," wrote Graham Stuart in 1925, "the president of Peru may rule as despotically as any tyrant of ancient times." Leguía's actions sometimes demonstrated the truth of Stuart's observation. However, the frequent descriptions of his regime as vindictive, arbitrary, and totally repressive are overdrawn. The worst violations of civil rights occurred in the first term of the Oncenio when the regime was threatened by massive student demonstrations, violent strikes, military conspiracies, and attempts to assassinate the president. Some Leguía apologists have attributed these excesses to the dictator's cousin and prime minister, Germán Leguía y Martínez, a man called "the Tiger" by his foes. But the president probably approved the stern measures taken by his kinsman, whom he exiled in 1923, when Leguía y Martínez developed personal presidential ambitions. The dictatorship mellowed in later years. While some dissidents received harsh treatment, others were handled with considerable circumspection, obtaining rewards for holding their opposition within acceptable bounds. "Bread or the Club," Porfirio Díaz's formula for ruling Mexico, had an able practitioner in the wily Peruvian president.

Leguía jailed many political offenders, usually without trial, but he preferred to deport troublemakers. Exiled public officials and important politicians often continued to receive their salaries or pensions while abroad. Youthful critics frequently were offered "scholarships" for study overseas. In the second half of the Oncenio many exiles were permitted to return home. Leguía suppressed some unfriendly journals. Yet, other hostile publications, including a few that printed articles by exiles advocating revolution, continued to appear. Fear of police spies inhibited free speech. But throughout the Oncenio, criticism of the regime and its policies was expressed oratorically, in signed petitions, and by peaceful demonstrations without government reprisal. Apparently, Leguía applied the "clear and present danger" principle in determining his reaction to dissent.

Leguía attempted to maintain some semblance of constitutional government, but the frequent charges that this shell of republican legality was devoid of substance did not disconcert him. "Dictatorship is more popular than anarchy," he candidly told one journalist. Several foreign commentators also believed the country's choice was that simple. In his monograph on the Peruvian political system, Graham Stuart correlated authoritarian regimes with periods of intense crisis and viewed the Leguía dictatorship as an unfortunate but almost inevitable consequence of the industrial revolution in Peru. Constitutional government, he hoped, might return after the nation had adjusted to the new economic environment. Other North Americans in Peru, including diplomats and businessmen, often asserted that the president was justified in sacrificing the country's very imperfect republican institutions to achieve major social and economic change and avert Red revolution. Many Peruvians agreed. Although the broad base of support that Leguía enjoyed in 1919 quickly narrowed—his honeymoon with students and many workers was quite brief—he continued to seek and receive the backing of some labor unions, many white-collar employees, and most urban-based business groups until the twilight of the Oncenio.

Only three political parties functioned openly during the dictatorship: Leguía's own Democratic Reform party, the Constitutionalist party of his military supporters, and the now-senile Democratic party. Members of these organizations received cabinet posts and this coalition enthusiastically endorsed Leguía for reelection in 1924. The Liberal party died with Augusto Durand, its leader, in 1922. Enervated by deportations and defections to Leguía, the once-dominant Civilista party withered away. In addition to the formal political organizations, Leguía also courted the Catholic Church and the armed forces. He blocked implementation of civil marriage and divorce laws, invited the Church to participate in some of the state's social programs, and made an ill-fated attempt to dedicate the republic to the Sacred Heart of Jesus. Because of these efforts the president generally had the cooperation of the Peruvian hierarchy, and the Vatican decorated him.

The support of the armed forces, essential to the survival of the regime, was a special concern of the strongman. He lavished new equipment on the military services and made loyalty to the administration a major criterion for promotion. Still, several attempted coups threatened the government. Never sure of the soldiers, Leguía tried to divide and rule them. The administration created a well-armed *guardia civil* (national police) in 1924. Ostensibly organized to permit the regular military forces to concentrate on defending the nation's frontiers, the civil guard also counterbalanced the army. Similarly, the regime strengthened the navy and the new air corps, further reducing the dominance of the senior military service.

Beyond the maintenance of power, the *sine qua non* of every dictatorship, Leguía assigned top priority to the material advancement of his country. Ensnared in the economic optimism characteristic of the 1920s, the president believed that the development of Peru's vast natural resources would bring new and permanent prosperity to the nation. He attempted to accomplish this task with sizable public as well as private investment. Generous tax and concession policies attracted much new capital from abroad, especially the United States, where "dollar-decade" investors had confidence in the stability of the Peruvian regime. By the end of the Oncenio total foreign investment in Peru reached about 400 million dollars.

The government itself provided much of the infrastructure for material growth. State participation in economic development was not new to Peru, but under Leguía expenditures on public works increased nearly fivefold. Not until the Alliance for Progress of the 1960s, with its incentives from the United States government, would any succeeding administration devote a larger share of its budget to the Ministry of Development. Leguía obtained some of the necessary capital from domestic sources. New imposts and a reorganization of the tax collection system doubled the government's revenues in the decade after 1919. But most of the money for public works came from foreign banks. By the end of Leguía's administration, Peru's external debt had soared to 110 million dollars, eleven times its level at the start of the Oncenio. Large sums were squandered or lost through fraud and mismanagement. Juan Leguía, the president's son, negotiated several foreign loans and public works contracts and received generous "commissions" for his services. Nevertheless, the government employed much of its borrowed money productively.

Leguía spent almost 150 million dollars on public works and planned to devote another 100 million dollars to such projects during his aborted final term. To accommodate Peru's burgeoning foreign commerce, the regime began a major modernization of port facilities at Callao. The railway system was expanded by one-third and several older lines received extensive renovation. Supported by a government airmail contract Elmer J. ("Slim") Fawcett, a North American pilot, established the country's first commercial airline in 1928. Leguía's road program proved to be his greatest success in the area of transportation and one of the more controversial features of his administration. The Highway Conscription Act of 1920 required men between the ages of 18 and 60 to work without pay for six to twelve days each year on road construction and maintenance within their home districts. The law exempted several occupational groups from this service and the obligation could be fulfilled by the payment of a sum sufficient to hire a substitute. These provisions of the statute and its very uneven enforcement throughout the country placed the burden of the program upon the nation's poor, especially the Indians. Once again the state exploited the ancient labor-tax tradition. Nevertheless, these undemocratic methods produced impressive results. The Leguía regime constructed more than 10,000 miles of road and 300 bridges and improved the quality of existing arteries.

For the first time since the Inca Empire the state played a major role in the extension of irrigation. Under the direction of Charles W. Sutton, formerly of the United States Reclamation Service, the government surveyed the water resources of most large coastal valleys and initiated five important projects. By 1929, about 132,000 acres had been irrigated at a cost of sixteen million dollars. Hoping to create a new group of middle-class farmers, the government divided much of this land into moderate-sized parcels and sold these properties on long-term credit. The success of this program contrasted sharply with a myriad of dubious schemes to establish European and North American colonists in the Montaña. To encourage the modernization of agriculture the Leguía regime acquired the Molina Hacienda, near Lima, for the National Agrarian University and opened several experimental farms. The government also created an Agricultural Credit Bank and compiled the nation's first agrarian census.

In 1920, the Leguía administration announced an ambitious

program to provide thirty-three cities with paved streets and modern sanitation facilities. By the end of the Oncenio, however, most of the seventeen million dollars allocated for this purpose had been expended within the environs of the capital. In addition to improved water and sewer systems, Lima and its satellite towns received new plazas, parks, and monuments. The government paved thirty-five miles of thoroughfares, including the Avenida Leguía connecting Lima and Callao. The erection of several public buildings contributed to a general construction boom. Meanwhile, the Lima-Callao district strengthened its position as the nation's economic center. According to Peru's first industrial census, taken in 1923, this metropolitan area attracted two-thirds of the capital invested in manufacturing. Most of the country's banks, which increased in number from eight to thirteen and tripled their assets, also were located there. By 1930, much of the open space between Lima and its suburbs had disappeared. The population of the metropolitan area swelled from 225,000 to 375,000 during the decade of the 1920s.

The trend toward the consolidation and capitalization of Peru's coastal estates intensified during the Oncenio. The number of sugar plantations declined from 117 to 78, but production increased more than 50 percent. The output of cotton doubled with the nearly universal adoption of the Tangüis variety, and rice harvests expanded by almost two-thirds. The mining industry experienced even greater growth than agriculture. Petroleum production increased over 400 percent, the output of silver and gold more than doubled, and the extraction of copper climbed by 40 percent. For the first time several other minerals—lead, zinc, and vanadium—were exploited seriously. Under the Leguía administration Peru became one of the world's leading mineral producers, ranking first in the extraction of vanadium, fourth in silver, eighth in copper, and ninth in petroleum.

The outstanding performance of Peruvian agriculture and mining brought few rewards in the international marketplace, however. It was Leguía's misfortune to assume power as the republic's export-led economy approached the end of wartime prosperity. Between 1920, when the bubble of high prices burst, and 1929, the last "good" year before the Great Depression, the nation's exports more than doubled in volume while declining five percent in value. The country seemed to be racing on an economic treadmill. Although shipments of cotton and sugar increased 30 and 50 percent respectively, they earned one-third less money. Petroleum exports jumped more than eightfold, but only trebled in value. Copper alone among Peru's major trade items enjoyed relative price stability. The stagnation of the republic's export earnings contributed significantly to the fiscal problems that plagued Leguía's ambitious administration.

Critics of the Leguía regime frequently accused the dictator of misdirected priorities. He did little to improve the wretched condition of the nation's humble citizens, they asserted, while lavishing favors on foreign capital and spending vast sums on projects that increased the wealth of Peru's comfortable classes. Leguía argued that money invested to foster economic growth benefited all Peruvians and helped induce needed social change. The development of the republic's human resources, therefore, was an integral part of his plan for modernization. More directly, a comparison of Leguía's ordinary budgets with those of his predecessors shows little difference in the share of revenues devoted to "people programs." However, the higher level of government spending during the Oncenio brought a large absolute increase in expenditures within the social area.

The Church and private charities, often with subsidies from the national treasury, continued to play a major role in easing some of Peru's human problems. But under Leguía, the state itself assumed a much greater responsibility for the well-being of the nation's citizens. The government opened several new medical facilities, including a model children's hospital named in memory of the president's wife. The Leguía regime established a Bureau of Public Health, and this agency undertook impressive campaigns against smallpox, yellow fever, and other diseases. The government initiated a new program for Peru's many orphaned and abandoned children. Most importantly, legislation and administrative machinery fashioned during the Oncenio provided a foundation for more comprehensive efforts in Indian affairs, education, and labor relations.

In the election campaign of 1919, Leguía promised that his New Fatherland would provide a better life for Peru's native population and the Constitution of 1920 repeated this pledge. Article 58 announced that the state would "protect the indigenous race and . . . enact special laws for its development and culture." Candidate Leguía's *indigenista* credentials were suspect, however. As president a decade earlier he had signed a law prohibiting the exaction of forced Indian labor by public offi-

cials. But the first Leguía administration also had been lackadais-
ical in its attitude toward the infamous rubber-slavery scandal in
the Putumayo region. Whatever the depth of his feelings for the
natives, the president was a practical politician. The ever-
increasing influence of the Indianist movement made reform
politically attractive and Leguía appointed several prominent
indigenistas to public office.

A new wave of native uprisings in the southern Sierra soon
tested the sincerity of the regime's official Indianism. Leguía's
initial response indicated that the New Fatherland would be little
more than traditional paternalism and old repression. Several
dedicated reformers resigned their government posts. While the
civil guard crushed the peasant revolts, the president ignored the
recommendations of a commission he had established to investigate the roots of native unrest. In a similar vein, the Leguía
administration secured more Indian legislation during its first
term than all of its republican predecessors combined. But jux-
taposed with the mammoth injustices of the Highway Conscription Act, many of these measures seemed ludicrous.

The dictatorship added "Indian Day" to the calendar of national holidays and erected statues of Atahualpa and other native
heroes. Several unproductive Indian congresses assembled
under government auspices, affording "Little Inca" Leguía an
opportunity to pose for photographs with colorfully clad peasants. More substantive measures, such as the upward revision of
the minimum wage for Indian agricultural workers, often were
poorly enforced, ignored, or applied to the detriment of the
natives. An example of the latter was the Patronato de la Raza
Indígena (Guardianship of the Indian Race), an institution reminiscent of the colonial period. Established in 1922, the *patronato*
consisted of a central board in Lima, chaired by the archbishop,
and juntas at the departmental and provincial levels. The local
patronatos had general responsibility for the protection of the
natives and superseded the regular courts in some suits involving
Indians. Unfortunately, *gamonales* gained control of several of
these bodies and used their positions to further exploit the
peasants.

To a considerable degree the Leguía regime's vaunted Indianism proved to be political gimmickry or worse. Nevertheless, some of its actions in this area were significant. In 1921, the
government created the Bureau of Indian Affairs to study the
problems of the indigenous peoples, recommend reforms, and

coordinate state programs for the natives. A new Bureau of Indian Education developed a special curriculum for Quechua-speaking children and opened a few vocational schools for native youths. Of greatest importance, the state began to provide some protection for Indian lands. The 1920 constitution recognized the indigenous communities as legal corporations and declared their fields to be inalienable portions of the national patrimony. Supplementary legislation amplified the rights of the *comunidades* and provided that they receive their just share of precious water resources. Unfortunately, implementation of these measures required time-consuming cadastral surveys and complicated procedures for the official registration of the communities. Five years elapsed before the inefficient and under-staffed Bureau of Indian Affairs opened its registry office. At the end of the dictatorship less than 400 of the republic's thousands of indigenous communities had been registered.

In spite of Leguía's promises, the condition of Peru's Indians did not improve appreciably during the Oncenio. Yet, the regime did make a beginning. The Constitution of 1920 formally ended a century of official oblivion toward the special problems of the natives and government hostility for their communal traditions. If nothing else, the avalanche of Indian legislation enshrined *indigenismo* as an element of the republic's official ideology. It is a sad commentary on Peruvian government that, for three decades after Leguía, no succeeding administration would do more for the indigenous population.

Leguía promulgated the Organic Law of Instruction in June 1920, a major reorganization of the entire education system from kindergarten through the university. This intricate, utopian plan sought to provide training for the 80 percent of Peru's children who were not enrolled in school and fashion the curriculum and teaching methods to meet the country's special needs. Beyond basic literacy, the law emphasized vocational instruction. Dr. Harry E. Bard, a North American who had served in Leguía's first government, returned to Peru as director general of education. Bard remodeled the administrative structure of the school system and staffed the major posts with twenty-four educators from the United States. Hampered by inadequate funding, hostility from Peruvian traditionalists, and the incompetence of some of the Yankee "experts," confusion reigned and the program fell far short of its unrealistic objectives. Nevertheless, the Leguía government more clearly defined the goal of democratizing public education and recorded some quantitative advances toward this end. The regime constructed more than 500 primary schools and enrollment at this level grew from 180,000 to 300,000 pupils.

San Marcos University doubled its enrollment during the Oncenio, but most of this statistical increase resulted from political turmoil that prevented students from graduating on schedule. The student strike in June 1919 ended four months later when Leguía began to reward his young constituents for their assistance in his victory. Within a year, a series of laws met most of the student's demands for reform. The administration granted nominal autonomy to the universities and students received representation on the governing councils of their schools. The compulsory attendance requirement ended and a scholarship program for underprivileged youths began. Life tenure for faculty was abolished and more than a score of professors at San Marcos who had been blackballed by the students were summarily dismissed.

The rapport between the government and university youth was fragile and short-lived. The students distrusted and disparaged the largely self-educated president. Leguía, in turn, had little respect for the products of San Marcos—"dreamers, babblers and 'white collars'," he called them. Students and faculty who spoke out against the regime's disregard for civil liberties quickly discovered that "reform" could be used to purge the dictator's critics. Within two years the list of Peruvian exiles included the names of several prominent professors. Following a protest strike in May 1921, Leguía ousted the rector of San Marcos and closed the ancient institution for the remainder of the year. The government again suspended classes in 1923, 1924, and 1925. The provincial schools also experienced purges and closures. A reorganization of higher education in 1928 ended even the specious autonomy that Leguía earlier had granted the universities.

During those periods when San Marcos was open, its routine was disrupted by interminable politicking—protests against the government, faculty electioneering, and power struggles within the student federation. Professional student-politicians, academic ward heelers who registered year after year without attending classes, became fixtures on campus. To do battle with the government, the students strengthened their alliance with urban workers. University politicans assisted in the formation of new labor groups, organized strikes, and supported worker demands. In March 1920, Peru's first national student congress assembled at Cuzco with financial support from the government. Borrowing from earlier experiments in adult education, the delegates approved the establishment of the González Prada Popular Universities, a free night-school program for workers. In addition to the three R's, the university students and other intellectuals who staffed the *universidades populares* dispensed large doses of political propaganda to their pupils.

The Oncenio was the gestation period for Peru's modern labor-left parties—the Communists, Socialists, and the nation's own APRA party. In the myth of creation shared by these groups, Leguía is the major devil-figure, a reactionary ogre who brutally repressed the country's emerging proletariat. Actually, the diminutive autocrat's labor policy seems almost liberal when viewed within the context of the worldwide "Red Scare" after World War I and almost universal government malevolence toward unions. Urban labor assisted Leguía in his rise to power and he hoped to retain their support. Soon after taking power the new president released the workers imprisoned during the May 1919 general strike, and labor made significant gains in the early months of his administration. In rapid succession Leguía decreed the eight-hour day in manufacturing, amplified the workmen's compensation law, and set more rigid health and safety standards for factories. Several new statutes regulated the employment of women and minors, including provisions for maternity leaves and a requirement that the textile mills operate day-care centers for the children of their female employees. In 1920 and 1921, the government imposed price controls on foodstuffs and other necessities and placed rent ceilings on workers' housing, satisfying the two most important demands of the labor movement.

While Leguía dispensed rewards to the workers, he attempted to avert costly strikes, and his regime was determined to check antigovernment activity within the labor movement. The Constitution of 1920 provided for state mediation of labor disputes and, when necessary, compulsory arbitration. Leguía entrusted enforcement of these measures to the greatly expanded Office of Worker Affairs, which also received broad powers to fix wages and hours of work. In spite of the state's new interventionist role in labor relations, many strikes, including long and damaging walkouts by railroad, port, and public utility workers, were allowed to run their courses. Government involvement in other strikes frequently produced victories for labor. In the first years of the dictatorship even the agricultural workers, through the efforts of state conciliators, exacted important concessions from the heretofore largely unorganized sugar plantations of the north coast.

During the early years of the Oncenio, Leguía favored peaceful labor organizations, and several new unions appeared. But the regime's romance with the workers began to fade between May and September 1920, when a flurry of disputes erupted in violence and threatened to become a general strike. Armed with strike-breaking decrees, the president met this crisis with a carrot-and-stick strategy. To detach the more moderate organizations from the movement Leguía offered generous concessions combined with threats of repression should they reject his terms. Uncooperative unions had their meetings disrupted and their leaders imprisoned. The government closed newspapers supporting the strikers. Protected by police, struck factories reopened with scab labor and cavalry patrolled the streets of Lima. A labor congress that assembled the next year with Leguía's blessing hotly debated the movement's future attitude toward the government. Several unions desired to cooperate with the regime. But a strong current of anarchism still pervaded many others and they would not brook any compromise. Viewing government as the major obstacle to human betterment, these revolutionary activists were on a collision course with Leguía, for whom the state was an instrument of progress.

After the 1920 confrontation between Leguía and labor, the unions did not seriously challenge the regime until May 1923. Hoping to win Church support for his reelection, the president planned a formal ceremony dedicating the republic to the Sacred Heart of Jesus. This proposal served as a catalyst in bringing together several disparate opponents of the government—the anticlerical students, many unions, some disgruntled Civilistas, a handful of Protestants, and even a few Catholic laymen like Víctor Andrés Belaúnde, who called this attempt to link God with the dictatorship of high-degree Mason Leguía a "repugnant comedy." When police attempted to disperse a large group of demonstrators near San Marcos University on May 23, a riot occurred. A student and a worker were killed and many others were wounded. The next day a general strike paralyzed Lima, while an emotional crowd in the Plaza Mayor heard impassioned funeral orations for the movement's two "martyrs." Police and troops rapidly cleared the area. The government arrested several leaders of the demonstration and closed San Marcos.

A new wave of strikes began and reached a climax in October and November 1923, when more than twenty walkouts by transportation and public utilities unions brought commerce to a standstill. The president responded with a decree authorizing the induction of workers in key industries into the armed forces. Thereafter, strikers could be shot for desertion. Although Leguía did not invoke this law, the threat of militarization, the arrest of several labor leaders, and the suppression of some unions defused this explosive situation. Strikes continued to take place throughout the remainder of the Oncenio. But disorganized and purged of its militant leadership, the labor movement no longer threatened the stability of the regime. The influence of anarchism within the unions became supplanted almost entirely by Marxism, an ideology that permitted greater tactical flexibility in the struggle against the capitalist state.

With the exception of a few blue-collar unions that endorsed Leguía for reelection in 1924 and 1928, the dictator lost the support of Peru's manual laborers. But he had considerable success in mollifying the *empleados,* the white-collar employees, who formed their own associations. Following a strike in December 1919, the "friendly intercession" of the president brought the employees wage increases of 10 to 65 percent, a shorter workday, a longer lunch break, and a ban on Sunday work. While Leguía's benevolence toward the blue-collar unions ended after 1923, the government did not molest the more tractable employees' associations. Perhaps to reward these groups for their cooperation and detach them from the increasingly hostile labor movement, the regime enacted the Employees' Statute in 1924, a measure that drew a sharp line between the manual *obreros* and the more prestigious *empleados.* Extended in 1925 and 1928, this code provided for sufficient notice of dismissal, severance pay, improved workmen's compensation, widows' pensions, and employer-paid medical care for some white-collar employees. Throughout the Oncenio the notable expansion of industry, commerce, and government services increased the employment opportunities for this class, and a small decline in the cost of living protected salaries.

Leguía's most lasting accomplishments occurred in the field of foreign relations and he took great pride in his diplomacy. In the words of one of his adulators, Peru was a nation "without frontiers" when the little autocrat first took power in 1908. The republic had territorial conflicts with all five of its contiguous neighbors. The resolution of these disputes was the primary objective of Leguía's foreign policy. The president concluded boundary agreements with Bolivia and Brazil during his initial term and the Oncenio produced treaties with Colombia and Chile. Progress also was made toward ending a dangerous dispute with Ecuador. Ironically, the strongest opposition to Leguía arose from his relations with other countries.

The dictator's love of foreign ideas, his generosity toward foreign capital, and his dependence on foreign expertise rankled many Peruvians. At a time when "Yankee imperialism" had become the principal watchword of Latin American nationalists, Leguía's benevolence toward the United States was especially offensive to many of his countrymen. Besides large loans from banks in the United States, the government granted the most lucrative concessions and public works contracts to North American businessmen. By 1929, the "Colossus of the North" had replaced Great Britain as Peru's major source of foreign capital. Spaniards trained the *guardia civil,* Frenchmen advised the army, British officers held key posts in the air corps, and Lima had a German city planner. But Leguía once asserted that wherever possible, he tried to "put an American at the head of every public work or public institution" in Peru. United States citizens directed the irrigation, public health, and sanitation programs. North Americans dominated the customs service and the school system. A United States mission trained the navy, and countless other Yankees filled lesser posts. The president even imported his personal physician and dentist from the north.

Leguía's employment of foreign capital and technicians was defensible, but some of his efforts to please Washington bordered on pandering. Columnist Drew Pearson described the Peruvian leader as "the chief booster and gladhander [of] the United States . . .in the length and breadth of South America." The Fourth of July, the North American Independence Day and the anniversary of Leguía's 1919 coup, became a national holiday for the celebration of United States-Peruvian friendship. The regime decorated Herbert Hoover and erected a statue of George Washington. A portrait of James Monroe adorned the president's office. Moreover, Leguía frequently consulted with United States embassy officials about sensitive domestic as well as foreign problems. Peru generally supported the unpopular

North American position in the stormy inter-American meetings of the 1920s. The Leguía regime, alone among the Latin American governments, endorsed United States military intervention in Nicaragua. North American officials frequently returned these compliments. Ambassador Alexander Moore ascribed to Leguía the "courage of Caesar, the power of Napoleon and the diplomacy of Richelieu" and nominated the "Little Giant of the Pacific" for the Nobel Peace Prize.

There can be little doubt that Leguía sincerely admired the United States. However, the "Silver Fox" also had ulterior motives for solidifying his ties with Washington. In November 1919, Leguía informed Peru's ambassador to the United States that the main reason for giving priority to Yankee investors was to secure North American diplomatic support in the republic's longstanding dispute with Chile. According to the Treaty of Ancón, a plebiscite was to have been held in 1894 to determine whether the Chilean-occuppied departments of Tacna and Arica were to be returned to Peru or be ceded permanently to Chile. Unfortunately, the treaty did not specify procedures for the election nor establish eligibility for voting. Obviously, native-born residents of Tacna and Arica could participate. But what would be the status of the thousands of Chileans who had settled there after the war and the many Peruvians who had left the region? The Peruvian government distrusted any election held under Chilean supervision and Santiago was in no hurry to decide the matter. Attempts to resolve the dispute through new negotiations failed, producing only increased bitterness. In 1910, President Leguía severed diplomatic relations with Chile. Both countries undertook expensive armaments programs and war seemed dangerously close on several occasions. Meanwhile, the "Chileanization" of Tacna and Arica continued.

By 1919, Peru had lost confidence in its ability to win even an honest election in the two disputed departments. Therefore, the Leguía regime insisted that the plebiscite provision of the peace treaty had expired in 1894, and that a new settlement must be made. Confident of success, Chile demanded that an election be held. In 1922, the two nations agreed to submit the plebiscite issue to arbitration by the president of the United States. Three years later, Calvin Coolidge announced his decision: the long-overdue election would be held under North American supervision and persons who had established residence in Tacna and Arica since the War of the Pacific could vote along with natives of the disputed territory. Stunned by the adverse decision from Washington, Peruvian nationalists denounced Leguía for placing this vital question in the hands of the Yankees. A general strike paralyzed Lima, students rioted, and a mob attacked the United States Embassy. A North American commission headed by Gen. John J. Pershing and then Gen. William Lassiter attempted to arrange the plebiscite. But in June 1926 the commission reported that Chilean harassment of Peruvian voters made a fair election impossible. Peru rejoiced.

Assuming the role of mediator, the United States suggested several compromises, but Peru and Chile rejected all of these proposals. Any settlement short of total victory would have angered powerful nationalist elements in both countries. With this new impasse, Chile prepared to annex Tacna and Arica unilaterally, an action that might have brought war. Then, through a chance, shipboard meeting of Peruvian and Chilean diplomats enroute to an inter-American conference, informal discussions of the problem began and the two nations resumed diplomatic relations shortly thereafter. Direct negotiations finally produced a sensible solution to the problem—a division of the territory. Both Leguía and President Carlos Ibáñez of Chile feared public reaction to the compromise, so the new president of the United States, Herbert Hoover, agreed to announce it as his own formula. After a proper show of reluctance, Leguía and Ibáñez "magnanimously assented" to the settlement in the interest of peace. On June 3, 1929, the Treaty of Lima was signed, ending a half-century of hostility over the "Alsace-Lorraine of South America." Arica remained with Chile; Peru recovered Tacna. In addition, Chile paid Peru six million dollars and agreed to provide port facilities for Peru at the Bay of Arica, Tacna's traditional outlet. Although Leguía and Ibáñez continued to express misgivings about the settlement in public, their legislatures understood the true feelings of both presidents and quickly ratified the document. The treaty was as good as Peru could have reasonably expected and probably a majority of informed citizens accepted it. But the compromise aroused the anger of a large number of ultranationalists.

An almost universally unpopular treaty with Colombia magnified the risks of compromise with Chile. Peru's boundary with Colombia in the remote, northern Montaña had been disputed since independence. Although the territory in question was vast—about 50,000 square miles between the Río Caquetá and the northern watershed of the Napo River—it had few civilized inhabitants and scant economic importance until the late nineteenth century. Then, the rubber boom brought bloodshed between Peruvian and Colombia tappers in the region and a full-scale war threatened. By 1919, the collapse of the rubber industry had greatly reduced the value of the territory, but tension between the two countries remained high. The United States government used its good offices to bring the contestants together and in March 1922 they signed the Salomón-Lozano Treaty. An apparent victory for Colombia, the agreement established the Putumayo River as the boundary between the two nations. Peru received somewhat less than half of the disputed land. But most importantly, the nation also ceded a 4,000-square-mile corridor extending southward from the Putumayo to the Amazon, giving Colombia, for the first time, a 60-mile frontage on the mighty river. Called Leticia after the name of the principal town in the district, this region seemed unquestionably Peruvian.

Realizing that the Salomón-Lozano Treaty would be very unpopular, Leguía kept its details secret. Meanwhile, he used every excuse to delay ratification, including a protest by Brazil, whose territory abutted on Leticia. The United States repeatedly prodded Lima to finalize the pro-Colombian document. Relations between Washington and Bogotá had been strained since 1903, when the United States assisted Panama in gaining its independence from Colombia. Because of this hostility, North American businessmen had been frustrated in their attempts to obtain oil concessions from the Colombian government. Through the efforts of the United States, Brazil withdrew its objections to the Salomón-Lozano Treaty and, in March 1925, Peru signed an agreement to ratify the pact without further delay. But Leguía continued to procrastinate and Colombia threatened to sever its diplomatic ties with Peru. With its prestige now deeply committed to the settlement, the United States increased its pressure on Lima. Leguía finally relented and submitted the document to his congress in December 1927. The treaty was ratified over the protests of a handful of legislators, primarily representatives from the Amazonian departments. The dictatorship still attempted to suppress news of the agreement, but the details gradually became known, especially after the demarcation team began its work in November 1929. On August 17, 1930, Peru formally transferred Leticia to Colombia. One week later, a revolution ousted Leguía.

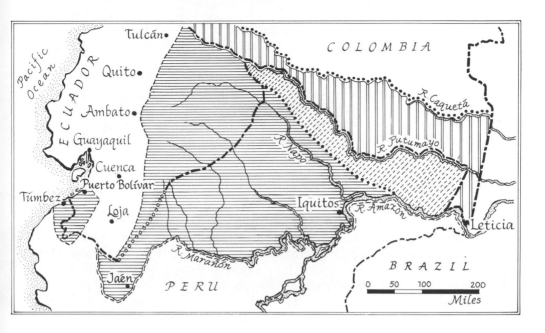

Peru's Northern Boundary Disputes

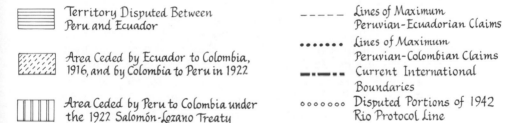

The Salomón-Lozano Treaty, almost always viewed in isolation, has invited a very damning picture of Leguía: overly solicitous of the United States and Yankee capitalists, the Peruvian dictator surrendered his nation's vital interests to Colombia.
The Leticia settlement, however, was an integral part of a very
complex diplomatic effort. Leguía's desire to please Washington
in this matter arose from more than his well-known Yankophilia.
The Salomón-Lozano Treaty was negotiated in 1922, while
preparations were being made for the United States arbitration

171

of the Tacna-Arica plebiscite controversy. Peru signed its 1925 pledge to expedite ratification of the Colombian treaty the same day that President Coolidge announced his decision to proceed with the election in the Chilean-occupied territory. From that time until the ultimate settlement with Chile, Leguía was highly dependent upon the friendship of Washington. The Salomón-Lozano Treaty, therefore, might be considered part of the price for an acceptable solution to the far more serious dispute with Chile.

The Salomón-Lozano Treaty itself had considerable merit. Leticia had minimum real value for Colombia. Surrounded by swamps and lacking direct river links with the rest of the nation, it provided its new owner with only a "psychological port" and dubious status as an Amazonian nation. Similarly, Leticia was of negligible economic importance to Peru. It did, however, afford Colombia a position from which to harass Peruvian river traffic if the Colombians chose to ignore the treaty's guarantees of free navigation. In return for the cession of Leticia, Peru obtained significant diplomatic and strategic advantages. Lima's international position was unenviable when the Salomón-Lozano Treaty was negotiated in 1922. While the nation faced a war with militarily superior Chile, its northern flank was insecure. In addition to the controversy with Colombia, Peru had a more serious boundary dispute with Ecuador. Traditionally, Ecuador and Chile had supported each other in confrontations with Peru, their common rival. In 1916, Ecuador had concluded a boundary settlement with Colombia that strengthened Quito's position against Peru in the Amazon Basin. By the Salomón-Lozano Treaty, however, Colombia relinquished to Peru territory obtained from Ecuador in 1916. The Ecuadorians now were surrounded on the east by Peru. A sharp blow to its aspirations, Ecuador broke diplomatic relations with Bogotá when Colombia ratified the treaty in 1925. Negotiating from a new vantage point, Peru agreed to settle its boundary controversy with Ecuador *after* resolving the Tacna-Arica question, when Santiago's support for Quito presumably would end. In the interval, Quito's ability to assist Chile against Peru diminished considerably. Formerly friendly Colombia was now a potential enemy at Ecuador's rear. Peru and Ecuador did not reach an amicable solution to their territorial dispute. In 1941, a vastly stronger Peru overpowered largely friendless Ecuador and dictated peace terms. The advantages gained by the Salomón-

Lozano Treaty were important factors in the eventual triumph of Peru.

Unfortunately for Leguía, many of the successes of his diplomacy were not visible, while his concessions were glaringly apparent. Although the settlement with Chile had significant support, the Salomón-Lozano Treaty had few defenders and its provisions became public at the worst possible moment. The Colombian agreement outraged Peruvians of all classes, but discontent was perhaps greatest within the nationalistic armed forces. At a time when Leguía desperately needed the support of the soldiers, he could not command their loyalty.

The crash of the New York stock market in October 1929 signaled the onset of the Great Depression and hard times for Peru and Leguía. The prices paid for the republic's exports plummeted, foreign trade declined sharply, and the value of the *sol* dropped precipitously. The service on the swollen foreign debt loomed larger and larger. Leguía no longer was able to secure new loans to keep his regime afloat. Public works programs halted, unemployment mounted, and the salaries of government employees slipped further in arrears. Much of the popularity that the president had enjoyed evaporated with the nation's prosperity. Emboldened by defections of former Leguía supporters, the autocrat's old enemies now picked at the emaciated carcass of the dictatorship. Students and workers taunted Leguía defiantly, and civilian politicians plotted his overthrow with the military.

Lt. Col. Luis M. Sánchez Cerro raised the banner of revolution at Arequipa on August 22, 1930, and garrisons throughout the country began to join the movement. Leguía fled three days later on a Peruvian warship. But the revolutionary government persuaded the commander of the vessel to return to Callao. The fallen dictator was imprisoned in a dank, dirty cell on San Lorenzo Island in Callao harbor, a place where he had confined some of his own enemies. The new regime quickly organized a Tribunal of National Accounting to consider criminal charges against the Leguía regime. Denied an opportunity to defend themselves, the former president and three of his sons were found guilty of corruption and were fined seven million dollars. The charges against the younger Leguías were substantially true, but the dictator apparently left office a poorer man than when he had seized power. The imprisoned president complained of a painful prostate infection, but his captors denied him medical attention until November 1931, when they moved him to a naval hospital. Still, an operation was not authorized until it was too late to save his life. Protesting his innocence of all crimes and proclaiming his patriotism, the sixty-eight-year-old autocrat died on February 6, 1932. He weighed sixty-seven pounds.

7

A Doleful Decade: The Thirties

I N REFUGES THROUGHOUT THE WORLD Peruvian exiles
heard the resounding crash of the Leguía dictatorship and
scores of expatriates began their journeys home. Among those
awaiting this moment was Víctor Raúl Haya de la Torre, the
dominant personality of twentieth-century Peruvian history. Far
more controversial than even Leguía, Haya de la Torre would
struggle for more than four decades to achieve the presidency.
Although he did not gain this objective—in fact, he has never
held any elective government office—Haya's very presence
shaped the major political events of Peru until the 1970s.

❧ *The Rise of the Revolutionaries*

"Víctor Raúl," as his admirers call him, was born in the
northern coastal city of Trujillo on February 22, 1895. Friendly
biographers have traced his ancestry back to the conquistadors
and have noted the moderate wealth of his mother's family. But
Haya's immediate home environment was distinctly middle
class. His father, Raúl Edmundo, was a sometime politician,
newspaper publisher and editor, printer and, finally, a salaried

accountant for a large sugar plantation. The fortunes of the elder Haya had declined, like those of most of his neighbors in the shadows of the Gildemeister and Grace plantations. Trujillo had prospered during the initial rise of the modern sugar industry. As the giant enterprises became dominant and absorbed the smaller planters and crop farmers, however, the community began to suffer. The integration and greater self-sufficiency of the large-scale operations hurt the region's independent craftsmen and merchants. Their distress became acute after 1915, when Gildemeister purchased a special license from the government to import goods for its own use duty free at a nearby port. The firm opened its own plantation stores, eliminating the shops of the labor contractors who had purchased their wares from local wholesalers. Worse, the inexpensive goods from these plantation outlets flooded the town markets, further injuring local merchants.

Under these adverse circumstances, Trujillo's once prosperous middle class struggled to maintain appearances. At considerable sacrifice to his family, Víctor Raúl attended the best private school in his hometown and enrolled at the National University of Trujillo in 1913. His social life at this time centered on a literary club of middle-class students, many of whom would remain Haya's lifelong associates. Already at this early age, Víctor Raúl exhibited considerable political talent and ambition. Elected secretary and then president of his school's student organization, his friends called him the "Prince of the Grand Venture." Within a few years Haya's companions in the "Trujillo Bohemia" would make common cause with the sugar workers in their often bloody battles with the plantation owners, and the north coast would become Víctor Raúl's partisan stronghold. But Haya apparently had only a passing interest in the problems of the laboring class in 1917, when a small inheritance enabled him to depart for the Peruvian capital.

After a few weeks in Lima, Haya secured the post of secretary to the prefect of Cuzco department. During a seven-month sojourn at the ancient city of the Incas, Víctor Raúl made acquaintances at the local university, became introduced to the world of the Indian, and acquired a smattering of Quechua. Returning to Lima in 1918, he entered San Marcos University and took a part-time job as a legal clerk. In the library of his employer's law office, Haya first read Marx and became interested in revolutionary politics. Víctor Raúl quickly established himself within the inner circle of the Peruvian Student Federation (FEP). First serving as Trujillo's representative to the federation, he then became a member of the committee that coordinated the FEP's support for the workers' January 1919 general strike. The following October, after the major battles for university reform had been won, Haya was elected president of the FEP. In this new capacity the fledgling politician presided over the national student congress at Cuzco in 1920, and gained that body's endorsement for his plan to establish the González Prada Popular Universities for workers.

Haya spent the next three years building a coalition of workers and students from which to launch his career in national politics. He supported himself by teaching at the Colegio Anglo-Peruano, a secondary school operated by Presbyterian minister John MacKay. At night he helped reestablish a textile workers' federation in Lima and opened several *universidades populares* for his blue-collar constituents. With funds borrowed from MacKay and perhaps financial aid from the government, Víctor Raúl traveled to Montevideo, Buenos Aires, and Santiago to represent the FEP at international student conferences. His reputation soared back home in Trujillo, but Haya needed a dramatic stroke to achieve national prominence. The opportunity arrived in May 1923 with Leguía's plan to consecrate Peru to the Sacred Heart of Jesus. Víctor Raúl, like most other students and young intellectuals, apparently had supported Leguía in 1919. According to some, Haya's links with the dictator continued at least until 1922. But the campus politician was the principal organizer of the protest rally on May 23 and the major speaker at the public funeral for the movement's fallen heroes the next day. Leguía's troops dispersed this gathering and arrested most of its leaders. Haya eluded capture until October, when he was imprisoned on San Lorenzo Island. That very day the FEP held its election. Manuel Seoane defeated the controversial Víctor Raúl for the presidency. But when the students learned of Haya's incarceration, they annulled the original contest. In new balloting, the imprisoned leader unanimously won the top post. Seoane, who later became Haya's most important lieutenant, received the vice-presidency. After a week of agitation by students and workers and a hunger strike by Víctor Raúl, Leguía decided to deport his troublesome young adversary. On October 9, 1923, the twenty-eight-year-old apprentice revolutionary sailed for Panama, the beginning of a remarkable eight-year odyssey.

Two months before the May 1923 disturbances, another

young leader returned from European exile with "a woman and some ideas." José Carlos Mariátegui, unlike Haya de la Torre, had personally experienced the privations of Peru's humble classes. Born in the southern Department of Moquegua on June 14, 1894, his father was a minor government clerk; his mother, a mestiza seamstress. The elder Mariátegui soon abandoned his family and José Carlos, his brother, and sister moved to the port of Huacho, their mother's hometown. The impoverished family went to Lima in 1902, probably to seek medical attention for a knee that José Carlos had injured. After several unsuccessful operations, Mariátegui was condemned to constant pain. For twenty years he walked with a pronounced limp. His friends called him the "Lame One." An infection forced the amputation of his good leg in 1924, immobilizing him for the remainder of his short life.

Childhood was brief for the poor of early twentieth-century Peru. In 1909, with only a primary-school education, fourteen-year old José Carlos took a job with a Lima newspaper. Advancing from office boy and typesetter's assistant, Mariátegui in 1914 began writing his own columns under various pseudonyms. He contributed to several publications during the next four years, reporting local events and writing literary criticism. Not until 1918, however, did he publish his first serious piece of social commentary. The next year José Carlos and a friend began publication of their own journal, *La Razón,* which strongly supported the workers and students in their struggle with the expiring Pardo regime. Unlike most young intellectuals of the period, Mariátegui did not endorse Leguía's candidacy. After the July 1919 coup, *La Razón* sharply criticized the new president's program. In August, the magazine's printer refused to produce further issues. Two months later José Carlos accepted a small government "scholarship" and departed for Europe. Although he visited several countries, Mariátegui spent most of his four-year exile in Italy, where he married Anna Chiappe. In the course of his travels the young writer was transformed from a vaguely socialistic, humanitarian reformer into a tough-minded Marxist theoretician.

Mariátegui brought his bride and their new son home to Lima in March 1923. In his absence, the infant student-worker alliance of 1919 had matured under the influence of the newcomer Haya de la Torre. Mariátegui and Haya cooperated in the publication of *Claridad,* the new official journal of the González Prada

Popular Universities. But from the beginning, their relationship was uneasy. A conflict of personalities, ambitions, and ideologies would make the two men bitter foes by 1928. The expansive, ruggedly handsome Haya, with his "good family" and university education, excelled at both public oratory and intimate conversation. "There flowed from him," admitted one of his enemies, an "almost juvenile gayety, fresh, warm, contagious. . . . He was charming and brilliant; he made each person he talked with feel specially loved, apart from the others."* First and foremost, Haya was a *político*—a practical politician to his admirers, an unprincipled opportunist to his detractors. A man of action, ideas were a secondary consideration for Víctor Raúl. Mariátegui was quiet, serious-minded. Dark-skinned and self-taught, José Carlos felt out of place and somewhat uncomfortable with the San Marcos set. He communicated effectively within his circle of close associates, but physically handicapped and high-pitched in voice, Mariátegui shunned public speaking. José Carlos considered Haya a pretentious pseudo-intellectual, a demagogue whose egomania drove him to create a premature political movement. Mariátegui's revolution could proceed only after he had prepared the workers for their historic Marxian mission. In the end, neither Haya nor Mariátegui would submit to the other's leadership.

Mariátegui refused to support actively the anti-Leguía demonstrations of May 23, "a liberalizing struggle," he called it, "without any revolutionary sentiment." His new family obligations and a reluctance to board Haya's bandwagon also may have tempered his decision. But with the exile of Víctor Raúl and some thirty other student leaders, José Carlos became the dominant figure of the leftist movement in Peru. In the afternoon, young intellectuals gathered around him at his home, dubbed the "Red corner" by police. At night, Mariátegui sometimes lectured at the popular universities, whose directorship he assumed until their suppression by the dictatorship in late 1924. Largely because of his influence, Marxism replaced anarchism as the major ideological current of the workers' movement.

Mariátegui founded the famous journal *Amauta* in 1926. Although most of its contributors were Marxists, during its first two years the magazine carried articles on a wide range of sub-

---

*Eudocio Ravines, *The Yenan Way* (New York: Charles Scribner's Sons, 1951), p. 21.

jects by reformers as well as revolutionaries, including a few items submitted by the exiled Haya de la Torre. Leguía was relatively tolerant of Mariátegui and his journal. He arrested the editor and confined him to a hospital for a week during a "Red scare" in 1927 and closed *Amauta* for six months. But this harassment was mild compared to the experiences of other opponents of the regime. Perhaps the dictator understood that Mariátegui's concept of revolution was, as the detainee explained in the pages of two Lima newspapers, "very different from its traditional association with conspiracies" and posed no immediate threat to the government. *Amauta* attacked the capitalist system and predicted its demise, but it avoided direct criticism of Leguía and his administration.

Mariátegui assembled several of his articles in 1928, and published them in book form as *Seven Interpretive Essays on Peruvian Reality*. One of the earliest systematic studies of the country's fundamental problems, the *Siete ensayos* examined the tandem questions of the Indian and the land, public education, the conflict between regionalism and the centralized state, the religious factor in the nation's development, and Peruvian literature. In this, his most famous work, and other articles written after his return from exile, José Carlos established himself as perhaps the most creative Marxist theoretician of Latin America. But he was also a great *Peruvian* thinker. Combining his own ideas with the disjointed observations of González Prada and other writers, Mariátegui molded a coherent analysis of Peruvian life. His nationalism set him apart from most of his Marxist contemporaries and later brought him the condemnation of orthodox Communists.

For Mariátegui Marxism provided an analytical framework for the systematic study of the past, a method for interpreting the present, and an aid for charting future actions. It was not an intellectual straitjacket, but a personal, basic tool to be modified with the addition of new knowledge and adapted to the needs of different environments. In its application to "Peruvian reality," Marxism had to be adjusted to allow for the nation's communal Indian traditions and its precapitalist socioeconomic structure. The achievement of socialism in Peru, he hoped, would not have to await distant bourgeois and then proletarian revolutions as in Marx's Europe. Properly prepared, the country's small industrial working class along with a few "conscious elements of the middle class" (that is, the intellectuals) might rekindle the latent revolutionary spirit of the Indians. Ultimately, Peruvian socialism would combine modern technology with compatible indigenous practices. Like other Marxists Mariátegui believed that the interplay of material factors determined the evolution of society. But he viewed socialism as a spirtual force and the inevitability of revolution as the prime article of faith. Socialist redemption would return Peru to the virtues and values of the past but with the economic rewards of modern science. Mariátegui did not present a detailed program for achieving his goal. His thought, however, influenced the more specific proposals of other revolutionary nationalists, including Haya de la Torre.

Following his deportation in October 1923, Víctor Raúl went to Mexico at the invitation of that country's dynamic minister of education, the *indigenista* José Vasconcelos. For six months the young Peruvian served as an aide to his host, embellished his own Indianist credentials with a brief stint as a teacher in a rural school, and absorbed the exhilarating atmosphere of the blossoming Mexican Revolution. At a student congress in Mexico City on May 7, 1924, Haya announced the formation of the Alianza Popular Revolucionaria Americana (American Popular Revolutionary Alliance), soon to become famous under its acronym—APRA. Víctor Raúl originally conceived his *alianza* as an independent, Pan–Latin American united front embracing a wide spectrum of reformist and revolutionary groups. Although he unfurled a flag for his new organization in May, it was not until the end of 1924 that he enumerated his famous five-point "Maximum Program" for the hemisphere. Broad enough to encompass the divergent views of Latin America's entire left wing, APRA's international platform made its strongest appeal toward anti–United States sentiment, the largest common denominator of that variegated group. Specifically, Haya called for:

(1) Action of the countries of Latin America against Yankee Imperialism.
(2) The political unity of Latin America.
(3) The nationalisation of land and industry.
(4) The internationalisation of the Panama Canal.
(5) The solidarity of all the oppressed people and classes of the world.*

*Víctor Raúl Haya de la Torre, "What Is the A.P.R.A.?" *Labour Monthly* 8 (December 1926): 756.

Within this framework the aspirant continental leader envisioned the creation of national Aprista parties that would formulate more detailed "minimum programs" for their individual countries.

Soon after the founding of APRA, Haya left Mexico for a three-year adventure in Europe. Already recognized as a leader of great potential, he had received an invitation to observe the Fifth World Congress of the Communist International which assembled at Moscow in July 1925. Víctor Raúl met several heroes of the Russian Revolution, including Leon Trotsky, but he politely declined their invitations to affiliate APRA with the Soviet-directed Third International. Flirtation between the Russians and Haya continued for the next few years as both parties attempted to use each other. While the Communists desired to swallow APRA, the Peruvian *político* contemplated the incorporation of the Latin American Communists into his own Aprista international.

After a four-month stay in the Soviet Union, Víctor Raúl visited Switzerland, Italy, and France before establishing his base in Britian. He enrolled at Oxford and the prestigious London School of Economics. But the organization of APRA, rather than academic life, consumed most of his bountiful energy. He made several trips to the Continent as his life became a hectic round of public lectures, conferences, and meetings with fellow exiles. Meanwhile, Haya published more than a score of magazine articles and countless items in newspapers of Europe and the Americas. He maintained an active correspondence with friends on three continents.

When Víctor Raúl left Peru in 1923, his ideological baggage consisted of elementary Marxism and a few amorphous ideas about social justice, nationalism, and revolution. In that era of "isms," however, Haya needed a systematic doctrine to acquire respectability as a major political leader. From a purely practical standpoint, the unimaginative, orthodox Marxism that characterized his early writings became inadequate to justify APRA's independence from the Communist International. Politics was Víctor Raúl's natural ambience, but he also had considerable intellectual curiosity and he read widely. Borrowing ideas here and there and translating them into terms intelligible within the Latin American environment, Haya fashioned his own ideology— "Aprism." By 1927, when he attended the Communist-sponsored World Anti-Imerialist Congress at Brussels, Haya de la Torre's Marxist views had become pronouncedly revisionist. An exchange of bitter invective at that meeting initiated a blood feud between APRA and the Communists that continues to this day.

A published attack on APRA by a Cuban Communist greeted Haya's return to Mexico in late 1927. The *alianza*'s founder responded with *El Antimperialismo y el APRA,* the first extensive statement of his major ideas. Víctor Raúl asserted that Aprismo was fundamentally Marxist. It accepted dialectical materialism—the constant clash of economic forces—as the mainspring of history; the division of society into economic classes and the inevitable struggle between these groups until the triumph of the proletariat; and, finally, the world's ultimate arrival at classless, stateless socialism. But while Marx had correctly plotted Europe's revolutionary course from the middle of the previous century, Haya believed that Latin America's road toward socialism began at a different point in its historical evolution and passed through a different socioeconomic environment. To emphasize the separateness of the New World experience, the Aprista theoretician nearly eliminated the words "Latin America" from his vocabulary. Pointing to the fact that many countries of the region were more Indian than Latin, Víctor Raúl appropriated the term "Indoamerica" from his friend José Vasconcelos. For the developed world, as Marx had said, imperialism was the last stage of capitalism. But for backward areas like Indoamerica, according to Haya, foreign capital actually planted the seeds of modern industry and commerce. Therefore, imperialism was the necessary *first* stage of capitalism. Víctor Raúl condemned the "dogmatic and infallible Marxism of the Muscovite synods," with its almost total ignorance of the Americas and the "genuflecting creole Communists" who parroted the line of the Third International in the New World.

In addition to his last-stage, first-stage theory, Haya made several other alterations to adapt Marxism to the "Indoamerican reality." In Europe, he wrote, an independent bourgeois capitalism long ago had supplanted feudalism and had given birth to the revolutionary proletariat. In the New World, however, the feudal class continued to survive in an alliance with imperialist capitalism. This powerful combination controlled the governments of the region and used the state to assist in the exploitation of the other classes. Furthermore, the imperialists encouraged international conflicts among their victims in In-

domamerica to prevent the unification of its people in defense of
their independence. Because of the great strength of the
imperialist-feudalist enemy, Indoamerica's common foes could
be defeated only through an Aprista alliance of "anti-imperialist
states."

The vanguard in the struggle to gain control of the government machinery would not be the proletariat. Haya believed that
the industrial working class of predominantly agarian Indoamerica was too small to accomplish this task. Also, incipient
capitalism initially improved the workers' condition and rendered them more docile than their European contemporaries.
Latin America's middle class, according to Víctor Raúl, had the
greatest revolutionary potential. Unlike Europe's bourgeoisie,
Indoamerica's small landowners, merchants, industrialists, and
professional men were still fighting against feudalism and, therefore, had not lost their vitality. Drawing upon the writings of
others and perhaps his own experiences in Trujillo, he asserted
that the middle class, precariously dependent upon the feudal
oligarchy and foreign capital, suffered the most from imperialism. Indoamerica's bourgeoisie was being proletarianized
without ever capturing the apparatus of the capitalist state.

Haya declared that the middle class could immediately lead
the proletariat in the struggle against imperialism and its feudal
allies. It then could provide the expertise to direct the anti-
imperialist state, which the Aprista leader vaguely described.
Land would be taken from the feudal lords and given to those
who till the soil. The state would nationalize basic industries and
transform them into workers' cooperatives. These would operate alongside private enterprises owned by the new, independent bourgeoisie. Foreign capital might continue to invest in
Indoamerica but only under the strict supervision of the anti-
imperialist state. Although not explicitly stated by Haya, his
anti-imperialist revolution apparently replaced the bourgeois
revolution within the classic Marxist schema. Eventually, Indoamerican capitalism would develop sufficiently so that the
revolution of the proletariat could occur and produce classless,
stateless socialism. Víctor Raúl courted *indigenista* sentiment
with frequent references to the natives, whom he promised to
redeem. The Indian's role within the grand design of Aprismo,
however, was to be entirely passive. Aboriginal Americans
would receive benefits from the anti-imperialist state, but they
would not have any important function in its establishment.

Haya did not explain how the Apristas would "capture power." But his actions soon demonstrated that both ballots and bullets were acceptable means to achieve the desired end.

After a round of lectures in Mexico, Haya began a whirlwind tour of Central America in July 1928 organizing a few small Aprista groups. In his speeches he lashed out against the United States, whose marines were chasing the guerrilla leader Sandino through the backlands of Nicaragua. At the same time, Víctor Raúl prepared for his triumphant return to Peru. The preceding January, he had announced the formation of the Peruvian Nationalist party, an APRA affiliate, and his intention to challenge Leguía in the presidential election of 1929. One of the more obscure episodes in Haya's often mysterious career, this essay at electoral politics was apparently a subterfuge. While his friends in Lima distracted the government with the motions of a peaceful campaign, an army of 2,500 oil workers at Talara was to begin a revolution to overthrow the regime. Víctor Raúl's plans went awry. In December 1928, United States officials in the Panama Canal Zone refused to let the anti-imperialist orator disembark from his ship. The Aprista leader was forced to continue the voyage to Germany, where he spent the remainder of his exile. Six months later, Leguía's police captured the agent charged with organizing the Talara revolt.

The fragile peace between Haya de la Torre and Mariátegui shattered in 1928. José Carlos criticized Víctor Raúl's theory of the revolutionary middle class and he objected to APRA's apparent transformation from a loose "alliance of free spirits" into a "petty-bourgeois . . . nationalist party." Mariátegui scoffed at Haya's claims to leadership over a vast Latin American movement. APRA, he said, was no more than a "pompous letterhead." Declaring that *Amauta* was not a "publicity agent for any pretentious performer," the editor announced that he no longer would accept Aprista articles for publication. José Carlos refused to support Haya's election campaign and he became very angry when he discovered that this movement was to have been a diversionary tactic for an Aprista revolution. Mariátegui asserted that Haya's thirst for power would bring a fascist reaction. Víctor Raúl answered in kind. He called Mariátegui a provincial "Lima socialist" and a Leguía puppet, while at the same time accusing him of subservience to Moscow and its unrealistic European revolutionary model. José Carlos was guilty of "excessive intellectualism," "mental masturbations," "tropical illusions and absurd sentimentalism." As a cripple, declared Haya, Mariátegui could not lead a revolution—"He cringes from the idea of action." Víctor Raúl blamed his rival for the failure of the anti-Leguía revolt.

The open warfare between Haya and Mariátegui produced a great schism within the Peruvian political left, many of whose members had ties to both men. Mariátegui had been in contact with Moscow since 1927, when the Communist International suggested that he establish a party in Peru. José Carlos, however, believed that his country's proletariat was not prepared for that step. But his break with Haya and the start of a more militant phase of APRA's activities in Peru forced Mariátegui to organize a formal party to hold his followers together. Perhaps Víctor Raúl's attacks on his "useless semantics" and his own deteriorating health—the infection that had taken his leg had not been checked—prompted Mariátegui to advance his revolutionary timetable. In September and October 1928, José Carlos and his friends founded the Peruvian Socialist party (PSP). A few months later, the new party grouped its followers within the labor movement into the General Confederation of Peruvian Workers (CGTP). Although the PSP publicly was described as a broadly based front for the working and middle classes, Mariátegui and the other members of the party's executive committee formed a secret, seven-man Communist cell and affiliated the PSP with the Third International.

Amauta now became almost entirely an organ of the Moscow line. Still, its editor hoped to maintain some of his intellectual and operational independence. With the triumph of Stalin in the Soviet Union, however, the Communist International became increasingly intolerant of "nationalist deviations" from its official Marxism. It demanded that the PSP abandon Mariátegui's theory of the revolutionary Indian, submit to the discipline of Moscow, and adopt the name "Communist party," a label José Carlos studiously avoided for tactical reasons. Mariátegui wrote a careful defense of his position which his representatives read before the First Latin American Communist Conference at Buenos Aires in June 1929. That body rejected the ideas of the Peruvian leader, however, and censured his party. Mariátegui then prepared to confront the Communist officials at Buenos Aires in person. Intriguingly, he also arranged to see a specialist there about an artificial limb to restore his mobility. But he was too ill to travel.

With black-framed pictures of its founder *Amauta* announced the death of José Carlos Mariátegui on April 16, 1930, at the age of thirty-five. What he might have done if death had not taken him is a matter of conjecture. Today, several parties claim that his ghost resides with them. A month after Mariátegui's demise Eudocio Ravines, the new leader of the PSP and a long-time Moscow agent, submitted to the directives of the International and adopted the Communist label. The Communist party of Peru lists José Carlos as its founder. But Ricardo Martínez de la Torre, the lone opponent of Ravines's submission to Moscow, was also Mariátegui's closest associate. Shortly after the death of José Carlos, Luciano Castillo reestablished the PSP as an independent Marxist party. The new socialist organization asserted that it was the true heir of the "Lame One." The Apristas soon declared that the feud between Haya and José Carlos was only a fraternal spat and that Mariátegui eventually would have joined their camp. Other leftists and even some conservative groups now pay homage to the editor of *Amauta*. Ideological differences notwithstanding, the sincerity of his convictions, his love for his homeland, and the indomitable spirit painfully imprisoned within his crippled body have endeared the memory of Mariátegui to his countrymen.

Civil War, 1930–1933

The "best people" of the Peruvian capital crowded the airstrip of the country club in suburban Miraflores on August 27, 1930. At 5:00 P.M., "Slim" Fawcett's trimotor airplane arrived from Arequipa carrying the man whose revolution had toppled the Leguía dictatorship. Cheers greeted the opening of the aircraft's door, but the well-wishers were startled at their first glimpse of Lt. Col. Luis Miguel Sánchez Cerro, who emerged dressed in a rumpled campaign uniform. He was short, slender and very dark; he jokingly called himself "El Negro." The angular, Indian features of his face were dominated by a gaping, undisciplined smile that revealed large, widely spaced teeth—like an "orangutang," recalled one contemporary. Had the Huns arrived? The few members of the Lima elite who knew the "Hero of Arequipa" assured their friends that he was "safe." Furthermore, his principal civilian adviser, Dr. José Luis Bustamante i Rivero, was one of staid Arequipa's most distinguished citizens.

Sánchez Cerro boarded a convertible and departed for the capital. More than 80,000 humbler citizens cheered the motorcade as it wound its way through the main streets to central Lima. A man long imprisoned by Leguía rushed the automobile to personally thank the soldier. Women threw flowers, and placards proclaimed Sánchez Cerro the "Second Liberator of Peru." Soon after reaching the presidential palace, the Supreme Chief appeared on the balcony and briefly addressed the throng below. His declaration of the end of "eleven years of oppression" under the "monster named Augusto Leguía" produced pandemonium. It seemed too good to be true—a leader whom the wealthy could trust and yet a man of the people, a "*cholo* president" who could undermine the appeal of the radicals.

Barely forty-one years old at the time of his revolution, Sánchez Cerro was the fourth of eight children born to a notary in Piura, on the north coast. Educated at public primary and secondary schools, he was one of the few Peruvian presidents who had not attended a private academy. At the age of sixteen, Sánchez Cerro was accepted for admission to the Chorrillos military school. Arriving in Lima three months before the next class began, the penniless youth enlisted as an army private and spent this period as a common soldier. Sánchez Cerro graduated as a second lieutenant in 1910, and served with several units in all three of Peru's major geographical regions. He was a competent officer, but associates remembered him primarily for the personal qualities that later would make him attractive to the masses. The little caudillo had all the "manly vices." Although his written correspondence demonstrated that he was not the dullard that his enemies depicted, his speech employed the coarse language of the barracks. Sánchez Cerro loved gambling, drinking, and female companionship. Impetuous and physically courageous, he fought several duels in defense of his honor. He was a generous, fun-seeking comrade to his brother officers and a benevolent father to his troops. Honest but careless with both public money and his own salary, Sánchez Cerro had no interest in acquiring a personal fortune.

The "Hero of Arequipa" was a congenital conspirator. He first gained notoriety in the 1914 overthrow of Guillermo Billinghurst. Awakened by the sound of troop movements, he rushed to the presidential palace, where machine-gun fire had halted the revolutionary forces. Unarmed, Lieutenant Sánchez Cerro rushed one of the entrances to the building, forced open the door so that his friends could follow, and lunged at the startled defenders. This action cost him three fingers and the partial paralysis of his left arm, but it earned him a promotion to captain and a brief assignment as a military attaché in Peru's Washington embassy. Participation in an unsuccessful revolt against Leguía in 1922 brought no rewards for Sánchez Cerro. After a short imprisonment on desolate Taquila Island in Lake Titicaca, he was removed from the army. Through the intercession of a friend in the war ministry, however, the president was persuaded to reinstate his young adversary, whom he promptly dispatched to far-off Italy for training with Mussolini's army. Permitted to return home after two years, Sánchez Cerro received a promotion to lieutenant colonel in early 1930, and was placed in command of one of four army units based at Arequipa. He immediately began to conspire with his fellow officers and prominent civilians to overthrow the tottering Leguía dictatorship.

The success of the September 1930 revolution again demonstrated the audacity of Sánchez Cerro. He and other middle-rank officers first removed the commanding general at Arequipa and then issued a nationalistically worded manifesto urging support from other military units throughout the country. Although Leguía resigned two days later, he entrusted the government to a junta of generals who were reluctant to relinquish power to the upstart lieutenant colonel in the south. But Sánchez Cerro would not be denied the presidency. After five days, the caudillo won endorsements from several garrisons and received the junta's invitation to make his ceremonious entrance into Lima.

Sánchez Cerro continued to be the hero of the masses, but he quickly alienated many of the nation's most powerful groups. The Supreme Chief's military cabinet, composed entirely of politically inexperienced majors and colonels, caused consternation among the generals. A decree legalizing divorce angered the Church. A sweeping purge of Leguiísta bureaucrats and the vindictive treatment of the fallen dictator by the new regime drove supporters of the former president into the opposition camp. At the same time, the revolutionary government became locked in a struggle with Leguía's old enemies—organized labor and university students. Like many other officers of his generation who had been employed to quell violent strikes, Sánchez Cerro viewed the workers' movement as a dangerous arm of international communism. When a wave of strikes tested the new administration, the president suppressed them with a degree of severity unmatched during the Oncenio. The students petitioned the government for the reenactment of the 1919 university reforms, and Sánchez Cerro agreed to grant most of their requests. But when the students occupied buildings at San Marcos to press for all of their demands, police violently evicted them and closed the school.

In the early weeks of the new administration, political prisoners were released and many exiles returned to the country. This "democratic springtime" rapidly faded, however, as opposition to the regime intensified. Convinced the APRA was a Communist front, Sánchez Cerro curbed the party's activities and denied Haya de la Torre permission to enter Peru. To be sure, many members of the old elite agreed with this policy. But they were appalled when the *cholo* colonel announced that he would seek election to a constitutional term as president while remaining at the head of the provisional government. A series of army revolts and a naval mutiny brought Sánchez Cerro's resignation on March 1, 1931. Before departing for diplomatic exile in France, the "Hero of Arequipa" promised that he would return for the next presidential election.

The anti-Sánchez Cerro forces installed a new provisional government under the civilian presidency of David Samánez Ocampo, an old Piérolista. Except for the military ministries, moderate civilians staffed the cabinet posts. The interim regime immediately began preparations for elections in October to choose a constitutional president and a national assembly. This body would draft a new constitution and sit as a temporary legislature until the charter was adopted. A commission of prominent jurists and representatives of various political parties prepared a model electoral code, the most democratic in the nation's history. The law made voting compulsory for all literate males aged twenty-one to sixty. It provided for the careful registration and identification of voters, the secret ballot, and guarantees for the honest and open canvassing of returns, free from government influence. Although the code banned the Communist party, it established very liberal rules for the participation of other parties and the nomination of candidates.

Peru experienced a partisan campaign in 1931 like none before or since. With the old party system destroyed by Leguía, many new groups appeared. Eventually, two coalitions formed to support moderates Arturo Osores and José María de la Jara. The government maintained official neutrality in the contest, but a majority of the junta's members apparently favored La Jara, as did the Roman Catholic hierarchy. Because of poor organization and internal bickering within the moderate alliances it soon became apparent that the next president would be one of two charismatic leaders—Haya de la Torre or Sánchez Cerro. Many members of Peru's old political parties adroitly aligned themselves with these front-runners. The Leguiístas, persecuted by Sánchez Cerro, generally supported Haya, while most of their Civilista adversaries backed the "Hero of Arequipa."

Of the two leading candidates, the government was most adverse to the former president. The minister of war and strongman within the regime, Lt. Col. Gustavo Jiménez, was especially hostile to Sánchez Cerro. Aptly nicknamed "The Fox," this ambitious officer had been instrumental in ousting the former president and feared his return to power. At the urging of Jiménez, the provisional government denied Sánchez Cerro permission to return home for the campaign. But once again, the indomitable caudillo would not be turned aside. While his supporters in the capital staged protest demonstrations, he defiantly sailed for Peru without an entry visa. Finally, after the pesky little soldier promised to abide by the results of the election, he was allowed to land at Callao on July 3, 1931. Sánchez Cerro lacked sufficient time to organize his own political apparatus. Therefore, he adopted the banner of the Revolutionary Union (UR), a small group of right-wing nationalists.

APRA already had created a formidable electoral machine. Haya's lieutenants established local Aprista units throughout the country, assembled regional conventions, and launched *La Tribuna,* the party's official newspaper. A tumultuous crowd at Talara welcomed APRA's Maximum Chief to his homeland on July 12, and he began a triumphal speaking tour down the coast to Lima. One month later, Víctor Raúl opened the First National Convention of the Peruvian Aprista party (PAP)—theoretically, only one affiliate of the hemispheric *alianza*—and accepted its nomination.

Haya elaborated APRA's "Minimum Program for Peru," the party's platform, in a masterful, three-hour speech to 30,000 persons jammed into Lima's Plaza de Acho bullring. This remarkable document contained many old political clichés— promises of a democratic, decentralized government; honest, efficient public administration; a sound currency and a balanced

budget. Several other proposals were neither entirely new nor
revolutionary by themselves. But never before had so many
specific reforms (almost 300) been advocated. Moreover, AP-
RA's radical image and the apparent sincerity of its enthusiastic
young leaders indicated that the party intended to keep its
promises.

The PAP's *programa mínimo* had two salient characteristics: it
placed the Peruvian economy within a global context and made a
commitment to rapid economic and social change through the
massive intervention of a technocratic state. These features arose
from the party's universalistic, Marxist orientation, the exposure
of its exiled leaders to state capitalism and advanced social-
welfare programs in other countries, and the devastating impact
of the worldwide Great Depression. A few of the Aprista proposals were naïvely utopian, while others seemed unrealistic in the
political environment of the period. With some major exceptions, however, the party officially would continue to campaign
on the same platform for the next forty years. Many of its
programs would be implemented by non-Aprista regimes.

APRA called for the assembly of an economic congress,
composed of experts in various fields, to examine the nation's
resources, identify its needs, and set basic goals. Using these
guidelines, the government would implement programs carefully formulated with the assistance of a state planning agency.
Through a new national bank, the government would become a
major source of development capital. Peru would continue to
welcome foreign investment but only in certain industries and
under close regulation to protect the nation's interests. The
Apristas promised to eliminate all harmful monopolies and cancel government concessions and contracts that compromised the
nation's sovereignty. Protective tariffs along with state financial
and technical assistance would be employed to encourage native
mining, manufacturing, and agriculture. The government also
would foster workers' cooperatives in these economic activities.

The Minimum Program advocated the gradual nationalization of transportation facilities and insurance companies. The
Apristas pledged to expropriate gold and vanadium mines immediately and prepare for the nationalization of other extractive
industries in the "near future." Until that time, the state would
require mining companies to refine more minerals in Peru and
invest a portion of their profits in other sectors of the economy.
APRA proposed an agrarian reform, paying "just compensation"

to affected landowners. Excessively large estates, those controlled by absentee landlords, and inefficiently exploited properties would be expropriated first. Small farms and cooperatives would replace the archaic haciendas. The party promised to end the treasury's traditional reliance on regressive, indirect taxes and institute a system of progressive, direct taxation.

The Apristas called for the creation of a "functional parliament," a variation of Mussolini's corporate state in Italy. Under this system legislators would not represent political subdivisions or citizens as individuals but would be spokesmen for national economic sectors. All persons engaged in various branches of manufacturing, mining, agriculture, commerce, and the liberal professions would organize associations. These corporate bodies would elect representatives of their industry or profession to congress. APRA proposed to lower the voting age to eighteen, grant suffrage to women, and end the literacy requirement that disenfranchised a majority of the nation's citizens. The PAP platform demanded the complete separation of Church and state. It proposed to depoliticize the armed forces while improving their military capabilities and living conditions. In peacetime the soldiers would be employed in public works and social action programs. Under a new civil service system, bureaucrats would be hired on the basis of merit alone, and they could not be dismissed for political reasons. All public officials would be required to disclose their economic interests before assuming office and submit to an investigation of their finances at the end of their tenure.

Reflecting the influence of Magda Portal, the Aprista poetess, the party's platform had a strong feminist plank. In addition to full political rights for women, it advocated an end to the restrictions on the civil liberties of wives and demanded equal pay for women performing the same work as men. Similarly, the party proposed to remove all legal disabilities imposed upon illegitimate children. APRA espoused a complete reform of the educational system, with emphasis on vocational training and literacy programs for adults. All education would be free, limited only by the ability of the student. The party called for the reinstitution of the 1919 university reforms. The *programa mínimo* pledged ambitious public works and health programs. It recommended extensive new labor legislation, including provisions for agricultural workers, and the rudiments of a social security system. The party promised to protect the Indians, improve their standard of living, and incorporate the natives into the mainstream of Peruvian society. Finally, the national platform acknowledged the pledges made by regional Aprista conventions.

The program presented by Sánchez Cerro's Revolutionary Union appeared surprisingly similar to that of APRA, at least on the surface. It included promises of advanced social-welfare legislation to assist labor, education, and the nation's Indians. The party recommended several measures to combat the depression and encourage economic development. But the UR platform was much less detailed than APRA's Minimum Program and lacked the more radical proposals of Haya de la Torre. It declared that every farmer should own the fields that he worked but suggested that the nation possessed enough vacant public land to accomplish this without expropriating private estates. The program espoused state ownership of public utilities, but it did not call for the nationalization of mines or other industries. Although the Revolutionary Union called for higher tariffs during the economic emergency, it declared itself opposed to the principle of protectionism. In the end, Sánchez Cerro's deemphasis of the platform in his campaign and the presence of Peru's most conservative men in his camp cast doubts upon the sincerity of the party's promises.

Between July and October 1931 both major candidates spoke to huge crowds throughout the country. Haya even traveled to Iquitos. Although APRA stressed the superiority of its platform and promised to transform Peruvian society, the party also made vicious personal attacks on the *cholo* colonel, whom they depicted as an illegitimate, illiterate savage and a tool of the Civilista "oligarchy." Sánchez Cerro branded APRA an anti-Peruvian, international organization and a front for the Communists. He promised to "pulverize" the PAP and all other revolutionary enemies of society. Emphasizing his own nationalism, the UR candidate denounced Leguía's unpopular boundary treaty with Colombia. During the campaign opposition agitators frequently disrupted political rallies, riots occurred, and both Apristas and Sanchezcerristas were assassinated.

Because of strict security measures, the election of October 11, 1931, was surprisingly peaceful. The early returns placed Haya de la Torre in the lead, and his partisans complimented the government for supervising an honest expression of the popular

will. But Víctor Raúl's tally soon fell behind that of Sánchez
Cerro and APRA charged that fraud had been committed. The
PAP challenged the vote in virtually every department carried by
the opposition and fears arose that the canvass would not be
completed by the December 8 inauguration date. In late
November, however, the National Election Board announced
the official results of the balloting. Sánchez Cerro had won the
presidency with 152,000 votes, Haya de la Torre had received
106,000 ballots, and the candidates of the two moderate coalitions had polled a combined total of 41,000 votes. Although the
electoral tribunal made some questionable decisions, recent
scholarship had upheld the basic impartiality of the panel and the
validity of the election's results. Today, some Apristas begrudgingly admit the defeat of their party in its first contest. In 1931,
however, APRA was convinced that it had been cheated. It
seemed incomprehensible that the electorate favored a return of
the "oligarchy" rather than Víctor Raúl's promised revolution.
Furthermore, the party was certain that it would have been the
choice of the two-thirds of Peru's adult citizens denied the
franchise because of the literacy requirement.

The 1931 electoral census indicates that APRA was rejected
by large segments of the very sectors toward which it had directed its strongest appeal—the middle class, blue-collar workers, and the nation's youth. Peru's poorest folk, including the
bulk of the native population, did not vote. However, the election was by no means a rich man's contest. Less than 15 percent
of the voters were "white." Astoundingly, the registrars listed
almost a quarter of the electorate as "Indian." Eighty-five percent of the citizens that registered for the contest (82 percent
actually voted) had only a primary-school education or less.
Slightly more than 3 percent had received training beyond the
high-school level. Sixty percent of the registered voters were
thirty-five years of age or younger. The geographical distribution
of the vote and APRA's share of the total—about one-third—
were very similar to the pattern that would characterize Peruvian
elections for the next three decades. With the exception of
Sánchez Cerro's home department, Piura, and the Socialist party
stronghold of Túmbez, APRA swept the north, gaining huge
majorities in Haya's native La Libertad department and other
zones of heavily capitalized agriculture along the coast. In general, Sánchez Cerro won substantial victories in the less developed southern and central portions of the country, including

those departments where "Indians" comprised a significant element of the electorate. But the soldier also captured the vote of Lima-Callao and other urban areas outside of APRA's "solid north," regions with large concentrations of industrial workers and members of the middle class.

Tension filled Peru during the ten-day interval between the announcement of the election results and the installation of the new regime. Street fights, protest strikes, noisy demonstrations, and assassinations continued. Rumors of coups abounded. The president-elect feared that the provisional government would annul the election as APRA demanded. The Apristas anticipated a Leguía-style preinaugural coup to suppress congress and install their enemy with dictatorial powers. The "Hero of Arequipa" formally received the presidential sash on December 8, but partisan passions and violence only increased. The new president, as he declared in his inaugural address, was determined to tame the radicals and restore order. In Trujillo, meanwhile, Víctor Raúl refused to accept the mandate of Sánchez Cerro and claimed the "moral presidency" of Peru for himself. Filled with self-righteous indignation, APRA seemed determined to press the administration and win the laurels of martyrdom.

The constituent assembly installed in December 1931 had 64 supporters of Sánchez Cerro and 23 Apristas. Members of nearly a score of other parties divided the remaining seats in the 145-man, unicameral legislature. Through their intemperate behavior, the Aprista congressmen quickly alienated enough of their independent colleagues to give the regime a working majority. In early January, after ten days of sharp debate and questionable parliamentary procedures, the assembly approved an Emergency Law requested by the executive. Giving the government broad powers to end internal disorder, the measure was used to suppress APRA. The regime silenced the party's newspapers, closed its meeting halls, and arrested hundreds of Apristas. Independents who protested against the abuse of the law and others who criticized the regime received similar treatment.

In February 1932, the government announced the discovery of an Aprista plot to overthrow the regime. Violating the constitutional immunity of legislators from arrest, police invaded the chambers of the national assembly and seized the Aprista congressmen. A staccato of violent events now began. The administration ordered the arrest of Haya de la Torre on March 5. The next day José Melgar Márquez, an eighteen-year-old Aprista, shot and seriously wounded Sánchez Cerro at a church in Miraflores. The regime accused Juan Seoane, the brother of APRA leader Manuel Seoane, of supplying the weapon used in the attack. A military court condemned Melgar Márquez and Juan Seoane to death. Under pressure from congress and world opinion, however, Sánchez Cerro spared their lives. On May 6, police captured Haya de la Torre, who had hidden in the house of a friend. One day later, pro-Aprista sailors mutinied at Callao and seized two warships, but loyal navy and army forces quickly quashed the rebellion. The government arbitrarily selected 8 of the 300 mutineers and executed them by firing squad in front of the other insurgents. The regime rapidly purged the armed forces of suspected APRA sympathizers and closed San Marcos University.

Beginning in February 1932, or earlier, APRA made plans for a revolution to be led by Col. Gustavo Jiménez, Sánchez Cerro's old adversary. Armed Aprista civilians and the party's supporters within the armed forces simultaneously were to attack military posts and seize key urban centers throughout the nation. Originally scheduled for June, organizational problems produced a series of postponements. These delays caused great anguish in Haya's native Trujillo. A court martial had found the Surpeme Chief guilty of treason for leading an outlawed, communistic, and international party that endangered Peru's sovereignty. He was sentenced to death. According to rumor, Víctor Raúl was being tortured and his execution was imminent. Without orders from APRA's high command, 1,000 armed Apristas assaulted the O'Donavan army barracks near Trujillo in the early morning of July 7, 1932. Led by Manuel Barreta, called "Búfalo" (Buffalo), they took the garrison after a battle of several hours. The victorious rebels marched their prisoners into Trujillo where thousands of unruly sugar workers from the nearby plantations joined the movement. The Apristas stormed the police headquarters and other public buildings in the city and jailed several prominent civilian supporters of the regime along with the captured military and police personnel. Agustín Haya de la Torre, Víctor Raúl's brother, replaced the local prefect.

The premature uprising at Trujillo doomed the national conspiracy. Although Aprista units at Huaraz, in the Sierra northeast of Lima, and a few other isolated towns sprung into action, the government was able to prevent uprisings in other cities and concentrate its forces in the north. Soldiers soon ringed Trujillo. Military aircraft indiscriminately bombed and strafed the city. At this critical juncture, the rebel leaders fled, leaving their hysterical followers in control of the town. On July 10, shortly before the government assault, 60 prisoners—army officers, policemen, and civilians—were murdered at the city jail. The bodies of some were mutilated. Enraged by these atrocities, the troops that stormed Trujillo a few hours later immediately shot most captured rebels. During the next several days, the army arrested hundreds of suspects. Those whose trigger fingers and shoulders showed evidence that they had fired weapons were condemned en masse by a military panel. These unfortunates were executed at the ruins of Chan Chan, the ancient Chimu capital, a few miles from town. Estimates of the number killed range from 1,000 to 5,000 persons.

The tragic events at Trujillo poisoned Peru's political atmosphere. The military establishment viewed the Aprista assault on the O'Donavan Barracks and the slaughter in the jail as an attack upon the armed forces as an institution. Although Gustavo Jiménez was able to recruit a few officers for another abortive revolt the following March, APRA lost many friends among the professional soldiers. More importantly, the party made implacable enemies of military men who later might have become allies in the struggle for change. In succeeding years, anti-Aprismo became entrenched within the armed services. Instruction in the evils of APRA became part of the curriculum for cadets at the military academies. For the next four decades, the armed forces would hold annual services commemorating the "Trujillo Massacre." Nor did the Apristas forget Trujillo. With the party's membership and leaders drawn primarily from the north coast, the horrors of the military reprisals have been etched in the collective memory of the organization. APRA, too, honors its fallen heroes in ceremony and song. Aprista leaders denied responsibility for the senseless murders in the Trujillo jail, but they have been slow to forgive the army for its excesses. The deep hostility between Peru's largest political party and the nation's most powerful institution would stifle the country's democratic aspirations for many years.

Startling news that reached Lima on September 1, 1932, diverted the country's attention from the bloodshed at Trujillo. The previous evening 300 armed Peruvian civilians had seized the town of Leticia in the Amazonian territory recently ceded to Colombia. Sánchez Cerro at first denounced this action as an Aprista-Communist plot to embarrass his regime. He soon learned, however, that the attacking force consisted of nationalistic citizens of the Department of Loreto who resented Leguía's surrender of Leticia to the Colombians. A difficult decision confronted the president, who had denounced the Salomón-Lozano Treaty during his election campaign. The retention of Leticia would bring badly needed support for his regime. Conversely, an order to return the captured town might have sparked a separatist rebellion in Loreto and placed his already weakened administration in grave jeopardy.

Although Peru was not prepared for hostilities with Colombia, Sánchez Cerro adopted a belligerent attitude, perhaps hoping that he might gain concessions without bringing a full-scale war. The president ordered troops from Iquitos to reinforce the civilians at Leticia. Unfortunately, Bogotá would not relinquish its new river port without a struggle. In February 1933, Peruvian and Colombian forces clashed on the Amazon and the two countries broke diplomatic relations. Sánchez Cerro rejected offers of mediation from the United States, Brazil, and other third parties, and Colombia refused to renegotiate the Salomón-Lozano Treaty as Peru demanded. A major war seemed imminent.

During these months of domestic and international crisis Peru's national assembly labored on a new constitution which it promulgated on April 18, 1933. This fundamental law, the republic's most recent, contained several interesting departures from previous charters. It provided for a government that outwardly resembled both the presidential systems of the New World and the parliamentary regimes of Europe. In actual operation, however, the Peruvian government has more closely followed the American pattern. The president, under the 1933 document, was to be elected by the direct, compulsory vote of literate males aged twenty-one or older for a term of five (later extended to six) years. He could not be reelected before the intervention of another full term. With the consent of the legislature, the chief executive appointed a cabinet that had its own presiding officer, called a prime minister or premier. The ministers were permitted to hold seats in congress, participate in its debates, and introduce legislation to that body. Cabinet members also could be called before congress to answer questions and the legislature could remove them from office through a vote of no confidence. The charter denied the president his traditional power to veto legislation.

The legislative branch of government, usually called parliament, was bicameral. As in the past, the chamber of deputies represented regional constituencies and was apportioned on the basis of population. But breaking with tradition, the Constitution of 1933 called for the organization of a "functional senate," a body representing economic sectors like that which APRA proposed in its Minimum Program. The Apristas believed that a single-chamber, functional parliament would permit greater coordination in efforts to foster economic development. Peru's conservatives, like the European fascists, favored functional representation primarily because they hoped that it would promote national solidarity and discourage class conflict. Instead of struggle between the proletariat and their capitalist employers, the owners, managers, and workers of various enterprises would unite to further the interests of their particular industries. The corporatist theories of both the Apristas and the conservatives went untested, however, because this provision of the constitution was never implemented. Similarly, articles creating elected municipal and departmental councils would be ignored during most of the next three decades.

The Constitution of 1933 again proclaimed Roman Catholicism the religion of the state, but it expressly recognized the right to practice other faiths. The new charter included safeguards for other basic freedoms, however the president was empowered to suspend many of these during periods of emergency. Article 53 outlawed "political parties of international organization." Under this provision, APRA's participation in elections would be restricted for several decades, and the Peruvian Communist party has always been kept off the national ballot. The charter repeated most of the "social guarantees" of the 1920 constitution as well as the state's mandate to intervene in economic matters. In addition, the document encouraged the government to extend free public education to the secondary school and university levels and vaguely endorsed the idea that workers should share in the profits of their employers. At the conclusion of its main task, the drafting of the new constitution, the national assembly proclaimed that it would continue to serve as the republic's provisional legislature until the end of the presidential term in 1936.

President Sánchez Cerro reviewed 25,000 new army conscripts at the Santa Beatriz Racetrack near Lima on April 30, 1933. As his open automobile began to depart, a young Aprista stalwart named Abelardo Mendoza Leiva rushed from the crowd and shot the "Hero of Arequipa," who died a short time later. The forty-three-year-old soldier's personal estate consisted of some clothing and inexpensive jewelry, a few military decorations, and thirty dollars in cash. He bequeathed his nation a dangerous international confrontation and a bitter legacy of civil strife.

⋘ The Failure of Moderation, 1933–1939

The Constitution of 1933, unfortunately, had not provided for a vice-president. In the event of a vacancy in the office of president, the charter required congress to elect a successor within three days. A few hours after the assassination of Sánchez Cerro a nearly unanimous vote of the national assembly gave Gen. Oscar R. Benavides, the former provisional president, a mandate to complete the term of the fallen chief of state. Benavides, who recently had served as ambassador to Great Britain, returned to Peru only a few days earlier to assume command of Peru's army during the conflict with Colombia. Ironically, the general legally was ineligible to succeed Sánchez Cerro. The constitution barred active members of the armed forces from election to the presidency. The political realities of the moment, however, were far more compelling than the dictates of the twelve-day-old charter. As commander of the army, de facto power already rested with the officer. But more importantly, the general was a respected national figure with strong ties to prominent Civilista families and he had governed the country creditably during a similar crisis in 1914. The strong hand of a soldier seemed desirable to prepare for war with Colombia, bring peace at home, and resolve Peru's economic problems.

In a brief inaugural address, the new president asserted that a desire to serve his country rather than personal ambition prompted his acceptance of the executive burden. He pledged to establish a nonpartisan government of "peace and concord" to heal the republic's civic wounds. His first task, however, was to defuse the explosive conflict over Leticia. Shortly after his installation Benavides received a congratulatory message from his personal friend Alfonso López, who soon would be elected president of Colombia. Benavides invited López to visit Lima and by the end of May, the two leaders had reached an agreement for a cease-fire supervised by the League of Nations. Diplomats from both nations quickly began discussions of their conflict at Rio de Janeiro. Militarily and economically unprepared for war, Benavides was willing to return Leticia to Colombia if Bogotá would make a few face-saving concessions to Peru. Unfortunately, many of the president's countrymen did not share his attitude. The Leticia issue deeply divided the congress, the cabinet, the armed forces, and the nation as a whole.

In May 1934, after a year of difficult negotiations, Peru and Colombia signed a Protocol of Peace, Friendship, and Cooperation. Peru recognized the inviolability of the Salomón Lozano Treaty and agreed to withdraw from Leticia. Colombia promised to discuss with Peru, at a later date, unresolved disputes between the two nations in the Amazon region. With considerable difficulty Benavides secured his congress's ratification of the protocol in November 1934, but Colombia did not ratify the agreement until ten months later. Within the context of this diplomatic imbroglio the president charted his course through the hazardous waters of Peru's domestic politics.

Benavides's moderate approach to his country's internal and external conflicts quickly brought him the hostility of powerful right-wing and nationalist groups. A whispering campaign accused him of complicity in the assassination of Sánchez Cerro. Although apparently unfounded, these rumors gained credence from the new president's words and actions. At a press conference in Washington on his way home from the London embassy, the general had criticized the government's harsh repression of APRA. Minutes after the death of Sánchez Cerro, Benavides dispatched troops to take control of the Lima penitentiary. This action thwarted the plans of Interior Minister Luis A. Flores to execute Haya de la Torre, whom he branded the "intellectual author" of the presidential assassination. Benavides retained Sánchez Cerro's cabinet until he had secured his position. Then, at the end of June 1933, he installed a new, conciliatory panel of ministers under the premiership of Jorge Prado y Ugarteche. A few days later, Prado announced that elections would be scheduled to fill the vacant congressional seats formerly held by APRA. Benavides proclaimed a partial political amnesty on August 10, and Premier Prado personally released Haya de la Torre and many other Apristas from prison.

The administration's foreign and domestic policies were denounced by Sánchez Cerro's Revolutionary Union, which became increasingly fascist in its orientation. Now under the leadership of Luis A. Flores, whose admiration for Mussolini extended to wearing black-shirted uniforms, the party organized several antigovernment demonstrations during the next three years. The president also was criticized by Lima's leading newspaper, *El Comercio*. Owned by the nationalistic and virulently anti-APRA Miró Quesada family, this journal reflected the opinion of Peru's most conservative elements. Benavides hoped for Aprista support in defending his regime from these attacks, but the party gave him little aid and no comfort. In the face of the administration's announced policy of "peace and concord," APRA proclaimed an attitude of "serenity and vigilance." While the party endorsed the negotiations with Colombia, it asserted that the president merely had adopted the "old Aprista policy" of Indoamerican harmony. APRA also refused to praise Benavides's efforts to heal the nation's political wounds. They complained that he had not completely dismantled the dictatorship of his predecessor and that the regime's concessions had been forced by the overwhelming power of public opinion in favor of APRA.

Benavides held three personal meetings with Haya de la Torre. In these talks and in the Aprista press the party presented several demands to the government. APRA called for the revocation of the Emergency Law, the full restoration of civil liberties, the reopening of San Marcos University, and pardons for all Apristas convicted of crimes by military courts. Most importantly, the party demanded the reinstallation of the twenty-three Apristas who had been ousted from the legislature in 1932. Following that, APRA wanted congressional elections to replace the entire national assembly whose mandate, the party claimed, had expired with the promulgation of the new constitution. Benavides refused to overturn the Emergency Law, but he promised not to abuse its powers. He agreed to open the university in the near future. A general amnesty for all Apristas sentenced by courts martial was politically impossible. Included in their number were military personnel involved in various rebellions, persons convicted of participation in the "Trujillo Massacre," and the two men condemned for the first, unsuccessful attempt to assassinate Sánchez Cerro. Benavides would not reseat the Aprista assemblymen. However, he pledged prompt elections to fill these vacancies. But as the regime came under attack from both the right and left, the president became increasingly reluctant to see an influx of either Apristas or Flores's fascists into congress. Stressing the need to maintain domestic calm until a settlement of the Leticia dispute, Benavides repeatedly postponed the promised congressional elections. These frustrating delays intensified partisan passions and cast doubts upon the sincerity of the president's promises.

Late in the Sánchez Cerro dictatorship some of APRA's enemies boasted that the party had been destroyed as a viable political force. They were mistaken. In 1934, Haya claimed that the PAP had doubled its membership during the previous three years and that it numbered 600,000 persons of all ages and both sexes. Although Víctor Raúl probably exaggerated, the movement certainly had not declined in strength. Furthermore, adversity seemed to increase party loyalty and intensify the devotion of the rank and file to their leaders. Imprisonment gave an aura of revolutionary sainthood to the image of Haya de la Torre. Persecution in and out of jail greatly enhanced the stature of his lieutenants. Soon after Benavides's amnesty proclamation, APRA began to rebuild its organization. The party's newspapers reappeared, Aprista headquarters opened throughout the country, and propaganda committees of skilled orators toured the nation addressing rallies in every important town.

The APRA that emerged from the "catacombs" of the Sánchez Cerro period bewildered contemporary observers. One sympathetic North American described it as a political "cocktail" of communism, fascism, and democracy. In this strange mixture the strong flavor of the two totalitarian ingredients frequently made the last element barely discernible. Haya and other party leaders scoffed at traditional political democracy, the system under which Peru's humble classes long had been oppressed. They proclaimed the goal of achieving "functional democracy," in which some individual liberties would be sacrificed to bring greater economic and social justice for all citizens. The party demanded a return to constitutional government, but denounced the 1933 charter as an outmoded "Civilista" imposition. APRA spoke vaguely of establishing a "school state," with the government politically educating the electorate.

To prepare for new hostilities with the government, APRA was restructured by Ramiro Prialé, the Huancayo schoolteacher who became the party's master strategist. The new, highly touted "vertical organization" concentrated power in the hands of Haya de la Torre and his closest associates who comprised the party's National Executive Committee (CEN). Secretary General Haya was assisted by a cabinet that was both the PAP's directing apparatus and a shadow Peruvian government. Several of the nineteen "national secretaries" headed "ministries" that formulated programs to be instituted when the Apristas gained power. Other members of the CEN directed internal party affairs, including recruitment, finance, and even defense. APRA's soldiers, called *"búfalos"* in honor of the leader of the Trujillo uprising, were organized into "defense brigades."

Key members of the CEN formed the party's "political bureau," the unit that planned major strategy. In times of crisis, members of this inner circle became the Aprista "action committee." Other leaders would hold the post of secretary-general in later years, while Víctor Raúl—as "Supreme Chief"—became party prophet, standing above the regular organization. Intermediate strata within the party structure, including departmental committees, received their instructions from the secretary-general. At the lowest level, individual Apristas were grouped into "cells," with each member assigned a specific function. The party stressed obedience to superiors. Disciplinary committees judged and punished errant members. In the early years of the movement, APRA did not grant full membership until fledgling Apristas had proven their loyalty. A major test of the latter was the payment of party dues to support the APRA bureaucracy and the movement's activities.

The PAP brought the masses into Peru's political life, articulated their desires and provided important social services for them. But to traditional liberals APRA seemed an enemy of the pluralism associated with an open, democratic society. The lives of its members revolved around party activities. Aprista headquarters, the "houses of the people," were social centers, complete with recreational facilities and lunchrooms that dispensed low-cost meals. Apristas patronized businesses owned by other party members, whom they addressed as "companion." In addition to the regular party organization, APRA had its González Prada Popular Universities, a feminist wing, and its own labor unions grouped in an Aprista labor federation, the Central Sindical de Trabajadores Peruanos. Most controversial was APRA's youth arm, the Federación Aprista Juvenil (FAJ). Formally inaugurated in January 1934, it sought to develop boys aged twelve to twenty-one into future party leaders. The "Fajistas," as its members were called, swore allegiance to APRA and followed a rigorous personal code that stressed healthful living, mental discipline, and puritanical morality. Party leaders described the FAJ as a harmless social organization. But critics were alarmed by the sight of marching files of Fajistas, sometimes in uniform, and their slogan: "APRA Youth, Prepare Yourself for Action and not for Pleasure!"

From the totalitarian parties of Europe, whose rise Haya had witnessed during his exile, APRA borrowed the heavy use of symbolism, the emotional rallies, and the cult of the leader—very effective devices for a mass-based party in a country with a low level of literacy. A typical Aprista extravaganza bore a frightening resemblance to Hitler's festivals of mass madness taking place at that time in Nuremberg. A torchlight parade would convey the Apristas to a large open area, where bonfires illuminated APRA flags, seals, posters bearing party slogans and larger-than-life pictures of Víctor Raúl. Songs from the party's own songbook—including the Aprista anthem and the "March of the Búfalos"—would warm the crowd. Perhaps the faithful might recite the "Credo Aprista," a bizarre rewording of the Apostles Creed. Then, the party leaders would arrive, flanked by armed *búfalos*. They would greet the multitude with the APRA salute—a raised left arm with the palm of the hand facing outward—and the party's principal slogan: "Only APRA Will Save Peru!" Then the speeches would begin.

The rejuvenated APRA made its public debut on November 12, 1933, three months after Benavides's amnesty proclamation. Some 40,000 zealots packed the Lima bullfight arena to hear Haya and a half-dozen other leaders. The spectacle thoroughly frightened the nation's conservatives, who demanded that the government check the party's activities. By the end of the month, Benavides had replaced Jorge Prado's conciliatory cabinet with a ministry under José de la Riva Agüero. A descendant of Peru's first president and a leading intellectual, the new premier had been a liberal in his youth. By 1933, however, Riva Agüero had shifted to the far right. He called himself the "Marquis of Aulestia," his family's old Spanish title of nobility. Within a few years he would become Peru's foremost admirer of the Italian and Spanish fascist regimes. The sensitive Ministry of Government, charged with maintaining internal security, was entrusted to Commandant Alberto Henroid, an outspoken, rabid anti-Aprista. APRA viewed the selection of the new cabinet as a declaration of war against the party, an interpretation shared by the country's moderate politicians. Within hours after the installation of the new ministry, four democratic, centrist parties announced the formation of the National Alliance. Under the leadership of Amadeo de Piérola, a son of Nicolás de Piérola, the new coalition pledged to work for the restoration of APRA's twenty-three congressmen to the national assembly.

APRA's fears concerning the Riva Agüero ministry were well-founded. Within three months the new administration had closed the party's headquarters, newspapers, and popular universities. Police harassed Aprista leaders, and the party accused the government of an attempt to assassinate Haya de la Torre. For its part, APRA prodded the regime, hoping to provoke an embarrassing overreaction. The party encouraged a plethora of labor disputes and attempted to organize a general strike in January 1934. Defying bans on demonstrations, APRA staged boisterous celebrations of Víctor Raúl's birthday in February that resulted in street clashes with the police. The government charged the party with complicity in a military plot to overthrow the regime and arrest 400 Apristas. As relations between APRA and the administration steadily deteriorated, Benavides continued to promise that congressional elections would be held in June.

A preliminary agreement on the Leticia dispute in early May 1934 brought an abrupt shift in Benavides's domestic political strategy. An almost total surrender of Peru's demands, the protocol with Colombia was denounced by Riva Agüero. It seemed certain to encounter strong opposition in congress and throughout the nation. On April 30, the Revolutionary Union had staged a huge rally to commemorate the death of Sánchez Cerro, and its orators demanded that the government follow the hard line of the "martyred president." Benavides now determined that he would need Aprista cooperation to enlist popular support for the Leticia settlement and that his rightist cabinet would have to be replaced. The president cleverly forced the resignation of Riva Agüero and appointed a new, moderate ministry under Premier Alberto Rey de Castro. Through Amadeo de Piérola, Benavides approached Haya de la Torre and the two men reached a modus vivendi. The government would allow APRA to reopen its headquarters and newspapers, but this new freedom was to be exercised only to build popular support for the agreement with Colombia. On May 24, the regime publicly announced the signing of the protocol in Rio de Janeiro and a gigantic, "nonpartisan" peace parade was organized to demonstrate the nation's gratitude to the president. But as Benavides reviewed the throng from the balcony of his official residence, the marchers unfurled Aprista banners, demonstrating that the parade was largely an APRA affair.

Benavides's new essay at "peace and concord" quickly ended. Citing the need for tranquillity until the ratification of the protocol with Colombia, the regime postponed the congressional election until September. In July, the government demanded that APRA cancel its plans to commemorate the Trujillo rebellion. The party refused and on the seventh of the month, police disrupted Aprista rallies throughout the republic. A new round of strikes by Aprista unions began. In mid-August, the administration again closed the party's headquarters and newspapers. As the September election date approached, congress had not yet approved the Leticia settlement and the government delayed the balloting until November. Speaking for the National Alliance, Amadeo de Piérola warned that another postponement would bring a revolution. Late in October Haya de la Torre narrowly escaped death when an airplane he had chartered to fly him to Trujillo mysteriously malfunctioned. APRA charged that the government had sabotaged the craft. The national assembly ratified the protocol on November 2. But the preceding day the regime had announced the sixth postponement of the election—ostensibly to purge 4,000 fraudulent registrations (about 1 percent of the total) from the voting lists.

The predicted Aprista revolt began on November 26, 1934, under the direction of retired army colonel César E. Pardo, the party's secretary of defense. Informers apparently betrayed the movement in Lima, where police foiled an attempt to capture a military arsenal. A daring plan by a few Apristas to storm the presidential palace and seize Benavides also failed. In the Sierra, government forces turned back a vigorous assault on Huancayo, but Aprista units captured Ayacucho and Huancavelica after brisk battles with civil guard and army personnel. By the end of the month, however, the government had regained control over both cities. Attacks on Cuzco in early December, and Cajamarca a month later also failed and troops quashed general strikes in several southern cities. The regime arrested nearly 1,000 Apristas, including many top leaders, but Haya de la Torre eluded capture. During the next decade, the Supreme Chief lived clandestinely, addressing manifestos and intraparty correspondence from "Incahuasi" (the "house of the Inca"), the name given to Víctor Raúl's refuge of the moment.

Shortly after the suppression of the rebellion, Benavides secured new legislation that greatly increased his emergency powers and provided harsher penalties for political agitators and persons bearing arms against the government. The regime outlawed both the Aprista and Communist labor federations. Still, Benavides hoped to avoid the severity of the Sánchez Cerro dictatorship. Within a month after the uprising, all imprisoned Apristas had been exiled. Events of mid-1935, however, produced a hardening of the president's policy toward the party. On May 15, a twenty-year-old Fajista named Carlos Steer assassinated Antonio Miró Quesada, the publisher of *El Comercio,* and his wife. This act outraged the nation and Benavides gained the implacable hatred of the Miró Quesada family and their newspaper after Steer received a twenty-five-year prison term rather than the death penalty. In September, Aprista leaders Carlos Manuel Cox and Pedro Muñiz, men who had been deported to Chile the previous January, secretly returned to Peru to assume vacant posts within APRA's National Executive Committee. Police captured them two weeks later. Both men and most Apristas arrested after that date remained in prison until the end of the Benavides regime.

Benavides's mandate was to expire in December 1936, at the end of Sánchez Cerro's legal term. The president declared that he had no desire to remain in office beyond that time and scheduled elections for October 11 to choose a new chief executive and a parliament to replace the national assembly. Benavides hoped to organize a broad coalition, as he had done in 1915, to support Jorge Prado, the premier of the "peace and concord" cabinet of 1933. A moderate conservative of democratic views, Prado seemed capable of winning a majority vote from the center of the political spectrum. But the Prado family, one of Peru's wealthiest, long had been active in politics and had acquired many enemies. Furthermore, every Peruvian schoolboy had learned about Mariano Ignacio Prado, Jorge's father, the president who abandoned the republic during the War of the Pacific. Luis A. Flores, of the Revolutionary Union, and Manuel Vicente Villarán, a distinguished San Marcos professor and conservative politician, challenged the official candidate. Neither of these men, however, seemed likely to overcome the multiparty National Front created to elect Prado. To embarrass the regime, APRA had its friends submit nominating petitions for its presidential and vice-presidential candidates—Haya de la Torre and Col. César E. Pardo. As expected, the National Election Board disqualified the Aprista slate, citing Article 53 of the constitution which outlawed "international parties." Less than a month before the election APRA approached Luis Antonio Eguiguren, the highly respected leader of the moderately leftist Social Democratic party, and persuaded him to abandon Prado's National Front. Eguiguren hastily organized his own Democratic Front coalition and APRA instructed its members to vote for him.

Peruvians cast their ballots without incident on October 11, 1936. With three candidates appealing to the political right and only one man representing the left, the outcome of the contest was predictable. After two weeks of counting votes, Eguiguren apparently held a plurality sufficient for election, perhaps 40 percent of the ballots. Flores, Prado, and Villarán—in that order—divided the remaining 60 percent of the votes. Probably under orders from the president, the National Election Board suspended its canvass before the count had been completed. The tribunal then disqualified Eguiguren and the congressional candidates of his coalition on the grounds that they had received the votes of the proscribed APRA party. Benavides installed a new, all-military cabinet and called an emergency session of the national assembly, whose term was about to expire. The president presented that body with his formula for resolving the crisis: 1) the nullification of the entire election; 2) the extension of Benavides's term for an additional three years; and 3) the amplification of the President's powers, enabling him to legislate by decree. For ten days congressional orators, including Eguiguren, debated the executive's plan. The Revolutionary Union's delegation attempted to initiate impeachment proceedings against Benavides. Had the election been allowed to stand after the disqualification of Eguiguren, the black-shirted Flores might have become president. In mid-November, however, the national assembly assented to Benavides's wishes and dissolved itself.

Benavides's coup received little effective opposition outside of congress. A general strike proved to be unsuccessful because of the failure of Aprista and Communist unions to cooperate. The government broke the movement in three days. APRA almost succeeded in purchasing arms for a revolution from the leftist Bolivian government of Col. David Toro, but Benavides skillfully blocked this transaction. With APRA already repressed, the government moved to quiet its enemies on the right. Soon after the nullification of the election, frustrated candidate Flores publicly accused Benavides of complicity in the murder of Sánchez Cerro. The regime promptly arrested and deported the leader of the Revolutionary Union. On December 8, 1936, the day on which Peru was to have inaugurated a new president, Benavides issued a message to the nation. As in 1933, he denied any personal ambition in retaining power and asserted that he had acted only to save the country from anarchy. He recounted the achievements of his first three years in power and promised the country three more years of "peace, order and work." Armed with dictatorial powers, the general faced no major threat to his rule until the last year of his extended term.

In addition to the war with Colombia and Peru's internal strife, Benavides faced a third major crisis when he assumed power in 1933—the Great Depression. The worldwide economic collapse that began in late 1929 probably produced less human suffering in Peru than in the more developed countries of Europe and North America. The greatest portion of Peru's population still gained its livelihood from subsistence agriculture, artisan industry, and other archaic, relatively insulated activities. The already-austere lives of these people continued much as they had before. Conversely, the smaller, modern sector of the economy experienced extreme hardship because of the crucial role of foreign trade. Commodities which Peru sold abroad suffered from both declining prices and constricting markets as old trading partners raised tariffs and other barriers to protect domestic producers. Between 1929 and the trough of the depression in 1932, the value of Peru's exports fell from 335 million to less than 180 million *soles*. The government's income, highly dependent upon taxes related to international commerce, dropped by 45 percent during this same period. The labor force in the modern sector of the Peruvian economy, as in the more advanced countries, suffered considerably from unemployment and falling wages.

The three governments that held power for significant periods during the chaotic interval between the overthrow of Leguía and the death of Sánchez Cerro adopted several measures to alleviate the nation's economic distress. Generally in accord with the "sound money" principles of pre-Keynesian economics, these efforts had only limited success in combating the depression. Economic recovery after 1933 came primarily because of an upturn in the world market for Peru's exports. Nevertheless, some of the programs instituted by the two Sánchez Cerro administrations and the intervening regime of David Samánez Ocampo prevented the total collapse of some industries, improved the institutional framework for the republic's financial system, and initiated a trend toward economic nationalism.

The first Sánchez Cerro government hired Dr. Edwin Kemmerer, the Princeton University professor who advised many Latin American regimes during the twenties and thirties, to reform Peru's fiscal and monetary systems. Most of the recommendations of his report, issued in April 1931, were adopted by the Samánez Ocampo administration. The government slashed its budget to keep spending within the limits of the state's meager revenues. Peru suspended payment on its foreign debt of 180 million dollars, an obligation that would have consumed a third of the treasury's income. The government twice devalued the republic's currency by a total of 50 percent. These actions stabilized the *sol* and made Peru's exports more attractive to overseas buyers. A new Central Reserve Bank received broad powers to control the supply of money. The state reorganized the Agricultural Bank and authorized the establishment of an Industrial Bank to provide public funds for manufacturers. New legislation more closely regulated private banking.

To give immediate relief to the nation's planters, Sánchez Cerro declared a moratorium on foreclosures of mortgaged agricultural properties. The treasury also forgave delinquent taxes owed by farmers and small-scale miners and provided tax incentives for new investment in mining. Manufacturers received little new tariff protection. However, the government sought to encourage the consumption of their products through the establishment of a permanent industrial exposition in Lima and a requirement that all items made in the country be labeled "Peruvian Industry." Sánchez Cerro rescinded or renegotiated many of the contracts and concessions granted by Leguía and ordered the Peruvian Corporation to lower the rates on some of its railroad lines. To combat unemployment the government suspended immigration for two years and undertook a modest poor-relief program in Lima-Callao. New laws required that 80 percent of all jobs and an equal share of the total payrolls of most businesses in the country be reserved for Peruvian nationals and restricted certain occupations to native-born Peruvians.

The shadow cast by the impending war with Colombia made the early months of 1933 Peru's darkest hour of the depression. Benavides's prompt reversal of Sánchez Cerro's belligerent policy restored the confidence of investors. An almost simultaneous improvement in the world demand for Peru's products injected new life into the ailing economy, and the three-year decline in the nation's export earnings was reversed in late 1933. Within three more years, Peru's overseas sales would exceed pre-depression levels. In 1939, Benavides's last year in office, the value of the republic's exports surpassed the figures for 1929 by almost 35 percent. The small manufacturing sector of the economy grew rapidly during the 1930s. The country's scant export earnings in the first half of the decade greatly reduced its capacity to import finished goods and encouraged domestic entrepreneurs to fill the void. Although Benavides did not adopt protective tariffs, quotas restricted imports of Japanese textiles, the most important competitors of Peru's largest industry. In 1936, the new Industrial Bank began providing state capital for the development of manufacturing.

Benavides's budgets reflected the improvement in Peru's economy. Government spending nearly doubled during his tenure. Although state expenditures did not reach the levels of the flush years of the Oncenio, the general did not rely on "champagne loans" as did Leguía. His many significant projects were funded almost entirely from the treasury's regular revenues, including receipts from a new graduated income tax. Asserting that an adequate transportation system was the "axis of national progress," Benavides launched a major highway program. Other presidents had made similar statements, but none were so successful as the general in translating words into solid accomplishments. The efforts of the Leguía regime in this area had been substantial. However, most of the roads constructed during the Oncenio were disjointed projects, utilizing local resources to build rather crude links between isolated villages and regional market towns. Benavides's "Plan Vial" provided for a national system of modern highways to unite Peru's major regions. Realizing that ambitious undertakings in Peru often end abruptly with the tenure of their sponsors, the general strove to complete most of the work before he left office. He also created a separate highway fund with new gasoline taxes to encourage the continuance of the program by his successors. During its first four years, the regime constructed or substantially upgraded 1,200 miles of road. In his remaining two years, Benavides employed an average of nearly 40,000 workers per month to build an additional 2,500 miles of highway while renovating 4,000 miles of existing arteries.

Benavides expressed justifiable pride in his road-building

accomplishments at the end of his term. A Central Highway, paralleling the Central Railway, extended from Lima westward to La Oroya, in the Sierra. From that point, one branch extended toward the south to provide the first good links with Huancayo, Ayacucho, Abancay, Cuzco, and Puno. At the end of 1939, only one bridge then under construction and a few short sections of road were needed to complete this important artery. To the north of the junction at La Oroya, the Central Highway climbed to Cerro de Pasco and then descended to Huánuco, at the gateway to the Montaña. From there the road entered the Amazon Basin itself, cutting through jungle-covered, outlying ranges of the Andes and then pushing across rain-forested plains toward Pucallpa. When the bulldozers reached this Ucayali River port in 1941, Peru had its first dependable route to the eastern lowlands and a "transoceanic" highway: Large seagoing vessels from the Atlantic reach Pucallpa by way of the Amazon River.

A second major artery constructed by the Benavides administration, the 2,000-mile Peruvian section of the Pan American Highway, provided the first link between all the cities hugging the coast from Ecuador to Chile. From this trunk, east-west "penetration roads" connected the ports of Chimbote, Huacho, and Pisco with their Sierra hinterlands. In the far north, where the coastal region broadens to its maximum extent, all of the major urban centers were interconnected. At Camaná, on the south coast, a branch of the Pan American Highway climbed the Andes to Arequipa, Puno, and the Bolivian frontier. Prior to 1933, only roads in the Lima-Callao district and a few other cities were paved. Benavides provided asphalt surfacing for almost one-third of the Pan American Highway and the entire 125-mile portion of the Central Highway between the capital and La Oroya. Although the Benavides administration concentrated on the construction of roads to serve Peru's internal commerce, his government did not neglect the needs of the nation's foreign trade. The major port improvements at Callao begun by Leguía were completed in 1934. The Benavides regime also initiated work on the new port of Matarani, a deep-water facility that eventually would supplant Mollendo as the principal outlet of southern Peru.

Utilizing the resources of the reorganized Agricultural Bank, the Benavides administration continued to expand the republic's irrigation systems. About 130,000 acres of land were watered, while facilities serving 275,000 acres were improved. The state

ECUADOR

COLOMBIA

R. Napo

R. Putumayo

Túmbez

Iquitos

R. Amazon

S. José de
Saramuro

Nauta

Talara

Paita

Piura

Bayovar

R. Marañón

Moyobamba

Yurimaguas

Chachapoyas

BRAZIL

Chiclayo

Etén

Pacasmayo

Cajamarca

R. Marañón

R. Huallaga

R. Ucayali

Trujillo

Salaverry

Pucallpa

Chimbote

Yungay

Huaraz

Tingo
María

Huánuco

Cerro de Pasco

Huacho

La Oroya

Callao

Lima

Huancayo

Puerto
Maldonado

Madre de Dios

Departmental Capitals •
Other Cities •
Major Roads ———
Railroads ++++++++
Trans-Andean Pipeline ----
Head of Steam Navigation ⚓

Huancavelica

Ayacucho

Cuzco

Pisco

Abancay

BOLIVIA

Ica

Nazca

San Juan

Marcona

Juliaca

Titicaca

Puno

Peru:
Transportation

Camaná

Matarani

Mollendo

Arequipa

Moquegua

Toquepala

Ilo

Tacna

Arica

CHILE

0 50 100 150 200 250
Miles

also undertook studies to irrigate an additional 400,000 acres. Benavides's irrigation program included the first significant efforts to supply water for the parched croplands of the Sierra. To increase further the area available for agriculture, the regime established the Bureau of Montaña Lands and Colonization. This agency began the first practical projects to settle farmers in Peru's vast Amazonian territory, most notably around the state's colonization center at Tingo María, on the road to Pucallpa.

The Benavides administration provided modern water systems for twenty-five provincial towns, finally fulfilling the promises made by Leguía. The regime also constructed several government buildings, including a new official residence for Peru's chiefs of state. Appalled by the armed forces' lack of preparedness during the confrontation with Colombia, the general began a major program to improve the effectiveness of the nation's military establishment. He instituted a modern, efficient command system, purchased large quantities of equipment—including two destroyers and many aircraft—and built several barracks and airfields. The success of this undertaking would be demonstrated dramatically in 1941.

In his last official message to the nation Benavides recounted his efforts to bring social justice to Peru. He attributed the impetus for programs in education, labor, and welfare to his "humanitarian sentiments" and his "love for the working classes." Perhaps. But a desire to undermine the appeal of APRA and forestall a bloody social upheaval also were compelling motives. On this occasion, as throughout his regime, the general reminded the people that he had brought change "by evolution and not by revolution." Some of the government's programs were designed to replace services previously provided by the outlawed Apristas. The party's lunchrooms, for example, were supplanted by state-subsidized Popular Restaurants—three in Lima and one each in Callao and La Oroya—where workers could purchase wholesome, inexpensive meals. In Lima, the restaurants served an average of 6,000 persons each day. Government night schools for workers had less success in replacing APRA's popular universities.

The Benavides government made the first large-scale effort to meet the growing need for low-income housing in the Lima area. The administration constructed five workers' "neighborhoods" with a total of 732 units providing shelter for about 4,000 persons. During his last year in office, the general established the Superintendancy of Social Well-being. This agency regulated the prices of foodstuffs and other necessities and attempted to ensure adequate supplies of these items. It also set minimum wages for various industries and enforced new health and safety standards. Finally, this office was charged with investigating monopolies and business practices detrimental to the general welfare and reporting these offenses to the proper officials.

The regime's most notable achievement on behalf of the workers was the Compulsory Social Security Law. Submitted to congress in late 1935, it required six months of negotiations by a mixed executive-legislative committee to make the bill acceptable to the lawmakers. Benavides signed the measure in August 1936, two months before the national election. Funded by deductions of 1.5 percent from the wages of workers, a 3.5 percent payroll tax on employers, and a 1 percent contribution from the state, the program permitted those insured to retire at age sixty with pensions of 40 to 60 percent of their income. The plan also provided sickness, disability, maternity, and death benefits as well as free medical care in government hospitals and clinics. The system had a number of flaws. In spite of its title, the program was not "compulsory," excluding the greatest portion of Peru's labor force. Persons with substantial incomes were not covered and, more importantly, their salaries were not taxed to support the fund. The plan insured only "regular" workers and excluded all wage earners living outside of narrowly defined "industrial zones." The law made no provision for unemployment compensation, and the government was unable to supply sufficient medical facilities to treat adequately all of the insured. Nevertheless, the program was a beginning, a foundation upon which a more satisfactory system could be built. An estimated 200,000 workers were enrolled under the law by 1939.

The Benavides government created the Ministry of Public Health, Labor, and Social Foresight to supervise the social security system along with other labor and welfare programs. In addition, the Bureau of Public Instruction was separated from the Ministry of Justice and elevated to full ministerial status. The government constructed 900 schools between 1933 and 1939. While the number of pupils attending public secondary schools increased by 50 percent, enrollments in the primary grades grew at little more than half that rate. After a three-year suspension of classes, San Marcos University resumed operations in 1935.

Peru's foremost public institution of higher education had only 560 students, about the number at the beginning of the century.

As the year 1939 began, many Peruvians speculated that Benavides would not relinquish power as scheduled and would extend his already-amplified term. If the general harbored this ambition, events of February certainly dissuaded him. On the eighteenth of the month, the president departed from Callao on a three-day cruise with the navy. Among those bidding him bon voyage was the minister of government, Gen. Antonio Rodríguez. As soon as the executive's ship left port, Rodríguez returned to Lima, took control of the presidential palace, and proclaimed himself provisional chief of state. A rank opportunist, the usurper had brought both APRA and the Revolutionary Union, mortal enemies, into the conspiracy. Commanders of military units in Lima had either joined the movement or promised their neutrality, and important garrisons in other parts of the country were expected to approve the coup within a few hours. The Benavides regime appeared lost. But in the morning of February 19, Maj. Luis Rizo Patrón, the leader of the civil guard unit assigned to protect the president, confronted Rodríguez in the courtyard of the presidential residence and killed him with a burst from his submachine gun. Although Benavides had been saved, his confidence was shaken badly. One month later, the general announced that he had no intention of remaining in power and that elections would be held in October.

Before leaving office Benavides wanted to alter the constitution for the benefit of his successors. Under the 1933 charter, however, amendments required the approval of a majority of both chambers of parliament during two regular sessions. No legislature existed in 1939, so the president submitted ten "constitutional reforms" to the public in an extralegal national plebiscite. The proposed changes increased the power of the executive at the expense of the legislature. Parliament would be stripped of its authority to institute or abolish taxes independent of the president and suffer a reduction in its mandate to investigate the activities of the executive branch. Other provisions extended the chief executive's term to six years, broadened his decree powers, and permitted the president to veto legislation. A three-fifths vote of congress would be required to override the objections of the executive. The plebiscite, held on June 18, was compulsory and carefully supervised by the government to insure the desired result. The regime reported that almost 90 percent of the voters favored the reforms.

In preparation for the October 22 national election, Benavides endorsed the candidacy of Manuel Prado y Ugarteche. This fifty-year-old banker was the brother of Jorge Prado, the official candidate in the aborted election of 1936. The administration's choice received support from a dozen parties of moderate to conservative hues. José Quesada, an independent conservative, organized the Patriotic Front to challenge Prado, but gained significant endorsements only from the outlawed and badly divided Revolutionary Union. Both candidates approached APRA, which again was proscribed from entering either the presidential or the congressional races. Although most Apristas probably preferred the more moderate Prado, the party's high command contemplated an endorsement of Quesada to force one final embarrassment on the Benavides regime—the imposition of Prado on the country. This strategy produced considerable dissension within the party, however, and APRA finally ordered its members to abstain from voting. Nevertheless, a group of renegade Apristas defied this directive and published clandestine issues of *La Tribuna* endorsing the official candidate. The election returns indicate that many members of the party heeded this advice. With Quesada's newspaper closed by the government and Benavides's officials supervising the contest, Prado was declared the winner with 262,000 votes to 76,000 for his opponent.

Benavides transferred the presidential sash to Manuel Prado on December 8, 1939. The ceremony was clouded by the summary execution a week earlier of two Apristas convicted by court martial of murdering the army commandant at Trujillo, Lt. Col. Remigio Morales Bermúdez.* The departing chief executive declared that he always had acted in the best interests of the nation, that he was at peace with his conscience, and that he confidently awaited the judgement of history. In the waning hours of his rule the general, noted for his personal honesty and that of his administration, halted a subscription drive by the chamber of commerce to purchase for him the house he had rented in Callao. The new congress, however, rewarded him with a promotion to the military rank of marshal.

*Haya de la Torre vigorously denied Aprista responsibility for the crime, claiming that the commandant was a "friend" of the party.

History has been kinder to Benavides than were his contemporaries, who attacked him unmercifully from both the right and left. Obese and beady-eyed, the soldier cut a ridiculous figure in his medal-covered dress uniforms with their plumed hats. Mimics delighted in mocking his often self-serving statements delivered with the affected intonations of an opera soloist. In recent years, however, even some Apristas who earlier branded the general a tyrant of the Sánchez Cerro mold admitted that Benavides brought Peru through its gravest crisis since the War of the Pacific. His administration posted notable achievements in international, economic, and social affairs. Several parties share responsibility for the continued political strife of the period. Although APRA's actions in the early months of the regime were within the limits of constitutional tolerance for a democratic state in tranquil times, the party's politics of confrontation were grave provocations in the explosive Peruvian atmosphere of 1933 and 1934. The far right, especially Luis Flores and the Revolutionary Union, as well as the intemperate journalism of *El Comercio* contributed significantly to the climate of hostility. The difficulty of the political decisions that he faced evokes sympathy for Benavides. But the abandonment of his apparently sincere policy of "peace and concord" in November 1933 and his refusal to permit the often-promised elections the following year sparked the open conflagration with APRA. At worst, the strongman was guilty of a cavalier exploitation of the party; at best, he demonstrated a pardonable degree of political ineptitude.

8

Détente and Debacle

[1939–1948]

✒ Domestic Truce and Foreign Wars, 1939–1945

MANUEL PRADO Y UGARTECHE HELD POWER at a most propitious moment: the years of his presidency coincided with those of the Second World War. To be sure, the economic dislocations produced by this struggle caused some hardships for Peru, but the nation's wealthy elite—of which Prado was a conspicuous member—generally supported his regime. At the time of his inauguration many observers predicted that the new civilian government would be unable to rein the revolutionaries and soon would be supplanted by another military dictatorship. Fortunately for Prado, the Peruvian left muted its attacks on the government and imperialist capitalism to concentrate on the defeat of a more dangerous enemy, imperialist fascism. The Revolutionary Union and other elements of the country's own radical right dwindled as Peru supported the Allied cause against the Axis powers. The suave, banker-president proved to be a skilled political manipulator, playing right against left, Communist against Aprista. Not only did he complete his term, but in doing so presided over Peru's return to democratic government. Congress and the courts resumed their constitutional functions. Laws of the the previous decade restricting civil liberties remained on the books. Their enforcement, however, became increasingly lax.

The formal proscription of APRA continued, but the harsh persecution ended. Prado deported several long-imprisoned Apristas and quietly informed others that they might return home. Haya de la Torre remained in hiding, for the most part undisturbed by the government, which apparently knew the location of "Incahuasi." *La Tribuna* reappeared and the police showed little interest in finding the newspaper's "underground" plant. APRA held "clandestine" conventions in 1942 and 1944, assembling more than 300 delegates in Lima for several days. Prado gained great popularity and considerable personal satisfaction from a brief war with Ecuador. He became the nation's first successful wartime leader in eighty years and repaired the damage done to the family name by the actions of his father, President Mariano Ignacio Prado, during the War of the Pacific.

The conflict between Peru and Ecuador concerned their common boundary for almost its entire length and possession of some 170,000 square miles of territory. In the west the two nations contested ownership of 500 square miles fronting on the Pacific in Peru's Department of Túmbez. Farther to the east, in the Andes, the neighbors vied for control of Jaén, a district of about 3,000 square miles in the upper reaches of the Marañón River. Finally, an estimated 167,000 square miles were at stake in the remote jungles of the Amazon Basin. Rooted in the ambiguities of colonial boundaries, the controversy dated from the early years of independence. In the ensuing century the two republics and third parties made several unsuccessful attempts to resolve the problem through direct negotiations and arbitration. In its legal complexities, the dispute was second to none in Latin America. Both nations, of course, produced mountains of old documents that "irrefutably proved" their rights to the territory. Independent scholars are divided on the issue of de jure ownership, but they generally concur that Peru had the best de facto title. Túmbez and Jaén had been administered from Lima since the initiation of the republic. Their residents considered themselves Peruvians. Peru's effective national control over most of the disputed territory in the Amazon Basin began only in the second half of the nineteenth century. Nevertheless, with greater economic and population resources and easier communications with the trans-Andean zone, Peru firmly established its presence in this region almost to the complete exclusion of Ecuador. Peru's occupation of most of the disputed land was an important element of its legal case in the efforts to resolve the problem through diplomacy and a decisive strategic advantage when the test of arms occurred.

In 1924 Peru agreed to hold talks with Ecuador to settle some of their boundary problems through direct negotiations and determine which remaining issues would be submitted to arbitration by the president of the United States. Because of the Tacna-Arica controversy with Chile and, later, the Leticia conflict with Colombia, Peru delayed discussions with Ecuador until 1936, when delegations from the two countries met in Washington. Evidently confident that it had the strongest de jure position, Peru insisted upon a "judicial arbitration" in which the decision would be based entirely on the legal merits of the case. Ecuador called for an "equitable settlement," one giving the arbiter broad latitude for compromise. After two years of wrangling, the negotiations ended in a chorus of diplomatic invective. Border skirmishes between the Andean neighbors during the next three years brought renewed attempts by the United States, Argentina, and Brazil to arrange a peaceful settlement. Ecuador, by far the weaker of the contestants, encouraged third-party intervention. Peru discouraged these efforts. Although the details of Peruvian diplomacy cannot be given with certainty, a preponderance of evidence indicates that Lima was determined to end the dispute on its own terms, even at the cost of war. If Peru had decided to resolve the question militarily, the nation chose an ideal time to do so. By mid-1941, the rapidly widening global conflict preoccupied the United States and Ecuador's Latin American neighbors. Quito could expect little effective aid from the outside.

An undeclared, general war erupted at several points along the frontier on July 5, 1941. Both sides claimed that the other fired the first shot. The struggle was a most uneven contest. Ecuador's unstable government had made only minimal preparations for hostilities. Many of the nation's 3,000 defenders, concentrated primarily in the west, were raw recruits who lacked sufficient ammunition for the poor arms they possessed. Ecuador's communications with the front were very inadequate. The republic had no air forces engaged in the fight and the Ecuadorian navy wisely kept its one effective warship out of the combat zone. Peru's armed forces had made great progress since their embarrassing state of unpreparedness eight years earlier during the Leticia crisis. Lima put 15,000 men into the field against its adversary. Under the overall command of Gen. Eloy

G. Ureta, the well-disciplined and organized Peruvian army was equipped with modern weapons. A new network of paved roads facilitated the movement of supplies to Peru's forward positions. Twenty-five military aircraft and a naval force of two cruisers, two destroyers, and a pair of submarines supported the army in the north.

The Peruvians quickly overran Ecuadorian defenses along the western front. The key victory came at the battle of Zarumilla on July 24, under the direction of Lt. Col. Manuel A. Odría. In the next week the army occupied almost all of Ecuador's southernmost maritime province, El Oro. Meanwhile, the navy blockaded Ecuador's south coast and shelled Puerto Bolívar, the principal port in the region. The air force bombed and strafed transport facilities and dropped propaganda leaflets on urban centers. In the eastern theater, river gunboats and amphibious airplanes based at Iquitos carried Peruvian troops to isolated Ecuadorian garrisons. Weakened by aerial bombardment, these positions soon fell to the attackers. All effective resistance by Ecuador had ceased when the United States, Argentina, and Brazil arranged a truce, scheduled to begin on July 31. In the final hours before the cease-fire Peru launched a blitzkrieg to capture strategic objectives and sufficient Ecuadorian territory to impose its boundary demands on Quito. For the first time in the western hemisphere airborne troops were employed in war. Transport planes landed Peruvian infantry on roads and other flat surfaces and dropped paratroops into Puerto Bolívar. Motorized units quickly secured points taken from the air. The army was within striking distance of Guayaquil, Ecuador's largest city and major port, when the truce began. In violation of the cease-fire agreement, the fighting continued for another two weeks in the Amazon, until Peru had taken several more Ecuadorian posts.

The Peruvian army remained in control of all territory captured in the war when the Third Meeting of Ministers of Foreign Affairs of the American Republics assembled at Rio de Janeiro in mid-January 1942. Called because of the entrance of the United States into the world war the previous month, Washington wanted to secure a resolution requiring all American nations to sever diplomatic relations with Germany, Italy, and Japan. To further enhance the image of inter-American solidarity, it was hoped that a peace could be arranged between Peru and Ecuador. Chile now joined the three original mediators—the

United States, Argentina, and Brazil—in new efforts to achieve this goal. More concerned with obtaining a quick settlement than with the actual terms of the agreement, the mediators, with Brazil playing the most prominent role, pressed Ecuador to accept a boundary based upon the military situation. To a lesser degree the four peacemakers urged Peru to drop its more extreme territorial demands. On the last day of the conference, January 29, Peru and Ecuador signed a Protocol of Peace, Friendship, and Boundaries. Peru gained slightly more territory than it had held prior to the war. Ecuador relinquished little land that it previously had occupied. Nevertheless, the defeated nation renounced its claims to about 80,000 square miles in the Amazon Basin, an area almost as large as Ecuador's effective national territory. In addition, the 5,000 square miles that Quito actually surrendered to the conqueror included the more navigable, lower portions of its Amazonian tributaries. The loss of this land hindered Ecuador's access to the mighty river. Peru's parliament unanimously ratified the agreement, while the Ecuadorian legislature approved it by only a plurality.

Ecuador soon regretted its decision to sign the Rio Protocol, denouncing it as an "illegal imposition." The Ecuadorians discovered a minor error in the document's geographical description of the boundary. Utilizing this, Quito prevented the final demarcation of the frontier in 1945, thus keeping the issue alive. Ecuador then brought its dispute with Peru before the Organization of American States and the United Nations. President José María Velasco Ibarra declared the Rio agreement null and void in 1960. Official Ecuadorian maps continued to depict Quito's sovereignty over the territory won by Peru and government publications bore the inscription: "Ecuador Was, Is and Shall Be an Amazonian Nation." Peru, meanwhile, insisted that the Rio Protocol had irrevocably settled the boundary controversy. But a series of frontier incidents after 1945 testified to the contrary.

The administration of General Benavides had been cool in its relations with the United States while showing an affinity for the fascist regimes of Franco's Spain and, especially, Mussolini's Italy, where the president had served as military attaché. Washington, therefore, welcomed the election of the Francophile and pro-Allied Prado. In accordance with a resolution adopted at the Rio Conference, Peru broke diplomatic relations with the Axis countries in January 1942. Although Lima did not declare war until three years later, Peru strongly supported the Allied war effort. Prado permitted Washington to build an airbase at Talara for the defense of the Panama Canal, and the Peruvian navy cooperated with United States naval forces in patrolling the zone south of that vital waterway. Like other nations of the hemisphere, Peru seized the assets of Axis nationals within its boundaries. The government, however, reserved special treatment for citizens and residents of Japanese extraction. Within hours after the attack on Pearl Harbor the Prado administration, with the assistance of United States officials, arrested about 10 percent of the 17,000 Japanese in the country. These people were sent to the United States for internment along with Japanese residents of the North American republic. Peru denied readmittance to most of these expatriates after the war.

Peru contributed most significantly to the Allied cause by providing the United States with strategic commodities. Government agencies of the two nations cooperated to increase production of industrial metals and other raw materials. A new Mining Bank, like those previously established for agriculture and manufacturing, supplied state funds for the expansion of this industry. Another public entity, the Peruvian Amazon Corporation, increased the output of rubber, quinine, and insecticide base in the Montaña. The United States provided Peru with loans, technical assistance, and large quantities of war materiel under the Lend-Lease program.

The world war caused severe economic problems for Peru. Unlike some other Latin American republics, its foreign trade did not prosper. In dollar terms the value of the nation's exports for the 1941–45 period grew by only 5 percent over the total for the previous half decade, while its imports rose by 28 percent in value. Rising prices rather than a greater volume of purchases from abroad accounted for the latter increase. Peru, in fact, could not obtain some of the products it traditionally imported and domestic industry attempted to fill this void. The nation's manufacturers increased their share of the national income from less than 15 to more than 26 percent between 1942 and 1947. Still, Peruvians suffered from shortages of finished goods, foodstuffs, and other items. In spite of a cumbersome system of government controls, the cost of living climbed 80 percent during the Prado presidency. The regime itself contributed to the inflationary spiral. With its revenue from taxes on foreign trade sharply reduced in the early years of the conflict, the treasury relied on loans and large emissions of paper currency to pay its bills. As a result, the supply of money increased nearly threefold. Although the national budget more than doubled during the Prado years, most of this increase was lost because of the declining value of the *sol.*

Peru's national census of 1940, the first in more than sixty years, underscored several problems among its seven million citizens that competed for the treasury's meager resources. Almost 46 percent of the population were Indians, by definition a class living on the margin of society. About 35 percent of the people did not understand Spanish. Sixty-two percent of all Peruvians gained their livelihood from agriculture and stockraising. Slightly more than one citizen in three lived in a town as large as 2,000 persons. The census verified the visible shift of the population from the highlands to zones with greater economic opportunity on both flanks of the Andes. Since the last enumeration in 1876, the Sierra's share of the republic's inhabitants had declined from 73 to 65 percent. The Montaña had enlarged its portion from less than 4 to more than 8 percent of the total. Notwithstanding the loss of Tarapacá and Arica to Chile, the coast reported an increase from 23 to 26.5 percent of the population. Much of the growth in the latter region was concentrated in the Lima-Callao metropolitan area, which counted 700,000 residents.

Although primary education had been free and compulsory for more than three decades, the census indicated that 60 percent of the population was illiterate. Moreover, the quality of literacy was poor among the minority that could read and write. For every 1,000 Peruvians over five years of age, only 247 had attended primary school, 31 of these advanced to the secondary level, 3 received training at a vocational school, and 6 persons entered a university. The nation seemed to be making little progress in the battle against illiteracy. Only one-third of Peru's children were enrolled in classes in 1940, and boys were 50 percent more likely to attend school than girls. A great disparity in education existed between the coastal region and the highlands. While almost two-thirds of the people on the coast were literate, barely one Serrano in four could read and write. Three-quarters of the children in Lima-Callao went to school. In five predominantly Indian departments of the southern highlands, less than 15 percent of the children attended classes.

Shocked by the magnitude of the illiteracy problem, the Prado administration made its most notable endeavors in this

area. An increase of 338 percent in the budget for the Ministry of
Education permitted the construction of 4,000 primary schools,
an average of almost two per day during the six-year Prado
regime. The government opened 27 normal schools to provide
teachers for these new classrooms. The administration made a
remarkable effort to bring instruction to the Indians of the
Sierra. Seventeen rural normal schools were established to train
a special corps of teachers for this task. Most of the students were
of Indian background and received state scholarships. In addition, the regime opened 35 improvement centers which conducted workshops to train experienced teachers in new methods
for instructing Indian children. To reach the nation's two million
unlettered adults—mainly Indians—the government launched a
national literacy campaign in 1944, a year after the publication of
the census. Almost 12,000 teachers, civil servants, and private
citizens joined "acculturation brigades" that staffed 7,200 literacy centers. More than 360,000 illiterates enrolled in the program during its first year. Forty percent of these persons learned
to read while many others acquired a knowledge of spoken
Spanish.

Except for education, Manuel Prado initiated few new programs for Peru's social development. Instead, his regime continued and improved the work of its predecessor in this field.
The number of persons included in the social security system
expanded considerably, and the government made notable progress in supplying the medical facilities required by the plan. The
administration completed several housing projects for workers,
opened three more Popular Restaurants, and significantly expanded a free-lunch program for the public schools. Similarly,
parliament drafted little new labor legislation, but Prado removed many of the restrictions placed upon worker organizations in the 1930s. With greater freedom, Peru's trade unions
enjoyed a new period of growth.

To compensate for increased expenditures by the military
and the ministries of education and labor, Prado cut the public
works budget by almost 50 percent. Nevertheless, the regime
completed the new port at Matarani and, at a reduced rate,
continued Benavides's programs in irrigation, highways, and
municipal improvements. With the construction of 2,400 miles
of new roads, the administration nearly finished the basic network planned by its predecessor. Efforts to settle the Montaña
intensified. The government built penetration roads, coloniza-

tion centers, and agricultural experiment stations for tropical crops.

The Prado administration did begin one ambitious, long-term project—a plan to transform the Santa River Valley, 250 miles north of Lima, into a major industrial zone. With a multipurpose program similar to that of the Tennessee Valley Authority in the United States, the government created the Santa Corporation to undertake this task. The heart of the endeavor was the construction of a large dam at the Cañón del Pato that would provide water to irrigate 250,000 acres of land and supply 125,000 kilowatts of electric power for industry. The plan designated the sleepy little port of Chimbote, at the mouth of the Río Santa, to become the "Pittsburgh of Peru." The finest natural harbor in the nation, Chimbote Bay received modern port facilities while the city itself benefited from new water, sewer, and street systems and the eradication of malaria in the district. The Santa River Valley project called for the establishment of several factories in the area, including one to produce badly needed cement. But most significantly, the administration selected Chimbote as the site for Peru's first steel mill. High-grade iron ore was to be supplied from state-owned deposits at Marcona, on the western rim of the southern Sierra. The nearby port of San Juan would be modernized to accommodate large ore-carrying vessels. Although electric power was to heat the furnaces of the government-owned steel mill, anthracite beds in the upper Santa River Valley would provide the coal needed as a raw material in the steel-making process. Hampered by a shortage of machinery, the Santa Corporation had completed only one-third of the hydroelectric project when Prado left office. The agency employed more than 6,000 men per month on other phases of the program, however, and these progressed rapidly.

Peru suffered another seizure of its chronic, preelection jitters during the final year of Prado's term. Although the president announced his intention to transfer power peacefully to a freely elected successor, many Peruvians doubted the sincerity of the incumbent. Prominent among the skeptics was a group of Arequipa natives who, in late 1944, organized the Frente Democrático Nacional (National Democratic Front). The FDN labored to mobilize public opinion in support of honest elections and provide a vehicle for a concensus candidate who would restore unrestricted democracy. While the *frente* searched for a suitable standard-bearer, former President Oscar Benavides re-

signed his ambassadorship to Argentina and returned home to
test his political popularity. In a manifesto to the nation, the
marshal apologized for the authoritarian excesses of his administration. This conciliatory gesture, however, did not mollify his
old enemies on the left. Meanwhile, influential conservatives
endorsed Marshal Eloy G. Ureta, the hero of the war with
Ecuador, who became the nominee of the Revolutionary Union.
Anxious to maintain peace with the armed forces, Prado initially
appeared to favor Ureta. But behind the scenes the president
joined with Benavides to find a centrist candidate for the FDN.

Dr. José Luis Bustamante i Rivero, Peru's ambassador to
Bolivia, agreed to accept the presidential nomination of the
FDN in March 1945, with the condition that APRA be legalized
and invited to join the *frente*. Manuel Prado was reluctant to meet
this demand. But Benavides, who had been instrumental in
persuading Bustamante to enter the race, now arranged a meeting with Haya de la Torre in which the two old adversaries made
a gentlemen's agreement: neither the Aprista leader nor the
soldier would become candidates and both men would endorse
Bustamante. Benavides also promised to use his influence with
Prado to lift the ban on APRA, enabling the party to present
congressional candidates on the FDN slate. In mid-May, the
National Election Board granted legal recognition to APRA,
which had adopted the name Partido del Pueblo (People's party)
in deference to the constitutional proscription of "international"
parties. On June 10, 1945, Peru enjoyed its first relatively free
and fair election in almost a decade and a half. Bustamante i
Rivero won about 300,000 votes, twice the number polled by
Ureta. Marshal Benavides died less than a month later. Perhaps
the sixty-nine-year-old soldier-statesman believed that he finally
had brought his nation a regime of peace and concord.

The willingness of Benavides and Prado to cooperate with
APRA arose, in considerable measure, from a moderation of the
party's ideology during the world war. Haya de la Torre charac-
teristically denied that his *alianza* had altered its fundamental
principles or abandoned its goals. According to the supreme
pontiff of Aprismo, the party's enemies had repented and
adopted norms of conduct more acceptable to APRA. The party
merely responded by extending its forgiveness to these sinners.
At the same time, "Aprista realism" required the use of new
tactics to achieve victory in a changed political environment.

The first and most notable alteration occurred in APRA's

posture toward the United States. As the shadows of Hitler's Third Reich darkened Europe, Haya warned of the dangers of Nazi expansionism. He urged Latin America to join the United States in the fight against fascism when the war began. For the Aprista leader the imperialism of the totalitarian Nazis, supported by their racist doctrines, posed a far greater threat to the mixed peoples of Indoamerica than did the imperialism of the western democracies. Furthermore, the United States—heretofore the major threat to Latin America—had changed radically since the inauguration of Franklin D. Roosevelt in 1933.

In a simplistic interpretation of North American politics, Haya described the Republican party as the bulwark of domestic conservatism and the driving force of Yankee imperialism. Roosevelt's Democratic party, by contrast, was a spiritual sister of APRA. Haya called the New Deal a "revolutionary" program to bring social justice to North American workers, much like Aprismo's grand design for Indoamerica. The Good Neighbor Policy, the inter-American corollary of the New Deal, coincided with the *alianza*'s goal of Indoamerican unity to combat imperialism. The United States had renounced its policy of unilateral intervention in the Americas for a program of multilateral cooperation in the defense of the continent. The State Department, according to Víctor Raúl, no longer gave unstinting support to Yankee investors in their disputes with Latin American governments. Washington, for its part, cultivated the friendship of APRA. While the United States embassy in Lima was notably sympathetic to the party and urged President Prado to relax the campaign against the organization, several Aprista leaders enjoyed red-carpet treatment during visits to the United States under State Department auspices.

APRA officially modified its Maximum Program for Indoamerica at the party's 1942 convention. The delegates deleted the word "Yankee" from the *alianza*'s call for "action against Yankee imperialism," and the Apristas now proposed to "inter-Americanize" rather than "internationalize" the Panama Canal. At the same meeting, the party formally adopted Haya's twelve-point "Plan for the Affirmation of Democracy in the Americas," which he had issued in May 1941. This document, which APRA claims inspired many subsequent developments in inter-American relations, stated that the world was confronted by a choice between two conflicting political systems—

totalitarianism and democracy. The New World nations, asserted Víctor Raúl, were fundamentally democratic in their origins and aspirations. Freedom in the Americas was indivisible and the death of liberty in any nation of the continent threatened democracy in the others. Therefore, all American republics needed to unite in combating dictatorship at home as well as in the Old World.

Haya's plan envisioned the convening of an inter-American congress to compile the liberties guaranteed by the several American constitutions into a common, internationally binding code for the entire hemisphere. Thereafter, an inter-American assembly, with each national delegation democratically selected to represent its country, would enforce the laws of the Americas through collective intervention. Víctor Raúl also proposed the formation of an inter-American economic congress. Utilizing plans drafted by national economic congresses, this international body would formulate a program of hemispheric cooperation to improve the material well-being of all Americans. This new relationship would include a customs union, a development bank, and a common currency backed by gold, silver, and primary products. The adoption of this plan, declared Haya, would replace the "tutorial Pan Americanism" dominated by Washington with "democratic inter-Americanism without empire."

APRA's rapid rapprochement with the United States accompanied the initiation of a more gradual transformation of its official attitude about capitalism and foreign investment. The party's new friendship with Washington, of course, required some softening of its antagonism toward "Yankee economic imperialism." However, the shifts in APRA's policy were more than mere tactical adjustments. The *alianza*'s attacks on capitalism and its advocacy of a socialistic "anti-imperialist state" had broad appeal among the working and middle classes during the dark days of the Great Depression. But contrary to the diagnoses of many Marxists, the old economic order arose from its deathbed more vigorous than before. Meanwhile, new social legislation and more enlightened attitudes toward labor, especially by foreign investors, brought increased rewards to the workers. The new enterprises spawned by overseas and domestic capital often became strongholds of Aprista labor unions and important sources of employment for the party's middle-class following. Under these new circumstances, a radical change in the economic system seemed less desirable. While Víctor Raúl minimized the dangers of Yankee imperialism, he began to emphasize the positive aspects of foreign investment which—according to his last-stage, first-stage theory—would hasten the development of capitalism and, therefore, the revolution of the proletariat.

As APRA enlisted in the crusade against totalitarianism, the party sought to develop a more democratic image for itself. There was less public mention of "functional democracy," with its fascist overtones, and greater stress placed upon liberal democracy. Allied propaganda during this second "war to make the world safe for democracy" appeared to have a significant effect on Latin America. The demise of several dictatorships in the mid-1940s seemingly presaged a new democratic era. In Peru, APRA's legalization and participation in the FDN coalition conformed to this trend. Many observers predicted that Haya de la Torre would become president in the election scheduled for 1951. The Partido del Pueblo might "capture power" by ballots rather than bullets. In accord with its new, pacific stance, APRA did not fill the post of defense minister within its National Executive Committee in 1944, and the party officially dropped this office from its secretariat four years later. APRA also softened the anticlericalism of its early days. In a 1941 manifesto, several party leaders declared that "the majority of Peruvians are Apristas in politics and Catholics in religion." Other party spokesmen, including Haya, simply stopped talking about those portions of their program that offended the Church.

To meet the inevitable charges that APRA had radically altered its fundamental principles, Haya refined his "historic-space-time" theory, and obscure exposition of historical relativism that he had unveiled in 1935. Purporting to combine Marxism with Einstein's theory of relativity and Arnold Toynbee's "challenge and response" interpretation of universal history, Víctor Raúl continually elaborated the concept until he elevated it to the status of a full-blown philosophy. Basically, Haya argued that all history and philosophies of history were relative. He criticized orthodox Marxism and all other universal theories that postulated historical laws based upon the experience of Europe or other single regions. The pattern of historical evolution varied with different cultural areas and their individual stages of socioeconomic development. Furthermore, Haya asserted that Marx had contradicted the fundamental idea of his philosophy—the constant, dialectic clash of forces—by envision-

233

ing an ultimate, static condition: classless, stateless socialism. Víctor Raúl declared that Marxism itself was subject to the same inevitable process of change as it confronted new developments in science and philosophy. The "historic-space-time" theory allowed Haya maximum tactical and ideological flexibility while retaining Aprismo's appeal as a "scientific" system.

Deadlocked Democracy, 1945–1948

President José Luis Bustamante i Rivero was a distinguished legal scholar from Arequipa. Fifty-one years old at the time of his inauguration in July 1945, he came from a staunchly Catholic, middle-class family. The new chief executive desired to guide his nation along a course of decentralized, democratic government, ending the cycle of domination by the self-serving coastal "oligarchy" and the extraconstitutional regimes of military strongmen. Bustamante feared that Peru was approaching a cataclysmic revolution. Unless social justice was brought to the masses by peaceful means, it would come on the crest of a violent upheaval that would smash indiscriminately all of the nation's institutions and traditions. Although he shared APRA's professed concern for the poor and endorsed some of he party's specific proposals, the new president was apprehensive about the *alianza*'s anticlerical origins, Marxist ideology, revolutionary élan, and authoritarian overtones. Nevertheless, Bustamante believed that APRA had provided a necessary vehicle for mass participation in politics and that it would triumph at the polls in the near future. He hoped to have a moderating influence on the party, so that it would act more responsibly when it gained power in its own right.

Bustamante proudly asserted that he was not a "politician." He previously had held public office, but never as a member of a formal party, nor at the sacrifice of principle to partisan or even personal concern. He had helped Sánchez Cerro draft the manifesto for the Arequipa revolution that toppled Leguía and served in the caudillo's first cabinet. Bustamante resigned, however, when the *cholo* colonel appeared to be fashioning a long-term dictatorship. Similarly, he had accepted the ambassadorship to Uruguay from Benavides. But after the annulment of the 1936 election, he refused to recognize the dictator's authority and gave up his post. Unfortunately, Peru required the leadership of a skillful, practical politician, a man willing to compromise to make the imperfect system work. Bustamante believed that he had to govern the country within the strict limits imposed by the constitution to restore respect for the rule of law. Excessively legalistic at first, he later probed the limits of constitutionality, exposing himself to charges of hypocrisy.

While the president desired to prepare APRA for the future exercise of power, the Partido del Pueblo assumed that it already had reached that objective. The party claimed that its votes had provided Bustamante's electoral landslide and that he should act as their agent in carrying out the Aprista program. Some of the party faithful envisioned Bustamante as a figurehead chief of state performing ceremonial functions, while Haya de la Torre ran the government as prime minister. The president acknowledged that APRA was the largest component of his FDN coalition, but he believed that non-Aprista and even anti-Aprista votes might have provided his margin of victory. In any event, Bustamante stated that the constitution's separation-of-powers principle required the executive to maintain his independence from both party and parliament. As Aprista Manuel Seoane described the situation, the party believed that it had elected Bustamante "captain of the team," but the president thought that he had been chosen to "referee the game."

Observers detected a coolness between the gregarious Haya and the reserved FDN presidential candidate at their first meeting prior to the election. Disputes over the composition of the coalition's congressional slate followed by a series of petty personal effronteries brought their relationship to the breaking point by inauguration day. Then, Bustamante surprised APRA by appointing Rafael Belaúnde to the premiership without consulting the party. A fellow native of Arequipa and a founder of the FDN, Belaúnde was a political moderate with a conciliatory attitude toward APRA. The party, however, distrusted the new prime minister, largely because his brother, the Catholic intellectual Víctor Andrés Belaúnde, had been an outspoken critic of the *alianza*. Bustamante did consult with Haya concerning the remaining cabinet postions. The president said that he wanted to entrust a half-dozen important portfolios to his personal followers, none of whom APRA considered friendly. Bustamante then offered to place Apristas in two politically non-sensitive ministries. Perhaps, as the president later explained, he had attempted to bargain with Víctor Raúl. Bustamante opened with a low bid of two posts, expecting eventually to relinquish about half of the eight civilian ministries to the Apristas. Haya, however, rejected this meager offer and abruptly terminated the discussion without making a counterproposal.

The Partido del Pueblo did not participate in Bustamante's initial cabinet, but it dominated parliament. In the senate the Aprista bloc held a small absolute majority. The party fell slightly short of this mark in the lower chamber. However, APRA frequently received the votes of several non-Aprista members of the FDN, including that of young Fernando Belaúnde Terry, the son of the prime minister. Furthermore, the party's rigid discipline gave APRA's "parliamentary cell" a single, unified voice on all major issues. Aprista congressmen caucused at party headquarters, where they also deposited signed but undated resignations with Haya de la Torre. If APRA could not institute its program from the executive branch, it would do so from the chambers of parliament.

Conflict between the president and the Aprista-dominated congress began on the first day of the legislative session, with the passage of a sweeping amnesty bill that Bustamante reluctantly signed. Although he did not object to the release of all political prisoners, the president disapproved of a provision restoring rank and command to military officers—primarily Apristas—who had been removed from the armed forces for revolutionary activities. The repeal that same day of the 1932 Emergency Law and other measures restricting civil liberties led to greater friction. With the end of press censorship, Peruvian journalism reverted to the jurisdiction of an 1822 law described as archaic by the Apristas. Long angered by the often distorted reporting and editorial attacks of conservative newspapers, APRA proposed a new Press Law that became the subject of intense partisan debate. It provided stiff penalties for libel, required that the name of the responsible editor appear on the masthead of newspapers, and that journals report the identity of their major stockholders, ostensibly to prevent foreign manipulation of public opinion. After the enactment of the law in December 1945, its opponents organized a protest rally at San Marcos University. Unfortunately, an even larger crowd of Apristas staged a counterdemonstration. A bloody riot erupted and concluded with an attack by the Apristas on the offices of *El Comercio* and *La Prensa*, Lima's most important conservative newspapers. APRA leaders denied responsibility for the violence, which they attributed to overzealous workers and students. The party's enemies, however, denounced the incident as organized terrorism perpetrated by the infamous *búfalos*.

An almost complete rupture existed in the relations between Bustamante and APRA by the end of 1945. From the files of its own secretariat, the party introduced an avalanche of legislation. The president denounced most of these measures as technically unsound, fiscally irresponsible, or sheer demagoguery. But he could do little to halt the Aprista program. Congress quickly nullified the illegal constitutional reforms secured by Benavides in 1939, including the presidential veto. Bustamante then employed a transitory provision of the constitution, of doubtful validity in 1945, permitting him to return bills to parliament with his "observations." This tactic only delayed promulgation of the laws by the president of the senate. Once enacted, the executive branch sometimes refused to implement the new statutes. Parliamentary committees frequently grilled cabinet members. A censure motion brought the resignation of the minister of agriculture after only two months in office. Aprista legislators demanded statistical data and other information from executive departments, while congressional commissions investigated several state agencies. Bustamante accused the Partido del Pueblo of partisan harassment. APRA maintained that it merely was performing its constitutional duties in a conscientious manner. As the struggle between APRA and the president intensified, most of the non-Aprista members of the FDN coalition joined with their colleagues on the right and the far left to fight the dominant party.

Prime Minister Belaúnde attempted to maintain political peace, but attacks from both the right and left brought his resignation in January 1946. However, a compromise between Bustamante and APRA now seemed to offer hope for the future. Julio Ernesto Portugal, a political moderate acceptable to the Partido del Pueblo, became the new premier and three Apristas were named to head the ministries of finance, development, and agriculture. APRA used these posts to strengthen its partisan position. Apristas replaced civil servants who refused to join the party. Members of APRA employed by other agencies organized party "cells" and followed orders issued from Aprista headquarters. Outside of government, party organizers intensified their activities. In bitter and sometimes bloody struggles with the Communists and Socialists, APRA gained control of the

237

labor movement. Under a new, liberalized University Statute the Aprista-led Peruvian Student Federation resumed its intense politicking. Luis Alberto Sánchez, APRA's foremost academician, was elected rector of San Marcos. The Peruvian Aprista Youth (JAP) replaced the old FAJ—Fajista sounded embarrassingly similar to *fascista*—and began a vigorous recruitment campaign in the secondary schools. Several high schools now experienced student strikes similar to those at the universities.

Bustamante accused the Aprista-controlled congress of infringing upon his powers as president. Parliament promoted high-ranking military officers who had not been nominated by the executive and closely scrutinized candidates favored by Bustamante. A similar jurisdictional dispute arose from an Aprista bill to create a national economic congress. The president said he favored the establishment of such an entity as a consultative body, but he charged that the measure supported by APRA would have illegally granted legislative and executive functions to this assembly. Another important conflict concerned municipal government. Although the Constitution of 1933 provided for the election of city officials, Peru's urban centers continued to be administered by presidential appointees. APRA and Bustamante, both avowed proponents of municipal autonomy, agreed that the constitution should be respected in this matter. However, a municipal election law did not exist. The Apristas suggested that while a new electoral code was being prepared, the cities should be governed by temporary juntas consisting of representatives elected by various civic, social, and economic organizations. The president denounced this plan as an Aprista power grab. But parliament prevailed and APRA-controlled juntas were elected in several municipalities.

The Partido del Pueblo and Bustamante did cooperate on one important project. In his 1946 annual message to congress, the president asked the legislators to prepare a contract permitting the International Petroleum Company to explore the Sechura Desert, on the north coast, for oil deposits. A complicated contract was drafted and a bitter debate in parliament and the national press followed. Opponents of APRA used the issue to embarrass the Partido del Pueblo. APRA's Socialist and Communist critics charged that the *alianza* had betrayed its anti-imperialist ideology. Conservatives accused the Apristas of a treasonous giveaway of the national patrimony, granting the IPC perpetual ownership of the surface and subsoil minerals of four northern departments. APRA retorted that the contract was in harmony with Aprismo's concept of the "anti-imperialist state," which welcomed foreign investment under strict government supervision. Both the Apristas and Bustamante insisted that the arrangment only allowed the company to explore the region for a reasonable period of time and that the exploitation of any petroleum discovered would require separate contracts. The government might negotiate concessions with the IPC, other private firms, or enter the petroleum business itself through a newly created state oil agency. A clever parliamentary maneuver by opponents of the plan prevented its approval in the 1946 legislative session. Whatever the merits of the Sechura Contract, it greatly intensified the level of partisan bitterness in Peru and produced considerable dissension within APRA itself.

In the evening of January 7, 1947, two assailants driving a green Buick assassinated forty-five-year old Francisco Graña Garland. Peru had witnessed a rash of political beatings, bombings, and murders in recent months. Although some of this violence had been directed against APRA, most of the victims were enemies of the party. Both sides accused their opponents of terrorism. But the death of Francisco Graña caused a national furor far surpassing that produced by previous incidents. The socially prominent and personally popular Graña was director of *La Prensa,* the conservative newspaper that had led the campaign against the Sechura Contract. Remembering the assassination of *El Comercio*'s Antonio Miró Quesada by an Aprista gunman a dozen years earlier, the public immediately directed its outrage at APRA. The party protested its innocence and *La Tribuna,* the Aprista newspaper, offered a large reward for the apprehension of the murderers.

In the middle of this political storm, Bustamante secured the resignations of the three Aprista cabinet ministers, an act that heightened public suspicion of the party's complicity in the Graña affair. The new ministry included five military officers. The president entrusted the key Ministry of Government, which controlled the police, to APRA-hating Gen. Manuel A. Odría. Apristas complained that the investigators seemed determined to lay responsibility for the murder at the doorstep of their party. To protect himself from charges of persecution, Bustamante hired a respected Canadian detective and placed him in charge of the Graña investigation. Eventually, two Apristas—a member of the party's congressional delegation and an employee of the

239

agriculture ministry—were charged with the crime. APRA accused the police of employing torture, illegal drugs, and incompetent witnesses to fabricate a tenuous case against the suspects. While the judicial proceedings moved at a glacial pace, partisan hatreds continued to deepen.

Prior to the beginning of the 1947 legislative session, APRA's congressional opponents on the right and left devised a plan to block the enactment of the Aprista program. The bylaws of the senate required a quorum of two-thirds for the constitutionally prescribed election of officers. Although APRA held a majority in the upper house, it lacked the quorum necessary to organize that body. The senate's anti-Aprista minority, calling itself the Parliamentary Union, boycotted the opening of congress on July 28, and continued to absent itself. The chamber of deputies could not function legally unless the senate was in session. Under the constitution, the president was empowered to issue provisional decree-laws while the legislature was in recess. APRA charged that Bustamante had conspired with the striking senators to obtain dictatorial powers. The president certainly enjoyed the respite from the Aprista legislative onslaught, but qualms of constitutional conscience at first restricted his use of decree powers to the most urgent needs of the government. Meanwhile, Bustamante's efforts to end the congressional boycott brought attacks against him from both APRA and its enemies. The parliamentary strike effectively halted legislative progress in Peru, leaving in abeyance the Sechura Contract, a municipal election law, and other important measures.

The Bustamante-APRA government had registered some achievements in the preceding two years. However, partisan turmoil and economic problems frustrated the optimistic predictions made at the time of the regime's inauguration. The administration continued to open primary schools at the rapid rate set by Manuel Prado. Lima acquired a giant soccer stadium and a new National Library building. The government created a National Tourism Corporation that constructed several hotels throughout the country. The republic's medical facilities were expanded considerably, with emphasis placed on maternity clinics. But after a decade and a half of Aprista promises to attack vigorously the nation's fundamental problems, the efforts of its congressional bloc disappointed many Peruvians. APRA did not sponsor comprehensive programs for agrarian reform, labor, or the country's Indians. The party's piecemeal legislative proposals in these areas often had the appearance of cynical political demagoguery. One highly touted achievement, the "Yanacona Law" regulating farm tenancy, was so complicated that it could not be enforced.

The Peruvian economy experienced great difficulty readjusting to peacetime conditions. After a sharp though brief upturn in exports at the end of the world war, the republic's international commerce and the economy in general stagnated. Per capita income actually declined. The complicated wartime controls on foreign exchange, imposed to hold down prices and establish priorities for scarce imports, continued. This system taxed exporters, subsidized importers, and presented tantalizing opportunities for graft to the officials that administered the program. In spite of these controls inflation mounted rapidly, reaching 30 percent in 1947. Price ceilings on certain staples produced shortages and gave impetus to a flourishing black market. Debate concerning economic policy contributed to the political strife of the period.

With parliament inoperative after July, 1947, Peru's partisan struggle intensified in the streets. APRA called a general strike in August to protest the senate boycott. Bustamante responded by declaring martial law and postponing special congressional elections scheduled for the next month. The general strike failed, but a wave of walkouts stalled many important industries and public services. The president employed the army to operate the struck Central Railroad. Marches protesting food shortages and high prices in Lima and Cerro de Pasco developed into bloody riots. In the latter city, the provincial governor was killed in the violence. Hundreds of lesser incidents, magnified by the nation's highly partisan press, thoroughly poisoned the civic atmosphere.

In February 1948, Bustamante announced that he had uncovered an Aprista plot to overthrow the government. He condemned the party in a hard-hitting radio address and added three more military officers to his cabinet. A few days later, the regime ousted the APRA-dominated municipal juntas and replaced them with city officials appointed from Lima. In mid-June, six weeks before the scheduled start of the 1948 legislative session, Bustamante's military cabinet urged him to outlaw APRA. The government then could purge the party's congressional delegation and end the parliamentary deadlock. The president, however, still hoped for a compromise solution to the problem. Led by General Odría, the cabinet resigned and Bustamante appointed a new civilian ministry. Three weeks later, ultraconservative Col. Alfonso Llosa issued a call for revolution from the important garrison at Juliaca, in the southern Sierra. But the nation's other military bases remained loyal and the regime survived its first major test.

The anti-Aprista senators again failed to appear for the opening session of parliament on July 28, 1948, and Peru's congressional strike entered its second year. Both Bustamante and APRA accused each other of foiling their attempts to reach a compromise with the leaders of the boycott. Peru's legalistic president now devised a formula of questionable legality to resolve the constitutional crisis. He announced that a special election would be held the following March for 107 representatives. These men would sit with the regular members of parliament in a constituent assembly which could assume legislative functions. At the same time, Bustamante urged the nation's anti-Apristas to unite in a coalition for the special election and friends of the president quickly organized the Popular Democratic Movement.

A badly divided Partido del Pueblo faced this challenge. Significant dissension within APRA, already apparent by the late 1930s, increased notably after 1945. While external critics charged the organization with undemocratic methods in parliament and the destruction of civil liberties in the streets, disenchanted Apristas decried the authoritarian control of the party by Haya de la Torre and the clique around him. Disaffected middle- and lower-level leaders accused the party chieftains of losing touch with the people. Left-wing Apristas deplored their *alianza*'s new friendship with the United States and winced at Haya's two visits there during Bustamante's term. With the pride of a small-town newspaper over the success of a native son, *La Tribuna* gave massive coverage to Víctor Raúl as he was courted by the State Department and feted by Wall Street moguls, the often-excoriated villains of his earlier speeches. The Aprista left also condemned the rightward shift in the party's economic program demonstrated by the Sechura Contract, the *alianza*'s unrevolutionary legislative proposals, and Haya's pronouncement of a new "Aprista maxim": "We do not want to take away the wealth of those who have it," Víctor Raúl declared in 1945, "but create wealth for those who do not have it." APRA's 1948 convention, furthermore, made another important change in the five-point Maximum Program for Indoamerica. The adjective "progressive" was inserted before its call for the "nationalization of land and industry."

Aprista militants disapproved the leadership's newly avowed goal of gaining power by nonviolent methods. Rather than a means to an end—revolution—APRA seemed to have become an end in itself. The heroic leaders of the 1930s now seemed addicted to expensive food and drink, silk suits, comfortable homes, and chauffeured limousines. Party stalwarts who had suffered persecution under Sánchez Cerro and Benavides chafed at the influx of new members, often former enemies, anxious to reap the fruits of electoral success. Haya, himself, seemed to have changed, a transformation that his more generous critics attributed to years of exile, imprisonment, and hiding. The image of the fighting revolutionary gave way to that of the detached philosopher. Worse, "the Old One," as they already called Víctor Raúl at age fifty, seemed almost senile at times. Indecisive one moment, he was rashly precipitious at others. Disgruntled Apristas charged that Haya followed the last advice given to him by members of his intimate circle—the "bureau of confusion," they called it.

By 1948, several prestigious party members had abandoned the movement with embarrassing public denunciations. Other disenchanted Apristas, however, remained within the organization, hoping to return the *alianza* to its old revolutionary course. With party morale and discipline in disarray, APRA's highly centralized "vertical organization" became a liability. The administrative machinery was too unwieldy for effective control, and the party's increasingly conservative National Executive Committee could not check the activities of militant subordinates. While Haya publicly ascribed the terrorism of the period to Communists and other groups attempting to discredit APRA, he privately suspected the party's old paramilitary units, which he began to disband. But as political tensions increased in the second half of 1947, and fear of a right-wing military coup mounted, Haya ordered the reorganization of APRA's fighting forces.

Party members with military expertise, including young Maj. Víctor Villanueva, were instructed to procure arms, establish liaison with Aprista sympathizers within the armed forces, and prepare contingency plans for a revolution. The men charged with this assignment met frustration at almost every turn. Party chieftains refused to provide sufficient funds for the movement.

Haya lacked confidence in APRA's own military resources and selected a non-Aprista general to head the uprising. Víctor Raúl could not decide whether to launch the revolution from Lima or Arequipa and he postponed the rebellion each time that political developments offered a ray of hope for a peaceful solution to the crisis. Haya departed for the United States in January 1948. He entrusted military affairs to a Defense Committee dominated by militants and political matters to an Action Committee composed of more conservative, old party confidants. Both groups claimed supreme authority to initiate the revolution. The Defense Committee wanted to strike and issued orders to commence operations on February 6. The Action Committee, however, refused to cooperate. The movement faltered and Bustamante began his crackdown on the party.

Haya de la Torre returned to Peru in May 1948 for the Aprista national convention. Again, he ordered preparations for a revolution. But in August, high-ranking army officers who had discovered the plot informed Víctor Raúl that the military was planning an institutional coup against Bustamante. The armed forces would topple the regime without bloodshed and promptly hold elections in which all political groups could participate. Haya agreed to delay the Aprista uprising and await the generals' revolt scheduled for late September. APRA's own plotters did not trust the military, however, and their suspicions increased when the generals postponed the coup until October 8. Placing old party warrior Col. César E. Pardo at the head of their movement, the young militants decided to strike on October 3, without the knowledge of Haya and the cautious politicians around him. The conspirators believed that these leaders would be forced to cooperate once the revolution started. Hesitation after that time would bring the destruction of the party.

At 2:00 A.M. on Sunday, October 3, Aprista cadres within the navy seized most of the fleet anchored at Callao and quickly stormed several military installations on shore. At the same time, *búfalos* captured the central telephone exchange in Lima. But suborned elements of the air force, army, and civil guard along with several of APRA's own paramilitary units failed to carry out their assignments. Former Secretary General Luis Heysen and Pedro Muñiz, the party's *ad hoc* minister of defense, noted suspicious movements of rank and file Apristas and then heard the naval guns at Callao. They frantically issued orders dispersing the other groups. Heysen and Muñiz later claimed to believe that the unauthorized revolt was the work of Communist or right-wing infiltrators, a plot to provoke government suppression of APRA.

Haya de la Torre apparently did not receive word of the revolt until two hours after it began. According to his account, he rushed to the leaders of the armed forces' conspiracy and begged them to launch their coup immediately. The officers, however, insisted that they were unable to strike at that time. They would have to take action against the Callao mutiny, but the generals promised to overthrow Bustamante forty-eight hours later. Víctor Raúl claimed that he considered calling the Aprista masses into the streets, but it was Sunday morning, a very bad time to mobilize the students and workers. Therefore, he agreed to wait for the generals to act. Two days passed. The institutional coup did not take place. In the meantime, tanks and air attacks pounded the Callao insurgents into submission and President Bustamante issued a decree outlawing APRA. Troops seized the party's headquarters, newspapers, and radio stations. Within a week more than 1,000 Aprista leaders had been arrested. APRA's top officials charged the authors of the revolt with treacherous insubordination. The perpetrators of the uprising and other militants accused Haya and his advisers of cowardice and treason. The party was in shambles.

For several months prior to the Callao mutiny, Gen. Manuel A. Odría, the former minister of government, had plotted with other officers and conservative civilians to oust Bustamante and crush APRA. Although the party no longer posed a threat, Odría decided to proceed with his plan. From Arequipa on October 27, he issued a manifesto that accused the president of being "soft on APRA" and failing to provide the leadership needed to meet the country's economic, social, and moral crisis. Odría's pronouncement quickly received endorsements from the commanders of several provincial garrisons. Bustamante defended his regime in a dramatic, nationwide radio broadcast and ordered his generals in Lima to suppress the movement. But they refused to take up arms against their brother officers. On October 29, 1948, José Luis Bustamante i Rivero was placed on board an airplane bound for Argentina.

From exile in Buenos Aires the deposed president explained his actions in a book entitled *Tres años de lucha por la democracia en el Perú* [Three years of struggle for democracy in Peru]. A few years later Luis Alberto Sánchez, APRA's court historian, used the same phrase to head the appropriate chapter of his *Haya de la*

Torre y el APRA. Several other works concerning the 1945–48 period have appeared, but most of these are even more polemical than the aforementioned, obviously biased accounts. No objective, thorough examination of the Bustamante administration has been published and many basic facts of this very complicated story remain obscured in a morass of secrecy, blind partisanship, distortion, and outright falsehood. Therefore, conclusions about this period must be tentative. It is apparent, however, that Bustamante, APRA, and especially the striking parliamentarians all contributed significantly to this debacle, which might better have been described as "three years of struggle *against* democracy."

9

Conservatives Triumphant

[1 9 4 8 – 1 9 6 2]

G EN. MANUEL A. ODRÍA DEMONSTRATED González
Prada's maxim that the presidency was the ultimate rank
in a successful military career. But Odría's rise to power was
quite different from the dishonorable path described by the old
Peruvian anarchist. He was a model scientific soldier in an army
striving for increased professionalism. Born in the central Sierra
town of Tarma in 1897, his parents named him to honor the
memory of Col. Manuel Odría, an uncle who had fallen before
Spanish guns during the battle of Callao a quarter century earlier.
Virtually inheriting his vocation, the young Odría entered the
military academy at Chorrillos in 1915 and graduated at the head
of his class four years later. Odría spent most of his career in the
classroom. After advanced study at the Superior War College, he
joined the Chorrillos faculty and then taught at the national war
college, where he later became superintendent. Lieutenant Colonel Odría's skillful direction of Peru's victory at the battle of
Zarumilla in 1941 made him a popular hero and earned him two
training tours at United States army schools. Five years later,
Brigadier General Odría became army chief of staff and then
minister of government in the Bustamante administration. In
1951, President Odría's compliant congress elevated him to the
rank of division general, a title he always used with great pride.

Odría's personal life as chief of state contrasted sharply with the spartan virtues of the soldier. Wealthy friends gave him a mansion in Lima's exclusive Monterrico district, and he indulged in a passion for fine clothes and expensive cars that was scandalously inconsistent with his rather modest salary as president. Official corruption became a salient feature of Odría's eight-year dictatorship, a period called the "Ochenio."

இ The Ochenio of Odría, 1948–1956

Immediately after assuming the provisional presidency on October 30, 1948, Odría instituted a harshly authoritarian regime. The government proclaimed a state of emergency and suspended all constitutional guarantees for the maximum thirty-day period permitted by the national charter. Odría repeated this action every month until his election as "constitutional president" in 1950. The new administration reaffirmed the law banning APRA and the Communist party. The unions, the universities, and the armed forces were purged of all suspected Apristas and their sympathizers. Political prisoners crowded the nation's jails—the regime arrested an estimated 4,000 persons during its first eight months. The biggest fish of all, however, eluded Odría's dragnet.

In January 1949, Haya de la Torre rushed into the Colombian embassy in Lima and was granted political asylum. It was assumed that arrangements quickly would be made for Víctor Raúl to leave the country under a safe-conduct pass from Odría. But ignoring this time-honored Latin American tradition, the government charged that the APRA leader was a common criminal, not a political refugee, and demanded that the Colombians surrender their guest. Relations between the two countries became badly strained as several attempts to resolve the controversy, including adjudication by the World Court, failed. Trenches (ostensibly for street repairs) were dug around the embassy and the haven was encircled with barbed wire. Barricades blocked the streets leading to the building and soldiers trained spotlights and machine guns on all exits to prevent a dash for freedom by Haya. Víctor Raúl remained an "exile" in his own country for five years, until April 1954, when Colombia and Peru reached an agreement for his deportation to Mexico.

Anti-Aprismo continued to be a major theme of the

Ochenio. A military tribunal investigating the Callao mutiny declared that Haya de la Torre had instigated the rebellion and passed sentence upon him along with 245 others. The government broadened its probe into the assassination of Francisco Graña Garland, eventually convicting ten Apristas of the crime. The army's annual services commemorating the 1932 Trujillo Massacre became more elaborate than ever and the Ministry of Government published several anti-Aprista tracts replete with pictures of the party's arsenals and rogues' galleries of fierce-looking *búfalos*. Non-Apristas also felt the heavy hand of the dictatorship. The Internal Security Law of June 1949 permitted the forcible entrance by police into the homes of suspected political criminals and the search of these premises without warrants. Opponents of the regime could be summarily imprisoned or exiled, and the death penalty was restored for persons convicted of rebellion, sedition, or conspiracy against the government. In addition, the measure severely restricted the rights of free speech, press, and assembly.

For two years Odría presided over a military junta that exercised both executive and legislative powers. The continued recess of parliament, explained the government, was part of a "political moratorium" designed to end the chaos of the Bustamante period, and it saved the treasury two million dollars per year. Once secure in his position, Odría announced that "free elections" for president and parliament would be held in July 1950. Receiving endorsements from a half-dozen political parties, the dictator expected little opposition in his bid for a regular six-year term. APRA and the Communists could not present candidates and only Ernesto Montagne, the nominee of the hastily organized National Democratic League, challenged the incumbent. An old retired general from Arequipa, Montagne posed no threat by himself. But Odría remembered the embarrassing electoral fiasco of 1936 and feared that APRA would instruct its members to vote for his opponent. Less than a month before the balloting, the Odriísta-dominated National Election Board disqualified Montagne, charging that his nominating petition contained forged signatures. This action produced a revolt in Arequipa by the thwarted candidate's supporters, which the army suppressed with the loss of more than 200 lives. The government accused the Apristas and Communists of inspiring the uprising and imprisoned Montagne. On July 2, Peru's electorate exercised the privilege of voting yes or no for General

Odría. The regime reported that more than 80 percent of the voters answered affirmatively while giving the administration a comfortable majority in parliament. Odría became less repressive after his election and some of his critics began to praise the president's "moderation." The government, however, continued to be frankly dictatorial.

Programs designed to end the nation's postwar economic slump received top priority from the Odría administration. Adopting the recommendations of Klein-Saks, a conservative* United States consulting firm, the government abandoned the cumbersome system of controls and subsidies in favor of a "free economy." Peru became the first nation of Latin America and one of a few in the world to abolish all exchange controls. The treasury devalued the *sol*, making the republic's exports more competitive in the international marketplace. Resumption of service on the foreign debt, in default since the 1930s, improved the country's credit rating and enabled Odría to obtain substantial loans from the World Bank and the International Monetary Fund. Private United States investment in Peru doubled between 1950 and 1955, reaching a book value of 300 million dollars. The market value of North American holdings may have been twice that amount. Total foreign investment approached 800 million dollars at the end of the Ochenio.

A cover story about Peru appearing in *Fortune*, the prestigious United States business magazine, praised the Odría regime for its "scrupulous respect for private property" and asserted that the republic had "held up a standard in international economic conduct to which far richer nations . . . might repair."† The administration's capitalist morality and liberalized mining and petroleum codes attracted massive capital investments in Peru's extractive industries. Under a slightly modified version of the original Sechura Contract the International Petroleum Company began drilling exploratory wells on the north coast. Several other oil firms received concessions to search millions of acres in the Montaña for petroleum. Although new oil and natural gas deposits were discovered east of the Andes, most of these were not large enough to warrant the high cost of their development. The IPC's efforts in the Sechura Desert produced only dry holes.

*Julius Klein, the company's senior partner, had served as assistant secretary of commerce in the Hoover administration.
†John Davenport, "Why Peru Pulls Dollars," *Fortune* 54 (November 1956): 131–32.

Greater success attended the quest for metallic minerals. Two United States enterprises formed the Marcona Mining Company and obtained a contract to extract a billion tons of high-grade iron ore from the Marcona Plateau, twenty miles from the southern port of San Juan. In return for supplying Peru's modest domestic needs at low prices, the company was permitted to export ore on generous terms from the state-owned deposit. During the same period four North American corporate giants (Cerro de Pasco, American Smelting and Refining, Phelps-Dodge, and Newmont Mining) created the Southern Peru Copper Company to invest more than 200 million dollars developing a mammoth copper-mining complex at Toquepala, sixty miles from the port of Ilo. Boasting 12 percent of the non-Communist world's reserves of copper and the largest open-pit mine anywhere, Toquepala would treble Peru's output of this metal in 1960, its first full year of operation.

Odría's Leguía-like benevolence toward foreign capital, especially in the sensitive area of mineral resources, conflicted with a strong current of economic nationalism in Latin America. The dictator partially disarmed his anti-imperialist critics, however, with a few cautious essays at state capitalism under a five-year plan for "economic independence" announced in 1950. The Empresa Petrolera Fiscal (EPF), a state oil agency created by the previous administration, received jurisdiction over Peru's petroleum resources and began operating its own oil fields and refineries. According to the new Petroleum Code, private oil concessions with all of their surface installations eventually would revert to the EPF. The regime undertook several hydroelectric projects and launched a fifty million dollar highway program. The construction of a fifty-mile railroad eliminated a transportation bottleneck at the new port of Matarani, and improvements also were made at Callao Harbor. The capital's international airport, Limatambo, became the first in South America to be fully equipped for instrument flights.

At the request of the Odría administration a United Nations team studied the agricultural sector of the economy, which had been falling further behind in the struggle to feed the republic's burgeoning population. The world organization's report recommended a fundamental agrarian reform, including the expropriation and redistribution of inefficient Sierra haciendas. Pressure for a major change in the pattern of land tenure intensified following the bloody mass uprising of 1952 in neighboring

Bolivia, where land-hungry peasants seized many estates. Odría, however, was unwilling to attack the latifundia of the highlands. He hoped to ease the agrarian problem by expanding the area available for cultivation. The government drafted a five-year plan for irrigation that proposed to provide water for 1,250,000 acres of desert. Texas millionaire Robert G. LeTourneau, a fundamentalist lay preacher and promoter of "industrial-missionary enterprises," obtained a concession of almost one million acres of jungle near Pucallpa. In return, LeTourneau agreed to build a fifty-mile road from Tournavista, as he called his holding, to the Central Highway and clear land for colonists with the heavy construction equipment manufactured by his firm. In addition, army engineers and private contractors built roads to open other sections of Amazonian Peru to settlers.

The success of Odría's massive dose of free enterprise in restoring health to the country's ailing economy cannot accurately be determined. National income statistics for Peru are unreliable for precise analysis, often varying considerably among different reporting agencies. More importantly, external forces largely beyond the influence of state policy strongly affected the performance of the export-led economy. The regime's new fiscal and investment programs coincided with the outbreak of the Korean War in 1950. The prices commanded by Peru's exports, which had slumped drastically the previous year, suddenly surged upward, only to drop precipitously after the 1953 armistice. Trade surpluses again became deficits, red ink replaced black in the treasury's ledgers, and the administration's fleshy budgets were cut to the bone of austerity. Nevertheless, major economic indicators for the country as a whole suggest some impressive gains during the Odría years. The value of both imports and exports more than doubled and the nation's manufacturers increased their output by almost two-thirds. The gross national product grew at a healthy annual average of perhaps 6 percent. Unfortunately, the prosperity reflected in these indices was not universal. While the modern portion of the economy advanced, artisan industry and agriculture for the domestic market declined. The economic benefits of the period, including government spending, accrued primarily to the coast, while per capita income decreased in the interior departments. The gap between comfort and misery widened.

Odría attempted to win popular support for his regime and undercut APRA's mass appeal through new labor and social-welfare programs. In his first public address after seizing power he declared that the achievement of "effective social justice" would be the primary goal of his administration. Almost immediately, reports from Peru began comparing the new strongman with his famous Argentine contemporary, Gen. Juan Domingo Perón. The Odría program, in fact, bore little substantive resemblance to Perón's "Revolution." The Peruvian president contemplated neither significant changes in the economic system nor a major redistribution of income, and the creation of a totalitarian state was beyond his ambitions. In the early years of the Ochenio, however, Odría seemed to be imitating the Perón style and the two governments had some striking though superficial similarities. Large, well-organized rallies of friendly workers, much like those of Perón's "shirtless ones," heard Odría proclaim the "Fundamental Rights of the Peruvian Worker" and announce new labor laws. Taking her cues from "Evita" Perón, the president's wife was depicted as the nation's foremost philanthropist, "the scale of love balanced between General Odría and his people." Her María Delgado de Odría Social Assistance Center distributed Christmas toys to poor children and performed other highly publicized acts of charity.

Organized labor, an Aprista stronghold, received the government's special attention as Odría reverted to the old strategy of curbing the power and independence of the unions, while paternalistically granting favors to the workers. The administration banned strikes with "political objectives" and legal walkouts were discouraged in favor of mediation by the new, cabinet-level Ministry of Labor and Indian Affairs. With the tacit approval of the regime, the officially outlawed Communist party gained control of several Aprista unions. Those that remained loyal to APRA, along with the Aprista-dominated Peruvian Workers' Confederation, were suppressed. The number of legally recognized labor organizations declined sharply. Nevertheless, Odría enjoyed considerable support among the working class, especially during the early months of the Ochenio. Nineteen days after taking power, the government reorganized the social security system, significantly increasing the number of persons covered and amplifying the benefits provided by the plan. A short time later, the regime promulgated a new labor code that established the rights of workers to share in the profits of their employers. The administration raised the minimum wage and Odría decreed seven blanket pay increases to keep salaries apace with prices. The government also initiated many labor-intensive public works projects that eased unemployment in Lima-Callao.

The Odría administration instituted a ten-year national education program in 1950. New taxes tied to the support of public instruction paid for the construction of 1,500 new schools. Many of these were *unidades escolares,* large modern plants that housed both primary and secondary schools while providing recreational facilities for the community. Enrollments in the primary grades grew by more than 50 percent. The government also established a National Fund for Health and Social Welfare to finance many projects, including municipal water and sewer systems, hospitals, and an extensive network of maternity clinics. A large-scale public housing program fell far short of its goal. However, a decree granting squatter's rights to the residents of the *barriadas* that now ringed the capital endeared Odría to many occupants of these makeshift communities.

The president boasted about his administration's accomplishments in education, public works, health, and welfare. Expenditures for the armed forces, however, regularly exceeded those for social programs. The dictator granted generous pay increases to the military and constructed many comfortable barracks and officers' clubs as well as new academies for each of the three armed services. To modernize the nation's military establishment the government procured large quantities of surplus war materiel from the United States, purchased six submarines for the navy, provided the air force with its first jet aircraft, and established the Center for Higher Military Studies. Responding to the desires of some officers, especially the younger men, for a more active role in the nation's economic and social development, Odría organized two battalions of army engineers for road construction and other public works.

The relative prosperity of the Ochenio's middle years purchased Odría the acquiescence of a considerable portion of the working and middle classes along with the support of most of the nation's wealthy elite. But the president's popularity faded along with the deterioration of the economy in the later years of the regime. Many Peruvians, of course, never had approved of the government's authoritarian cast. When Odría relaxed his dictatorship following the 1950 election, demands for greater freedom increased rather than subsided. The administration eased its controls on the unions in late 1952, and a wave of strikes ensued. The strongman broke these in a ruthless manner, tarnishing his image as the workers' benefactor. In the face of mounting economic and political problems after 1953, the president spent less and less time at his desk and became an almost permanent fixture at Lima's night clubs. Reports of widespread graft in high office scandalized the nation.

By the middle of 1954, most of the electorate looked forward to the expiration of Odría's presidency in two years. Rumors that the dictator planned to seek an unconstitutional, second successive term generated much anxiety, however, even among the favored armed forces. In August 1954, Odría quashed an army plot and exiled a dozen senior officers, including Gen. Zenón Noriega, his prime minister and heretofore most trusted collaborator. Four months later, the government reported the discovery of a military-civilian conspiracy against the regime. Although unsuccessful, these movements produced the desired effect. In February 1955, the president announced that elections would be held in June of the next year and that he would relinquish power to the choice of the people. Odría permitted the formation of political parties and eased his censorship of the press. From the pages of *La Prensa* conservative publisher Pedro Beltrán campaigned for free elections and the repeal of the Internal Security Law so that APRA could participate in the contest. Odría refused the latter request, but in December 1955 he issued a general amnesty. Many exiles, including several prominent Apristas, began returning to Peru.

Odría approached several groups to the right and center of the political spectrum, urging them to nominate a common candidate. But Pedro Beltrán and his friends in the newly formed National Coalition rejected this appeal. As friction between Beltrán and the president increased, close associates of the dictator organized the Restoration party, rekindling fears that Odría planned to extend his stay in office. In mid-February 1956, Gen. Marciano Merino, the army commander at Iquitos, "pronounced" against the government. Appealing for support from other garrisons, the rebel officer charged that Odría planned "to use the armed forces as an instrument of terror against the people" in continuing his dictatorship. The president imposed a state of siege upon the nation and moved quickly to crush the revolt. The government accused Pedro Beltrán of complicity in the movement and imprisoned the journalist along with other members of his National Coalition. This action caused the regime considerable international embarrassment. The charges against Beltrán proved to be insupportable. During the editor's month-long imprisonment, the Inter-American Press Association nominated him for its Freedom of the Press Award, an honor that he subsequently won.

Odría and his Restoration party eventually endorsed the candidacy of Hernando de Lavalle, a conservative bank executive and board member of some thirty corporations. But many conservatives disapproved of the official candidate and they approached sixty-seven-year-old former President Manuel Prado y Ugarteche. In April 1956, he entered the race under the banner of his own Pradist Democratic Movement (MDP). The two rightist presidential aspirants were challenged on the left by Fernando Belaúnde Terry, the dean of San Marcos University's School of Architecture. A member of a prominent Arequipa-based family, the forty-four-year-old Belaúnde spent most of his youth in Europe, Mexico, and the United States, where he attended the University of Texas. During the Bustamante administration, in which his father had served as prime minister, Fernando held a seat in the chamber of deputies as a member of the president's National Democratic Front. He frequently had voted with the Apristas and was one of the few politicians who publicly protested against the suppression of the party in 1948. Considered the candidate of the "intellectual left," Belaúnde campaigned on a reformist platform similar to that of APRA.

Although Belaúnde's National Front of Democratic Youth was poorly organized, his uncontested appeal to the political left frightened Odría. Less than three weeks before the election, the regime induced the National Election Board to disallow the architect's candidacy. At a huge rally in Lima's San Martín Plaza, Belaúnde delivered an emotional address and then led his supporters on a march to the headquarters of the election tribunal. Police attempted to halt the procession, but Belaúnde grabbed a Peruvian flag and raced to his destination. On the steps of the building that housed the election officials, Belaúnde warned that his followers would overthrow the dictatorship if his name were not placed on the ballot. A short time later, the election panel reversed its earlier decision and approved the architect's candidacy. Odría's clumsy meddling greatly enhanced the reputation of this charismatic leader, a new "democratic caudillo" reminiscent of Nicolás de Piérola.

Five other presidential candidates also entered the race, but by the end of May, all of these had withdrawn in favor of the three front runners—Lavalle, Prado, and Belaúnde. Neither these endorsements nor the popularity of the candidates themselves, however, would decide the contest. Again, the support of APRA would be crucial. Although Odría had allowed the Apristas to hold their third national convention, he continually denied them permission to run their own candidates. APRA leaders offered to support Lavalle in exchange for his explicit pledge to lift the ban on the party after the election. The official candidate, however, would give only vague assurances of a "return to democracy" in the event of his victory. From the standpoint of ideology, Belaúnde was the logical choice for an Aprista endorsement, and he openly asserted that he would legalize the party. But APRA viewed him as a serious rival for the votes of its traditional constituency. Furthermore, it seemed likely that Odría would not permit Belaúnde's inauguration, especially if his election was achieved with Aprista support. The late surge in the architect's campaign, however, raised fears that he might be elected in his own right if APRA failed to back another candidate. The election's unpredictability was compounded by the fact that for the first time Peruvian women would exercise the franchise at the national level.

During the first week of June, Aprista leaders met with Prado and Odría at the dictator's home and entered into the "Monterrico Pact." The president unofficially transferred his support from Lavalle to Prado, probably in return for a pledge that the MDP candidate would not vigorously investigate the corruption of the outgoing regime. APRA agreed to endorse Prado and instruct its partisans to vote for the MDP parliamentary slate. The former president promised to legalize the Partido del Pueblo following his victory. To weaken Belaúnde, several Apristas were permitted to run for congress as independents in four important departments.

In the election of June 17, 1956, the National Election Board proclaimed Manuel Prado the victor with 586,000 votes. Belaúnde polled 457,000 ballots, and Lavalle, 222,000. The MDP candidate also won comfortable majorities in both chambers of parliament. During the five-week interval between the election and the inauguration fears arose anew that Odría would not abide by the results of the contest. APRA called a general strike at the end of June to demonstrate its support for Prado. The lame-duck regime responded with a thirty-day suspension of the constitution and the arrest of several Apristas. But on Independence

Day, July 28, Manuel Prado y Ugarteche was installed as president. Still, skeptics charged that Odría relinquished power only because the dictator had broken his leg shortly before the inauguration.

Convivencia, 1956–1962

Immediately after taking the oath of office, Manuel Prado began to dismantle the oppressive instruments of the Odría dictatorship and fulfill his election promise to the Apristas. Shortly before the inauguration parliament had passed bills legalizing the Partido del Pueblo and granting a general political amnesty. The new president signed these laws in his first official act. Prado then issued a series of decrees nullifying the infamous Internal Security Law, lifting press censorship, ending controls on union activity, and eliminating other abuses of the Ochenio. True to its word, APRA's few congressmen joined with Prado's MDP to organize the legislature. Although the Apristas sought to maintain their freedom of action and disassociated themselves from some of the administration's more unpopular measures, the party supported Prado on most critical issues and used its influence to reduce labor unrest. The Aprista-dominated Peruvian Workers' Confederation threatened the government with several general strikes, but only one materialized. Haya de la Torre spent most of the period abroad to avoid personal conflicts with the president.

APRA received ample consideration for its cooperation with Prado. While the regime hampered the activities of the Communists, the Apristas had a free hand to work within the labor movement. The party organized many new unions, and membership in these groups soared. Concentrating on economic issues rather than political goals, the trade unions won several important victories. New labor legislation provided for annual bonuses and implemented the profit-sharing program formulated by Odría. APRA shunned sensitive political posts within the executive branch of government but accepted appointments to a number of pleasant, largely ceremonial offices, including the ambassadorship to the United Nations General Assembly. This working arrangement between Prado and APRA was christened "Convivencia"—"living together." The president also applied this concept to his relations with other political groups. Playing the role of peacemaker, Prado appointed several of his personal antagonists to high office and labored to end old feuds between other influential public figures.

Prado needed all of the political support he could muster. The new president was beset by serious economic problems, some of which he inherited from his predecessor. Odría had spent his last days in power attempting to purchase goodwill for his future political ventures. He granted large pay increases to the armed forces and authorized fifty new public works projects. The dictator encumbered the incoming administration with these burdensome commitments and an empty treasury. Furthermore, Prado assumed office during a period of mounting inflation and budget deficits. Soon the nation's already-declining export trade would suffer additionally from the recession of 1957–58 in the United States, which constricted Peru's traditional market and brought a 44-percent drop in copper prices. Natural disasters also contributed to the president's woes. While a severe drought destroyed crops in the southern highlands, floods ravaged the central Sierra. In January 1958, the worst earthquake in nearly a century rocked Arequipa.

Prado promised to meet the economic crisis with a program of fiscal stringency, but he was unwilling to pay the political costs of such measures. The budget for 1957 proved to be 30 percent higher than that for the last year of the Ochenio, and government spending increased another 12 percent in 1958, producing huge deficits. The nation continued to import more than it exported. By 1958, Peru's overseas sales were 20 million dollars less than when Prado took office. At the same time, per capita income declined while the price of consumer goods rose by 10 percent each year. The deterioration of the economy seriously weakened Prado's hold on the reins of power. Four cabinets resigned during the administration's first two years. A rash of strikes, including one by the police, led to four suspensions of the constitution between November 1957 and August 1959. Rumors of impending military coups permeated the capital and the president's personal popularity eroded rapidly. Crowds watching the Independence Day parade in 1958 pelted Prado's limousine with tomatoes.

Pedro Beltrán was the leading critic of the administration, denouncing Prado's economic policies almost daily in the editorial page of *La Prensa*. Tired of this constant sniping, the president appointed the publisher finance minister and premier in

July 1959. Beltrán instituted an austerity program, asking each citizen to "pay a quota of sacrifice" for the nation's welfare. Peru's working classes, however, soon complained that their quota was disproportionately large. Following a token wage increase, pay scales were frozen. The government ended subsidies that stabilized the cost of bread and meat, producing a 30-percent rise in the price of the latter item. The International Petroleum Company, the supplier of most of the country's oil products, declared that the administration's ceiling prices were too low to allow a profit and ceased its drilling operations. Faced with the unpleasant prospect of importing oil, Beltrán permitted the IPC to raise prices on various petroleum products by 30 to 350 percent. This action quickly translated into hikes in bus and taxi fares, evoking loud public outcries. To balance the government's accounts, Beltrán cut state spending by one-third, largely at the expense of the public works program.

The premier's fiscal policies made him one of the more unpopular men in Peru, but they produced the desired economic effect. In 1960, for the first time in almost a decade, the government reported a budget surplus, and the regime continued to live within its means during the remaining two years of Prado's term. The gross national product rose by more than 7 percent in 1960 and climbed 9 percent during the last year of the administration. Meanwhile, the rate of inflation was reduced to an acceptable 5 percent and in 1960, the nation ended its seven-year deficit in foreign trade. The improvement in Peru's international commerce resulted from the opening of the Toquepala copper mine and the dramatic addition of fish meal to the list of the republic's major exports.

During the Second World War Peru developed a small modern fishing industry that supplied tuna to a few domestic canneries. Although most of the tinned fish was consumed at home, some of the output entered the United States market. Fish meal, a protein-rich flour made by applying intense heat and pressure to tuna scraps, was merely a by-product of the canning operation. The market for this substance was limited, however, because it had a strong, fishy taste that was transferred even to the meat of animals fattened on the product. Peru's total fish catch was small, less than 50,000 tons in 1948. Three years later, the industry's export market collapsed when the United States sharply increased its tariff on canned tuna. Coincidental with this setback, however, came technological advances in fish meal production that rendered the commodity suitable for animal feed and, later, for even more direct consumption by humans. Peruvian fishermen rapidly turned their attention from tuna to the abundant anchovies of the Humboldt Current that supplied an ever growing number of fish meal plants. When Manuel Prado took office in 1956, his nation recorded a fish catch of less than a quarter-million tons. But almost incredibly, Peru became the world's foremost fishing nation in 1962, when its fishermen extracted more than six million tons of marine life from the coastal waters. Before the end of the decade the country's annual harvest from the sea would surpass ten million tons and earn about one-third of the republic's foreign exchange.

The rapid flow of foreign capital into Peru during the Ochenio declined sharply after Prado took office. To encourage investment from both overseas and domestic sources, the administration secured passage of the Industrial Promotion Law in November 1959. This measure gave tax incentives to new industries deemed basic to the development of the economy. The law also sought to decentralize industrial activity by providing added benefits to businesses locating outside of the Lima-Callao district. After two years the government reported that 740 enterprises had been established under the provisions of the law. Most of these, however, were concentrated within the environs of the capital.

The financially pressed Prado regime curtailed state investment, funding public works projects at only half the rate of the previous administration. Many of Prado's programs, in fact, were extensions of those begun by Odría. The government budgeted seventy-nine million dollars to build new highways and upgrade a similar amount of old roads. In 1960, Prado announced an ambitious five-year plan to invest a half-billion dollars for the integrated development of the nation's agricultural, mineral, and power resources. The program emphasized greater utilization of the republic's hydroelectric potential to provide power for industry. The regime completed several dams begun by Odría and undertook some new projects, increasing Peru's output of electricity by almost 80 percent. Some of this energy heated the furnaces of the state-owned steel mill at Chimbote. The construction of this monument to economic nationalism, initiated during Prado's first term, was completed in 1957. Although the source of much pride, the metal produced by this small plant was more expensive than imported steel.

As in his first administration, Manuel Prado took special interest in the nation's schools. He appointed Jorge Basadre, Peru's premier historian, to head the Ministry of Education and significantly increased the budget for this agency. Between 1956 and 1959, the regime stressed improvements in the primary school system, where enrollments expanded by 30 percent. Emphasis shifted to the unversity level during the second half of Prado's tenure. In an effort to decentralize higher education and provide more specialized training in technical fields, the government increased the number of colleges from seven to twenty-one. Unfortunately, several of these new institutions were too small to maintain viable programs.

The Prado regime timidly approached Peru's two most pressing needs—adequate housing for the thousands of migrants now flooding Lima and agrarian reform. The president created the Commission on Agrarian Reform and Housing to study these problems and recommend solutions. This body included some of the country's largest landowners. A National Housing Institute, established in 1961, drafted a cautious, short-term housing plan for the remaining eighteen months of Prado's tenure and a far more expensive ten-year program for his successors. With a loan of 7.5 million dollars from the United States Agency for International Development, work began on 4,254 new housing units, only a token assault on the republic's tremendous shortage. Even less progress was made toward easing the agrarian problem. As anticipated, the Commission on Agrarian Reform and Housing's 1959 report concerning land tenure recommended that "previously deeded" property not be expropriated. The land hunger of the peasants should be satiated by opening new public lands to cultivation. The administration's agrarian reform bill, submitted to the legislature in September 1960, was somewhat more liberal than that proposed by the commission. However, this measure exempted most of the republic's large estates from expropriation and made unrealistic provisions for cash compensation to affected property owners, a feature that would have crippled the reform. Still, conservatives tenaciously fought the bill while the left attacked it as insufficient. Endless debate stalled the proposal in congressional committee rooms where it rested when Prado left office.

The government's very limited efforts toward agrarian reform were spurred, in part, by the activities of Hugo Blanco. In 1958, this young Trotskyite agronomist from Cuzco began work in the Convención Valley, a region on the fringe of the Montaña north of the ancient Inca capital, where about 100 haciendas produced coca, coffee, and cacao with the labor of tenant farmers. Establishing himself as a renter on one of these estates, Blanco organized nearly 150 agricultural unions and grouped them in a peasant federation. After the landowners rejected tenant demands for a reduction in their traditional labor service, Blanco's peasants called a strike. Neither court action nor the use of private armies sufficed to break the movement, and the tenants continued to occupy their plots without working for the *hacendados*. Emboldened by this success, other peasants formed syndicates in the southern and central Sierra and a wave of tenant strikes along with "invasions" of estates by squatters occurred. The government proclaimed martial law in October 1960 and ordered the civil guard to oust trespassers from a huge ranch owned by the Cerro de Pasco Corporation. In the following months, several violent confrontations between peasants and police produced many deaths. Meanwhile, other Trotskyite organizers from Argentina arrived in Lima and began recruiting students for a guerrilla army. The leftist group robbed two Lima banks to finance their revolution, but police quashed the movement before it could launch its "war of liberation" in the highlands.

The deepening crisis in the Sierra failed to dislodge the agrarian reform bill from parliament, but the administration attempted to placate the peasants through politically painless colonization ventures in trans-Andean Peru. Pioneer settlement in older frontier zones quickened and a decree of April 1960 reserved 50,000 square miles in the west-central Montaña for a new project called Plan Peru-vía. A road penetrating the region was rushed to completion and, shortly before Prado left office in mid-1962, the newly created National Institute of Agrarian Reform and Colonization began distributing a few plots to settlers.

Manuel Prado's foreign policy reflected growing hostility toward the United States in Peru during the 1950s. This animosity had several sources. The rapid influx of North American capital inspired frequent denunciations of "Yankee economic imperialism" in the nation's press and the speeches of its politicians. Peru's proclamation of a 200-mile fisheries limit in 1947 initiated a long and bitter dispute between Lima and Washington. Along with their neighbors, Peruvians shared a general disillusionment concerning the United States' attitude toward

Latin America. The McCarthy era's obsessive fear of communism seemingly led Washington to favor right-wing, authoritarian regimes in the hemisphere rather than reformist, democratic administrations. The award of the Legion of Merit to General Odría and other dictators by the Eisenhower government reinforced this view. Latin Americans also complained that Washington lavished financial aid on nations within the European and Asian arenas of the Cold War, while neglecting its long-time allies in the New World.

During this same period, Latin American economists serving on the United Nations Economic Commission for Latin America elaborated their thesis that the United States and other industrial countries had a fundamentally exploitative trade relationship with the raw-material producers of the underdeveloped world. This note of economic hostility intensified with the onset of the 1957–58 recession in the United States. To alleviate the distress of the North American mining industry, the Eisenhower administration contemplated new tariff protection for domestic mineral producers. Protracted congressional hearings concerning this topic caused growing anxiety in Peru, where a disastrous drop in metal prices already had produced hardship.

A dramatic demonstration of Peruvian disaffection toward the United States occurred in May 1958 during Vice-President Richard M. Nixon's brief stay in Lima. Nixon expressed a desire to visit San Marcos University and explain his government's policy to student critics. However, the Peruvian Student Federation issued a statement, replete with Marxist jargon, declaring that the North American emissary would not be welcome on their campus. Peruvian officials and the United States embassy urged Nixon to stay away from the school. But the vice-president asserted that to avoid San Marcos would give a victory to the Communists, whom he seemed certain were behind the recent surge in anti-Americanism. A large hostile crowd met Nixon's motorcade at the entrance of the university. For a time the students merely directed angry questions concerning mineral tariffs at the Yankee visitor. Then the throng began to hiss, shout, and throw stones, forcing the Nixon party to make a hurried retreat. Later, the vice-president appeared at the more conservative Catholic University in Lima. No rocks were hurled, but the mood of the students was ugly as they asked Nixon the same questions he had heard at San Marcos.

In September 1958, the Eisenhower administration rejected proposals for higher tariffs on minerals in favor of import quotas that reduced Peru's exports of lead and zinc by 20 percent. Although the United States viewed this measure as a compromise, the quota system enraged Peruvians. A short time later, the Soviet Bloc offered to purchase the republic's surplus lead and zinc along with its excess cotton. Almost immediately, the Peruvian parliament passed a resolution urging the executive to sell the nation's products to *any* customer. Washington's response came quickly. All of Peru's lead and zinc would be permitted to enter the North American market in spite of the recent quotas.

Peru's use of the Red bugbear to frighten Washington, so successful in the import-quota dispute, was limited by President Prado's own anticommunism. The regime, in fact, had severed the nation's diplomatic ties with Czechoslovakia, the republic's only link with the socialist world. However, Peru did make a brief attempt to chart a "third course" in international affairs. In October 1957, the president enunciated the "Prado Doctrine," calling for increased cooperation between the Organization of American States and NATO, a relationship that he thought would reduce Latin America's dependence upon Washington. At the same time, Peru's ambassador to the United Nations urged the formation of an independent bloc of Latin American and Latin European countries in the world body.

Relations between the United States and Peru improved notably after 1958. The economic recession ended, removing the source of much discontent. Partly as a result of Nixon's visit to Peru and his even more hostile reception in Venezuela, Washington began to reexamine its policies toward the hemisphere. The triumph of Fidel Castro in Cuba hastened this reassessment. In its last years the Eisenhower administration agreed to support an Inter-American Development Bank, and United States foreign aid to Peru and its neighbors grew significantly. The Alliance for Progress of the Kennedy government brought even more attention and financial assistance to Latin America along with a stronger official commitment to the support of democracy and reform in the region. As hostility between the United States and Cuba intensified, Washington ended that nation's huge sugar quota within the protected North American market. More than a half-million tons of the Cuban allotment were transferred to Peru in 1961. The Prado regime reciprocated with vigorous support for Washington's efforts to isolate the Castro government from the inter-American community.

Manuel Prado's critics characterized him as a do-nothing

president, a man who exercised little leadership in resolving the nation's major problems. The accomplishments of his administration would have been respectable by the standards of earlier times. However, the need for basic reforms in the republic's economy and society had become manifest in the 1950s. The very urgency of the country's problems could have provided the impetus for change, but Prado failed to utilize this opportunity. The president, nevertheless, took pride in his management of Peru's political crisis. In the more than four decades between 1919 and 1962, the country had experienced only sixteen years of relative democracy. Manuel Prado occupied the Palace of Pizarro during twelve of these. He left office enjoying considerable popularity and with fewer personal enemies than at the time of his inauguration.

Long before the conclusion of Prado's term in 1962, Peruvians began searching the political horizon for his successor. As in the previous three decades the role of APRA was central to these speculations. Unlike earlier times, however, the party's association with the Prado regime now evoked considerable ambivalence among citizens of all ideological hues. Leftists wondered if the Apristas still desired basic reform. Was *convivencia* apostasy or a clever ruse in the battle for change? Similarly, conservatives asked if the party truly had been tamed. Did the revolutionary wolf lurk beneath the sheep's clothing of moderation? In any event would the military, APRA's old nemesis, permit the party to take power?

The rightward trajectory of Aprista ideology, perceptible since the late 1930s, had continued during the repression of the Odría dictatorship and became even more pronounced in the years that followed. Fortunately for Haya de la Torre, who rarely has admitted a mistake or a change of mind, many early expositions of his ideas were couched in vague terms, allowing multiple interpretations. Less ambiguous portions of his old writings were made malleable by subjecting them to the crucible of the historic-space-time theory. Reviewing the first three decades of his party's history in *Treinta años de aprismo* (1956), Víctor Raúl protested his fidelity to the *alianza*'s original doctrines and accused his critics of misinterpreting his words.

APRA's Supreme Chief explained that the term "capitalism" in the Aprista lexicon was synonymous with "industrialization" and that private enterprise, "democratic captitalism," was superior to the "state capitalism" of the totalitarian Communists.

Haya insisted that he never had promised a "socialist revolution," but a "social revolution." If Franklin Roosevelt's New Deal had occurred prior to the formulation of Aprismo, wrote Víctor Raúl, it might have been used as an example of the "planned democracy" of the "anti-imperialist state." Concerning APRA's call for the nationalization of lands and industry, Haya placed this goal within its "logical scale," behind the still-unfinished task of Indoamerican unification. Moreover, asserted the party philosopher, Apristas had employed the term "nationalization" in a "general manner." It might only mean transferring the ownership of property or dominance within an industry from foreigners to "nationals" of Peru or greater governmental vigilance over certain economic activities. "Aprista nationalization," concluded Haya, "is inclined toward state ownership of development corporations . . . and the stimulation of agricultural and industrial cooperativism, but respecting and guaranteeing private property."

The deeds of APRA's leaders reinforced the more conservative tone of their words. The electoral pact between the Partido del Pueblo and Manuel Prado in 1956 surprised many rank and file Apristas. Even greater amazement attended the party's support for Prado after his inauguration. Haya de la Torre and other Aprista chieftains defended their actions on practical political grounds. They had traded their votes for legality. In their continued cooperation with the regime they sought to demonstrate that APRA had matured since the days of the Bustamante debacle. If Prado's program was not so progressive as the party would like, explained the leaders, the old conservative could be trusted to preside over free elections in 1962, and he might be persuaded to endorse the Aprista candidate. Support for the government also was designed to gain the party respectability in the eyes of the nation's elite and soften the antagonism of the armed forces.

APRA did acquire greater acceptability among the nation's upper class. Prior to the 1962 election, one prominent rightist described Haya de la Torre as "the conservative leader this country needs." But the party paid dearly for this new respectability, losing much of its already diminished radical wing. The rise of Cuba's Fidel Castro, the hemisphere's new revolutionary star, hastened the disintegration of the APRA left. At its fourth national congress in 1959, the party purged eight leaders who expressed opposition to the Convivencia with Prado. The next year, APRA lost control of the Peruvian Student Federation to a new leftist coalition. Another flurry of public denunciations of the *alianza*'s leadership by Aprista intellectuals further embarrassed the party. Vicious personal attacks on Haya earlier leveled by rightist critics now were echoed by ex-Apristas. Víctor Raúl was accused of direct complicity in several political murders, of being addicted to astrology, and of leading an international narcotics ring. One APRA renegade, the poet Alberto Hidalgo, claimed personal knowledge that lifelong bachelor Haya was a homosexual. Some discnchanted Apristas entered opposition political parties. Others joined former student leader Luis de la Puente Uceda's APRA Rebelde.

Aprista stategists considered by-passing perennial candidate Haya de la Torre in 1962 for a younger leader or at least someone less odious to the military. For the Aprista masses, however, Víctor Raúl was "Señor APRA." An enthusiastic crowd of 150,000 persons greeted the Supreme Chief at the Limatambo Airport when he returned home in January 1962 to accept his party's nomination. Hoping to continue the Convivencia, Manuel Prado's MDP endorsed the Aprista leader and Pedro Beltrán followed suit after his own candidacy failed to generate popular enthusiasm. Two small rightist organizations joined with those of Prado and Beltrán to further the cause of Víctor Raúl, who officially ran as the candidate of the Democratic Alliance. During the campaign Haya found himself in the awkward position of being welcomed in conservative circles while his appeals to former supporters on the left were met with skepticism and even open hostility.

Haya de la Torre had one serious challenger on the right, former President Manuel Odría who had organized his own Unión Nacional Odriísta (UNO). The general seemed likely to attract a considerable share of the conservative vote, especially among the provincial aristocracy of the Sierra and those members of the coastal elite who could not repress their old hatred of APRA. In addition, Odría expected to do well among the nonunionized, working-class elements of Lima-Callao who remembered his job-creating public works, his legalization of squatters' dwellings, and the charitable works of Señora Odría. The ex-dictator's opponents expressed indignation at his entrance into the contest. They charged that he had illegally amassed a fortune of three million dollars during the Ochenio and branded him a reactionary tyrant. Describing himself as a "socialist of the right," Odría neatly side-stepped this attack with a classic statement to the residents of Lima's *barriadas:* "Democracy is not edible." The old soldier campaigned as a vigorous foe of communism and APRA.

Fernando Belaúnde Terry, the third major presidential candidate, directed his appeal to the left and center of the political spectrum. He had begun his campaign soon after his defeat in 1956, organizing a new party—Acción Popular (AP). A heterogeneous group of intellectuals, students, workers, professionals, and businessmen, the AP gained a significant portion of its following from disaffected Apristas. Belaúnde worked diligently to build an effective political apparatus capable of challenging the APRA machine. The candidate spent much time on highly publicized tours of the interior, sometimes traveling to remote villages by mule and canoe. To emphasize his concern for Peru's neglected provinces, Belaúnde accepted his party's nomination at a national convention held in Iquitos.

Belaúnde expounded his program in a book entitled *Peru's Own Conquest.* Praising *mestizaje,* the mixing of races and cultures in Peru, the candidate advocated the creation of a "mestizo economy." This system would be basically capitalist, but with greater state intervention to eliminate injustice and ensure maximum benefits for the commonweal. Drawing heavily upon the idealized image of the Inca Empire, Belaúnde asserted that his programs had their roots in the nation's pre-Columbian past. Like the Cuzco rulers, Acción Popular believed in comprehensive national planning. Blending the ideas of the ancient Andean *minka* with John F. Kennedy's Peace Corps, the candidate proposed a self-help community development program called Popular Cooperation. With tools and technical advice provided by the government and the assistance of student volunteers, the people themselves would build roads, schools, and other public facilities. Acción Popular also promised the people a major public housing program, easier credit for small farmers and businessmen, tax reforms to obtain more revenue from the wealthy, and a comprehensive agrarian reform. AP's proposed attack on Peru's agrarian problem was largely the work of agronomist Edgardo Seoane, the party's vice-presidential candidate. Ironically, Belaúnde's running mate was the brother of Manuel Seoane, the popular Aprista liberal and his own party's nominee for vice-president. Belaúnde proposed to work toward Acción Popular's ambitious goals within the framework of a highly democratic administration. He promised greater autonomy for local governments as well as more tax money and influence in the national regime for the interior. The AP candidate courted military support with his advocacy of a prominent role for the armed forces in national planning, public works, and civic action programs. Belaúnde appealed to nationalist sentiment by pledging an "independent foreign policy" and a speedy resolution of an old dispute between the government and the International Petroleum Company over ownership of the La Brea y Pariñas oil field.

The personal qualities of Belaúnde himself attracted many followers. His rugged good looks and close association with reformist elements of the Catholic Church made him popular with women voters. At the same time, his displays of physical courage enhanced his image as a *macho,* a he-man that Peruvian males could admire. In 1957 Belaúnde had fought a duel with an opposition congressman, a contest that ended only after the swords of both men had drawn blood. Most spectacular, however, was his May 1959 confrontation with the Prado government. Because of a bank strike the president had proclaimed a thirty-day suspension of constitutional rights, including that of public assembly. Acción Popular had scheduled a convention at Arequipa for that period and the political gathering took place in defiance of Prado's decree. Police arrested Belaúnde and sent him to El Frontón, Peru's maximum-security prison on an island off Callao. During an exercise period a few days after his arrival, Belaúnde broke for the water, dove into the surf, and swam to the yacht of a friend. Unfortunately, the craft also carried a prison guard who returned the fugitive to the island. The incident received much publicity and Belaúnde was hailed as a great champion of civil liberties after the government failed to prove its case against him. Acción Popular's opponents charged that these escapades demonstrated that Belaúnde lacked the emotional stability to lead the nation. They also questioned his ability to control his more radical followers and accused him of being an unwitting tool of the Communists. AP had led a fight to legalize the Communist party and openly courted Marxist votes.

Several weeks prior to the election, Acción Popular accused the National Election Jury of favoritism toward Haya de la Torre. Several candidates of small rightist parties that would have drawn votes away from the Aprista leader were disqualified because their nominating petitions lacked the valid signatures of

20,000 qualified voters as the law required. Leftist competitors of Belaúnde, however, remained on the ballot even though at least two of these probably did not meet this test. In the end, the presence of four minor parties in the presidential race—the Christian Democratic party, the Peruvian Socialist party, the Social Progressive Movement, and the National Liberation Front, a Castroite group—determined the outcome of the 1962 election. Charges of electoral chicanery became more serious as the day of decision drew nearer. AP protested that APRA was attempting to rig the contest and asked the armed forces to investigate alleged irregularities in the registration of Aprista voters. The military complied with Belaúnde's request and quickly issued its report. Claiming to have found convincing evidence of violations in almost 40 percent of the registrations checked, the soldiers ominously declared that "the will to commit fraud was patent." The armed services announced that they would carefully scrutinize the balloting. Belaúnde threatened revolution if the election was not fair and asserted that he would accept the verdict of the National Election Jury only if its canvass was verified by the military.

On June 10, 1962, 1.7 million of Peru's 2.2 million registered voters went to the polls. Early returns gave the lead to Belaúnde, who hastily claimed victory. Later returns, however, put Haya de la Torre in front and Belaúnde's euphoria faded. The Lima press reported the final tallies of the National Election Jury on July 17. Haya de la Torre led the field with 557, 047 votes (32.98 percent); Belaúnde received 544,180 ballots (32.1 percent); Odría won 480,798 votes (28.45 percent); and the four minor party candidates had a combined total of 108,593 ballots (6.47 percent). Haya de la Torre, the popular choice by a margin of almost 13,000 ballots over Belaúnde, had not received the 33.3 percent of the votes required for direct election. Under the constitution, the contest would be decided among the top three candidates by a majority of the combined membership of the newly elected parliament, whose total of 241 senators and deputies was divided as follows: Democratic Alliance (Haya's coalition), 114; Acción Popular, 78; Unión Nacional Odriísta, 42; others, 7.

Barring a most unlikely pact between the Democratic Alliance and all of the minor party congressmen, two of the major organizations would have to form a coalition to elect a president. Meanwhile, rumors of an imminent military takeover induced rapid action toward that end. Desperate to to finish his term and transfer power to a constitutional successor, Manuel Prado worked feverishly to arrange a compromise that would place any one of the three contenders in the presidency. The major candidates also negotiated directly with each other. Throughout these proceedings, Belaúnde maintained an inflexible attitude toward proposed compromises with APRA. An alliance between the AP and the UNO was ruled out because their combined parliamentary strength fell two votes short of a majority. The only alternative to a coup seemed to be a marriage between the strangest of bedfellows—Haya de la Torre and Manuel Odría.

In a televized address on the evening of July 17, Gen. Manuel Odría indicated to the nation that APRA's congressmen would cast their votes for him. The announcement stunned the public, especially the Aprista faithful. Why should the presidency go to Odría, who had finished third in the election, and not to Víctor Raúl, the leading candidate? Two weeks earlier, high-ranking army officers had told President Prado that the military would not permit Haya to take office. The election of Odría at least would preserve APRA's large parliamentary bloc and give the party considerable power. Furthermore, the failing health of the aging former dictator encouraged hope that APRA's Manuel Seoane, who had won the first vice-presidency (Peru elects two vice-presidents), might succeed him in the near future. Even before Manuel Odría spoke to his countrymen, however, the armed forces had demanded that the National Election Jury annul the inconclusive contest. The panel refused.

In the early morning hours of July 18, a cordon of tanks and 200 army rangers, in camouflaged battle dress, encircled the Palace of Pizarro. After the guards refused to admit them to the grounds, a tank crashed through the heavy iron gate. From that point onward, the rite was formally correct. Col. Gonzalo Briceño led two four-man columns into the president's office. Displaying eight armed hand grenades and two satchels of TNT, the commandos "invited" Prado to come with them. Seated at his desk with his family and friends standing behind him, the beleaguered chief of state declined their request. In a voice that at first trembled but then firmed, he made a brief address, protesting the military's violation of the constitution. There were cheers and some angry shouts, followed by the singing of the national anthem. At its conclusion, Prado put on his coat and hat while the soldiers sent for his bags. The fallen leader and his family were taken to the Callao naval base where they were held until the expiration of Prado's term on July 28. The military then permitted the ex-president to fly to exile in Paris, where he died four years later.

Why did the coup occur? A number of different answers were offered in a plethora of literature addressed to that question. Only one thing seems certain: no single cause adequately explains the action of the armed forces. The military officially declared that it had intervened because gross fraud in the election had subverted the will of the people. With the benefit of hindsight, however, it appears that the contest was relatively honest, perhaps because of the close supervision of the soldiers. The military government later published a voluminous "white paper" to support its charges, but this document failed to demonstrate that voting irregularities had affected the outcome of the balloting. Nevertheless, the officers seemed convinced that an attempt had been made to rig the election and, on July 18, they probably believed that significant fraud had occurred. Furthermore, powerful elements within the armed forces strongly opposed the inauguration of either Haya or Odría under those questionable circumstances. If any one of the major candidates had received a clear constitutional plurality in an election above suspicion of major irregularities, the soldiers probably would not have interfered with the installation of the victor. Finally, Belaúnde demanded that the National Election Jury annul the contest and entrust the selection of a president to an extralegal "court of honor," a most unlikely prospect. Failing this, the AP candidate presented two alternatives: the establishment of a military government or a bloody popular uprising. With partisan passions at the flash point, fear of a civil war also contributed to the military's decision.

10

The Army and the Architect,

[1962–1968]

Dictablanda, 1962–1963

A COMMUNIQUE FROM THE ARMED FORCES' HIGH COMMAND on July 18, 1962, announced that the constitution had been suspended for an indefinite period, that the recent elections for both president and parliament had been canceled, and that a military government had assumed executive and legislative functions. The soldiers pledged that theirs would be a caretaker regime. New elections already were scheduled for June 9, 1963. The coup was described as an "institutional act" of the armed forces. Instead of a single dominant officer seizing power for himself or a small clique, a junta of four men had assumed control of the nation on behalf of the three military services. Each officer held a cabinet post and all were designated equal "co-presidents." The executive quartet included army generals Ricardo Pérez Godoy and Nicolás Lindley López, air force general Pedro Vargas Prada, and Vice-Adm. Francisco Torres Matos, representing the navy. High-ranking officers also staffed the remaining ministerial positions.

After one week in office General Pérez Godoy, the senior officer of the junta, relinquished his portfolio as finance minister and assumed the traditional ceremonial functions of Peru's chief of state, but his three co-presidents retained their share of executive authority. Pérez Godoy's colleagues forced his retirement in March 1963, and General Lindley López became titular head of state. Although rumors of an ideological rift in the regime abounded, the official explanation for this change was that Pérez Godoy—who relished public appearances and television speeches—attempted to enhance his personal power and failed to share authority with his co-presidents.

The military's assumption of power received little effective opposition. Belaúnde, Odría, and important business groups applauded the "patriotism" of the armed forces. The Supreme Court and the Church hierarchy recognized the de facto authority of the new regime. The Christian Democrats voiced their disapproval of the coup, but only APRA attempted any significant protest. The Aprista-controlled Peruvian Workers' Confederation called a general strike for July 23, but 3,000 anti-Aprista labor leaders pledged their support for the junta. Except for a few cities in APRA's "solid north," the walkout failed miserably. On July 28, the 141st anniversary of Peru's independence and the day on which a new president was to have been inaugurated, the junta proclaimed the restoration of all constitutional guarantees.

Diplomatic recognition of the military government came quickly from the major nations of Europe and most of Latin America. But the United States, which had applied pressure to forestall the coup, severed all formal ties with Peru and suspended military and financial aid to the regime. This action produced a storm of protest from many Peruvian leaders who charged the Kennedy administration with illegal political intervention and economic coercion. Washington's gesture on behalf of the Alliance for Progress's commitment to democracy ended in August with the appointment of a new ambassador. The United States lifted its embargo on aid two months later, but the level of funds disbursed to Peru declined by 75 percent during the year. The military administration responded with a declaration that Lima would become more independent in world affairs.

Many people anticipated that the installation of the junta would bring a return to the political repression associated with past military regimes and a concerted attack upon APRA in particular. There was little surprise, therefore, when troops vandalized the plant of the party's newspaper in the immediate aftermath of the coup. But the government quickly disavowed this action and promised to pay for any damages to *La Tribuna*'s facilities. The generals summoned Aprista leaders to the government palace along with representatives of other political parties and asked them to cooperate with the administration. APRA promised not to subvert the regime, but reserved its right of peaceful opposition. Although the junta did not harass APRA and continued to proclaim its neutrality toward the nation's political groups, some of the regime's action did favor non-Aprista labor unions.

Following the restoration of constitutional rights ten days after the coup, the junta generally respected basic personal liberties. Political commentators coined the term *dictablanda* ("soft dictatorship") to contrast the regime with the usual *dictadura* (" 'hard' dictatorship"). Nevertheless, a "Red scare" in January 1963 marred the administration's record for tolerance. Announcing the discovery of a plot to assassinate key leaders and overthrow the government, the generals suspended the constitution for one month and jailed many suspected Communists and other leftists. The government failed to produce convincing evidence of a conspiracy and soon released most of these persons. Nevertheless, the regime used this opportunity to invoke Article 53 of the constitution outlawing "international" parties. The generals declared that the Communist party, the Castroite National Liberation Front, and other "communistic" groups would not be permitted to participate in the forthcoming election.

Organized labor severely tested the restraint of the military government. In addition to APRA's abortive general strike, the junta was confronted with more work stoppages than at any comparable time in the nation's history. During the soldiers' first month in office, workers struck the Central Railroad and the Toquepala mines, two very important elements of the national economy. Instead of forceful intervention, the regime declared that it respected the right of peaceful strikes. A few days later, the junta decreed a higher minimum wage and extended the coverage of the law to include a larger number of workers. A series of violent labor clashes at the mining centers of the central Sierra, however, caused a thirty-day period of martial law in December. Police arrested about twenty-five union leaders, but released all of them before the end of the month, when peace was restored. Although previous military governments had not been consistently antiworker, the junta of 1962–63 was the first that was not obviously antiunion.

276

The junta continued to describe itself as a "caretaker government," but a flurry of reform decrees demonstrated that the officers intended to do more than light housekeeping during their year in power. The generals' most publicized efforts were directed at the nation's agrarian problem, as the crisis in the countryside entered a more explosive phase. In November 1962, peasant organizer Hugo Blanco attacked a police station near Cuzco and killed one officer. A massive campaign to apprehend the elusive leader culminated in May 1963, when he was captured and sentenced to twenty-five years in prison. That same month, a group of Peruvian students returned home from Cuba where they had received guerrilla training. Led by the young poet Javier Heraud, they crossed from Bolivia into the Montaña Department of Madre de Díos. From there they hoped to reach Hugo Blanco's peasants in Cuzco. After only a few days in the country, however, police at Puerto Maldonado killed half of the six-man team and captured the others. Although this threat had ended, it seemed that the revolutionary left was determined to fulfill Fidel Castro's prediction that the Andes would become the "Sierra Maestra of South America."

The regime relentlessly hunted guerrillas, but it did not suppress the peasant leagues. The government assigned sympathetic officers to each of these organizations to observe all meetings and explain the junta's programs for the land-hungry farmers. These were noteworthy, considering the soldiers' short tenure. In August 1962, the six-week-old administration claimed all unexploited arid lands for the state. Decree-law 14238 of November 16, entitled "Bases for an Agrarian Reform," outlined a comprehensive program for major changes in the agricultural sector of the economy. Although this plan was to be elaborated and implemented in the future, the decree immediately empowered the government to expropriate unused and mismanaged estates for the benefit of the "national economy and social progress." Land thus acquired could be distributed to landless peasants or those whose plots were insufficient for their needs. The law also prohibited the exaction of labor service from tenant farmers, provided for a minimum wage for agricultural workers, and promised to extend the social security system to the countryside. Another decree, issued in March 1963, established pilot agrarian reform projects in seven regions, including the tension-wracked Convención Valley. There, the government purchased twenty-three haciendas that had been seized by peasants. Divided into fifty-acre units, these properties were granted to farmers who agreed to pay for the plots over a twenty-year period. In addition to this initiative toward agrarian reform—the first real attempt in modern Peruvian history—the junta continued the colonization programs of preceding administrations.

The military regime gave considerable impetus to systematic government planning in Peru. The National Planning Institute, created in October 1962, was charged with drafting a comprehensive plan for the nation's social and economic development. The new agency also received authority over the planning activites of other state entities. From the efforts of the National Planning Institute emerged a ten-year plan for the entire country and several blueprints for the achievement of specific goals, including the integration of the Indians into the mainstream of national life. The government invited the Inter-American Committee for Agricultural Development (CIDA) to study the republic's agrarian problems and recommend reforms. Its authoritative report, a damning indictment of the nation's system of land tenure, would be employed in the elaboration of later agrarian reforms.

The generals also grappled with the problem of rapid urbanization, establishing a Housing Bank to finance the construction of homes for middle- and working-class families. The military augmented the budget for public works and economic development programs by almost 90 percent. The Ministry of Education enjoyed a sizable increase in its funds as the government ambitiously proclaimed 1963 the "Year of Education," the start of a campaign to end illiteracy. Perhaps to atone for the corruption of the Odría dictatorship, the junta sought to project an image of honesty and efficiency. The government prosecuted several members of the Prado administration for graft and launched an assault against speculators in foodstuffs. New personal and corporate income tax laws set stiff penalties for tax evasion.

Soon after taking power, the junta appointed a commission of prominent jurists and professional politicians to draft a new election code. This law, submitted to the government in late September 1962, made several important changes in Peru's electoral processes. To reduce fraud, the statute required all qualified voters to reregister and present positive proof of identity. A single, comprehensive ballot provided by the state replaced the previous system of multiple ballots supplied by the parties, a procedure that had facilitated the intimidation of voters. The code discouraged presidential campaigns by small parties like those that fractionalized the vote in 1962. Using the census of 1961, the law reapportioned parliament for the first time in forty years. The coast received an increase in its congressional delegation, but Peru remained far away from the one-man, one-vote ideal. As in the past, the code based representation on total population rather than the number of qualified voters (literate adults). Thus, persons who possessed the franchise in the largely illiterate Sierra continued to have a greater voice in the legislature than voters in the more literate coast.

The campaign for the presidential election of June 1963 began immediately after the annulment of the previous race, and it was almost a rematch of the 1962 contest. There was, however, an important difference. Only one minor-party candidate competed with Belaúnde, Haya, and Odría. In January, Acción Popular entered an alliance with the Christian Democratic party (PDC), promising them the second vice-presidency and two cabinet posts. Although not officially endorsed by the Catholic Church, the Christian Democrats employed the papal encyclicals *Rerum novarum* and *Quadragesimo anno* to justify a program of radical reform. A pact between the AP and the PDC seemed logical. Belaúnde had many friends within the Christian Democratic party, whose strength was concentrated in his family's native Arequipa. Furthermore, both Belaúnde and the PDC leadership had been followers of former President Bustamante i Rivero and their two parties appealed to essentially the same constituency. The government's elimination of the other small leftist parties that had campaigned in 1962 apparently diverted most of their votes to Belaúnde.

Haya de la Torre's renomination by APRA raised some intriguing questions. Did not the armed forces block his election for purely personal reasons in 1962? The military now denied that they had done so and indicated that the junta would permit Haya's inauguration should he win the required plurality in June. Still, if the generals' well-known abhorrence of Víctor Raúl threatened to damage the party's chances at the polls, should not the Supreme Chief have stepped aside in favor of another leader? Manuel Seoane thought so. In his race for the vice-presidency in 1962, he had run well ahead of Haya and he wanted to lead the ticket in 1963. When Víctor Raúl again became the party's nominee, the volatile Seoane refused to run for any subordinate political office.

During the campaign Belaúnde exploited the issue of AP-

RA's stillborn pact with the UNO, calling Haya "Odría's boot-lick." But both Víctor Raúl and the former dictator attacked each other vigorously in the new contest, underscoring their contention that the earlier arrangement had been made only to avert a coup. Although reregistration had trimmed 300,000 names from the voting lists, 100,000 more citizens cast ballots in 1963 than in the previous year. Odría alone among the major candidates suffered an absolute decline in popularity. Víctor Raúl increased his vote by 75,000, but this was insufficient to offset the even larger gains made by Belaúnde. The final returns awarded Belaúnde 708,000 votes (39 percent); Haya de la Torre, 623,000 (34.3 percent); and Odría 463,000 (25.5 percent).

The Revolution That Failed, 1963–1968

Throughout his campaign Fernando Belaúnde had promised to preside over a "revolution without bullets," the accomplishment of major change within the democratic process. However, the composition of the new parliament, elected for a six-year term concurrent with that of the president, indicated that Belaúnde's task would be difficult. The administration AP-PDC alliance controlled only 20 of the 45 senate seats and 50 of 140 posts in the chamber of deputies. Shortly before taking the oath of office on July 28, the president-elect approached General Odría and Haya de la Torre with an offer of a few cabinet posts in exchange for legislative support. The two opposition leaders rejected this overture. Instead, they formed a pact, called "La Coalición," which gave them comfortable majorities in both houses of congress. APRA and the UNO claimed that their coalition was arranged only to elect parliamentary officers and that they would pursue their own legislative programs. Nevertheless, the two parties consistently united in their efforts to frustrate the administration. La Coalición, in fact, exhibited greater solidarity than did the AP-PDC alliance.

Most Apristas apparently had accepted the logic of their leaders' earlier political pacts—the Convivencia with Prado and, following Haya's explanation, even the ill-fated arrangement with Odría in 1962. The new link between APRA and the ultraconservative UNO, however, appalled many party members. As the hostile parliament began to impede Belaúnde's program, including several reforms long advocated by Haya de la

Torre, APRA appeared to have sold its soul for the narrowest of partisan reasons. Forty prominent Apristas signed an open letter to the press denouncing La Coalición. Liberal leader Manuel Seoane urged his party to cooperate with Belaúnde and withdrew from active politics when his admonitions were not heeded. He died in 1964. A dramatic demonstration of Aprista disaffection came in December 1963. In fulfillment of a campaign pledge, Belaúnde ordered municipal elections, a privilege that most cities had not exercised in more than four decades. With APRA's legendary grass-roots organization, La Coalición seemed certain of adding control of local government to its domination of parliament. Nevertheless, AP-PDC candidates won most of these contests, scoring several victories even in APRA's "solid north." In the race for mayor of Lima, Christian Democrat Luis Bedoya Reyes defeated Señora María Delgado de Odría.

Belaúnde made a significant break with the past in the selection of his cabinet. President Prado's regime had had a distinctly aristocractic cast. Comprised primarily of older men from wealthy Lima families, most of his ministers had received traditional educations in law or the humanities and had long careers in politics. The new official family, by contrast, was largely middle class in origin and had an average age of only forty-five. A majority of the ministers were natives of the provinces, many of them had been trained in technical fields, and few had extended service in partisan politics or government. "El Arquitecto," as the president's friends called him, and his team of *técnico* advisers quickly submitted an ambitious legislative program to parliament. In spite of obstruction by the APRA-UNO coalition, several of these measures were adopted. With the economy experiencing unprecedented prosperity and an atmosphere of hope pervading the country, the new administration enjoyed great popularity.

Belaúnde's civic action programs, especially Popular Cooperation, aroused considerable enthusiasm. During the summer of 1964, the government selected 550 vacationing university students from among 4,000 applicants for volunteer work assisting backward villagers and *barriada* residents with community development projects. Belaúnde employed the armed forces in several programs. Army and air force civic action teams were assigned to Popular Cooperation. The air force delivered mail and emergency aid to isolated areas and its aircraft provided low-cost cargo service for regions with poor overland transport facilities. Ten days after taking office the administration created the Fluvial Civic Service. Four navy gunboats, carrying medical personnel, teachers and agronomists, were dispatched to the rivers of the Montaña. In 1966, these craft logged 15,000 miles, providing service to 50,000 persons in 278 villages.

A study completed early in Belaúnde's tenure reported that one-third of Peru's children had never attended school and that the dropout rate was very high for those who did. To correct this problem the government increased the Ministry of Education's budget by 140 percent, permitting Peru to boast that it devoted a larger share of its gross national product to schools than any other Latin American nation. The results were impressive. During the Belaúnde years, enrollment in the primary grades grew by 41 percent, attendance at the high-school level jumped by 127 percent, and the number of students receiving vocational training doubled. Between 1961 and 1972 illiteracy was reduced from 40 to 33 percent nationally. In the five predominantly Indian departments of the Sierra the rate of illiteracy fell from 71 to 57 percent. In an effort to improve the quality of instruction the administration secured a law to "dignify the teacher" in 1964. The nation's poorly paid instructors were promised a 100 percent increase in their salaries over the next four years and the law guaranteed jobs to all graduates of teachers' colleges. As a result, enrollment at the country's normal schools surged by 179 percent. Higher education continued to expand rapidly, encouraged by the elimination of tuition at this level. Belaúnde opened more than a dozen new colleges and the number of university students doubled to 94,000.

The government undertook several public housing programs and opened a network of small clinics in provincial towns. An increase of 400 percent in expenditures for irrigation between 1962 and 1965 supported projects designed to water 1,575,000 arid acres and improve existing systems serving 675,000 acres. Work on the hydroelectric programs of preceding regimes intensified. Belaúnde purchased several new vessels for the national steamship company. Improvements at Callao and many smaller harbors increased the loading capacity of the country's public ports by 50 percent. Of all the public works projects, however, Belaúnde took greatest personal interest in his Jungle-Margin Highway, a road extending north to south through the western valleys of the Montaña. From this axis, east-west feeder roads would open vast tracts of virgin land to agriculture. In October 1963, Belaúnde signed an agreement with Colombia, Ecuador, and Bolivia to extend this artery along the entire, 3,500-mile western rim of the Amazon Basin. The Bolivarian Highway, as the international project was designated, anticipated expenditures of a half-billion dollars. Peru's section of the highway, 970 miles in length, was estimated to cost 172 million dollars plus an additional 56 million dollars for access roads. When completed in 1979, about five million acres of land would be available to 500,000 Peruvian colonists. Work on the project progressed rapidly as Peruvian army engineers and private contractors bridged raging rivers and cut through jungle-covered mountains. Old, isolated communities along this route experienced an economic revolution, and pioneer farmers quickly established themselves in newly opened areas.

During his presidential campaign Belaúnde pledged that the colonization of the Amazon would be only one sally in the battle to alleviate the nation's agrarian problems. He indicated that the redistribution of estates in the Sierra and along the coast would be the major thrust of his attack. In August 1963, the two-week-old administration submitted its agrarian reform proposal to parliament. With some 240 articles, this extremely complicated measure called for the expropriation of large properties and the compensation of the owners with long-term bonds. Affected estates would be distributed in family-sized units to farmers who would pay for their plots over a twenty-year period.

Belaúnde's bill attempted to satiate the land hunger of the peasants without seriously disrupting the economy. The modern plantations of the coast would retain enough land to permit efficient operation. The first 375 acres of permanently irrigated land were exempted from nationalization. Holdings in excess of this basic limit were liable to expropriation on a sliding scale according to the original size of the estate. Very large enterprises might retain up to 3,700 acres. In addition, the most efficient plantations that practiced enlightened labor policies could receive an exceptional exemption allowing them to keep as much as 7,000 acres. Multiples of the limits for irrigated coastal estates were to be used in determining the maximum allowable size for less desirable croplands and pastures throughout the country. The proposed law also provided for the concentration of very small parcels into larger units, the formation of farm cooperatives, and the extension of financial and technical assistance to increase agricultural productivity.

Surprised by the swiftness of the administration's initiative, the APRA-UNO opposition stalled the agrarian reform bill while it labored to formulate alternatives. The UNO, representing the nation's most conservative landowners, unveiled its agrarian program three weeks later. This proposal emphasized colonization along with government financial and technical aid to stimulate production within the existing tenure pattern. Loathe to let the upstart Acción Popular gain credit for this long-awaited reform, APRA alternately labeled the government plan as "reactionary" and "Communist-inspired." Belaúnde's measure, they charged, permitted archaic haciendas to retain excessive amounts of land while destroying the efficiency of the modern plantations. APRA claimed that its agrarian reform, sent to congress in October, provided for greater administrative flexibility. The government might expropriate some estates in their entirety and leave others completely intact. When parliament adjourned in late November 1963, without enacting agrarian reform, the president called the lawmakers into special session. The proposal still failed to emerge from the legislative labyrinth, but parliament did amend the constitution to permit the compensation of landowners in bonds rather than exclusively in cash as the 1933 charter required.

In his efforts to dislodge the agrarian reform bill from congress, Belaúnde received the tacit cooperation of the nation's peasants and their activist leaders. Land invasions intensified in 1963, when an estimated 300,000 persons participated in the seizures. Front-page stories in the conservative press warned of the revolutionary potential of these disorders. Landowners strengthened their private armies and formed "self-defense leagues." The APRA-UNO coalition demanded that the administration oust the trespassers and censured the minister of the interior for failing to preserve the peace. Belaúnde at first minimized the danger and refused to take forceful action. He hoped to avoid a bloody confrontation, and the chief executive probably relished the leverage that the crisis gave him in his struggle with parliament. In January 1964, however, the first major invasion took place on the coast. About 10,000 persons occupied 30,000 acres in Piura, and the president sent the heavily armed civil guard to evict them. In the following weeks police killed 17 squatters in Cuzco and arrested 200 peasant leaders. Meanwhile, Belaúnde used the limited authority of the military government's agrarian reform decree to purchase and redistribute estates in regions of greatest turmoil.

As the situation in the countryside became increasingly volatile, the AP-PDC parliamentarians and their opposition formed a committee to reach a compromise on agrarian reform. Aprista amendments weakened Belaúnde's original proposal which was, itself, of doubtful effectiveness. Two of these changes virtually exempted from expropriation the great estates of the coast, the stronghold of APRA's labor unions. The final law, number 15037, was a vaguely worded administrative nightmare, dividing responsibility for its implementation between the executive and legislative branches of government. The 51 procedures required before the peasant obtained title to his new parcel provided numerous opportunities for bureaucratic sabotage. The reform severely taxed scarce resources. It necessitated an army of technicians to make preliminary studies and a large portion of the compensation was to be made in cash. These obstacles notwithstanding, it was estimated that, at best, the agrarian reform could provide farms for only one-tenth of the republic's land-poor peasants. The president, however, urged his followers to support the measure and signed the bill into law on May 21, 1964.

The agrarian reform law was both the last of Belaúnde's major successes and the first in a series of failures that clouded his remaining years as president. The general optimism attending the enactment of the measure soon faded into disillusionment as the administration failed to make the best of a bad law. The final bill provided that a scant 3 percent of the national revenues be used to finance agrarian reform. The government spent less than two-thirds of that amount for the program. By mid-1968, little more than 1.5 million acres had been affected and only 20,000 farmers had benefited from this action. Most of the land acquired, in fact, consisted of haciendas purchased outright and many of these transactions had been initiated by the previous regime. Peasants who had seized these lands, forcing the government's hand, were the principal beneficiaries.

Fortunately for Belaúnde the ineffectiveness of the agrarian reform had not become manifest by June 1965. In that month Luis de la Puente Uceda, who had transformed his APRA Rebelde into the Leftist Revolutionary Movement (MIR), began guerrilla operations in isolated pockets of the departments of Cuzco and Junín. In September, Héctor Béjar's National Liberation Army (ELN) undertook a similar task in the mountains and jungles of northern Ayacucho. Composed primarily of students, these armed bands used the promise of land to attract peasant volunteers. The local farmers, however, rejected the appeals of the revolutionaries. Instead, they frequently cooperated with counterinsurgency units of the Peruvian army which conducted a massive campaign to destroy these rebel groups. Puente Uceda was killed, Béjar was captured, and by January 1966 both the MIR and the ELN had been suppressed.

Army commandos could not be used to eliminate Belaúnde's peaceful critics. The failure of the agrarian reform program produced increasingly bitter denunciations from the left wing of Acción Popular, led by Vice-President Seoane, and from the Christian Democrats. At the same time, APRA and the UNO sharpened their attacks on the administration. The opposition-dominated parliament seemingly employed every opportunity to force the resignation of cabinet officers and used its control over appropriations to embarrass the president. By the end of 1965, Belaúnde's promised revolution had faltered.

Many of the administration's difficulties were financial in origin, but Belaúnde did not preside over a general economic recession. The republic's gross national product grew at a respectable annual average of more than 5 percent during the 1963–68 period. Peru's exports increased 60 percent in value. The nation's factories augmented their production by more than one-third and, in 1966, manufacturing surpassed agriculture as the largest component of the national income. Nevertheless, Belaúnde could not adequately fund his programs and he was unwilling to curtail them. During his tenure public spending soared from 14 billion *soles* to more than 30 billion *soles*. The treasury ended an old arrangement with a consortium of five private banks, the Caja de Depósitos y Consignaciones, which had collected various taxes for a handsome commission and assumed this function itself. In spite of this and other improvements in fiscal management, however, the government's revenues did not keep pace with its expenditures. State spending surpassed its regular income by an average of 17 percent a year.

To eliminate these budget deficits Belaúnde submitted a new revenue program to parliament. The package included an increase in the income tax, imposts on real estate, and a tax on the dividends of corporations. Adopting the slogan "No More Taxes!" APRA and its UNO allies blocked these measures for three years. Belaúnde, himself, contributed to the treasury's woes by eroding the government's already meager tax base. He amplified the Industrial Promotion Law, which granted tax exemptions to new factories, and extended this system of incentives to the countryside with a new Agricultural Promotion Law. Another measure permitted goods destined for enterprises in the Montaña to enter the country free of tariffs. Soon, Iquitos became the entrepôt for a booming contraband trade in luxury goods. The government paid its bills by resorting to the printing press—doubling the supply of paper *soles*—and to foreign loans. The external debt jumped from 187 million dollars to 750 million dollars during Belaúnde's tenure. Furthermore, because of frosty relations between Lima and Washington, Peru obtained relatively little long-term, low-interest money from the Alliance for Progress. Belaúnde secured several short-term loans from private banks in Europe and the United States. The repayment of these obligations haunted the executive during his last year in office.

The rapid expansion of public and private spending as well as the regime's monetary policies put great pressure upon the *sol* and the nation experienced a spiraling inflation. Between 1963 and 1966, the consumer price index climbed by 40 percent and the cost of living escalated 21 percent during the next year. The price of food rose even faster as Peru's farms failed to match the fecundity of its people. An unfavorable balance of trade soon complicated the monetary problem. Belaúnde hoped to induce large-scale foreign investment to increase the volume of Peru's mineral exports. A protracted tax dispute with the Southern Peru Copper Company, however, inhibited significant new capitalization of this industry. Still, the value of the republic's exports continued to rise throughout the period. But beginning in 1965, the country's sales abroad did not keep pace with its purchases. In that year Peruvian sugar earned 40 percent less foreign exchange. More importantly, the heretofore dynamic fish meal industry entered a two-year period of stagnation. The nation's trade deficit averaged almost sixty million dollars per year from 1965 to 1968. While inflation threatened to price Peru's exports out of the world market, dollars and other stable currencies became cheaper, encouraging Peruvians to purchase even greater quantities of goods from abroad. The trade deficit, heavy service on the foreign debt, and a serious flight of capital as wealthy citizens sought safer ground for their savings produced a drastic decline in the treasury's gold reserves. To reverse this trend the government devalued the *sol* by 35 percent in early

September 1967, and the national currency slipped another 10 percent in value by the end of the year. The republic's salaried workers, who saw the purchasing power of their wages drop precipitously, responded with a wave of strikes.

The worsening economic crisis and the policies adopted to combat it produced a severe strain on the already weakened government alliance. The Christian Democrats split into warring factions. In November 1967, the administration suffered a defeat in an important special election and the PDC withdrew its support from the regime. The rift within Belaúnde's own Acción Popular became almost complete schism. The party's national convention in late 1967 elected Edgardo Seoane secretary general, rejecting the president's personal choice. The next June, AP nominated Seoane to run for the presidency in 1969. During this same period, stories of widespread corruption in government, especially in the award of public works contracts, pervaded Lima. The exposure of a monumental civilian-military smuggling ring shocked the nation in mid-1968.

"El Arquitecto" had an inventive mind, a flare for bold concepts and catchy slogans that captured the imagination of the public. But he showed almost no interest in the drudgery of fiscal administration and little talent for resolving the related political problems. Belaúnde also displayed an unfortunate penchant for making foolish statements that delighted his partisan critics. Although devaluation of the *sol* seemed inevitable as early as 1966, the president repeatedly asserted that such a step would be "treasonous." Trying to present an air of optimism during the fiscal crisis, Belaúnde declared that some of Peru's most notable triumphs had occurred when the treasury was bankrupt. Thereafter, one caustic journalist dubbed him the "greatest economist since Marie Antoinette." As his problems intensified, the chief executive seemed to lose touch with reality. Opponents accused him of retreating more and more to the security of his study and the solace of his architectural models. He no longer appeared willing to continue the struggle for reform, but seemed anxious only to survive his full, constitutional term.

As reports of a military conspiracy against the regime began to circulate in 1968, the beleaguered Belaúnde received support from a most unexpected source—APRA. The party's harassment of the administration had been designed, in part, to weaken Acción Popular and secure the election of an Aprista government in 1969. However, fears now arose that the armed forces might oust Belaúnde, cancel the forthcoming elections, and establish a long-term military regime. APRA's UNO allies suffered a major defection early in 1968, and the coalition of the two opposition parties ended a short time later. The president appointed a new cabinet in May, under the premiership of Dr. Osvaldo Hercelles, a Lima physician with close ties to APRA. The next month, the Aprista parliamentary bloc joined Belaúnde's remaining partisans to pass a bill granting the executive broad authority for sixty days to decree fiscal reforms and other measures to resolve Peru's economic problems. The administration's tax program quickly became law, and a policy of funding public works only as revenues permitted eased the pressure on the treasury. Soon the trade deficit ended and the rate of inflation was halved. The government began negotiations to refinance the onerous foreign debt and secure large new investment in the mining industry. With the passage of a law limiting the participation of foreign capital in Peru's commercial banks, Belaúnde seemed to be reembarking on the road to reform. Although the austerity program produced some grumbling, the administration appeared to have weathered the economic and political storm. But then, the president signed a controversial agreement with the International Petroleum Company, setting in motion events that culminated in his ouster.

The dispute between Peru and the International Petroleum Company had a long and complex history. Two legal questions formed the crux of the issue: could a private party own subsoil minerals in Peru? More specifically, did the IPC have absolute title to the oil at its 640-square-mile La Brea y Pariñas field on the north coast? According to ancient Spanish law the crown owned all mineral wealth and granted concessions to individuals for the exploitation of mines. From almost the beginning of its independent existence Peru, along with the other Latin American nations, maintained that the sovereign state had inherited the prerogatives of the Spanish king, including ownership of subterranean minerals. In 1824, however, the indigent Bolívar regime authorized the sale of all forms of state property to raise revenue. Two years later the government granted the tar pits at La Brea to a Peruvian citizen in satisfaction of his claims against the treasury.

In the ensuing decades, the tar deposits changed hands several times and the adjoining hacienda of Pariñas was added to the original property. The oil beneath the estate first acquired commercial importance in the 1860s. New mineral laws adopted in the next decade required that all "concessions" be validated and appraised for taxes. But Genaro Helguero, the proprietor of La Brea y Pariñas, ignored this directive, claiming actual ownership of the property rather than status as a concessionaire. A few years later, however, Helguero attempted to clarify his unique legal position in preparation for a sale of the holding. In 1888, he apparently received a confirmation of his title and a special tax regime for La Brea y Pariñas. Helguero quickly sold the property to British interests who, in turn, leased the field to the London and Pacific Petroleum Company. Heavy capital investment now brought the first large-scale exploitation of the property.

The privileged tax status of La Brea y Pariñas came under fire in 1911. The government demanded that London and Pacific Petroleum submit to the same tax system that applied to other oil companies, an action that would have increased the firm's tax liabilities fortyfold. The British government was drawn into the controversy, which culminated in a 1921 agreement to submit the dispute to binding international arbitration. The next year, however, representatives of the oil company and the Peruvian government arrived at their own compromise and the arbitration panel announced this settlement as its official award. The British owners of La Brea y Pariñas sold the field in 1924 to the IPC, a Canadian-registered subsidiary of Standard Oil of New Jersey, a firm that had leased the property ten years earlier. The new owners believed that they had acquired valid title to the surface and subsoil of La Brea y Pariñas and a tax regime that was inviolable under international law.

In the early 1930s, however, the Peruvian government began to question the legality of the 1922 tax award. From that time onward, nationalists increasingly challenged the IPC's title to the property itself, maintaining that private ownership of the subsoil was impossible under Peruvian law. They asserted that even if the 1826 title to La Brea were valid, it applied only to the original tar pits and not to the then-unknown petroleum deposits under the much larger estate. In 1957, the company petitioned the state to exchange its title to La Brea y Pariñas for a standard concession under the 1952 Petroleum Code. The government denied this request. By 1968, criticis of the company claimed that the IPC owed the nation from fifty million to more than one billion dollars, depending upon whether the firm was merely "evading taxes" on its own oil or had "stolen" oil belonging to the state. Although lawyers for the company and government attorneys produced reams of documents to support their assertions, nationalistic rhetoric had transformed the legal question into a political issue of the first magnitude.

The IPC was a very vulnerable target, a highly visible example of "Yankee economic imperialism." The firm extracted almost a quarter of Peru's petroleum from La Brea y Pariñas and another 60 percent of the country's oil from the Lobitos field, a property operated by the IPC under a regular concession. The company's installations at Talara represented two-thirds of the nation's refining capacity. IPC's ubiquitous ESSO stations retailed most of Peru's gasoline and the firm was virtually the only source of aviation fuel. Although International Petroleum did not have a complete monopoly of the Peruvian oil industry, the firm demonstrated its dominant position in 1959, when its threat to suspend drilling operations forced the government to permit large increases in gasoline prices. The company used a similar tactic in 1967, when the devaluation of the *sol* slashed its income. Critics charged the company with all manner of wrongdoing, from exploiting its workers to bribing public officials and controlling the nation's press. They claimed that the IPC's tremendous economic power endangered the sovereignty of the state. With a book value of 190 million dollars, the company was the third largest enterprise in Peru. Furthermore, Standard Oil of New Jersey, the IPC's parent organization, earned annual revenues four times greater than the country's gross national product.

The IPC's management in the 1960s suffered from the sins of its fathers. In the early decades of the century, the firm had made huge profits. It also had loaned money to financially pressed regimes and purchased the favor of important politicians. These practices, however, were not uncommon in Peru and government officials exerted considerable pressure to exact funds from the oil company. Although IPC's workers always were well-paid by Peruvian standards, foreigners nearly monopolized the managerial positions while nationals of Peru supplied the menial labor. Talara and other company towns were rigidly segregated. The comfortable living quarters and recreational facilities of the foreign elite contrasted sharply with the hovels that sheltered the native workers. After the 1930s, however, the company worked diligently to improve its image. The firm engaged in a number of philanthropic activities and sponsored quality publications de-

voted to Peruvian history and culture. It assumed a "correct"
attitude in its relations with government officials. The IPC built
new housing for its common labor force and provided many
other fringe benefits, including perhaps the best schools in the
country.* Government price controls, in force after 1939, restricted the company's profits and made Peruvian petroleum
products among the least expensive in the world. By the 1960s,
the International Petroleum Company presented itself as a
model enterprise. With a payroll of 18,000 workers, the firm was
Peru's most important private employer. Seventy-two percent of
IPC's upper management personnel, including the company's
president, were Peruvian nationals. It was the republic's second
largest taxpayer.

In his July 1963 inaugural address President Belaúnde rashly
promised to resolve the IPC dispute within ninety days. Negotiations began immediately between the administration and the
company. International Petroleum offered to exchange its contested title to La Brea y Pariñas for a contract to exploit the field
for the government and a tax schedule that would permit an
adequate profit. Fearing the wrath of the Miró Quesada family's
passionately anti-IPC newspaper, *El Comercio,* and believing that
the Kennedy administration would not vigorously support the
company, Belaúnde presented a tough counterproposal to the
firm. It included a payment of fifty million dollars to satisfy
"delinquent taxes" and a tax regime that the IPC insisted would
absorb all of its profits. When ninety days passed without the
promised settlement, the embarrassed executive asked parliament to abrogate the company's 1922 tax award and follow one
of two courses: expropriate the IPC, reducing any compensation
by the amount of its alleged back taxes, or issue the firm an
operating contract for La Brea y Pariñas on the government's
terms. Congress did nullify the firm's special tax status, but then
tossed the political hot potato back to the president. The legislators authorized the executive branch to negotiate a "suitable
arrangement" with the company and report any action to parliament.

After six months of relative inactivity, negotiations resumed.
In July 1964, the government and the company reached an
informal agreement on the general terms of a settlement. The
IPC would renounce its title to La Brea y Pariñas in return for a

*Ironically, young Fernando Belaúnde had been one of the architects
who designed the new workers' facilities at Talara in the early 1950s.

quitclaim on any delinquent taxes. The company would continue to operate the field for the government, refine the state's oil at Talara, and receive a commission of 20 percent of the net profits from the sale of these products, which the IPC would market through its ESSO outlets. With hindsight it appears that Belaúnde should have finalized this arrangement. His personal popularity, at its peak in mid-1964, soon would decline, greatly increasing the political risks of accepting an even more advantageous settlement at a later date. The president, however, dreaded the inevitably caustic reaction to this compromise and refused to submit it to his hostile parliament.

The administration abruptly changed its bargaining position in December 1964. The government now demanded that the IPC simply renounce its claim to the disputed oil field without receiving an operating contract or a release from tax obligations. Stunned, the firm rejected these terms and suspended negotiations. The Belaúnde regime and the company engaged in sporadic, fruitless talks during the next three years. The administration insisted that the IPC tacitly acknowledge the illegality of both its title to La Brea y Pariñas and its special tax status. The company was prepared to make a substantial cash payment to soothe nationalist sentiment. But blistering under incessant charges that the firm had wrongly enriched itself at the expense of the Peruvian people, the company's officials balked at any settlement that did not implicitly recognize the validity of its title and the legality of the 1922 tax award. Inflexible Peruvian nationalism had found a peer in the IPC's stubborn company pride.

The diplomatic intervention of the United States government complicated negotiations between Peru and the International Petroleum Company. The Kennedy administration had welcomed the election of Belaúnde, whose reformist regime promised to become a showcase of the Alliance for Progress. Washington, however, wanted an amicable resolution of the IPC question. The United States feared that a less than equitable settlement would establish a precedent that might endanger North American holdings in other Latin American nations and around the world. Furthermore, private investment had a prominent role in the development strategy of the Alliance for Progress. The maintenance of a "favorable business climate" was deemed essential to attract this capital. The policy of the State Department concerning the IPC affair became increasingly rigid after the succession of Lyndon Johnson in November 1963.

Washington failed to provide Belaúnde with the generous

funding that it had promised at the time of his inauguration. Hoping that Lima quickly would realize that Alliance for Progress money was tied to the IPC dispute, United States officials initially attributed delays in loans for Peruvian projects to the State Department's bureaucratic inefficiency. Only in 1966, after Belaúnde had failed to "get the message," was he candidly informed that economic aid had been suspended because of the oil issue. The Peruvian press denounced this policy as economic intervention outlawed by the Charter of the Organization of American States and described United States envoy John Wesley Jones as the "Ambassador of IPC." Outraged public opinion greatly increased the difficulty of achieving a new compromise on the petroleum question.

Recognizing that further economic pressure would be counterproductive, Washington resumed small-scale aid to Peru in 1966. The next year, however, another dispute again strained relations between the two countries. Following the purchase of new military aircraft by Chile, Peru's traditional rival, and several accidents with Peru's dilapidated Korean-War vintage jets, Belaúnde attempted to purchase F-5 fighters in the United States. This relatively inexpensive craft was sturdy, easily maintained, and seemed suitable to Peru's needs. The United States congress, however, blocked the sale, asserting that Washington did not want to abet a new Latin American arms race. Under intense pressure from the armed forces and Peruvian nationalists, Belaúnde ordered very expensive, sophisticated Mirage jets from France. For a second time the State Department expressed its displeasure with an embargo on loans to Peru. Belaúnde later attributed many of his economic woes and the overthrow of his government to the "financial blackmail" of Washington.

In July 1967, the Peruvian parliament responded to the new suspension of United States aid by formally nullifying the IPC's title to La Brea y Pariñas and ordering the registration of that property as a national petroleum reserve. Although this action technically expropriated the holding, the law permitted the company to continue "temporarily" its exploitation of the field. In spite of this new prodding, the oil firm adamantly refused to meet Belaúnde's terms for a settlement until the middle of 1968, when the campaign for the next presidential election began. It seemed inevitable that nationalist passions soon would be aroused to the point that public opinion would force the uncompensated expropriation of La Brea y Pariñas and perhaps the firm's other properties as well. On July 25, the company informed the government that it would accept the president's proffered settlement. In his Independence Day address to the nation three days later, Belaúnde euphorically announced that the dispute had been "settled" and that he soon would take formal possession of the oil field.

The president was determined to end the IPC conflict before the expiration of his sixty-day authorization to decree economic reforms. Following arduous, around-the-clock negotiations that almost collapsed at the last moment, the government and the company signed an agreement at five o'clock in the morning of August 13, the day Belaúnde had set as the deadline for a settlement. A few hours later, the executive flew to La Brea y Pariñas where he signed the Act of Talara, formally proclaiming the nation's ownership of the property. Although he described the final agreement as a triumph for Peru, the settlement evoked considerable controversy as its provisions gradually became known. The International Petroleum Company relinquished its title to the subsoil minerals and surface installations at the field, but the firm retained possession of its refinery and storage facilities at Talara. In return for an agreement to enlarge the refinery, the government canceled its tax claims against the firm, now officially calculated at 144 million dollars. Under a separate contract Peru's national oil company, the Empresa Petrolera Fiscal (EPF), agreed to sell 80 percent of the petroleum that it extracted from La Brea y Pariñas to the IPC. The firm obtained the right to manufacture and market oil products for forty years. After that period, the Talara refinery complex would revert to the state. Critics of this arrangement charged that the price set for the sale of government oil to the IPC was too low, much less than the cost of imported Venezuelan crude. Furthermore, the EPF had assumed responsibility for the least profitable sector of the industry—extracting crude oil—while the foreign company retained the more lucrative refining and marketing operations. Finally, nationalists asserted that La Brea y Pariñas would be pumped dry before the nation gained ownership of the Talara refinery.

Carlos Loret de Mola, the president of the EPF, resigned his post on September 6 to protest the terms of the settlement with the oil company. Four days later, he made a sensational statement that magnified the controversy into a national scandal and doomed the Belaúnde regime. A participant in the recent negotiations, Loret de Mola avowed that he had signed an eleven-page contract with the IPC. The former bureaucrat claimed that on the final page he had noted the minimum price that the IPC must pay for the state's oil. The government, however, published a contract that had only ten pages. Furthermore, the original document had been lost! The mystery of the missing "page eleven" may never be solved. Belaúnde asserted that it never existed and that Loret de Mola, whom the president had refused to reappoint for another term as head of the national oil agency, manufactured the story for political reasons. Independent observers have suggested that page eleven might have existed and could have been lost in the last minute rush. In any event, it seems that Loret de Mola's *página once* would have been superfluous. It merely summarized the complex pricing formula contained in the first ten pages. Moreover, the IPC representative affixed his signature at the bottom of page ten, so Loret de Mola's notations on the following sheet were not binding upon the company. Finally, the price agreement was subject to renegotiation. The complexity of the contract, however, and the mysterious disappearance of the original document gave credibility to charges that a gross fraud had been perpetrated.

Edgardo Seoane denounced the IPC settlement in a televised address September 20 and disassociated Acción Popular from the actions of the president. Invoking his prerogative as founder of the party, Belaúnde declared a "reorganization" of AP and revoked Seoane's presidential nomination. A demeaning brawl ensued between the supporters of Belaúnde and Seoane for physical possession of Acción Popular's headquarters in downtown Lima. The Christian Democrats and the UNO joined in the attack against the IPC agreement and APRA now hedged its original support for the contract. Both *La Prensa* and *El Comercio* staged editorial assaults on the regime. Cardinal Juan Landázuri Ricketts, the Roman Catholic primate of Peru and an old friend of Belaúnde, asked the president to "clarify" the IPC matter. Most ominously, thirty-six generals issued a statement condemning the agreement with the oil company. Led by the military ministers, the cabinet resigned on October 2. The chief executive quickly appointed a new cabinet, but the members held their portfolios for only a few hours.

A column of tanks surrounded the Palace of Pizarro at two o'clock in the morning of October 3. A troop of soldiers entered the building without resistance and seized the president. Loudly denouncing his captors as "traitors," the pajama-clad Belaúnde was whisked from his official residence and placed on board an airplane bound for Buenos Aires enroute to eventual exile as a visiting professor at Harvard University. Several thousand students vigorously demonstrated their anger at the destruction of constitutional government and APRA called for a popular uprising. The armed forces responded by arresting 300 students and silencing APRA's radio station. Meanwhile, Argentine officials thwarted a quixotic attempt by Belaúnde to board an airliner departing for Lima. Within a few days, the military had established firm control over the country. On October 9, the government abrogated the settlement with the IPC and nationalized La Brea y Pariñas along with the Talara refinery complex, an action that brought broad public support for the new regime.

The Statute of the Revolutionary Government, issued on the day of the coup, declared that the armed forces had assumed power because of the "immediate necessity of putting an end to economic chaos, to administrative immorality and improvisation, to the surrender of our natural resources, . . . as well as to the loss of the principle of authority and [the Belaúnde government's] inability to achieve the urgent structural reforms demanded for the well-being of the Peruvian people and the development of the country." This official explanation of the revolution was rejected in many quarters. Belaúnde, APRA, and some foreign commentators unfamiliar with changing ideological currents within the armed forces initially branded the military intervention a right-wing reaction. Thus, the "oligarchy" had prompted the generals to oust the president because they resented his reforms, especially those concerning taxes and banking, and because the conservatives feared the election of a more radical regime in 1969.

Skeptics also questioned the high-sounding patriotic phrases of the revolutionary manifesto and explained the movement primarily in terms of the narrow, institutional interests of the military establishment or the personal ambitions and animosities of the coup's leaders. It was argued that the army, which played the key role in the takeover, resented the relative decline in its share of the defense budget due to the purchase of expensive equipment by the navy and air force. Some observers suggested that the generals overthrew Belaúnde because he planned to investigate corruption in the armed forces. Critics of the revolution often emphasized the fact that Gen. Juan Velasco Alvarado,

the army's senior officer, had been bypassed a few months earlier
for the post of war minister and that he would have been retired
from active duty in January 1969.

Although the officer corps, like most Peruvians, was hostile
to the International Petroleum Company and Belaúnde's contract with the firm, neither the military nor most other commentators attributed primary importance to the IPC affair as the
cause of the coup. Popular outrage at the oil settlement and the
subsequent "page eleven" scandal, however, determined the
timing of the revolution. The IPC incident grieviously weakened
Belaúnde and provided a *cause célèbre* which the armed forces
could exploit to gain public support for a coup. It also brought
into the movement several officers who had been reluctant to
strike at their commander in chief.

The Revolutionary Statute of October 3, although couched
in rather general terms, seems a far better explanation for the
coup than those that emphasized personalities or short-range
institutional advantages for the military. The armed forces had
favored Belaúnde's election five years earlier largely because
they agreed with his reformist platform. The soldiers continued
to support his government while it appeared capable of bringing
needed social and economic change. During the long deadlock
between the executive and parliament, high-ranking officers
repeatedly offered the president military assistance to suppress
congress and dictatorially institute reform by decree. This idea,
however, was anathema to the democratic Belaúnde. By late
1967, the armed forces had lost confidence in his ability to
govern the nation effectively. The promised "revolution without
bullets" had failed.

Political developments in 1968 offered little hope that significant reform would be achieved in the near future through
constitutional procedures. APRA's belated assistance to Belaúnde seemed designed only to keep the lame-duck regime
afloat until the next election, the approach of which distressed
the military. Acción Popular, the UNO, and even the small
Christian Democratic party had split into warring factions. Only
APRA remained united and it appeared likely that the conservative, Belaúndista wing of AP would enter an electoral pact with
the Apristas. And who would be the candidate of the Partido del
Pueblo? In June, APRA's national convention had nominated
seventy-three-year-old Haya de la Torre for a fifth presidential
race. Military antipathy toward the party and the aged leader who

personified it had intensified since 1962. Ideologically, the officers' hostility for APRA now rested almost exclusively on the party's increasing conservatism. While APRA had been retreating to the right during the previous decades, opinion within the military establishment had shifted to the left. Perhaps more important than conflicting ideas, however, the once revolutionary organization's sabotage of Belaúnde's reform program convinced the armed forces of the complete cynicism and civic bankruptcy of the party. APRA, for many officers, had demonstrated its unworthiness to rule the nation.

11

The Pragmatic Revolution:

Peru Since 1968

PERU'S REVOLUTIONARY GOVERNMENT OF THE ARMED FORCES quickly proved to be a novelty among Latin American military regimes. Unlike the conservative martial dictatorships most typical of the region, the administration of Gen. Juan Velasco Alvarado accomplished sweeping reform during the first phase of the revolution, from 1968 to 1975. With the exception of Castro's Cuba, no nation of the Western hemisphere experienced such dramatic change in so short a period. Furthermore, this was achieved largely without bloodshed or a complete suppression of personal liberties. Peru's ruling generals repeatedly asserted that their program was "neither capitalist nor communist" but distinctly "Peruvian." Indeed, the hallmark of the regime was its remarkable degree of innovation, a flair for experimentation that partially accounted for both its successes and failures. The complex reforms of the Velasco administration, of course, did not spring *sui generis* from the minds of a few military men. The government drew upon the expertise of many civilian advisers representing a wide variety of ideologies. The regime also dispatched observers to several different countries and received technical missions from all parts of the world. Although many reforms showed evidence of these foreign influences, the Velasco government was highly selective in the choice of ideas and considerably modified borrowed programs for application to Peru. The nation was not remodeled after any functioning system. The Peruvian armed forces brought a pragmatic revolution.

✑ The "New Generals"

A large body of literature concerning Peru's "new generals" appeared after they seized power in October 1968. Most of these studies attributed the reformist attitude of the armed forces to the social origins of the officer corps, their education and other professional experiences, the institutional interests of the military establishment, and to the growing pressure for change during the previous decade. The armies of Latin America, the dominant military service throughout the region, long had recruited their officers primarily from the middle sector of society and the Peruvian army did not deviate from this basic pattern. However, a very significant portion of Peru's career soldiers came from distinctly lower-middle-class or even working-class backgrounds, and a majority were natives of the neglected provinces. For some scholars these factors helped explain the apparent sympathy of many officers for the nation's humbler citizens, especially those in the underdeveloped interior. The army's often intimate contact with peasants during the civic action and counterinsurgency campaigns of the 1960s was thought to have reinforced the social consciences of the officers.

The desire of the armed forces to create a more open society with greater opportunities for the common man also was linked to the officers' own professional development. Although personalism undoubtedly played an important role within the armed forces, as it did throughout Peruvian society, the military career had been one of a few in which capable young men could appreciably improve their socioeconomic position without family wealth or political influence. The army was perhaps the most merit-oriented major institution in the country. Unlike the professional soldiers of the great powers, Peruvian officers had few opportunities to demonstrate their worth in combat. Therefore, the battle for promotion was waged in the classrooms of a series of schools. Nearly all army officers began their careers at the Chorrillos military academy, graduating as second lieutenants after four years. Promotion to captain normally required further training in a military specialty, and attendance at the Superior War College was mandatory for advancement to the rank of major. The more promising officers received additional instruction at foreign military schools, Peru's own Center for Higher Military Studies, and at civilian universities at home and abroad. Competition was keen for the advanced training that brought promotion, and these opportunities primarily depended upon previous academic performance. Consequently, the Peruvian army had a much higher correlation between educational achievement and professional advancement than did the United States army. In recent decades 80 percent of Peru's officers who attained the rank of division general graduated in the top quarter of their class at the military academy. Career patterns appeared to be similar in the navy and air force. While the nation possessed little expensive, sophisticated weaponry, Peru's military establishment was considered one of the more technically proficient armed forces in Latin America.

Much of the research probing the "new military mentality" stressed the influence of the Center for Higher Military Studies (CAEM), the institution that the deposed Fernando Belaúnde sardonically termed "the army's school for presidents." Beginning in the mid-1950s select groups of army and air force colonels and navy captains enrolled in the center's eight-month "national defense course," a program that transcended the limits of traditional military education. Destined for top positions within their services, these officers surveyed the nation's fundamental problems, explored remedial programs, and discussed the role of the armed forces in the formulation and implementation of high state policy. CAEM also functioned as the country's foremost "think tank," producing plans for several important reforms. Graduates of the school were strongly represented in the revolutionary government, but CAEM was not the only source of reformist sentiment within the armed forces. Several of the most ardent advocates of change—including President Velasco himself—had not attended the center, while some prominent alumni of the school were described as "conservatives." Still, CAEM acted as a lens, gathering certain ill-defined though broadly shared ideas of the officers and focusing these into a rather coherent body of doctrines. These frequently were expressed by spokemen for the military government.

According to CAEM theoreticians the armed forces were

responsible for the "integral defense" of the state, a charge that encompassed the maintenance of domestic order along with the protection of the nation's sovereignty and independence. Threats to the latter included overt armed attack, foreign-supported internal subversion, "economic aggression," and even "dependency." The military's duty to preserve domestic tranquillity was not a mandate to defend the status quo. CAEM doctrine asserted that the state existed to promote the "common good." Governments that did not effectively pursue this goal lacked legitimacy and, by implication, could justifiably be overthrown. The capacity of the armed forces to perform their integral defense function depended upon the realization of the "national potential"—that is, the maximum development of the country's material and human resources. The defense of the nation against external pressures required greater economic self-sufficiency and an improvement in the quality of Peru's manpower. Similarly, the preservation of internal peace necessitated the elimination of the extreme poverty and social injustice believed to foster violent revolution. CAEM summarized these ideas in the slogan "There Is No Defense Without Development!"

Many officers believed that the social and economic development needed to realize Peru's national potential required fundamental reforms. However, the governments prior to 1968 were unwilling or unable to undertake these changes. Spokesmen for the Velasco regime declared that powerful economic interests, both domestic and foreign, dominated the nation. Reformist and even avowedly "revolutionary" political parties along with their captive labor unions and peasant leagues were corrupt, self-serving bureaucracies—a "political oligarchy." Therefore, the armed forces took control of the state to bring social and economic justice to the people and restore morality, discipline, and patriotism to the government.

Altruism certainly was not the only motive for reform, however. For many officers the instinct of self-preservation may have been paramount in their desire for change. The "Peruvian Revolution" was also, in part, a preventive revolution. Although the army had been able to crush the guerrilla movements of the mid-1960s, the military intelligence services believed that the potential for internal subversion remained dangerously high. A mass, violent upheaval directed by militant Marxists could have destroyed Peru's professional military establishment along with other institutions revered by many soldiers, most notably the Church. In addition, such a movement would have imperiled the position of the middle class, the sector from which most officers emerged. Although the middle class opposed several programs of the Velasco regime, especially in its later years, this group generally maintained its standard of living. After 1968, economic benefits for the nation's poor were achieved largely at the expense of the upper class, a group that often snubbed high-ranking officers of low social origins.

Objectives less noble than reform undoubtedly attracted some officers to military rule: a wider arena to win professional recognition and promotion; increased budgets for the armed forces; the dual salaries—military and civilian—often paid to officers employed by state agencies; opportunities for graft; in short, the desire to wield power for good, evil or, simply, its own sake. Finally, many officers apparently disapproved of the imposition of military government in October 1968.

President Juan Velasco Alvarado typified Peru's "new generals." Born in Piura on June 16, 1910, he was among eleven children of a minor public employee. Velasco's family has been described as "working class" and his childhood one of "dignified poverty." A short, dark, emotional man of common speech and humble habits, he resembled in many ways Peru's other *cholo* president from Piura—Sánchez Cerro. In 1929, after attending public primary and secondary schools in his hometown, Velasco stowed away on a coastal steamer that carried him to Lima. He arrived too late for admission to Chorrillos, so the future president enlisted as a private in the army. The next year he won entrance to the military academy through competitive examination. Beyond this point, however, Velasco's career differed markedly from that of the arch-conspirator Sánchez Cerro. Graduating at the head of his infantry officers' class, Velasco shunned revolutionary politics and rose gradually through the ranks, becoming a division general in 1965. His assignments included teaching at the Superior War College and Chorrillos—where he served later as superintendent—military attaché in France, and Peru's representative on the prestigious Inter-American Defense Board.

Because of the institutional nature of the Revolutionary Government of the Armed Forces, General Velasco's role in the transformation of Peru often was underestimated. The president, unlike some of the officers around him, was not noted for his brilliance. Nor did he possess great charisma. Only his obvious sincerity made him an effective speaker. Short and somewhat stout with an Oriental cast to his face, the public called him "El Chino" and joked about his idiosyncracies. Nevertheless, many Peruvians could identify with Velasco. They were proud of the accomplishments of the revolution and respected its leader.

General Velasco's contribution to the revolution was more than symbolic, however. On Independence Day, 1974, the president made public the secret "Plan Inca," a document he claimed to have written personally prior to the 1968 coup. Drafted in admirable military style, the plan had thirty-one sections, each addressed to a particular national problem. After describing the "situation" in 1968, the document listed the "objective" of the revolution and outlined the "actions" needed to achieve this goal. Largely a statement of what the regime had accomplished by mid-1974, it seemed unlikely that Velasco could have composed the plan in its entirety six years earlier. The revolution had been shaped by forces unforeseen in 1968—the actions of foreign countries, the fluctuations of the international economy, the pressures of civilian interest groups, and the vagaries of nature. Most importantly, the armed forces often were deeply divided over the course of the revolution and many compromises were made to accommodate these discordant factions. That the revolution progressed so far without destroying the essential unity of the military establishment testified to Velasco's political skill.

Velasco, four other generals, and four colonels planned and executed the overthrow of the Belaúnde government. The conspirators initially bypassed several senior army officers and the leadership of the navy and air force. A desire to preserve the unity of the armed forces induced these elements to participate in the "institutional government." After October 1968, public declarations of solidarity with the "Revolution" became almost a ritual for Peru's military leaders. Most officers probably could have subscribed to a minimum statement of the regime's goals—the achievement of a modern, prosperous, and more just society free from foreign domination. But considerable difference of opinion existed within the armed forces concerning the magnitude of change required, the appropriate means to achieve these ends, and the revolution's priorities. A "conservative" sector placed economic development—requiring high levels of saving and investment—ahead of social justice on their list of priorities. They envisioned the continuation of a significant place for private enterprise, including closely regulated foreign capital, in the economy. A "radical" element called for a profound reordering of society. They emphasized a greater role for the state and various forms of worker-managed enterprises in the nation's economy and a more rapid redistribution of income. The radicals often were willing to slow the process of economic development to achieve greater social justice. Less well delineated were the positions of these groups concerning civil liberties and citizen participation in the restructuring of society. The conservative element included several senior army generals and most high-ranking naval officers. The radical tendency was strong within the army and among junior officers in the other services. Individuals not easily placed within these two loose categories were described as "moderates."

Until his removal from office in August 1975, General Velasco was the balance wheel of the revolutionary government. Sometimes described as a "moderate," he occasionally sided with the conservatives. But at critical moments the president supported the radicals, helping to effect a revolution within the revolution. Each major policy decision produced a shake-up within the regime. Several cabinet members were reassigned to different ministries and some were forced into early retirement. Within the upper echelon of the administration only Velasco continued to occupy the post he held in 1968. Yet the military coalition was maintained through strict adherence to seniority in promotions, especially within the command structure, and the judicious distribution of cabinet posts among the various factions. The second most important position within the regime—the combined office of prime minister and minister of war—was occupied by army generals associated with the conservative element. The other portfolios were distributed among the three military branches and staffed proportionately with officers reflecting the ideological tendencies of the different services. Some ministries, especially those controlled by the navy, had a reputation for "conservatism"; others were considered "radical." The crucial role of General Velasco in preserving the unity and equilibrium of the regime was demonstrated in February and March 1973, when the president became gravely ill. Following two emergency abdominal operations, circulatory problems forced the amputation of his right leg. Prime Minister Edgardo Mercado Jarrín assumed Velasco's duties, but this conservative general had considerable difficulty exercising authority over his colleagues.

Largely due to strong differences of opinion within the military establishment, the programs of the Velasco administration exhibited a high degree of ambiguity that baffled observers and made the word "pluralism" one of the more hackneyed terms of Peru's revolutionary rhetoric. The public pronouncements of government officials repeatedly expressed the regime's desire for the free expression of diverse ideas, a multiplicity of organized interest groups, friendly relations with both East and West, and a "plural economy" that would be "neither capitalist nor communist." The new economic system was to include small, family owned businesses; larger, "reformed" private enterprises; state corporations and joint public-private ventures; workers' cooperatives; and a novel "social property" sector.

The Velasco administration erected the framework of the plural economy in a series of sweeping "general laws" governing most of the country's major economic activities. Extremely complex and often vague, these measures initially attempted to harmonize the frequently conflicting goals of the revolution and the ideological countercurrents within the government. The ambiguities in these policy-laws evoked pleas from various quarters, especially private investors, for the regime to define more clearly the "rules of the game," so that plans could be made for the future. Much of the uncertainty in the reform decrees was purposeful, an element of "strategic indecision" that allowed the administration maximum flexibility. After measuring the political and economic repercussions of the general laws, the regime issued official "clarifications" and supplementary legislation modifying the original statutes. In some cases the state negotiated special contracts with individual companies exempting them from the general laws. Although the government demonstrated its willingness to compromise, it remained remarkably faithful to the spirit of the reform program. In fact, the Peruvian revolution "deepened" after 1968. The economy became increasingly statist and redistributive. This movement was gradual, however, as the Velasco regime labored to maintain the unity of the armed forces. The radicals and conservatives engaged in a revolutionary rumba—three steps forward and one step back.

2 The Revolution

"Peasant, the landlord will eat no more from your poverty!"
Employing these words attributed to Túpac Amaru II, General
Velasco announced a new agrarian reform on Peru's national
"Indian Day,"* June 24, 1969. The enabling act, Decree-Law
17716, repeated much of Belaúnde's 1964 agrarian law, but key
portions of the earlier measure were changed to permit a rapid
and profound transformation in the pattern of land ownership.
The decree plugged large loopholes in the old statute, significantly reduced the amount of cash compensation, and simplified
administrative procedures. The government pledged to eliminate all large private estates by mid-1975.

Decree-Law 17716 prohibited the ownership of farmland by
joint-stock enterprises. The government gave corporations a
period of six months to divest themselves of their agricultural
holdings. Individual owners of latifundia could retain a portion
of their property, the amount varying according to the region
and quality of the land. On the coast the legal limit was set at 375
acres of irrigated land, 750 acres for farms dependent upon
rainfall and 3,750 acres for pastures. In the Sierra the maximum
ranged from 37.5 to 295 acres for croplands or sufficient pasture
to carry 5,000 sheep. These rather generous allowances gave
solace to few *hacendados,* however. To qualify for the "basic
exemption," the land had to be worked primarily by the owner
and his family, employing a limited number of hired workers.
Furthermore, properties smaller than the legal maximums might
be taken if they were near land-poor indigenous communities or
their proprietors had violated Peru's much-abused labor laws. In
addition to land, the measure provided for the expropriation of
farm buildings, livestock, implements and associated facilities
for processing agricultural products, including sugar refineries,
cotton gins, and rice mills. A month after the agrarian reform
decree, the government nationalized all of the country's water
resources.

To permit a rational restructuring of the agrarian sector, the
reform was to be instituted by regions, with the government
condemning entire districts containing many large estates. Compensation was to be based initially upon the landowners' de-

*This date is now celebrated as the "Day of the Peasant."

clared valuation of their holdings for tax purposes, a feature that would punish the widespread practice of tax evasion. The law provided for cash indemnities of up to 2,300 dollars for land, 23,000 dollars for machinery and the full value of livestock expropriated. The remainder of the compensation would be made in bonds of three classes, bearing 4 to 6 percent interest, redeemable over twenty to thirty years. The agrarian reform bonds immediately could be converted into cash if the money was invested in industrial projects approved by the state, and if the entrepreneur obtained at least half of the required capital from other sources. Thus, the regime hoped to transfer capital from agriculture to other economic activities and use the agrarian reform to induce additional investment in high priority industries.

The agrarian reform envisioned three classes of beneficiaries: private proprietors of "family-sized" farms, indigenous communities, and, especially, cooperatives. Only those estates that could be divided without seriously diminishing their productivity would be distributed in individual parcels. Just 7 percent of the land eventually transferred under the program was distributed in private plots. Traditional indigenous communities received priority in the award of land, but they were encouraged to transform themselves into modern producers' cooperatives, the system favored by the regime. Large collective enterprises would enjoy the economies of scale, facilitate central planning for the agricultural sector of the national economy, and simplify the state's efforts to provide financial and technical assistance to farmers. In overpopulated rural districts the establishment of cooperatives rather than the parcellation of the land also would permit larger numbers of persons to receive benefits from the reform. The law required recipients of land, both individuals and collective entities, to pay for their new property over a period of twenty years. These remissions would be used to amortize the agrarian reform bonds.

The Velasco administration dramatically launched the agrarian reform by immediately expropriating the eight largest sugar plantations on the coast and converting them into cooperatives. The affected holdings included the Grace and Gildemeister enterprises along with estates belonging to powerful political figures. Because most of these properties also were strongholds of the Aprista labor unions, cynics hastily charged that the agrarian reform was merely a weapon to weaken the regime's opponents rather than a device to bring economic and social change. This skepticism quickly diminished, however, as the reform spread rapidly throughout the country. Although the program required one more year than the six originally anticipated, all privately owned latifundia had been eliminated by mid-1976.

Notwithstanding this success, the agrarian reform encountered serious problems arising from one fundamental fact: Peru did not have enough affectable farmland to satisfy the needs of the entire rural population. The government initially estimated that the program might distribute 25 million acres to 650,000 families, while an equal number of poor farmers would not receive land. The administration soon discovered, however, that peasant communities occupied significantly larger areas than had been thought; furthermore, many *hacendados* had subdivided and sold their holdings during the rural unrest of the 1960s. In the end about 17.5 million acres were transferred to only 286,000 farm families. The scarcity of land accentuated contradictions between the economic and social objectives of the program. The government desired to increase the efficiency of the nation's agriculture to improve the living standard of the rural population, supply the cities with sufficient food at moderate prices, and leave a surplus for export. At the same time the Velasco regime proposed to provide land for as many needy farmers as possible and allow them a great degree of independence in the management of their properties, features that probably would reduce efficiency.

The conflicts within the reform program were most apparent in the sugar cooperatives of the north coast. The law granted membership in these entities to the permanent wage workers and former tenants on these properties. However, the plantations also had provided employment for thousands of seasonal migrants and part-time workers who owned or rented small farms nearby. These unfortunates continued to work part-time for the new collectives but at inferior wages and without sharing in the profits of the enterprises. Not only did the cooperatives resist the admission of outsiders, they also sought to increase profits and dividends for their members through the purchase of labor-saving machinery. Ironically, the land invasions of the prerevolutionary period reoccurred as squatters defiantly established themselves on lands belonging to the cooperatives.

The military regime assumed that the transformation of private estates into worker-owned cooperatives would eliminate labor disputes and obviate the need for the old Aprista unions. But the agrarian reform accomplished neither of these objectives. Stressing the need for competent mangagement during the early years of collective operation, the government insisted upon appointing general managers for the plantations as well as a majority of the members of the policy-making administrative councils of the cooperatives. The degree of worker control was to increase as these enterprises funded their agrarian debts. Members of the cooperatives protested that state bureaucrats merely had replaced the old owners and managers. The unions demanded a voice in the operation of the plantations and organized a wave of strikes. In response to this agitation the government agreed to give the workers control over the administrative councils and held elections for these bodies in May 1972. The regime prohibited the use of old political party labels in the campaign, but candidates supported by the Aprista unions swept most of these contests.

The collectivization of the modern estates in the coastal region was, on the whole, an economic success. Favored by good weather and strong markets, production and profits steadily increased. Furthermore, a considerable amount of acreage was diverted from sugar and cotton to the cultivation of rice, which Peru began to export. The efficient sugar cooperatives were able to devote about one quarter of their income to amortize their agrarian reform debts. Unfortunately, other sectors of the reformed agricultural economy did not prosper. Production in the highlands remained stagnant, as most of the archaic haciendas of the past now became impoverished agrarian collectives. On the coast and in the Sierra many independent farmers who had received "family-sized" parcels under the reform were unable to improve their living standards appreciably and still meet the payments on their land. In 1973, therefore, the government forgave this obligation for about 75,000 peasants who held less than twelve and one-half acres of irrigated land or its equivalent.

The agrarian reform also encountered political problems in the less developed regions of the country. Many of the largest Sierra estates were transformed into cooperatives called "agricultural societies of social interest" (SAIS). In these organizations former tenants shared lands and profits with neighboring indigenous communities. Although created, in part, to end old boundary disputes between the former haciendas and *comunidades,* violent struggles soon occurred between the regular members of the cooperatives and the participating indigenous communities over land-use policy and the division of profits. In addition, both groups attacked the state-appointed managers and pressed for the cancellation of their agrarian debt. Under the banners of the old peasant federations, agricultural workers who did not obtain land from the reform law invaded the cooperatives and the medium-sized private holdings exempted from expropriation. They demanded a reduction in the size limits established for private parcels so that more land could be distributed. The freeholders became reluctant to improve their farms because they feared collectivization in the future. To reassure these independent agriculturalists, the government, borrowing from the experience of Mexico, issued certificates of "inaffectability," guaranteeing their farms from expropriation. But uncertainty remained as illegal peasant invasions continued.

The Velasco administration announced a major reorganization of its agrarian program in 1973. In addition to changes in the system of cooperatives, a five-year plan for 1974–79 emphasized bringing new areas under cultivation. Four irrigation projects, watering some 600,000 acres, were to be completed during the period. The colonization of the Montaña, downgraded after the overthrow of Belaúnde, also received increased priority under the new program. More than 1,200,000 acres were to be opened for settlement in the eastern portion of the country. On the fifth anniversary of the agrarian reform in June 1974, the government issued the Law of Native Communities and Agricultural Promotion for the Jungle Region. Extending the agrarian reform to the Montaña, this measure acknowledged the rights of tribal Indians to sufficient lands for hunting and shifting cultivation. The law limited individual properties in the region to 75 acres of cropland. However, "reformed enterprises" that distributed 30 percent of their profits to the labor force could retain up to 250 acres of arable land or 5,000 acres of pasture.

After 1970 the government assumed an increasingly larger role in agricultural marketing through EPSA, the Public Enterprise for Agricultural Service. This multipurpose agency attempted to ensure adequate supplies of food at moderate prices through various controls and subsidies. It purchased certain staples from producers, transported them to urban areas, and distributed this produce to retailers. The agency itself sold groceries through its own supermarkets and private outlets under contract to the government. This chain numbered about

312

1,000 stores in 1974. EPSA also regulated the import of foodstuffs and along with other government and semigovernment entities controlled the export of all major agricultural commodities.

The revolutionary government made the state the preponderant force in the nation's financial system. Control over credit was a major instrument in its programs for economic development. Continuing a process begun late in the Belaúnde administration, the Velasco regime decreed the Peruvianization of Banking Law in January 1969. Under this measure the government purchased several foreign-owned financial institutions and acquired a majority interest in all others dominated by overseas investors. These assets were transferred to the state's Banco de la Nación, which entered the commercial banking field in competition with private Peruvian banks. The Banco de la Nación quickly purchased stock in several of these and, by 1974, the state controlled all but one of the republic's major commercial banks. The government also began a gradual nationalization of the insurance industry, another important source of capital. In 1971 the administration created the Development Finance Corporation (Cofide). This agency served as a holding company, managing the government's interests in state enterprises and joint public-private ventures. Cofide also channeled funds from the treasury into the state system of sectorial development banks (for agriculture, manufacturing, mining, fishing, and housing). The regime used Cofide bonds to compensate the owners of expropriated businesses and sold these securities to raise capital for various projects. By 1974, the state banking system accounted for about three-quarters of the credit transactions and two-thirds of the money loaned in these operations.

The Velasco administration nationalized other elements of Peru's economic infrastructure and created an alphabet soup of state companies to manage them. In 1969 the government announced that it would nationalize the telecommunications industry. Entel-Perú, the new National Telecommunications Enterprise, quickly purchased the Lima telephone system from International Telephone and Telegraph along with a majority interest in all other telephone and cable companies. Under the General Telecommunications Law of November 1971, the state obtained a minimum 51-percent share in all television stations and a quarter interest in the nation's radio stations. Electro-Perú, the state power enterprise established in 1972, purchased at least majority control of all electric companies. The assets of the Peruvian Corporation, the foreign firm that had owned most of the nation's railway system since 1890, were acquired by the government in November 1972. The National Railway Enterprise, Enafer, was created to operate these lines and all others serving the general public. The regime significantly expanded the state merchant marine fleet, purchasing many vessels from a new government ship-building company, Sima-Perú. The administration also began to nationalize domestic air transportation.

An earthquake centered a few miles west of Chimbote rocked Peru on May 31, 1970. The worst natural disaster recorded in the western hemisphere, the tremor brought a torrent of water, ice, and earth rumbling down the once-beautiful Callejón de Huaylas, the valley that suffered the greatest damage. The city of Huaraz, the capital of Ancash department, was 90 percent destroyed. The historic city of Yungay entirely disappeared. As many as 75,000 persons lost their lives and some 400,000 were left homeless. The government estimated the physical damage at more than a half-billion dollars. The quake may have produced a significant shock within the Velasco administration itself, strengthening the arguments of those officers advocating increased state intervention in the economy. During the next few months the regime instituted a series of important reforms favored by the radical "earthquake generation."

The revolutionary government promulgated the General Law of Industries on Independence Day, July 28, 1970. This decree proclaimed the state's intention to control the nation's "basic industries"—the production of steel and nonferrous metals, primary chemicals, fertilizer, cement, and paper. Initially, private companies engaged in these activities were permitted to continue their operations under regulations imposed by the government. However, the state eventually would own these industries in their entirety or with minority participation by private capital. Industrial enterprises controlled by foreigners were required to divest themselves of all but one-third of their assets within fifteen years. Although the regime sought to end foreign domination of Peru's industry, it welcomed overseas investors willing to hold minority interest in new businesses. Such firms might be established with a maximum of 49 percent foreign money; but Peruvian capital, public or private, eventually would have to control two-thirds of the stock.

The industrial law created five priority classifications for all manufactures based upon their economic and social utility. Government financial and technical assistance, tariffs, and other taxes would be used to encourage high-priority industries and discourage those deemed less desirable. Thus, the tariff on an electric motor imported for use in the production of medicine would be much lower than the duty on the same item to be employed in manufacturing jewelry. In addition to these incentives, the regime offered other advantages to businesses locating outside of the Lima-Callao area and to firms entering mixed ventures with the state.

The General Law of Industries also introduced the "labor community" concept, an idea that later was amplified and extended to mining, fishing, and telecommunications. Every manufacturing firm employing more than five workers or generating annual sales of more than 24,000 dollars was required to establish an "industrial community" (CI). This entity would include all persons employed by the company, from the general manager to the janitor. Each year these firms would give 10 percent of their pretax profits to the CI in the form of cash. An additional 15 percent of the enterprise's annual gross profits would be transferred to the *comunidad industrial* in the form of company stock. Dividends from the stock together with the cash payment would be distributed by the CI to each of its members according to a formula based upon the employee's salary, seniority, and the number of days worked. These last two criteria were designed to discourage strikes, absenteeism, and transiency among the labor force.

The industrial community, which was to be organized democratically, immediately would place at least one member on the firm's board of directors. Thereafter, the group's representation would increase in proportion to the percentage of the stock it held. When the CI acquired 50 percent equity capital in an enterprise, the company would become a workers' cooperative. In theory, workers eventually could own most of Peru's modern manufacturing enterprises. But the CI's acquisition of majority control in heavily capitalized firms would require many years and might never occur if the company itself reinvested at least 15 percent of its profits in the operation. In businesses with more than 25 percent government ownership, the industrial communities were to receive Cofide bonds rather than equity shares. These CI's would place only two members on the boards of state or mixed state-private ventures. At the minimum, however, the *comunidad industrial* would increase the income of workers and give them a voice in management.

Following the enactment of the General Law of Industries, the Velasco regime began to issue decrees regulating specific areas within the manufacturing sector of the economy. For example, the Automotive Industry Law, decreed late in 1970, required all plants assembling automobiles to obtain at least 70 percent of their parts from Peruvian sources by 1973. The government also reduced the number of automobile manufacturers from thirteen to five firms and asserted the state's authority to regulate the prices and specify the models of motor vehicles produced in the country. Several similar laws attempted to "rationalize" other industries and encourage the use of Peruvian components. To help firms obtain industrial inputs not available within the country, the government created the National Industrial Trade Enterprise (ENCI). Taking advantage of the economies of scale, this firm imported raw materials and machinery which it distributed to manufacturers.

The military administration unveiled in 1973 a major plan for the development of the manufacturing sector. Employing both public and private capital, the program envisioned investments totaling more than a billion dollars by 1990. Although the plan called for further industrial expansion in metropolitan Lima and Chimbote—where the capacity of the national steel mill was to be increased considerably—emphasis was placed upon the decentralization of industry. Major new industrial complexes were projected for Iquitos, Pucallpa, Ilo, Tacna, Arequipa, Trujillo, and especially the Ica-Nazca district, which was selected as the site for Peru's second steel mill. The government planned to participate actively in these projects through Indu-Perú, the national industrial development agency organized in 1972. Modeled after the highly successful Chilean Fomento Corporation, Indu-Perú planned to build factories, nurture them during their initial stages, and then sell them to private investors. Indu-Perú also was charged with establishing plants in the "basic industries" sector for the state and providing management services to private enterprises.

The General Law of Fisheries, decreed in July 1970, gave the state considerable control over this important sector of the economy. In addition to establishing a system of priorities and incentives similar to those set for manufacturing, the fisheries law created ECHAP, a new government agency to market all fish meal and fish oil. The decree also provided for a reorganization of the structurally weak fish meal industry. Most firms in this sector were forced to modernize their plants, reduce excess capacity, and refinance their burdensome short-term debts through the state. The General Law of Fisheries and supplementary measures created a modified version of the labor community for the fish meal industry. All companies were to transfer 20 percent of their annual profits—8 percent in cash and 12 percent in stock—to "fishing communities" embracing all persons in their employ. Half of the cash and half of the dividends from the equity shares would be distributed directly to the members of the fishing community. However, the remainder would be assigned to a nationwide "fishing compensation community," an entity including all employees of every firm within the industry. The compensation community then would disburse its funds to the individual members of this national organization. Thus, the compensation community would help equalize the benefits received by employees of less profitable firms with those working for more efficient enterprises. The fishing communities, like the industrial communities, received representation on the boards of directors of the fish meal companies. These firms were to become cooperatives when the *comunidades* acquired 50 percent of the stock.

Ownership of the fish meal industry changed hands much sooner than anybody, including the government, anticipated. The warm El Niño current invaded Peru's cold coastal waters in 1972, dealing a nearly fatal blow to the fishing industry. The anchovies almost disappeared. To replenish this resource the government banned the harvesting of the few tiny fish that remained. This condition of scarcity persisted throughout the next year. Primarily to rescue the fish meal companies from bankruptcy, the Velasco regime nationalized the entire industry in May 1973. A new state fishing firm, Pesca-Perú, acquired all of the country's 100 fish meal factories and the nation's 1,500-boat anchovy fleet, becoming the largest enterprise in Latin America. In addition to its monopoly over fish meal and fish oil, Pesca-Perú formed mixed corporations with private firms to catch and can food fish, especially tuna.

Much of Peru's development potential was concentrated in the mining industry, a sector that required vast amounts of capital and technical resources. Therefore, the nation's pragmatic revolutionaries welcomed continued foreign participation under strict government control. In September 1969, the Velasco administration demanded that all holders of mining concessions granted prior to 1965 submit schedules within ninety days for the development of these properties and, if approved, begin exploiting the deposits by April 1970. Concessionaires that did not comply with this order would lose their mineral rights. In December 1969, the regime and the Southern Peru Copper Company—the North American conglomerate that owns Toquepala—signed a contract for the firm to develop its huge Cuajone concession, a project requiring a half-billion dollar investment. The administration also approved some smaller proposals. But more than 2,000 concessions, including giant mineral deposits assigned to Anaconda, American Smelting and Refining, Cerro de Pasco, and Southern Peru Copper, reverted to the state. The government planned to develop several of these properties itself or in cooperation with private capital. In all, the administration contemplated new investments of one billion dollars to double the nation's copper production by 1978.

A Normative Law of the Mining Industry, issued in April 1970, and a more detailed General Mining Law, decreed eighteen months later, amplified the state's powers over the mining sector of the economy and set new regulations for investment in the industry. These codes encouraged the formation of mixed private-state ventures. A new government mining agency, Minero-Perú, was to hold at least one-quarter of the stock in these enterprises. The mining legislation also established tax incentives to encourage large-scale investment, greater efficiency, and state participation in mining firms beyond the 25 percent minimum. Under this last provision, companies would give additional stock to the government in lieu of taxes. The new mineral statutes empowered Minero-Perú to establish a monopoly over the export of all mine products and reserved for state ownership all future copper refineries. Finally, the mineral codes provided for profit-sharing "mining communities" for each enterprise and an industry-wide "mining compensation community" similar to the *comunidades* in fishing.

Although the Velasco administration proclaimed its desire for the continued participation of foreign capital in the mining industry, the Cerro de Pasco Corporation feared eventual expropriation. The oldest of the major mining enterprises in Peru, Cerro had been a prime target for the attacks of Peruvian nationalists. In December 1971, the firm and the government began negotiations for the sale of the company's mining complex in the central highlands. Cerro reportedly asked about 150 million dollars for its holdings, which included the only copper smelter in Peru, while the state offered a much smaller amount. After these discussions deadlocked, the government demanded that the company upgrade the notoriously substandard workers' housing facilities as the new mining laws required. Cerro denounced this order as a scheme to force a sale at the administration's price, which the firm described as "confiscatory," or to justify expropriation. The Velasco administration nationalized the company in December 1973 producing jubilation throughout the country. Centromin-Perú, a branch of Minero-Perú, assumed operation of the former Cerro holdings. In August 1975, the regime expropriated the Marcona Company's iron-mining complex. Thereafter only Southern Peru Copper, through its partnership arrangement with the state, remained among the mining giants of the past.

The national oil agency, renamed Petro-Perú, greatly expanded its operations after 1968. In addition to the former properties of the International Petroleum Company, the state corporation acquired several smaller enterprises and significantly increased its own exploration and production activities. Nevertheless, Peru continued to depend upon Venezuela for about one-third of its petroleum needs. To gain self-sufficiency in this resource the Velasco regime signed exploration and production contracts with a score of foreign oil companies. Under these arrangements Peru was to receive 50 to 60 percent of all petroleum extracted and installations constructed by the firms would revert to the state after twenty-five to thirty-five years. By 1973 new wells were tapping deposits off the north coast, and more importantly, in the northern Montaña. Here, indications of seemingly vast pools of petroleum aroused hopes that Peru again would become a major exporter of oil. In mid-1974, the government secured loans in Japan and several other countries for the construction of a pipeline to transport oil from the Amazon Basin over the Andes to the Pacific port of Bayovar, where the administration planned to establish a petrochemical industry.

The agrarian reform and laws establishing the "labor communities" produced major changes in the ownership of the nation's productive capacity. Affecting economic activities generating about 45 percent of the national income, these programs could have brought a substantial improvement in the living standards of many people. Nevertheless, it soon became apparent that the early reforms would redistribute income almost entirely within the modern portion of the economy. The agricultural component of the national income was produced largely on the coastal plantations. Income transfers in this sector benefited the members of the cooperatives that had acquired these enterprises, about one-fifth of the country's farm workers. Similarly, the profit-sharing programs of the labor communities favored only the 8 percent of Peruvian workers engaged in fishing, mining, telecommunications, and modern manufacturing. The new *comunidades* did not include the thousands of commercial employees, artisans, peddlers, servants, and persons employed in small-scale businesses. During the first four years of the revolution, therefore, the most notable economic reforms promised significant rewards for only about 18 percent of the nation's labor force. These persons already ranked within the top quarter of the country's wage earners. Furthermore, the workers in the labor communities and wealthy cooperatives often demonstrated a reluctance to share their added income with new members.

The government instituted two programs in 1973 to provide benefits for groups excluded by the earlier reforms. Giant collectives called "integral projects for rural settlement" (PIAR's) were introduced to resolve the land and labor problems of entire districts. At a pilot project in the Ica Valley, for example, twenty-three cooperatives established during the initial phase of the agrarian reform were combined to form three PIAR's. To these large entities the government added newly created "service cooperatives" comprised of persons who did not belong to the original cooperatives—artisans, day laborers, and small freeholders who wanted part-time employment on the plantations. Each of the component cooperatives, both production and service units, contributed a share of its profits to the PIAR's for redistribution to individual members of the larger organization. Resembling the "compensation communities" in fishing and mining, the PIAR's shifted some income from the wealthy production cooperatives to the service workers. Unlike the labor communities and original agrarian cooperatives, however, the PIAR's received incentives to admit new members. The government also encouraged independent farmers, especially those with minuscule plots, to assign their lands to the PIAR's and become full participants in the profit-sharing program.

The revolutionary government proposed to create many new jobs in modern industry and commerce through a unique system of "social properties." First unveiled in broad outline by General Velasco in his 1972 Independence Day speech, the regime published a draft law for the program a year later and began experiments with the novel form of enterprise. The definitive Law of Social Property was promulgated on Labor Day, May 1, 1974. The most innovative and controversial reform of the revolution, the program is extremely complex and employs a special terminology to differentiate it from "individualistic capitalism" and "statist communism." The "social property enterprise" (EPS) is a collective, worker-managed business. It is neither a cooperative nor a state-owned entity, but theoretically belongs to all persons participating in the entire social property sector of the economy. EPS's can be initiated by the government. Ideally, however, a group of workers conceives of a useful and viable enterprise—manufacturing a product or providing a service—and presents this idea to the National Social Property Commission, the body that supervises the program. If approved, the state supplies the technical assistance and the initial capital to establish the business. Workers' assemblies in each EPS formulate basic policy and elect their own managers. In addition to their economic function, the social property enterprises often provide housing, educational programs, and a variety of other social services for their members.

The social property enterprises establish wage rates for their members based upon the function performed by the worker and his needs. However, the law discourages the payment of more than two "basic wages" to any individual. Incentives for productivity consist of merit points that can be used to obtain improved housing, special training, better jobs, and the higher salaries paid to persons with superior skill and greater responsibilities. Dereliction of duty can bring demotion and even expulsion from the organization. Ten percent of the "excess" (the capitalist word "profit" is never used) produced by the EPS's is contributed to a national pool for distribution to all members of every social property enterprise in the country. Additional profits are not shared by members of the individual EPS's. This feature and other regulations discourage the tendancy to restrict membership—the major problem of the cooperatives and labor communities.

In its first years the program was to be funded by Cofide. After meeting their operating expenses and contributing 10

321

percent of their surplus to the profit-sharing plan, the EPS's were to transfer their remaining gains to the National Social Property Fund, the institution that eventually was to supply much of the capital for new social properties. These payments were to continue even after the enterprises repaid their original debts. Thus, profits from successful EPS's would permit a constant expansion of the social property sector. The government planned to acquire additional money for the program from private investors. Under the law banks and other financial institutions were required to hold investment portfolios consisting of government bonds along with securities, called "share-bonds," in various social property enterprises. The banks, in turn, were to sell "participation certificates" in these portfolios to the public. Similar to mutual fund shares, these certificates were to yield dividends and be tax exempt.

The Velasco administration assigned top priority to the development of the social property program, a decision that caused great controversy both within and outside of the government. Although the government asserted that the social property sector would expand automatically until it became "predominant" within the "plural economy," this would require many years because about 90 percent of the EPS's were to be new ventures. Existing businesses could be transformed into social properties only upon a request by two-thirds of their owners and with the consent of the National Social Property Commission. These assurances notwithstanding, private entrepreneurs expressed anxiety over their ability to compete with the EPS's, which were to be favored in the award of government contracts and have preferred access to credit. Private businessmen along with the members of the labor communities and the wealthy agrarian cooperatives also feared the forced conversion of their enterprises into social properties at some future date.

Critics of the program raised questions about the degree of state control over the social property sector and the economic viability of the system. The Velasco administration described the EPS as an example within the economic realm of the spontaneous, democratic, self-directed institutions that the regime also envisioned for the nation's social and political life. *"Autogestión,"* the term used to denote this concept, soon became another popular cliché of the revolution. However, the state's control over funding for the EPS's and its domination of the National Social Property Commission created doubts about the degree of

322

autogestión. The program would be expensive. In its early years, at least, the social property sector would have to compete for scarce financial resources with other government projects. Furthermore, if the "autogestionary economy" encountered serious problems, the role of the state certainly would increase with a corresponding decrease in worker control. Small experiments in worker-managed enterprises had been made in several countries prior to Peru's adoption of the program. The system had been instituted on a nationwide scale only in Yugoslavia, where it enjoyed considerable success. But worker-managed firms in that country functioned largely within a command economy which responded to directives from the state. Peru's social properties were to be part of a free-market economy, with supply and demand providing the basic dynamic force. Finally, there was no functioning model to predict how the other sectors of Peru's "plural economy" would perform in competition with the EPS's, especially within a volatile political atmosphere.

Rapid, revolutionary change, whether achieved by violence or peaceful means, usually has brought severe economic dislocation and decline in its immediate aftermath. The Velasco administration, however, viewed the structural transformation of the economy as a prerequisite for substantial, sustained development. Through prudent and pragmatic management the regime accomplished major reform while registering respectable gains in the standard economic indices. The stabilization program initiated by Belaúnde in 1968 was continued through the following year. Austerity measures resolved the balance of payments crisis and reduced the rate of inflation from more than 19 to less than 7 percent. The administration began an expansionary economic program in 1970. During the next four years, the nearly stagnant gross national product grew by a cumulative annual average of almost 6.5 percent and per capita GNP by 3.7 percent yearly. Meanwhile, the annual increase in the cost of living was held to an average of under 7 percent. The government achieved this impressive record in spite of problems largely beyond its control: very costly strikes by copper miners in 1970 and 1971, accompanied by a sharp drop in export prices during the latter year; unfavorable weather for agriculture in 1972; and almost total inactivity in the key fishing industry during 1972 and 1973.

Many of the successes of Velasco's first five years can be attributed to improved public administration and one of the more effective national planning systems in Latin America. In

1969, the government reorganized the National Planning Institute (INP), making it the capstone of an extensive planning network extending throughout the bureaucracy. The elevation of the INP's director to ministerial rank indicated the new importance attached to this agency. In addition to a long-range Plan for Social and Economic Development, the institute prepared five-year and two-year plans for each sector of the economy and for the nation as a whole. These projections, unlike earlier plans, were formulated in close cooperation with the planning services of various ministries to set reasonable goals and ensure a sincere effort to meet stated objectives.

To increase administrative efficiency, the military regime began a major reorganization of the executive branch of government in 1969. The cabinet was restructured along more logical, functional lines. Thus, the catchall Ministry of Development and Public Works became three separate units—the ministries of Energy and Mines, Industry, and Housing. The Ministry of Finance and Commerce became the Ministry of Economy and Finance, while commerce and tourism were combined into a new cabinet post. Duties performed by several ministries were reassigned to the new Ministry of Transportation and Communications. The administration first divided the old Ministry of Agriculture and Fisheries into two portfolios and, in early 1975, a separate Ministry of Food was established to permit the agriculture ministry to concentrate on the problems of agrarian reform. The various subcabinet bureaus and agencies attached to the presidency were regrouped within this new structure. In addition, the regime created a Council of Interministerial Coordination, comprised of representatives from each ministry, and a Council of Economic and Financial Affairs, linking all cabinet posts within the economic area.

Senior generals and admirals—many of them conservatives—occupied the prestigious ministerial posts and directed the day-to-day administration of the state. Military radicals, however, had great influence in the formulation of basic policy through their domination of the strategically placed Advisory Committee of the Presidency (COAP). Most of the score of colonels and young generals who comprised this body served as liaison officers between the various ministries and the president. The committee screened all proposals for decree-laws submitted by individual members of the cabinet. With the aid of its own extensive secretariat of military and civilian experts, COAP refined these proposals and presented them to the full cabinet and General Velasco for final action. The director of COAP held ministerial rank. The revolutionary government also attempted reforms within the lower echelons of the bureaucracy to improve its efficiency, honesty, and responsiveness to the people. Toward this end a new National Institute of Public Administration undertook various studies and the regime established a Superior School of Public Administration to train bureaucrats.

The Velasco regime attributed many of Peru's social problems to economic causes—low productivity and the maldistribution of wealth along with the power it commands. For political as well as economic reasons the government gave implicit priority to the less difficult task of expanding the modern sector of the economy rather than the redistribution of income toward the nation's poorest citizens. Nevertheless, the administration did undertake several significant social-welfare programs. In May 1973, the government reorganized the social security system, combining a myriad of state pension plans into a single fund and vastly increasing the number of beneficiaries. Unlike the previous programs, which made the number of years worked the criterion for eligibility, the reorganized plan granted pensions to workers who reached retirement age—fifty-five years for women and sixty years for men. Furtheremore, high-salaried managerial personnel now were required to contribute to the new system. To make vital drugs available to Peru's humble classes, the regime established a Basic Medicines Program in 1972. Under this plan pharmaceutical companies competed for state contracts to supply huge quantities of 235 common medicines. These preparations were sold under their generic names by government health facilities and participating private pharmacies at a small fraction of the price of the drugs marketed under their trade names. In 1974 the administration promulgated a law providing free prenatal and postnatal care for all Peruvian mothers and their infants. A major reform of the nation's penal system was begun in 1969.

One indication that President Velasco's secret "Plan Inca" had not been drafted entirely prior to the overthrow of Belaúnde was a strong statement in favor of women's rights, a topic that probably would have received scant attention from Peruvian military men in 1968. In what was certainly the most "revolutionary" section of the published document, from a cultural standpoint, the plan called for reforms to give females "effective equality" with males and "eliminate discriminatory treatment which limits the opportunities or effects the rights and dignity of women." The publication of Plan Inca in July 1974 gave new impetus to Peru's small feminist movement. Within a few months the government took a small but symbolically important step toward fulfillment of its promise to women: females were granted admission to the armed forces.

The revolutionary government moved cautiously in its efforts to alleviate the problems of Peru's cities. A decree of September 1969 empowered the state to expropriate undeveloped real estate within municipalities and initiated endless rumors of an imminent "urban reform" that would nationalize rental housing. However, the administration insisted that it only wanted "urban renovation" and welcomed private investment in this expensive endeavor. A five-year Housing Plan for 1971–75 anticipated the construction of 463,000 new units, almost entirely by the private sector. The regime made attractive provisions for the use of agrarian reform bonds in financing housing projects. New tax incentives and penalties encouraged developers to build facilities for low- and middle-income families while discouraging real estate speculation. These inducements produced considerable success and housing construction became one of the more dynamic areas of the economy. Much of this activity occurred in Greater Lima, where the government estimated that almost six million persons would live by 1980. A new zoning ordinance for the capital sought to check "urban sprawl." Under a ten-year modernization plan, work began on a large hydroelectric project to give Lima the best power supply of any Latin American capital. The program also provided for new educational, recreational, and transportation facilities, including a network of modern freeways.

Peru's major urban problem continued to be the rush of migrants from the interior to the squatter settlements of the cities, especially Lima. The Velasco administration sought to slow this process while, at the same time, improving conditions within the "young towns" that already existed. To accomplish the latter goal, the National Organism for the Development of the Young Towns (ONDEPJOV) was established in December 1968. This agency coordinated the development efforts of the government, private social agencies, and, especially, the people of the settlements themselves. It trained community leaders, supervised elections for the bodies charged with local governance, and assisted in the organization of various cooperative projects, including the construction of houses and public works. ONDEPJOV also attempted to bring increased stability to the squatter settlements. Procedures for obtaining title to lots in the *barriadas* were simplified, and the regime encouraged legal marriages among couples living there.

The government understood that its programs to help the people of the young towns would encourage the formation of new squatter settlements. Therefore, the regime indicated that it would not tolerate future invasions. For over two years pressure for housing facilities in the capital mounted. Then, in April and May 1971, thousands of poor people invaded the Pamplona district of Lima and clashed violently with police sent to evict them. The squatters eventually agreed to move to a site prepared for them by the government, the Villa El Salvador. After the Pamplona incident the regime continued its hard line against illegal invasions while attempting to channel migrants into existing *pueblos jóvenes* or new, officially santioned settlements like El Salvador, which had 100,000 residents within less than a year's time. The Velasco administration realized, however, that the ultimate solution to the problems of the squatter settlements was the improvement of life in the backward interior of the country. The government launched a major community development program in 1969. Within two years more than 1,600 community centers had been opened throughout the country to provide a variety of social services.

The Velasco regime refused to give official recognition to an "Indian problem." The plight of the indigenous population was not attributed to cultural factors but to a socioeconomic system that also oppressed many non-Indians. To be sure, Túpac Amaru II was the principal symbol of the revolution. The ruling generals, like all good politicians, praised the ancient glories of the native race and, in 1975, proclaimed Quechua the second national language of Peru. But the word "Indian" in the nation's laws generally was replaced by *campesino* ("peasant"), a term that includes all of the country's poor rural folk. Although programs aimed at uplifting the peasant population were primarily economic in focus, the administration made necessary allowances for Peru's dual culture in the agrarian reform and especially in a new education law.

After three years of study, much public debate, and many revisions, the revolutionary government published its Education

Reform Law in March 1972. The most radical change ever implemented in the nation's school system, the reform sought to democratize education and provide training suited to Peru's social and economic needs. Instruction at all public institutions was to be free. Private academies, frequently condemned as elitist, were permitted to continue their operations, but they could not earn a profit. The law envisioned schools for all of Peru's children. Indians would learn Spanish, but they were to be instructed in their native languages. Providing considerable autonomy for schools, the statute emphasized community participation in the formulation of policy. Curriculum was to be tailored to regional needs. The reform also included extensive job-training and basic literacy programs for adults. The new education system was to be completely operative by 1980.

The law divided the formal school system into three levels: initial, basic, and higher education. Initial education encompassed nurseries, kindergartens, and day-care centers for children under six years of age. Although this level was free and strongly recommended, it was not compulsory. Centers for initial education were to emphasize the physical preparation of the child for school, providing nutritious meals and medical services. The basic education program replaced the old primary- and secondary-school systems and was compulsory. It consisted of three cycles totaling about nine years, from ages six to fifteen. However, pupils were to receive all of the time they needed to meet the minimum requirements for each grade, whereupon promotion to the next cycle would be automatic. This feature was designed to eliminate the dropout problem that plagued the old system.

Higher education, which was free but not obligatory, also consisted of three cycles. Requiring three or four years of study at new "high schools of professional education," the first cycle stressed vocational-technical training, even for students planning to attend a university. This program led to a "professional baccalaureate degree" and sought to supply skilled workers for Peru's developing economy. The government also hoped that this cycle would reduce the social distinctions between technicians and college graduates while encouraging students to undertake programs in science and technology at the universities, which were to provide the second and third cycles of the higher education program. The second cycle, leading to a teacher's certificate or a *licenciatura* (similar to a bachelor's degree in the

United States), required up to fourteen months of in-service training with state agencies in addition to the regular curriculum. The last cycle culminated with the doctorate.

An earlier Organic Law of the Peruvian University, decreed in February 1969, had united all of the nation's thirty-two senior educational institutions into a single system controlled by a powerful National Council of the Peruvian University. The decree called for radical changes in the internal structure of the universities themselves, with academic departments similar to those in the United States replacing the highly autonomous, career-oriented *facultades*. The measure sharply curtailed students' participation in university governance and banned partisan political activity on campus. Tuition, which had been eliminated by the Belaúnde government, was restored under a flexible schedule of fees based upon the student's ability to pay. The law evoked strong protests from both educators and students. Violent demonstrations produced the suspension of classes at several schools.

The 1972 education reform was a major compromise between the government and the universities. Although the concept of a nationwide university system survived, the structure was to be "autonomous and democratic," governed by a hierachy of representative assemblies and executive councils. Students were to comprise one-third of the membership in these bodies, while faculty received two-thirds of the seats. The individual universities were to determine their own internal organization until general statutes for the national system could be drafted by a special faculty-student commission. The law eased restrictions on campus political activity and again eliminated tuition. These concessions considerably lessened tensions between the Velasco regime and the universities. Nevertheless, government-imposed ceilings on enrollments, especially in the overcrowded teacher-training and humanities programs, continued to be a source of friction between the military administration and the students. In spite of these difficulties, the revolutionary government enjoyed considerable popularity among Peruvian youth during its early years because of Velasco's other domestic reforms and his nationalistic foreign policy.

The Diplomacy of the Revolution

The Revolutionary Government of the Armed Forces began its stewardship of the nation in the middle of a deepening diplomatic crisis with the United States. This confrontation was a mixed blessing for the generals. While it jeopardized the new administration's attempts to refinance the burdensome foreign debt and obtain international loans for its development programs, the dispute also provided an opportunity to demonstrate the regime's nationalism and build a broad base of popular support while it formulated its domestic policies. The imbroglio with Washington erupted on October 9, 1968, a date since celebrated as "National Dignity Day." The six-day-old government annulled Belaúnde's agreement with the International Petroleum Company and dramatically sent military units to take possession of the La Brea y Pariñas oil field and the refinery complex at Talara. Peru nationalized the company's remaining assests four months later. International law, of course, recognizes the right of sovereign states to expropriate private property, providing that adequate compensation is paid to the owner. However, the Velasco administration asserted that the Standard Oil subsidiary's 1924 title to La Brea y Pariñas was invalid. Therefore, the company had illegally extracted 690 million dollars worth of petroleum from Peru, a sum vastly exceeding the value of the IPC's facilities. No compensation would be paid to the firm.

Peru's actions against the IPC placed the new Nixon administration in a difficult position. Following Castro's confiscations of North American assets in Cuba, the United States Congress had legislated an arsenal of economic weapons to deter further seizures of Yankee businesses overseas. Most of these laws allowed the president great discretion in their application, but the 1962 Hickenlooper Amendment *required* the suspension of all economic and military aid to nations that failed to take "appropriate steps" within six months toward "equitable and speedy compensation" for expropriated American holdings. A 1965 amendment to the Sugar Act similarly required the cancellation of the sugar import quota for countries that made uncompensated seizures of United States firms.

Washington drastically curtailed its aid program for Peru and used its influence to check the flow of loans from international lending agencies to the Velasco government. Nevertheless, the Nixon administration determined that the formal imposition of economic sanctions against Lima would be counterproductive. The Peruvians repeatedly declared that they would not succumb to "illegal, economic aggression." The use of the punitive amendments probably would have destroyed any chance for compromise and might have caused a break in diplomatic relations. Furthermore, such actions would have been roundly condemned throughout Latin America, where the revolutionary government enjoyed widespread sympathy. The North American business community in Peru also opposed the imposition of sanctions. Attempting to maintain peace with these investors and protect its international credit rating, the Peruvian government insisted that the IPC case was "unique" and that other foreign firms need not fear the revolution. Although the Velasco regime acquired other North American holdings, it usually made reasonable and sometimes generous settlements with these companies.

Hoping to avoid invocation of the Hickenlooper Amendment, President Nixon appointed Wall Street lawyer John Irwin his special emissary and sent him to Lima in March 1969 for talks with the Velasco administration. Irwin achieved little progress toward resolving the IPC dispute by the April Hickenlooper deadline. Nevertheless, the State Department announced that it was deferring economic sanctions under the law because Irwin's talks with the Peruvians constituted an "appropriate step" toward indemnification and because the company still had recourse to Peru's administrative appeals process. The latter avenue closed four months later, when President Velasco rejected the IPC's appeal. But no further mention was made of the Hickenlooper Amendment nor was Peru's sugar quota revoked. The informal suspension of United States aid continued, however, as did the freeze on loans by the World Bank and the Inter-American Development Bank.

The attempt to resolve the IPC affair was complicated by a dangerous escalation of the "tuna war" between the United States and Peru. This long and vexatious dispute concerning fishing rights in the Humboldt Current was related to the development of the Peruvian marine industry, although not so directly as it might have seemed. Until the 1970 General Law of Fisheries provided incentives for the growth of Peru's food-fish industry, the fishermen of the two countries were not in direct competition. The North Americans restricted their activities to catching tuna, while the Peruvians concentrated on harvesting anchovies for their fish meal plants. Peru's national pride rather than its pocketbook was the country's principal stake in the controversy. A major maritime nation whose fishermen roamed the oceans of the world, the United States had a considerable economic interest in preventing the establishment of a precedent that could endanger its freedom to exploit the wealth of the seas. That nation's global military commitments also required the unrestricted use of the world's sea-lanes by the North American navy. Nevertheless, in early 1969, aroused United States indignation, rather than economic and strategic interests, threatened to combine with Peruvian nationalism and produce an armed confrontation.

Although never codified in general international law, the United States, Peru, and virtually every other nation traditionally claimed a three-mile "territorial sea"—that is, absolute control over their adjacent waters for the range of an eighteenth-century cannon. In 1945, however, the United States opened a new frontier in international maritime law. On September 28, President Truman issued two proclamations asserting that the United States possessed "jurisdiction" over its oil-rich continental shelf and also had the right to establish "conservation zones" for fisheries beyond its three-mile limit. Mexico quickly followed with similar declarations, which Washington approved. The next year Argentina claimed "sovereignty" over its continental shelf and coastal waters, introducing a semantical problem into the controversy. The English word "sovereignty" denotes absolute dominion. The Spanish *"soberanía,"* however, frequently is interchangeable with "jurisdiction," meaning limited authority for specific purposes. To protect whale herds off its coast, Chile made the first declaration of a 200-mile fisheries limit in 1947, and asked Peru to set the same maritime boundary. Lima's proclamation of *soberanía* came in August of that year.

After several months of silence, Washington attacked the Argentine, Chilean, and Peruvian declarations in strongly worded notes that seemed to dismiss contemptuously their legal arguments which, in fact, were similar to those employed by President Truman. Peru was especially offended because its proclamation had been drafted by incumbent President Bustamante i Rivero, a renowned authority in the field of international law who later would serve as president of the International Court of Justice. The United States took particular exception to Peru's 200-mile limit because Lima's declaration, unlike the others, made no mention of the rights of foreign nations within this zone. Actually, until that time, few foreign fishermen had exploited the marine life of the Humboldt Current. In the late 1940s and early 1950s, however, the rich California fisheries declined, and Yankee tuna clippers appeared in ever-increasing numbers off the west coast of South America.

Peruvian law required all vessels fishing within the country's 200-mile limit to be licensed. But Lima did not enforce this provision against foreigners, even after the United States tuna tariff of 1951—which almost destroyed Peru's nascent food-fish industry—brought demands for reprisals against the North Americans. The following year, however, Peru, Chile, and Ecuador signed the Declaration of Santiago, a statement of their common maritime principles. These included the exercise of "sole sovereignty" over the ocean, seabed, and subsoil minerals beneath it for a distance of 200 nautical miles. The signatory republics continued to recognize the right of "innocent passage" through this zone by other countries. Still, Peru did not enforce its fishing regulations against foreigners until the nation faced a public challenge to its authority. Aristotle Socrates Onassis, the Greek shipping magnate, announced in 1954 that he would test the Peruvian law. When his unlicensed vessels began fishing within the 200-mile zone, Peru's navy seized several of them and the government fined their captains.

After the Onassis incident Peru began to demand compliance with its fishing laws and fined the owners of several North American tuna boats who failed to purchase licenses. The United States Congress had prepared for his confrontation with the passage of the 1954 Fishermen's Protective Act, the first in a series of statutes that reimbursed Yankee fishermen for fines paid to the Peruvians and threatened Lima with various economic sanctions for enforcing its 200-mile jurisdiction against North American vessels. In effect, Washington encouraged United States citizens to defy Peru's claims and avoid recognition of this freedom-restricting precedent. Defiance of Peru's law caused considerable inconvenience for the North American fishermen, however, and in 1956 the American Tunaboat Association reached an agreement with the Peruvian government that brought a truce in the "tuna war." This organization promised to abide by Peru's laws and Lima pledged not to discriminate against foreign fishermen. Peru established reasonable regulations that applied equally to its own vessels as well as to those flying different flags. The government set moderate license fees and enforced a fishing calendar designed to protect the marine resources of the Humboldt Current from over-exploitation. All fines and fees collected were devoted to research in fisheries conservation.

The fisheries dispute flared anew in the early 1960s with the introduction of purse-seining to the tuna industry. Peru feared that this new technique, employing large nets, would endanger the marine life off its coast. At the same time, the use of nets freed the fishermen from the necessity of buying fresh bait in Peruvian ports, enabling them to avoid that nation's maritime officials. The "tuna war" again subsided in 1963, perhaps because of a widely rumored secret agreement with Belaúnde such as the United States did make with Ecuador.

Throughout the extended fisheries controversy many attempts to settle the dispute by direct negotiations and multilateral conferences had failed. The United States adamantly maintained that international law did not permit the unilateral regulation of maritime activities beyond the traditional three-mile limit. Peru insisted that international law was unclear on this issue and cited numerous precedents to demonstrate that it was evolving toward that nation's position. Meanwhile, Peruvian diplomats encouraged other Latin American republics to set 200-mile limits. The United States itself delivered a sharp blow to the three-mile limit in 1966, greatly strengthening Peru's argument. In response to demands by domestic coastal fishermen who were suffering serious losses from the incursions of Soviet trawlers into their fisheries, Washington proclaimed a 12-mile fishing limit. Several more Latin American states indignantly joined the "200-mile club," making that standard the most common in the Western hemisphere. As the dispute raged on it became apparent that the question could not be settled through appeals to existing international law and that a diplomatic agreement would be required to end the impasse.

Although a direct confrontation between Washington and Lima over the Hickenlooper Amendment had been averted in 1969, a new outbreak of the "tuna war" almost caused a complete rupture in United States-Peruvian relations. In mid-February of that year, a Peruvian gunboat attempting to capture two unlicensed California clippers fishing within the 200-mile limit collided with one of the vessels. The fishermen reported that their craft had been "machine-gunned" by the Peruvians; Lima acknowledged that "warning shots" had been fired with "rifles." Amid demands from west coast congressmen and their constituents that the United States navy protect the tuna fleet or arm the vessels themselves, Washington provisionally invoked the Pelly Amendment, suspending the sale of arms to Peru. This action, however, was not made public until discovered by the press in May, after the IPC crisis had passed. At that time, the Velasco administration responded by ordering the United States military missions to Peru out of the country. Lima also declared that New York governor Nelson Rockefeller, who was about to begin a Latin American tour for President Nixon, would not be welcome in Peru. After a month of quiet negotiations, the two nations backed away from the brink. Washington lifted its formal ban on arms sales to Peru (although it continued unofficially) and Lima agreed to hold new discussions with the United States concerning the fisheries question. These talks produced no significant change in the positions of either country, but the dialogue permitted passions to cool.

Within the context of the double-edged dispute with the United States, the revolutionary government vigorously pursued an "independent foreign policy" of friendly relations with all countries. Over the long run, the Peruvians hoped to reduce their dependence upon the North Americans by broadening their economic relationships with other countries. Lima's short-term diplomatic objective was to gain allies in its struggle with the State Department. In the face of the Nixon administration's "low profile" policy of reduced involvement in Latin America and other "noncritical" regions of the world, the Velasco regime labored to enhance Peru's international prestige. Increased visibility in world affairs, reasoned Lima, would inhibit Washington's exercise of power against Peru.

Peru established diplomatic relations with the Soviet Union in February 1969 and opened embassies in several other eastern European capitals shortly thereafter. Lima and Peking exchanged ambassadors in August 1971. Economic agreements—for trade, technical aid, loans, and credits—accompanied these new political ties. The revolutionary government also savored a few psychological victories. The joint communique announcing diplomatic relations between Peru and Communist China contained the familiar acknowledgment by Lima that Taiwan was an "inalienable" part of the People's Republic. In return, the Chinese recognized Peruvian sovereignty over the nation's adjacent waters for a distance of 200 miles. The Soviet Union, along with most of the other important seafaring countries, officially rejected Peru's fisheries claims. But during a visit to Lima in early 1973, Moscow's minister of fisheries declared that his nation always would "respect" Peru's 200-mile limit.

Peru also assumed a leadership role among the world's less-developed nations. In October 1971, the Velasco administration hosted a meeting of the "77 Group" (a very loose organization of nearly 100 Asian, African and Latin American states) and became an active spokesman for the Third World at other international forums. Peru was elected to a two-year term on the United Nations Security Council and supplied troops for the world organization's peace-keeping force in the Middle East. Peruvian diplomats exhibited their country's revolution as a model for rapid economic development and social change within the underdeveloped world. Emphasizing their nationalism and opposition to both capitalism and communism, Peru's leaders criticized the industrial nations of both the East and West for their economic policies toward the Third World suppliers of raw materials.

Closer to home the Velasco government worked within the Organization of American States to end the isolation of Cuba from its neighbors in the Western hemisphere. After these efforts failed, Peru unilaterally resumed diplomatic relations with the Castro regime in July 1972. While the bearded Cuban leader attested to the authenticity of the "Peruvian Revolution" and Chile's Marxist president Salvador Allende expressed warm regards for "comrade Velasco," Lima also maintained cordial relations with many of Latin America's conservative administrations. Avoiding ideological differences, Peru emphasized common interests that united Latin America in opposition to Washington. The position of the Peruvian government coincided with that of the rightist Brazilian regime in defense of the 200-mile limit. Lima supported Panama's demand for control over the isthmian canal. Peru was outspoken in its calls for a reduction of United States influence within the Organization of American States and a vociferous critic of North American trade and aid policies toward Latin America. The Velasco administration joined with those of Castro and Allende to denounce "Yankee economic blackmail."

Peru, Chile, Bolivia, Ecuador, and Colombia signed the Cartagena Agreement in June 1969, creating the Andean Group, a subregional component of the Latin American Free Trade Association. Venezuela subsequently joined the group in February 1973. Headquartered in Lima, this organization worked to hasten the economic development of its member states, whose industrial growth was to be coordinated so that their autonomous national economies would complement rather than compete with each other. Under a series of supplementary agreements this program was to be implemented gradually over a twenty-year period. By 1974 the Andean Group had made notable progress toward achieving its goal. A common tariff on the imports of nonmembers had been established, while provisions were made for the elimination or reduction of duties on goods traded among themselves. Each member state was assigned the exclusive right to manufacture and distribute certain items within the regional grouping. The organization adopted a uniform code for foreign investment. Strongly exhibiting the influence of Peru's General Law of Industries, it required that domestic capital eventually would own controlling interest in most enterprises.

The frigid relations between Washington and Lima thawed somewhat after Peru's May 31, 1970, earthquake. In cooperation with a massive international relief program, which included impressive efforts by the Soviet Union and Cuba, the United States temporarily lifted its embargo on aid on the Velasco government. The World Bank and the Inter-American Development Bank authorized emergency loans for the stricken nation. North American contributions, both public and private, totaled almost twenty-five million dollars. United States military personnel from Panama and helicopters from the carrier *Guam,* which anchored at Chimbote, participated in rescue missions. Mrs. Richard Nixon, who accompanied North American relief shipments and toured the devastated region, was received warmly by Peruvian officials.

Another natural phenomenon—the virtual disappearance of tuna off Peru's coast—also contributed to improved relations between the Nixon and Velasco administrations. These migratory fish did not move southward into Peruvian waters in 1970, and Peru's navy captured only one North American vessel. Tuna continued to avoid the Peruvian coast until late 1972. Farther to the north, however, the Ecuadorians seized many United States clippers and Washington reacted with a new punitive statute.

This measure automatically subtracted the amount of fines imposed upon North American vessels from the United States aid programs to the offending nations. In support of Ecuador, President Velasco loudly condemned this new legislative deterrent. It seemed likely that the dispute between the United States and Peru over fishing rights would return with the tuna.

The anticipated crisis occurred in January 1973, when the Peruvian navy seized more than a score of California-based boats fishing within the 200-mile limit. There was no United States aid program for Peru from which to deduct the one million dollars exacted in fines, and military sales to the Velasco regime virtually had ceased in 1968. Nevertheless, Washington announced that it again was placing arms sales to Peru "under review." Two months later a Soviet military mission arrived in Lima, and the revolutionary government placed a large order for Russian tanks and other weapons.

Then, almost as quickly as it began, the diplomatic struggle between Washington and Lima subsided. Apparently as the price for initiating a new dialogue, the United States ended its veto of loans to Peru by the international lending agencies. In April and May 1973, the Inter-American Development Bank approved almost 30 million dollars in loans to the Velasco regime. The next month, the World Bank authorized a whopping 470 million dollars in credits to Peru for a host of projects. Washington later approved a 15 million-dollar military aid program for Peru. In August President Nixon appointed investment banker James R. Green special envoy to the Velasco administration. A new round of negotiations concerning compensation for nationalized North American properties was complicated by more expropriations. Several United States firms were among those taken in the nationalization of the fishing industry the previous May. More troublesome was the dispute between the government and the Cerro de Pasco Corporation which culminated in the expropriation of that giant enterprise on the last day of 1973.

On February 19, 1974—only two days before Secretary of State Henry Kissinger was to address a meeting of American foreign ministers at Tlatelolco, Mexico—the United States and Peru settled the knotty compensation question. With the help of loans obtained from North American banks Peru agreed to pay 150 million dollars to several United States firms. Of this amount, Lima would give 74 million dollars directly to five companies, including Cerro de Pasco. The remaining 76 million dollars was to be placed in a special trust fund under the control of the State Department. The United States then would determine the amount of compensation due Peru's other claimants and disburse these funds on its own authority. This method, of course, would shield the Velasco administration from domestic criticism arising from the details of the compensation program. The agreement specifically identified eleven firms that were to receive indemnities. The International Petroleum Company was not among these. The Peruvian government asserted that it considered the IPC case closed. But the State Department apparently could indemnify the oil company if it chose to do so.

The United States and Peru also enjoyed a lull in their "tuna war" during the first half of 1974. Both nations, it would seem, attempted to avert a new confrontation over fishing rights in preparation for the United Nations Law of the Seas Conference held at Caracas between June 20 and August 30, 1974. Attended by delegates from nearly 150 nations, this meeting produced no concrete agreement concerning the many difficult questions on its agenda. However, a draft treaty submitted by the United States gained broad support and seemed to offer considerable hope for compromise. The North American proposal would have extended the territorial waters of coastal states from 3 to 12 miles. These nations also could exercise primary jurisdiction and preferential rights over natural resources in an "economic zone" extending for an additional 188 miles. Essentially, the draft treaty would have acknowledged Peru's right to exercise the kind of sovereign control over its coastal waters that the nation had practiced for two decades. Yet, licensed fishermen from other countries would have been permitted to exploit the marine life of the Humboldt Current, subject to Peruvian regulations, and the vessels of all nations would have been guaranteed the right of "innocent passage" through the economic zone. Ironically, the United States Congress weakened the bargaining power of the State Department in these negotiations. Throughout 1974, the North American legislators considered a bill, supported by coastal fishing interests, unilaterally extending the fisheries jurisdiction of the United States to 200 miles. In April 1976, President Gerald Ford signed this Fishery Conservation and Management Act into law. The "tuna war" apparently had ended, most unexpectedly, in a vindication of the Peruvian position.

ae The Troublesome Challenge: A Revolution with Liberty

Students of Peruvian affairs had difficulty plotting the political destination of the country's revolutionary journey. The signposts provided by the military regime—its words and actions—often appeared to point in opposite directions. Employing a singularly martial non sequitur, President Velasco dedicated his administration to a "revolution with liberty until the last cartridge is fired." He and other leaders repeatedly pledged to maintain the nation's "ideological pluralism" and respect the freedom to express these diverse views. The ultimate goal of the revolution was said to be a social, economic, and political democracy of "broad, full, popular participation" through "autogestionary" organizations which the people would create and direct by themselves. It seemed clear, however, that the political system envisioned for the future was not to be a traditional liberal republic.

Whatever its intentions for the future, the Velasco administration, in fact, was a military dictatorship. Furthermore, the president indicated that the armed forces planned to retain power until the fulfillment of the revolution was guaranteed, an objective estimated to require at least two decades. During its first six years the regime was not notably oppressive, resembling the *dictablanda* of 1962–63. Yet the tendency toward arbitrary decisions and intolerance for opponents—universal characteristics of dictatorship—were exhibited with increased frequency. To the extent that the generals made no concerted effort to implant an official doctrine within the national consciousness, the administration respected Peru's "ideological pluralism." But the liberty to express discordant ideas, from within the regime and without, was steadily restricted. Similarly, continually contracting "revolutionary parameters" confined the activities of the country's old political parties, labor unions, peasant leagues, and other organized interest groups. Stressing the primacy of social and economic democracy over representative political processes, members of the military regime increasingly spoke of "broad, full, popular participation" in reference to the workplace and local community, not the national government.

The Velasco administration governed Peru under the provisions of the Revolutionary Statute, issued on the day of the coup, and those portions of existing laws not superseded by that document and subsequent decrees. These measures vested executive power in a Revolutionary Junta comprised of the three military service commanders, who also held the cabinet portfolios for their respective branches of the armed forces. Theoretically, General Velasco served as president of the junta at the discretion of the army, navy, and air force commanders, with whom he shared executive authority. The Revolutionary Statute assigned functions previously performed by the legislature to the cabinet, a body selected entirely from the military establishment. Decree-laws were approved by a majority of the ministers and issued under the signatures of the Revolutionary Junta. The central government appointed most local officials, again drawing heavily upon the armed forces for executive personnel. Civilians continued to predominate in the lower levels of the bureaucracy and several held important advisory posts in high government councils. But military men headed most state agencies.

The administration instituted a major reorganization of the judicial system in December 1969. Undertaken primarily to increase the efficiency of the notoriously sluggish courts and improve the integrity of the magistracy, the generals undoubtedly hoped that the reform also would create a judiciary more sympathetic to the revolution. The government obtained the resignations of all 16 members of the Supreme Court, most of whom were approaching the mandatory retirement age. The reconstituted high-court panel included four of the younger judges from the old body. Under the new system Supreme Court justices were to serve renewable five-year terms rather than for life or until age sixty-five as before. The reformed Supreme Court immediately undertook a review of all judges presiding over inferior courts, removing 184 magistrates of questionable honesty or ability. To continue the reform process, the government appointed a blue-ribbon National Council of Justice. This body was to investigate charges of corruption in the administration of justice, reform judicial procedures, and fill all vacancies in the nation's judiciary, including those on the Supreme Court. After 1969, the generals usually respected the decisions of the courts. In a few celebrated cases, however, the officers overruled the judges, demonstrating that "the Revolution is the source of the law" and, therefore, supreme.

In the absence of functioning republican institutions, Peru's political parties lost much of their vitality. The National Odriísta

Union disbanded even before the death of General Odría in February 1974. Of the remaining partisan organizations, only the conservative, Belaundista wing of Acción Popular and a few small groups on the far left consistently criticized the regime. The left wing of AP (calling itself Acción Popular Socialista) and the Christian Democrats supported most of the administration's reforms. The Peruvian Communist party, taking its cues from Moscow, officially endorsed almost every action of the government. However, the nation's small independent Marxist groups—which official spokesmen termed the "ultras"—denounced many of the reforms as insufficient. They frequently questioned the sincerity of the generals, or charged that the revolution merely was modernizing the exploitative apparatus of imperialist capitalism. Although the opposition of the far left was largely verbal, sporadic guerrilla activity occurred and the regime accused the "ultras" of fomenting violent strikes and antigovernment demonstrations.

On May 7, 1974, the American Popular Revolutionary Alliance celebrated its fiftieth anniversary. Even before this event stimulated reflection about the movement's past, several Apristas and independent commentators noted the uncanny resemblance between the *alianza*'s maximum and minimum programs and the foreign and domestic policies of the Velasco administration. Peru's ruling generals indignantly rejected any inference that their revolution was Aprismo in epaulets. Indeed, those portions of the old Aprista platforms that most closely resembled the reforms of the military regime long ago were abandoned or distorted beyond recognition by the party's leaders. The brief and often vague promises of the early Apristas, furthermore, could not be compared realistically with the concrete actions of the revolution. Nevertheless, the PAP had popularized many of the reforms of the Velasco administration. A Peruvian Rip Van Winkle, awakening in the 1970s after a forty-year slumber, might well have assumed that APRA had succeeded in establishing its "anti-imperialist state." Perhaps a later generation would view Víctor Raúl as a prophet of the revolution, the "Peruvian Moses" whose political sins and personal failings prevented his entrance into the promised land of the presidency. But during the Velasco years he was a prophet with little honor in his own country.

The military administration placed several prominent leaders of Peru's old political parties in important state posts. The government insisted, however, that it appointed these men as individuals and not as representatives of their partisan organizations. Thus Héctor Cornejo Chávez, the Christian Democratic presidential candidate in 1962, became chairman of the National Council of Justice and former Vice-President Edgardo Seoane, the leader of Acción Popular's left wing, served as head of the Agricultural Development Bank. The founder of the small Social Progressive Movement, Alberto Ruiz Eldridge, was one of General Velasco's principal civilian advisers and headed Lima's diplomatic mission in Brazil. At Christmas 1970, the revolutionary government issued an amnesty for all political prisoners, including imprisoned guerrilla leaders Hugo Blanco and Héctor Béjar. Blanco soon became involved in a nationwide teachers' strike and was deported to Chile. Béjar, however, accepted a high post in the peasant affairs division of the administration's new social mobilization program. The labor union section of the same agency was headed by a longtime organizer for the Communist party. Even a few repentant Belaundistas and ex-Apristas received government appointments.

Some of the nations's old special interest associations, including the once-powerful national societies of agriculture and industry, were dissolved or gravely weakened by the regime. The Velasco administration, however, treated the Catholic Church with great deference. Several religious leaders enjoyed considerable influence in high government circles and Cardinal Juan Landázuri Ricketts regularly previewed important reform decrees. With the notable exception of a messy dispute between the auxiliary bishop of Lima and the minister of the interior during the 1971 Pamplona squatter invasion, conflicts between Church and state were rare. The Peruvian hierarchy and especially the National Office of Social Information, an association of liberal priests, strongly endorsed most of the regime's programs.

Peru's organized labor and peasant movements, with their close ties to the nation's political parties, had ambivalent relationships with the government. The Aprista-controlled Confederation of Peruvian Workers (CTP) opposed the nationalization of the north coast plantations and then struggled with the regime over the administration of the new sugar cooperatives. Like APRA itself, the CTP sharply criticized several other portions of the military's program—especially the social property Law—while proclaiming its fundamental sympathy for the revolution. The Communist-dominated General Confederation of Peruvian

Workers (CGTP), the country's largest labor federation, officially voiced almost unreserved support for the regime. Nevertheless, the parent organization seemed to have great difficulty maintaining discipline over its component unions, particularly those in the mining industry. The Confederación Campesina Peruana (CCP), the Communist-linked peasant federation, also exhibited considerable independence in its attacks on Velasco's agrarian policies.

Peru's prerevolutionary labor legislation remained in effect, for the most part, and the government recognized the right to strike within the limits established by these laws. Walkouts, in fact, occurred with greater frequency and idled many more workers than during the Belaúnde administration. However, the Velasco regime acted forcefully and sometimes brutally in suppressing several "illegal strikes," notably among copper miners and the very militant schoolteachers. Police and troops clashed with strikers while threats of dismissal were employed to force workers back to their jobs. The government frequently arrested labor and peasant leaders and deported some of the more recalcitrant officials. In spite of frequent denials, the generals apparently envisioned no place for the existing labor unions and peasant leagues in the revolutionary future. The agrarian cooperatives, labor communities, and social property enterprises were designed, in part, to eliminate the need for these organizations. But the Velasco administration avoided the turmoil that certainly would have resulted from a frontal assault on the old unions and leagues. These groups together with the political parties were expected to atrophy and gradually die of natural causes.

For two and one-half years the Velasco regime resisted pressures to establish a civilian-based political apparatus. The generals spurned the overtures of old partisan organizations that wanted to participate in the government. The nation's existing parties, the "political oligarchy," already stood condemned by the armed forces of moral and civic bankruptcy. The military also objected to the formation of a single government party to "institutionalize" the revolution. According to administration ideologues, such mechanisms invariably became self-serving, bureaucratic automatons that destroyed the revolutionary dynamic and oppressed the people they were meant to assist. In fact, a government party—the armed forces—already existed and the generals perceived no threat requiring the mobilization of the masses in defense of the regime. The "Peruvianization of banking," the agrarian reform, and the nationalization of other enterprises severely weakened the old conservative elite. The administration's reforms at home and its nationalistic foreign policy undercut the appeal of the badly fragmented revolutionary left. In the political field between these partisan poles, the generals skillfully pitted the Communists against the Apristas and used government jobs to co-opt the leadership of the other parties.

Many humble citizens, however, felt a need for greater identification with the process that was profoundly changing their country. "Committees for the Defense of the Revolution" (CDR's), similar to the neighborhood surveillance units of Castro's Cuba, appeared soon after the 1968 coup as the public rallied behind the regime's expropriation of the IPC and its vigorous defense of the 200-mile limit. In the following months, feeble opposition to the agrarian reform and conservative reaction to a drive for the unionization of Lima's domestic servants spawned a large number of new CDR's. Some of the committees were spontaneous in origin, but many were organized by the Communist and other parties. Producing consternation among conservative officers, these groups first were placed under government control and then disbanded.

By 1971 it became apparent that the Velasco administration would have to provide a vehicle for popular participation in the revolution, or risk the mobilization of the masses under the direction of civilian politicians. At the same time, the regime increasingly recognized the value of organized civilian support. Tensions within the military establishment heightened as the requirements for rapid economic development and the promise of social justice came more clearly into conflict. Difficult decisions concerning the future of the revolution threatened to destroy the unity of the armed forces and drive disaffected officers into alliances with the regime's civilian opponents, whose parties and pressure groups had not been dismantled. A series of violent strikes and mounting rural unrest, moreover, demonstrated that these organizations still possessed considerable disruptive potential. To bolster its position, weaken its civilian adversaries, and provide for limited popular participation in the revolution, the Velasco administration fashioned a new political mechanism that purportedly avoided the pitfalls of traditional political parties.

On the second anniversary of the agrarian reform decree, June 24, 1971, President Velasco announced the establishment of the Sistema Nacional de Apoyo a la Movilización Social (National System of Support to Social Mobilization). The regime purposefully crafted this unwieldly title to achieve the acronym "Sinamos" ("without masters"), a phrase that conveyed the official philosophy concerning political participation. Although headed by generals holding ministerial rank, Sinamos became the governmental arm where civilian leaders were the most conspicuous. Chief among these was Carlos Delgado, the organization's major theoretician and frequent spokesman. A sociology professor prior to the revolution, Delgado began his political career as an Aprista youth organizer. He later became a private secretary to Haya de la Torre before abandoning APRA along with other disenchanted left-wing intellectuals in the late 1950s. In addition to his duties with Sinamos, Delgado served as an adviser and speech writer for President Velasco. Some of Delgado's ideas, especially those concerning the evolution of Peruvian society, and the language he employed to express his views had strong overtones of Aprismo.

According to its creators Sinamos was not a political party but an "infrastructure of participation." Its primary task was to assist the people in establishing "autonomous, self-directed, basic institutions" for their involvement in every aspect of the nation's political, economic, social, and cultural life. Sinamos was not to become a self-perpetuating bureaucracy, however. Its life would be transitory, fading from existence after achieving its objective of a "social democracy of full participation." The agency promised to exert its greatest effort aiding Peru's humblest classes to become active citizens. But because these marginal groups had little experience in self-government, their "responsible" and "constructive" participation in the national life first required "ideo-political capacitation" by Sinamos. The agency would begin this educative process by involving the people in the affairs that directly affected their daily lives—at work and in the local community. Eventually, the masses would become full participants in national politics through their own "autogestionary" organizations.

The government protested against the use of standard political labels to describe the new system, asserting that it would be uniquely Peruvian. But obviously, the basic model employed was the corporate state. Unlike the familiar right-wing, fascist regimes of Europe, the new Peruvian edition was to be leftist, the predominant inclination of corporatist experiments in the Americas. Peruvians would be organized hierarchically according to functional, economic sectors. Cutting across class lines, this structure would encourage national solidarity and inhibit independent revolutionary activity by the masses. In its initial stages, at least, the corporate state would be controlled by a military elite with the assistance of civilian technocrats. Such a system could have had considerable flexibility, permitting a greater degree of popular participation in national affairs than ever before. Ultimately, however, the degree of self-government within the new order would depend upon the willingness of the armed forces to relinquish their monopoly of power.

Ironically, Sinamos came into existence with one of the larger bureaucracies in the Peruvian government. It initially incorporated eight offices previously responsible to the president plus several entities detached from various ministries. Sinamos quickly created additional units for popular involvement in a broad range of activities. By late 1973, the mobilization program employed nearly 5,000 persons in its central office in Lima and at thirteen regional centers throughout the country. Sinamos was beginning to open district headquarters for its "promoters," agents who worked within local communities. The jurisdiction of Sinamos included peasant communities, agricultural cooperatives, community development programs, regional development corporations, associations of *barriada* residents, trade unions, labor communities, peasant leagues, and the promotion of agrarian reform. Under a broad mandate to make the entire national bureaucracy more responsive to the needs of the people, the agency also performed the role of public ombudsman, attempting to "humanize" other state offices. In short, Sinamos interjected itself into all significant areas of organized popular activity and served as the only legitimate channel for citizen demands upon the government.

Sinamos immediately became a source of great discord in Peru and one of the more controversial creations of the revolution. The formulation of the mobilization program itself required nearly a year of debate within the administration. Other branches of the government resented the meddling of Sinamos and accused it of bureaucratic empire building. Meanwhile, the agency experienced considerable dissension within its own ranks. Staff members inherited from the Belaúnde administration opposed several Sinamos projects, while the excesses of enthusiastic young employees often embarrassed the agency. The wealthy cooperatives accused Sinamos of organizing peasant invasions of their lands. Independent farmers charged that the agency's agrarian reform "promoters" used bullying tactics to force them into collectives. The government claimed, with some justification, that the political right fought the mobilization program from the outside, while left-wing infiltrators sought to sabotage it from within.

Although the Velasco regime insisted that Sinamos was not a political party and that it would not become one, the program was designed to assume many functions of the old partisan groups. The parties viewed it as their mortal enemy. The labor unions and peasant leagues had an equally jaundiced attitude toward the competing organizations fostered by Sinamos. Fierce infighting occurred between the government-supported Confederation of Revolutionary Peruvian Workers (CTRP) and the workers' federations of the Communists and Apristas. The interference of Sinamos in union elections caused riots. Violent confrontations also took place in the countryside between the original peasant leagues and those associated with the officially sanctioned National Agrarian Confederation (CNA). Sinamos experienced considerable success in organizing previously unorganized elements of the population, but the agency often encountered solid resistance in its attempts to supplant existing associations with approved "autogestionary" bodies. In elections arranged by the agency, the nation's teachers overwhelmingly voted to maintain their own union and reject one supported by Sinamos. Sometimes, prerevolutionary interest groups captured the government's new participatory structures. When the first congress of the National Confederation of Industrial Communities (CONACI), held in March 1973, demonstrated that the old unions dominated this new entity, the regime ordered a "reorganization" of the confederation.

Critics quickly charged that Sinamos was not an "infrastructure of participation" but an instrument of manipulation. They doubted the "spontaneity" of Sinamos-assisted mass demonstrations in support of the regime and the tumultuous welcomes arranged for President Velasco and other military leaders during their visits to the provinces. More suspicious were the Sinamos-aided attempts of progovernment unions to silence publications critical of the regime. The administrative structure of Sinamos indicated that internal security, rather than social mobilization, may have been its principal objective. The boundaries of the agency's districts corresponded to those of the nation's military zones and the local army commander often doubled as the head of Sinamos in his region.

The National Agrarian Confederation opened its first congress in Lima on October 3, 1974, the sixth anniversary of the revolution. A showcase for the regime's program of "autogestionary democracy," delegates claiming to represent three million farmers assembled in the old chambers of parliament and elected a peasant from Huánuco president of the organization. Skeptics who expected the congress to provide uncritical support for the government were somewhat surprised. As anticipated, the assembly refused to seat delegates from the leftist peasant leagues and condemned the selfishness of the largely unrepresented sugar cooperatives. But while the peasants expressed general approval of the revolution, they sharply attacked several aspects of the agrarian reform and issued a plan calling for major changes in government policy.

The administration described the CNA congress and its "constructive criticism" as a great triumph for Sinamos. But obviously, the generals were beginning to view the popular participation program as a disaster. Sinamos had not notably augmented civilian support for the regime, and the activities of the agency brought increased political turmoil. The new "autogestionary" organizations failed to weaken the old parties, unions, and peasant leagues. On the contrary, the challenge from Sinamos seemed to revitalize these groups. Notwithstanding the official pronouncements of the government and the undoubtedly sincere convictions of some leaders, the immediate objective of Sinamos had been the *controlled participation* of the masses in the nation's politics. The newly mobilized sectors, however, demonstrated their unwillingness to accept the minor role in the system that the military envisioned. For many generals and admirals a new and largely unwanted dynamic—a Frankenstein monster—had been added to the revolution.

The revolutionary government's treatment of the press evoked censure from journalists around the world and caused great dissension within Peru itself. During their first difficult weeks in power, the generals seized specific issues of various journals, temporarily suspended publication of some periodi-

349

cals, and arrested several editors for printing "malicious news." It seemed likely, however, that the regime would become increasingly tolerant of the press after its hold on power had firmed. But in December 1969, the administration decreed its Liberty of the Press Statute which regulated both the print and broadcast media. This measure declared that freedom of expression would have "no other restriction than respect for the law, truth and morality, the demands of the security of the state and national defense and the safeguard of personal and family honor and privacy." The decree enumerated several press offenses: the publication of materials endangering the nation's security and economic stability; the dissemination of official secrets or false documents; and the printing of articles prejudicial to the honor and reputation of persons or organizations. Although the statute stated that no form of official censorship would be imposed except in wartime, journalists charged that the vagueness of the edict established an inhibiting self-censorship upon the press.

The press law also required that all stockholders, editors, and proprietors of journals published within the country be Peruvian citizens and reside in Peru for at least six months per year. A controversial interpretation of this provision in early 1972 forced Pedro Beltrán to relinquish his control of *La Prensa.* Nevertheless, that conservative Lima daily continued its editorial criticism of the revolution under the direction of Beltrán's nephew, Pedro Beltrán Ballén. Two years earlier, the government had silenced the opposition of *Extra* and *Expreso,* newspapers owned by former Belaundista minister Manuel Ulloa. Following strikes by left-wing employees, the regime expropriated both journals and transformed them into workers' cooperatives. *Extra* and *Expreso* immediately became the most uncritical supporters of the administration. In succeeding months several other publications were threatened with takeovers by their workers and many journalists were arrested, fined, and deported. The regime's most persistent journalistic thorn-in-the-side was Enrique Zileri Gibson, publisher of the magazine *Caretas,* who was arrested repeatedly for testing the Liberty of the Press Statute. His "offenses" included publication of an "obscene" cartoon of President Nixon, reporting generous increases in military salaries, and describing the administration as "paranoic."

In spite of these difficulties, newspapers and magazines expressing a broad range of political opinion—from extreme conservatism to Trotskyism—continued to appear. These publications analyzed and criticized the reforms of the revolution. Until 1974, a casual foreign reader of the Peruvian press might not have suspected the existence of any form of censorship. Yet certain topics, most notably struggles within the regime, were reported only at great risk by the country's journalists. As a result, a vigorous underground press appeared, and the notoriously unreliable Lima rumor mill became an increasingly important source of information and misinformation. For example, while the nation's newspapers in early 1973 attributed President Velasco's nearly fatal illness to a "ruptured aneurysm," many Peruvians believed that the general had been shot by a brother officer during a heated argument. Lead poisoning rather than the officially reported "circulatory problems" was thought to have forced the amputation of his leg. The regular press reported neither the rumor nor the official reaction to it.

The Telecommunications Law of 1972 and supplementary decrees established regulations for radio and television broadcasting. Some of the new rules drew far more praise than criticism. Programs emphasizing sex, violence, and crime could not be aired before 9:00 in the evening. Restrictions were placed upon the number and content of commercial messages. All broadcast advertising and at least 60 percent of regular programming had to be produced in Peru. But like the press law, other regulations imposed upon radio and television were vague and suggested an attempt at thought control. The government required broadcasts to "reaffirm the values of the human being, . . . entertain healthily, . . . and take into account the sectorial policies of the state and cooperate in bringing them about." Children's programs were to promote "national values" and inculcate "civic virtues." The Ministry of Education demonstrated the absurdities permitted under the law at Christmas 1972 by banishing Santa Claus from the airwaves. The administration condemned the jolly fellow as an antichristian, merchant's conspiracy, and a Nordic myth. Papá Noel pictured among snow-covered pines during the Peruvian summer allegedly demonstrated the nation's cultural dependence upon the northern hemisphere.

The Revolution in Crisis

The conflict between the administration and the press reached a climax in 1974. The denouement badly damaged the credibility of the "revolution with liberty" and contributed to a political crisis that would culminate in the ouster of President Velasco the following year. On March 5, the regime created the National System of Information (SINADI) under the direction of a general with cabinet rank. Established to "rationalize and standardize" the state's activities in radio, television, motion pictures and the print media, the system also included a Central Information Office charged with gathering, processing, and diffusing news to both the national and foreign press. Fears immediately arose that this agency would interpose itself between the Peruvian press and the international news services, which the regime had criticized for their coverage of the revolution. The government partially confirmed these suspicions in mid-April, when it banned the LATIN news agency. A wire-service consortium of Britain's Reuters and a half-dozen major Latin American newspapers, including Lima's *El Comercio*, LATIN was accused of vilifying the Velasco administration abroad.

Meanwhile, several journals which had given uncritical support to the government and often reflected its point of view—most notably *Expreso* and *Extra*, the newspapers previously transferred to Communist-dominated workers' cooperatives—launched an unrelenting editorial campaign against the *"gran prensa,"* Lima's major dailies. The self-styled "revolutionary press" charged that the *gran prensa* championed the reactionary political views and economic interests of the "oligarchy" and called for their expropriation. Amid these attacks, which were echoed by production workers at the beleaguered newspapers, and rumors that the regime planned an "integral solution" to the problem of free expression, the *gran prensa* fought back. Strongly worded essays defending freedom of the press and decrying "communistic tendencies" within the administration soon moved from the editorial sections to the front pages of the large dailies.

The *gran prensa* of Lima received support from many provincial newspapers, *Caretas* and most notably, *Oiga*, a popular news magazine. Francisco Igartua, *Oiga*'s independent socialist director, had been an ardent defender of the revolution. His journal enjoyed lucrative advertising accounts with state agencies and exclusive interviews with top leaders of the regime. But as the magazine intensified its campaign in defense of free expression, it lost its government advertising, became the target of police harassment, and encountered severe labor problems. *Oiga* survived by raising its subscription rates and successful appeals to its friends, who purchased ads supporting the magazine's editorial position. In mid-June, however, the government again closed *Caretas* and issued a deportation order against its publisher, Enrique Zileri, who went into hiding.

The press controversy sparked a heated dispute within the administration as conservative officers defended the independent newspapers in high government councils. On May 25, Vice Adm. Luis Vargas Caballero, the navy minister, aired this internal feud in public. In a speech lamenting the growing tendency to label all criticism of the regime "counterrevolutionary," he called for a reaffirmation of the commitment to ideological pluralism. President Velasco, in his weekly press conference a few days later, charged that the admiral had violated an administration rule restricting statements on political matters to the president and prime minister. He strongly suggested that the navy minister's resignation was expected. Almost all of the navy's flag officers, including two others holding ministerial posts, signed a letter defending their commander. But Vargas Caballero resigned on May 31, and the other protesting cabinet members surrendered their portfolios five days later. The government filled these vacancies with admirals who had been out of the country during the crisis and, therefore, had not signed the letter in defense of Vargas Caballero. The new navy minister, hastily flown to Peru from his attaché's post in Washington, reaffirmed his service's support for the revolution and its solidarity with the army and air force. But obviously, the unity of the military regime had been damaged badly.

Criticism of the recently proclaimed Social Property Law, the press dispute, and the ministerial crisis brought a hardening in the administration's relations with civilian opposition parties. During its first six years, the revolutionary government had arrested and deported several political leaders, especially members of the Belaundista wing of Acción Popular. The regime, however, had avoided harsh repression. No party had been suppressed and amnesties had freed political prisoners while permitting exiles to return home. Fernando Belaúnde, himself,

continued to receive his presidential pension in the United
States and was allowed to visit Peru for three weeks following the
death of his mother in December 1970. But, in May 1974,
leaders of Acción Popular attacked the government's treatment
of the press, praised Admiral Vargas and, again, called upon the
military to restore constitutional processes. On May 31, the
regime banned Acción Popular and deported its secretary general and secretary for political affairs. From Paris, AP leader
Manuel Ulloa vowed that the party would "carry on our struggle
clandestinely, until we have overthrown the anti-constitutional,
personalist and socializing government led by General Velasco."

Early in the morning of July 27, steel-helmeted riot police
invaded the offices of six Lima newspapers, ousted their management personnel, and replaced them with government-
appointed editors. In addition to an expropriation decree, providing compensation to the former owners, the administration
issued a new press law. This measure repeated most of the old
Liberty of the Press Statute, but also outlawed clandestine publications and prohibited the private ownership of nationally circulated daily newspapers that sold more than 20,000 copies—the
gran prensa. The decree did not affect the smaller dailies, weekly
newspapers, or the nation's magazines. After one year, the expropriated journals were to be transferred to "significant" organized sectors of the population. Thus, *El Comercio* would belong
to the peasants and *La Prensa* would express the views of the
labor communities. Professional associations, cultural organizations, educational groups, and entities representing service
workers also were to receive their own organs. It was clear,
however, that only groups organized or approved by the regime
would be given newspapers. Until the transfer was accomplished, the "reformed press" would be directed by four-man,
state-appointed editorial committees. These caretaker panels
included several of the nation's more notable journalists and
intellectuals. Although some of the new directors had criticized
certain actions of the military regime, all were basically sympathetic toward the revolution.

President Velasco defended the "Peruvianization" of the
press in his July 28 Independence Day address and in later
statements. Noting that the action had been a longtime objective
of the secret Plan Inca, he denied that the measure was designed
to stifle criticism of the regime. The president declared that the
"reformed press" was to be completely independent and that the

government expected "neither obsequiousness nor flattery." Velasco asserted that the old *gran prensa* had served foreign interests and had failed to represent the authentic views of a majority of the nation's citizens. Free expression had existed only for "businessmen and for small families and groups. There were newspapers of bankers, newspapers of exporters, newspapers of great landowners." Many Peruvians and some outside observers familiar with the Lima press agreed with the general's assessment of the *gran prensa*. But considerable sympathy was expressed for *El Commercio,* Peru's oldest daily. Operated for generations by the Miró Quesada family, the newspaper blended conservatism with extreme nationalism. After leading the campaign against the IPC, it had supported the Velasco administration until the 1969 press law. The Miró Quesadas, unlike the owners of the other expropriated journals, engaged in no significant business outside of their newspaper. The house arrest for several days of Luis Miró Quesada, the ninety-three-year-old family patriarch, evoked outrage from several quarters.

"NO," screamed the blackened cover of *Oiga* in response to the seizure of the *gran prensa*. The "rape" of the Peruvian dailies was condemned as "totalitarian" by the Inter-American Press Association, an organization that already had been highly critical of the Velasco administration. The IAPA also attached significance to the appearance of Cuban Defense Minister Raúl Castro and new Russian tanks at Peru's Independence Day parade. The expropriation of the Lima press drew further censure from the International Press Institute, the Inter-American Association of Broadcasters, and the presidents of Mexico and Costa Rica. After an eight-hour conference with government officials concerning the press, Peru's bishops issued a statement studiously avoiding comment on their obvious displeasure with the takeover itself. The episcopacy credited the regime with good intentions and expressed hope that the nationalized journals would become "authentic channels for free expression" by their assigned sectorial organizations. But the churchmen indicated their apprehension that the newspapers might express only the views of the new editorial committees. Perhaps most embarrassing to the Velasco regime was the response of the National Agrarian Confederation. Its spokesmen declared that *El Comercio,* the newspaper assigned to the peasants, did not represent their views but those of its new director, Christian Democrat Héctor Cornejo Chávez. The farmers' group asked the government to give them radio stations, far more effective channels for reaching illiterate *campesinos.*

For three nights following the seizure of the *gran prensa,* antigovernment demonstrations took place in the middle- and upper-class suburbs of Lima. Rioters, primarily young people, stoned state-owned banks and burned vehicles. Police quelled the unrest and jailed almost 500 persons, including several leaders of Acción Popular, who were charged with instigating the disturbances. Meanwhile, the administration also attacked Peru's Communists, perhaps partially to allay fears of growing Marxist influence within the government. The generals accused the Communist party of "opportunism" and charged that its labor unions and peasant federations were attempting to undermine the revolution. *Expreso* and *Extra,* the Communist-controlled Lima dailies, already had been seized along with the other major newspapers.

Peru's "reformed press" quickly attempted to demonstrate its independence. Although the newspapers defended the new press law, they published letters denouncing the measure. Within a week, editorials in two of the journals strongly criticized the administration for its closure of *Caretas.* The previously banned magazine reappeared a short time later with a scathing attack on the government's press policy by Peru's senior statesman, former President José Luis Bustamante i Rivero. Lima's newspapers then reported that three leaders of Acción Popular arrested during the antigovernment riots had been tortured by the Peruvian Investigation Police. The administration quickly obeyed writs requiring the release of the victims and dismissed the police chief. In preparation for the October anniversary of the revolution, the regime issued an amnesty for 190 persons accused or convicted of political offenses, including those arrested during the press riots. The president's annual message to the nation again proclaimed the revolution's commitment to "ideological pluralism" and the right of all Peruvians to "act politically in liberty." It appeared that a chastened administration had backed away from a policy of repression. But a series of crises quickly brought a reversal in this new essay at revolution with liberty.

In October 1974, an embarrassing scandal filled the pages of the nation's newspapers and magazines. Officials of EPSA, the state agricultural marketing agency, and Peruvian customs personnel were charged with smuggling millions of dollars worth of subsidized foodstuffs to buyers in Ecuador, Bolivia, and Chile. The government arrested more than 100 officials and ousted the ministers of agriculture and commerce. The next month, however, Peru's journalists pressed the generals too hard. Following the publication of articles concerning the deterioration of the economy, the administration closed *Oiga* and *Opinión Libre,* a new magazine staffed by the former editors of *La Prensa.* The English-language *Andean Times* was silenced a few days later for revealing the terms of a controversial contract between the government and a Japanese firm to construct the trans-Andean pipeline. After the Lima Bar Association protested that this agreement violated the constitution and endangered Peru's sovereignty, the regime deported three of its officers.

With channels for peaceful protest increasingly restricted, the regime's critics expressed their discontent by violent means. In the last weeks of 1974 several government offices were bombed, apparently by conservative groups, while two cabinet ministers narrowly escaped death at the hands of left-wing assailants. The administration responded with a decree authorizing the use of military tribunals to try suspected terrorists. The sentences of these panels—including the heretofore rarely invoked death penalty—were to be imposed within forty-eight hours.

A strike by the 18,000-man civil guard in early February 1975 afforded opponents of the administration an ideal opportunity to vent their hostility. On the fifth and sixth of the month, while most of Lima's policemen barricaded themselves in their headquarters, rioting youths rampaged through the unprotected streets of the capital. The offices of two "reformed" newspapers and the military club were burned along with many private buildings. Thousands of people from the *barriadas* of Lima quickly joined the original protestors in looting the shops of the business district. President Velasco decreed a thirty-day suspension of the constitution and, for the first time since coming to power, used regular troops to restore order in the capital. The soldiers stormed the barracks of the striking policemen and attacked the rioting civilians. An estimated 100 persons were killed and another 1,000 were injured during the unrest.

The February riots dramatically demonstrated the growing unpopularity of the dictatorship and the failure of Sinamos. In April 1975, the regime announced the "reorganization" of the social mobilization agency. The administration hastily grouped some of its friends into a makeshift Movement of the Peruvian Revolution to provide immediate backing for the regime. At the same time, representatives from government agencies and the officially sponsored sectorial confederations began planning a more structured Political Organization of the Peruvian Revolution.

The rapid growth of popular discontent was rooted, to a large degree, in the nation's economic difficulties. After several years of excellent performance, the Peruvian economy began to falter in 1974 and deteriorated badly in 1975. The cost of living increased by at least 15 percent in 1974 and jumped 40 percent the next year. A trade deficit that would exceed one billion dollars in 1975 deeply eroded the treasury's reserves of foreign exchange. The government borrowed heavily to balance its international payments and finance its development programs. By the end of 1975, the overseas debt would surpass 3 billion dollars and require 500 million dollars to service.

The economic crisis had both internal and external origins. The failure of the fishing industry to recover as anticipated along with lower prices and contracting markets for Peru's metallic minerals limited the nation's export earnings. Meanwhile, because of worldwide inflation, the country paid higher prices for an expanding volume of imports, especially fuel and foodstuffs. The government generously subsidized both of the latter items to ease the pain of inflation for the vocal urban population. For this same reason the administration maintained low prices for foods grown within the country, a policy that discouraged domestic agriculture and contributed to rural unrest. The state's revenues suffered from mismanagement and costly strikes in public enterprises, especially the copper mines, and low prices for government-owned export commodities. In spite of some tax increases and improvements in the collection system, the regime had avoided a thoroughgoing reform in this area and the favored middle class remained lightly taxed. While demands on the treasury mounted, the administration was forced to expand its already burdensome investment program to compensate for a serious decline in activity by the private sector.

Peru's entrepreneurs were badly frightened, and the government was unable to restore business confidence. It had broken too many promises in the past. In addition to their growing apprehension about competition from the social property sector, the businessmen nervously awaited major changes in the Industrial Reform Law. In August 1974, the press reported that contemplated revisions would require the conversion of all "reformed private enterprises" (those with labor communities) into cooperatives within ten years. Uncertainty about the future contributed to a drastic drop in private investment and a rash of bankruptcies. Speculation grew that the administration would be forced to undertake wholesale nationalizations within the lagging manufacturing sector to prevent economic collapse. Thus, Peru's entrepreneurial class seemed locked in a suicidal, self-fulfilling prophesy.

Government spokesmen generally refused to acknowledge the regime's share of responsibility for the economic decline. They predicted even greater difficulty until 1977, when earnings from newly opened copper mines and Amazonian oil would bring relief. Independent observers were more pessimistic, however. During 1975, the latest Amazonian oil boom showed ominous signs of becoming another bust. Among the score of organizations exploring for "liquid gold" beyond the Andes, only the state's Petro-Perú and one private company had discovered petroleum in commercial quantities. Fears arose that the amount of oil ultimately discovered might be insufficient to pay for the trans-Andean pipeline, the anticipated cost of which had soared from the original estimate of 300 million dollars to 900 million dollars. The gloomy forecast for the growth of Peru's export earnings and the troubled domestic economy produced uncertainty in previously favorable international banking circles. Furthermore, in August 1975, the government nationalized the Marcona Company's iron-mining complex and indicated that, because of alleged contract violations and other misdeeds, the North American firm would not be compensated. It seemed possible that Washington might respond as it had after past confiscations, with a "credit squeeze" that would further hamper Lima's attempts to refinance its foreign debt.

To resolve some of the nation's economic problems the administration instituted an austerity program on June 30, 1975. These measures granted moderate pay raises in partial compensation for recent inflation but placed a low ceiling on future wage increases. In addition, the government reduced or eliminated import subsidies for many items, hiked domestic food prices, and eased controls on the country's agriculture. A wave of strikes now swept the country. On August 5, the regime deported nearly thirty union leaders, magazine journalists, and top offi-

359

cials of APRA accusing them of fomenting the walkouts. Quickly, many of Peru's unions and student groups announced that they would launch a nationwide general strike on August 28, one day before the scheduled start of a major meeting of Third World foreign ministers in Lima.

Although a general strike in the glare of an international conference would embarrass the administration, more substantive international problems confronted the nation's diplomats. Relations between Peru and Chile had been uneasy since early 1973, when Lima began making large purchases of Soviet weapons. The replacement of the Marxist Allende regime by the conservative government of Gen. Augusto Pinochet in September of that year further increased tensions. Santiago reversed its earlier support for the Andean Common Market's strict foreign investment code, a move that threatened to scuttle the heretofore successful organization. Of greatest concern, however, were signs of an emerging right-wing, anti-Peruvian axis linking Brazil, Bolivia, and Chile. Armchair geopoliticians spun various scenarios for a war, especially with the latter country. The most plausible of these, from Lima's perspective, envisioned a Chilean attack on southern Peru to eliminate that region's rapidly expanding copper industry, an important competitor of Chile's principal export. Such an adventure, furthermore, might have aroused Chilean nationalism and generated badly needed domestic support for Pinochet's brutal dictatorship. Describing his nation's elongated neighbor as a "tube," one Peruvian general warned that "when there is pressure in the tube, its only escape valve is Peru."

A ghost from the past also haunted the peace of the Pacific. During 1975, Chile and Bolivia conducted talks to improve their frigid relations. Chile considered granting the claustrophobic Bolivians a corridor to the sea through the province of Arica, a cession which—under the 1929 Treaty of Lima—would require Peru's assent. Acquiescence to the transfer of this territory, lost during the War of the Pacific, certainly would anger Peruvian nationalists. A rejection of the proposal would harm Peru's relations with Bolivia and perhaps drive that nation into an alliance with Chile. In the face of these difficulties, Peru took steps to acquire several new warships and military aircraft. Both Lima and Santiago strengthened their forces in the frontier region.

The increasing level of tension within Peruvian society as a whole was reflected in the armed forces and their government.

The economic and political crisis brought into bold relief contradictions within the revolutionary program. The regime's policy options narrowed, leaving little maneuvering room for the compromises which heretofore had maintained peace among the officers. The administration faced difficult decisions on fundamental, interrelated problems. With the failure of Sinamos, the issue of popular participation again came to the fore. Should the military relinquish some of its control over the revolution? Civilians could have been allowed an increased role in the political process through a new participatory mechanism that would replace the discredited Sinamos, or through the old political parties. Conversely, the administration could have opted to control civilian opposition through increased repression and closer supervision of the press. If the path toward participation were followed, which public should the regime satisfy? The relatively comfortable classes, including groups favored by the early reforms, struggled to maintain their privileged position. Other Peruvians still awaited an improvement in their lives and demanded a further "deepening" of the revolution.

The answers to these political questions were tied to the even more perplexing problems of economic development. The "plural economy"—with its poorly synchronized private, public, and "social" sectors—was grinding to a halt and needed a major overhaul. It seemed likely that the revolution would have to move to the right or left. Should Peru place even greater emphasis upon the rapid growth of exports and heavy industry? This strategy, favored by conservatives, would require increased reliance on private capital, both foreign and domestic. Alternately, should the nation stress slower "development from within," shifting investment and income to domestic agriculture and other labor-intensive activities? This radical approach probably would entail the expansion of the public and social property sectors through the nationalization of many manufacturing firms and wealthy cooperatives. For Peru's pragmatic generals the issue concerned not only the desirability of these alternatives but also their viability. Which course of action was likely to succeed within the context of the nation's economic and political realities and the international setting? In their deliberations the officers certainly must have been sobered by recent events in Chile—the near collapse of the economy, the extreme polarization of society, the bloody coup and the ensuing reign of terror that brought infamy to the armed forces.

The debate on these issues gravely threatened the unity of

the military establishment. Reports of schisms and rumors of conspiracies became commonplace. Analysts closely scrutinized the pages of the controlled press for clues concerning the power struggle within the regime. Most observers noted a strengthening of the radical sector of the armed forces following the annual round of retirements and promotions at the end of January 1975. The conservatives were weakened by the retirement of Gen. Edgardo Mercado Jarrín, the prime minister and minister of war, who had been the central figure in speculations concerning a possible right-wing coup. He was replaced by Gen. Francisco Morales Bermúdez, a reputed "moderate." Meanwhile, several young generals—the colonels who had helped bring Velasco to power and, as members of COAP, had pressed for radical reforms—reached positions of importance within the cabinet and military command structure. They seemed destined to inherit complete control over the revolution within a few years.

During the first half of 1975, the military conservatives appeared to score several victories: the scuttling of Sinamos in April; the ouster of a radical navy minister in June; and, the next month, the removal of several left-wing editors along with a one-year postponement of the transfer of the press to popular organizations. Then, in late July, the radicals seemed ascendant as Velasco announced the uncompensated expropriation of the Marcona Company and a decision to convert the sugar cooperatives into social properties. All of these speculations were clouded, however, by the ambivalent role of General Velasco, who apparently preferred radical policies but had close personal ties to conservative officers.

The president, himself, had become a major source of apprehension within the military establishment. The sixty-five-year-old soldier had not recovered completely from his nearly fatal illness of early 1973. His public appearances and personal meetings with other leaders became more and more infrequent. In February 1975, two weeks after the Lima riots, the general suffered a serious attack of hypertension or, perhaps, a mild stroke. Although Velasco resumed his executive duties a week later, this crisis heightened concern about presidential succession in the likely event of Velasco's sudden death or disability. Two ambitious and controversial officers associated with the conservative faction appeared to be building bases of personal support among labor groups and the Apristas. Illness and the strains of leadership seem to have taken their toll on General

Velasco's personality as well as his body. More volatile than ever before, the president's colleagues complained of his erratic behavior, his stubborn inflexibility, and the increasingly personalist tone of the administration. Velasco's friends and relatives were accused of influence peddling and other improprieties. Although the general had promised a campaign to "moralize" the bureaucracy, the investigation of the EPSA scandal slackened and new frauds were uncovered in several state agencies. The mounting evidence of corruption embarrassed officers who took pride in the high moral standards of the administration's early years. By mid-1975, the desire to remove Velasco from office may have become so compelling that it subordinated, for the moment, the ideological dispute within the military leadership. Moreover, the replacement of Mercado Jarrín with Morales Bermúdez in the prime ministry had positioned a widely acceptable alternative to Velasco in line to succeed the president.

Born in Lima on October 4, 1921, Francisco Morales Bermúdez Cerrutti came from a prominent military family. His grandfather, Col. Remigio Morales Bermúdez, served as president of the republic from 1890 to 1894. Lt. Col. Remigio Morales Bermúdez, the prime minister's father, had been assassinated, allegedly by Apristas, while stationed at Trujillo in 1939. Trained as an engineer, General Morales Bermúdez was a *"técnico."* He shunned ideological disputes and stressed sound planning and efficient administration. The premier had been a founding member of the army's Department of Research and Development and budget director for the Ministry of War. During the military regime of 1962–63, he was assigned the highly sensitive task of reorganizing the nation's electoral system. Morales Bermúdez served as Fernando Belaúnde's finance minister from March to June 1968, a brief but productive tenure that produced a resolution of that administration's fiscal crisis. He held the same portfolio under Velasco from 1969 until early 1974. The general received much of the credit for the economic successes of this period and gained the respect of the international financial community. In addition to his managerial skills, Morales Bermúdez seemed well suited to repair the damaged unity of the military establishment. While enjoying the confidence of conservative officers, his long and close friendship with Gen. Jorge Fernández Maldonado—the regime's minister of mines and leading radical—made him acceptable to the left.

Between February and August 1975, Morales Bermúdez

strengthened his political base within the army, making special efforts to cultivate the radicals. Meanwhile, he assumed control over the regime's economic policies through his chairmanship of the newly created Inter-Sectorial Commission of Economic and Financial Affairs. Reports from Peru indicated that General Velasco was being reduced to the status of a figurehead and soon might be eased into dignified retirement. But if the president was given an opportunity to step down gracefully, he did not take it.

On August 29, 1975, the commanders of Peru's five military districts issued a joint communique removing Velasco from office and proclaiming Morales Bermúdez president. The document promised that the new administration would continue the revolution and "eliminate the personality cults and the deviations that our process has been suffering under those who made mistakes and who did not appreciate the true revolutionary feeling of all Peruvians." In a radio broadcast later that day, the fallen chief of state expressed satisfaction with his performance in office, pledged his continued dedication to the goals of the revolution, and called upon the people to support the new regime. The transfer of power had been bloodless, encountering neither military nor civilian opposition.

Within a few months after seizing power, Morales Bermúdez would reverse the radical trajectory of the revolution. Nevertheless, the overthrow of Velasco does not appear to have been the product of a conservative plot. Leftist commanders provided critical troop support for the coup and, within the cabinet, only the radical Fernández Maldonado seems to have been privy to the conspiracy. Rather than attempting to push the revolution abruptly to the right or left, it appears likely that the conspirators primarily desired to eliminate an erratic president, neutralize the power of some of his close associates, and preserve the institutional character of the government. Perhaps the men who ousted Velasco also hoped to buy time, postponing major decisions concerning the future. They may have believed that Morales Bermúdez's reputation for moderation along with a few alterations in the revolutionary timetable might have restored the confidence of the private sector. New foreign loans, including debt refinancing, and a resumption of investment by domestic business could have kept the economy afloat for a few critical years, until the future of Peru's fishing, copper, and oil industries became clearer. A change in leadership also would have provided opportunities to improve the government's badly deteriorated relations with the public. Finally, a moratorium on the ideological struggle within the regime may have seemed necessary to avert an irreparable breach in the military coalition and the collapse of the government.

✌ *Phase Two and a Final Look*

Morales Bermúdez moved rapidly and skillfully to consolidate his power. A new cabinet, appointed three days after the coup, had a decidedly more moderate complexion. It included several "nonpolitical" officers noted for their administrative abilities rather than their ideological positions. During the next three months another reorganization of the cabinet, the forced retirement of several close collaborators of Velasco, and the arrest of officers implicated in recent scandals eliminated a number of prominent military ideologues. Although both radicals and conservatives were ousted, the net result of these changes was a lessening of leftist influence within the administration. Therefore, the president made a special effort to assuage the fears of the radicals. In his first public statements the general asserted that the revolution's goals and priorities had not changed, only its leadership and methods. He pledged not to deviate "one millimeter" from the revolutionary course, while "consolidating" and making "irreversible" the gains of the previous seven years. Morales Bermúdez retained two radicals in the cabinet and announced that General Fernández Maldonado would become the next prime minister in January 1976. The president frequently praised the social property program and elevated the head of the National Social Property Commission to ministerial status. In December the administration revised the Agrarian Reform Law, significantly reducing the size limits on private holdings.

The new executive also labored to win popular support for his administration. Proclaiming a return to "ideological pluralism," his first decree granted a broad political amnesty. Previously banned publications reappeared; several critics of the Velasco regime were released from prison; and many exiles, including Fernando Belaúnde Terry, were permitted to return home. Dr. Luis Barúa Castañeda, a respected economist, became finance minister and the first civilian cabinet officer since 1968.

The president indicated that the military would begin to relinquish its control of the government at the municipal level and
might return to the barracks in six years. Morales Bermúdez gave
a series of "fireside chats" on the radio and made numerous
speeches throughout the country. At Trujillo, the bloody arena
of countless Aprista-army conflicts, the general dramatically declared that it was "time to forget the struggles between brothers"
(APRA and the armed forces) that had occurred forty-five years
earlier. But while the president called for "national conciliation,"
he prepared to meet violent civilian opposition by repairing the
tattered bonds of loyalty between the military and the police. A
civil guard general was brought into the cabinet and the internal
security forces received increased authority within the Ministry
of Interior.

Morales Bermúdez's first months in office were notable for
his studied avoidance of controversial decisions about economic
matters. The president obviously desired to secure his political
position before instituting major changes in policy. Furthermore, the general probably hoped to defuse the potentially
explosive confrontation with Chile so that he might concentrate
on domestic problems. In October, Peruvian and Chilean military leaders finalized an agreement for periodic consultations
about security matters. To avoid misunderstandings, they also
arranged for frontier commanders to exchange information concerning troop movements along their borders. Tensions arising
from the question of a Bolivian outlet to the Pacific subsided in
December 1975 when Santiago presented a formal offer to La
Paz. Chile would relinquish to Bolivia an eight-mile-wide corridor extending along the Peruvian border to the ocean. But this
zone would be demilitarized and the Bolivians would be required to compensate Chile with territory in southwestern
Bolivia equal in size to the ceded land area as well as the 200
miles of territorial sea fronting on the corridor. Bolivia seemed
likely to ponder this niggardly offer for several months and, thus,
Lima could delay its decision on the matter.

In his many "dialogues with the people" during the final
weeks of 1975, Morales Bermúdez spoke of a forthcoming
"second phase" of the revolution. This new epoch would bring a
consolidation of previous gains, resolve the pressing problems of
the moment, and "institutionalize" the revolutionary process for
the future. The president promised that "Plan Túpac Amaru," an
outline of the program, soon would be ready for public debate.

This document, however, failed to emerge from administration councils, where it undoubtedly caused great controversy. Morales Bermúdez's words and actions suggest that he wanted to make a moderate, rightward adjustment in the revolution. Unlike his early statements, the president's speeches now called for a temporary, tactical reordering of priorities to resolve the nation's economic crisis. He apparently envisioned increased fiscal austerity along with changes in the earlier reforms to rectify imbalances in the economy and restore the government's "credibility" with private capital. When Peru's economic health returned, the administration could reemphasize the ultimate goal of social justice for the masses. Civilians would be given an ever-increasing role in the government. At the end of Phase II, the military would submit a new political charter to the people in a national plebiscite and restore constitutional rule.

On January 12, 1976, the Morales Bermúdez administration launched Phase II with a series of economy measures. Taxes were increased, subsidies were eliminated, strict controls were placed upon nonessential imports and, following a wage adjustment for inflation, salaries again were frozen. Although the regime continued to pay lip service to the social property concept, it curtailed the expansion of this sector. State financial support for new EPS's was reduced drastically and Morales Bermúdez rescinded, at least temporarily, Velasco's decision to convert the sugar cooperatives into social properties. In February and March, the administration issued decrees favorable to small- and medium-sized businesses. New tax laws granted generous investment credits and simplified bookkeeping procedures for these firms. Most importantly, companies with annual gross profits of less than a half-million dollars no longer were required to contribute stock to their labor communities. Workers would continue to receive a share of the profits and enjoy improved pensions, but the companies would not become cooperatives.

The government announced in January that it had reached a preliminary agreement to compensate the Marcona Company for its expropriated holdings. This action ended a boycott of Peruvian iron ore by the firm's overseas customers and improved Peru's chances of refinancing its foreign debt. Official figures released in May indicated that the nation immediately required 400 million dollars for this purpose and even larger loans during the next four years. The regime also signaled its desire for new

367

inflows of overseas capital by establishing a commission to reexamine Peru's policies toward foreign investment. In addition, Morales Bermúdez attempted to lure more companies into the search for Amazonian oil with offers of generous contracts.

Notwithstanding frequent appeals by Morales Bermúdez for sacrifice and national solidarity, his economic policies received little support from the public. Peru's entrepreneurs pressed for further concessions. Organized labor protested against austerity with a wave of strikes and peasant agitation increased. Although General Fernández Maldonado labored to sell Phase II to Peruvian radicals, left-wing journalists severely criticized the program. In mid-March, the government again purged the editorial staffs of the "reformed Press." The second phase apparently came under a similar crossfire within the military establishment. While viewed with suspicion by the weakened radical faction, the increasingly powerful and restive conservatives demanded a more rapid and pronounced shift to the right.

On June 28, the Morales Bermúdez regime decreed a severe new austerity program. The *sol* was devalued a whopping 44 percent, while pay scales were adjusted by less than 15 percent. Moreover, the government sharply increased prices on foodstuffs, gasoline, public transportation, and utilities. New taxes and trade controls were instituted to preserve the treasury's dwindling reserves of foreign exchange. A drastic cut in public expenditures and a six-month suspension of all labor contracts indicated that the administration planned wholesale dismissals of workers employed in public enterprises. During the next week, riots occurred in Lima and several other cities. The regime proclaimed a state of emergency and arrested hundreds of persons. All strikes and unauthorized union meetings were prohibited. Protesting agricultural cooperatives were threatened with the loss of their benefits from the agrarian reform. On July 3, the administration closed a dozen magazines, whose editorial viewpoints spanned the entire ideological spectrum, accusing them of fomenting the disturbances.

On July 9, while widespread civilian unrest continued, a crisis erupted within the military leadership. Prime Minister Fernández Maldonado demanded the resignation of Gen. Carlos Bobbio Centurión, the ultraconservative director of the Chorrillos military academy. Bobbio was charged with insubordination and conspiring to overthrow the government. The general denied these accusations and refused to give up his command until paratroops prepared to storm the military school. Although the armed forces initially supported Fernández Maldonado in the struggle with Bobbio, conservative officers later rejected the prime minister's explanation of the affair. On July 16, Morales Bermúdez reluctantly accepted the resignation of Fernández Maldonado and the remainder of the cabinet. The reconstituted ministry included a second civilian—career diplomat José de la Puente Radbill, who became foreign minister—but not a single military radical. Moreover, the new prime minister, Gen. Guillermo Arbulú Galliani, as well as the new army chief of staff were noted conservatives.

The government reported in August that it had foiled a plot by a dozen junior officers to restore Fernández Maldonado to power. A concerted campaign now began to check radical influence within the armed forces and among the civilian population. The state of emergency was extended month after month throughout the remainder of the year. With basic civil liberties in abeyance, the number of political detainees and exiles mounted rapidly. Most of the nation's magazines remained closed and government permission was required to publish new journals. State-appointed editors continued to control the *gran prensa* and the regime postponed "indefinitely" the transfer of the newspapers to popular organizations.

The rightward retreat of the administration's economic policies quickened with the decline of radical influence. In late July, the government announced that Pesca-Perú would divest itself of the state's unprofitable 1,000-boat anchovy fleet and remove their crews from the public payroll. The vessels were to be sold to private firms, but companies formed by the unemployed fishermen would receive preference in the purchase of the boats and government financing. Pesca-Perú would continue to provide support services for the fleet and maintain its monopoly on the manufacture and sale of fish meal. At a conference of Peruvian businessmen in November, President Morales Bermúdez reported that forthcoming revisions in the Industrial Reform Law would remove the threat of collectivization from all manufacturing firms. Under the contemplated changes, labor communities would be permitted to acquire a maximum of one-third equity in their enterprises.

Following the ouster of radical Foreign Minister Miguel Angel de la Flor in July, Peru adopted a lower profile among Third World nations and concentrated on improving its relations within the Western hemisphere. The strident attacks on the United States, which typified the Velasco years, ceased. Lima's ambassador to Washington called for better understanding between the two countries. Peruvian diplomats also labored to gain new friends among the military dictatorships of Argentina and Brazil. But the imbroglio with Chile over the Bolivian corridor intensified as La Paz tentatively accepted Santiago's terms. Rather than simply approving or disapproving the cession, as Chile demanded, Lima proposed its own formula for resolving the problem. In addition to a Bolivian outlet to the Pacific, Peru's initiative called for joint control by the three nations of a coastal strip extending southward for about fifteen miles, from the Peruvian border to below the port of Arica. Bolivia could establish a new port for its exclusive use and would have sovereignty over the territorial sea fronting on the entire trinational zone. Although perhaps a sincere effort to end the dispute, Lima's proposal also seemed calculated to delay a settlement until the delivery of thirty-six fighter-bombers purchased from the Soviet Union strengthened Peru's bargaining position. Hopefully, the centenary of the War of the Pacific would not be observed with a reenactment of that bloody struggle.

As the tarnished Peruvian revolution began its ninth year in late 1976, the nation continued to be plagued by rampant inflation, lagging economic growth, high unemployment, and a staggering foreign debt. The generals still employed the rhetoric of the revolution and insisted that the process begun in 1968 had not ended. But barring a left-wing coup, bold new reforms were not anticipated. Military morale and discipline were in shambles, and civilian discontent mounted as the regime degenerated into the most repressive dictatorship since the Ochenio of Odría. Although Morales Bermúdez had indicated that Phase II would require six years of his stewardship, speculation grew that the president might return the government to civilians at a much earlier date.

Peru seems likely to continue its retreat from the radical course of the Velasco period, at least for the next few years. But the revolution will not be routed. Some reforms cannot be reversed. Peru's nationalistic officers will not permit others to be undone. Although instituted by a military dictatorship, many programs were the products of the nation's best minds, civilian as well as military. These changes were necessary and they continue to enjoy considerable popular support. Thus, the Peru that the generals and admirals return to civilian hands will be significantly different from the nation which the officers sought to transform in 1968.

Within the economic realm the state has greatly reduced the power of private capital and has itself assumed primary responsibility for increasing the nation's wealth. Notwithstanding Morales Bermúdez's efforts to resuscitate private enterprise and the government's withdrawal from some economic activities, the state almost certainly will continue to perform the role of national entrepreneur that it assumed after 1968. The major export industries, finance, and utilities probably will remain within the public sector along with some other "basic industries" identified in the Industrial Reform Law. By 1976, the state accounted for 90 percent of Peru's exports and 50 percent of its imports. A resurgence of private investment could reduce the relative contribution of the government to the nation's foreign trade, but the state will maintain its preeminence within this key sector. Giant multinational corporations no longer have direct control over Peru's most important industries and they are unlikely to regain their old position. The economy, however, is still dependent upon the outside world for markets, technology, and development capital. Indeed, because of heavy overseas borrowing by the public sector, indirect foreign investment has increased sharply since 1968. The wisdom of this policy ultimately will be determined by the results of the regime's investment programs. In any event, the state has become the principal agent in Peru's international economic relations. The concentration of economic power in the hands of the government has strengthened the country's negotiating position with foreign capital, and national interest rather than private gain now motivates these transactions.

In the early years of the revolution the military government implicitly subordinated the rapid pursuit of social justice to the more easily attainable goal of economic development. This decision, which the social property program seemed to question, has been reaffirmed and made explicit by the Morales Bermúdez administration. The government may permit the embryonic social property sector to survive; it might even create a few new EPS's, if only to support its assertion that the "revolution continues." But this form of enterprise seems unlikely to become significant within the foreseeable future. Neither will privately owned factories become cooperatives. However, the workers in these establishments are likely to retain their claim to a share of the profits and a limited voice in management. Profit-sharing also could be extended to commercial enterprises.

Because of political constraints and the dualistic structure of the economy, the revolution has not brought a significant redistribution of wealth from the very rich to the very poor. The major beneficiaries of the ownership reforms—the workers in the modern factories, mines, and plantations—already ranked among the upper quarter of Peru's wage earners. This group has and will continue to resist further transfers of income from itself to the less fortunate workers in the traditional sector of the economy. Nevertheless, some progress has been made toward the goal of social justice. The wages of the modern labor force were relatively high only because of the country's general poverty. In absolute terms, the standard of living for most of these workers remains modest. Peru's privileged proletariat, moreover, seems unlikely to be so tenacious or successful in blocking the aspirations of the marginal masses as was the old economic elite. The ownership reforms destroyed much of the power of this latter group. The agrarian reform has not yet produced appreciable material gains for Peru's poorest farmers. But the land now belongs to those who till the soil. This change along with the education reform were important steps toward making the social and political environment more conducive to the economic development of the countryside. The revolution also seems likely to improve the quality of life in ways that are difficult to measure monetarily: greater independence and dignity for the peasants, a more democratic and effective school system, a more active citizenry.

The success or failure of the process begun by General Velasco in 1968—and, indeed, the legitimacy of its claim to the label "Revolution"—will be debated for many years. For the moment, we only can say that the revolution remains unfinished. Much needs to be done to fulfill the promise of a more prosperous, just, and independent Peru. If it chooses to do so, a greatly strengthened Peruvian state can utilize its control over the nation's economic resources along with its fiscal and pricing policies to achieve these objectives. How the government uses its power will be determined by the political process which will function in an environment that has undergone considerable change since the overthrow of Belaúnde. The center of gravity has shifted to the left. The old conservative groups have been severely weakened. The armed forces and the Church have been liberalized. The military regime succeeded in mobilizing many humble Peruvians but failed to control their participation in the national life. The voice of the masses within the political arena will become louder in the years to come.

In spite of its many failures, the dictatorship strengthened the state and established new standards for effective government by which a more expectant public will judge future administrations. Rather than becoming despondent over the revolution's shortfalls, it is hoped that the considerable achievements recorded since 1968 will inspire Peruvians with a new confidence in their ability to overcome the problems that confront their nation.

A GUIDE TO FURTHER STUDY

INDEX

A GUIDE TO FURTHER STUDY

THE RESEARCH FOR THIS VOLUME employed some 5,000 items—primary and secondary sources, published and unpublished materials. What follows is a selection of about one-fifth of the author's working bibliography along with a few titles not consulted but known to be valuable. In choosing items for this essay, I have considered the importance of the topic treated, the quality and accessibility of the work, and the availability of alternate sources of information. Wherever possible, emphasis was placed upon secondary sources published in English. Frequently cited publications have been abbreviated as follows:

AUFS-WC   *American Universities Field Staff, Reports Service* (West Coast of South America Series)

HAHR   *Hispanic American Historical Review*

IAEA   *Inter-American Economic Affairs*

JLAS   *Journal of Latin American Studies*

MP   *Mercurio Peruano*

RH   *Revista Histórica* [Lima]

RMN   *Revista del Museo Nacional* [Lima]

❧ Peru—General

THE BEST PLACE TO BEGIN THE STUDY OF PERU and its neighbors is Preston E. James, *Latin America*, 4th ed. (New York: Odyssey Press, 1969), an outstanding geography text. Emilio Romero, *Geografía económica del Perú*, 6th ed. (Lima: Editorial Gráfica Pacific Press, 1968) is the standard Peruvian treatment of the subject. Useful compilations of social and economic information are David A. Robinson, *Peru in Four Dimensions* (Lima: American Studies Press, 1964); R. J. Owens, *Peru* (London: Oxford University Press, 1963); American University, Foreign Area Studies, *Area Handbook for Peru* (Washington, D.C.: United States Government Printing Office, 1972); and Perú, Oficina Nacional de Estadística y Censos, Dirección de Estadísticas Contínuas, *Indicadores demográficos, sociales, económicos y geográficos del Perú*, vol. 2 (Lima: ONEC, 1974).

Valuable works on the economy include José A. Guerra et al., *The Current Economic Position and Prospects of Peru* (Washington, D.C.: International Bank for Reconstruction and Development, 1973); Milton C. Taylor, "Problems of Development in Peru," *Journal of Inter-American Studies* 9 (January 1967): 85–94; Myron J. Frankman, "Sectoral Policy Preferences of the Peruvian Government, 1946–1968," JLAS 6 (November 1974): 289–300; Jurgen Westphalen, "Peru: Population Explosion and Development Policy," *Inter-Economics* (April 1969): 112–16; Frits C. M. Wils, "Agricultural and Industrial Development in Peru: Some Observations on Their Interrelationship," *Development and Change* 5, no. 21 (1973–74): 76–100; Arthur J. Coutu and Richard A. King, *The Agricultural Development of Peru* (New York: Praeger, 1969); C. T. Smith, "Problems of Regional Development in Peru," *Geography* 53 (July 1968): 260–81; Robert C. Eidt, "Economic Features of Land Opening in the Peruvian Montaña," *Professional Geographer* 18 (May 1966): 146–50; United Nations, Economic Commission for Latin America, *Analyses and Projections of Economic Development: VI. The Industrial Development of Peru* (Mexico, D.F.: United Nations Department of Economic and Social Affairs, 1959); Hernán Horna, "The Fish Industry of Peru," *Journal of the Developing Areas* 2 (April 1968): 393–406; Bobbie B. Smetherman and Robert M. Smetherman, "Fishmeal and the Peruvian Economy," *Quarterly Review of Economics and Business* 10 (Autumn 1970): 35–45; J. R. Coull, "The Development of the Fishing Industry in Peru," *Geography* 59 (November 1974): 322–32; and Michael Roemer, *Fishing for Growth: Export-led Development in Peru, 1950–1967* (Cambridge, Mass.: Harvard University Press, 1970). The reasons for the recent decline of the fishing industry are explained in César N. Caviedes, "El Niño 1972: Its Climatic, Ecological, Human and Economic Implications," *Geographical Review* 65 (October 1975): 493–509.

A large body of literature exists on the Indian and various aspects of the "Indian problem." Good introductions to this subject are Alfred Métraux, "The Social and Economic Structure of the Indian Communities of the Andean Region," *International Labour Review* 79 (March 1959): 225–43; and Jacob Fried, "Indian and *Mestizaje* in Peru," *Human Organization* 20 (Spring 1961): 23–26. The current "official" position is reflected in Fernando Fuenzalida Vollmar and Enrique Mayer, *El Perú de las tres razas* (New York: Instituto de las Naciones Unidas para Formación Profesional e Investigaciones, 1974). Also useful are Henry F. Dobyns, *The Social Matrix of Peruvian Indigenous Communities* (Ithaca, N.Y.: Department of Anthropology, Cornell University, 1964); Oscar Núñez del Prado, "Aspects of Andean Native Life," in Dwight B. Heath and Richard N. Adams, eds., *Contemporary Cultures and Societies of Latin America* (New York: Random House, 1965): 102–23; François Bourricaud, "Indian, Mestizo, and Cholo as Symbols in the Peruvian System of Stratification," in Nathan Glazer and Daniel P. Moynihan, eds., *Ethnicity: Theory and Experience* (Cambridge, Mass.: Harvard University Press, 1975): 350–87; Philip Mason, "Gradualism in Peru: Some Impressions on the Future of Ethnic Group Relations," *Race* 8 (July 1966): 43–61; Stephen Clissold, "The Indian Problem in Latin America: Changing Attitudes in the Andean Republics," *Race* 7 (July 1965): 47–57; José Varallanos, *El cholo y el Perú* (Buenos Aires: Imprenta López, 1962); Fernando Silva Santisteban, "Mestizaje y aculturación," RH 28 (1965): 27–35; A. Arias Larreta, "Indios y cholos," *América* [Havana] 47 (January–March 1956): 36–50; and François Bourricaud, "Castas y clases en Puno," RMN 32 (1963): 308–21. For the contrast between Indian and mestizo values see Ozzie G. Simmons, "The *Criollo* Outlook in the Mestizo Culture of Coastal Peru," *American Anthropologist* 57 (February 1955): 107–17. The *International Journal of Comparative Sociology* devoted its September–December 1974 issue (vol. 15) to "Class and Ethnicity in Peru." Especially useful is Pierre L. Van Den Berghe's introductory essay which analyzes the literature on the topic.

The process of social and cultural change has been emphasized in many community studies by anthropologists, sociologists, and political scientists, including Henry F. Dobyns, Paul Doughty, and Harold D. Lasswell, eds., *Peasants, Power and Applied Social Change: Vicos as a Model* (Beverly Hills, Calif.: Sage Publications, 1971); Richard N. Adams, *A Community in the Andes: Problems and Progress in Muquiyauyo* (Seattle: University of Washington Press, 1959); Paul L. Doughty, *Huaylas: An Andean District in Search of Progress* (Ithaca, N.Y.: Cornell University Press, 1968); William W. Stein, *Hualcán: Life in the Highlands of Peru* (Ithaca, N.Y.: Cornell University Press, 1961); F. LaMond Tullis, *Lord and Peasant in Peru: A Paradigm of Political and Social Change* (Cambridge, Mass.: Harvard University Press, 1970); and Edward Dew, *Politics in the Altiplano: The Dynamics of Change in Rural Peru* (Austin: University of Texas Press, 1969).

The most comprehensive study of Peruvian land tenure and associated problems prior to the 1969 agrarian reform is Comité Interamericano de Desarrollo Agrícola (CIDA), *Tenencia de la tierra y desarrollo socio-económico del sector agrícola, Perú* (Washington, D.C: Unión

379

Panamericana, 1966). A synopsis in English is Jacobo Brodsky and Jacob Oser, "Land Tenure in Peru: A CIDA Study," *American Journal of Economics and Sociology* 27 (October 1968): 405–21. The economics of the *colono* system is analyzed in I. G. Bertram, "New Thinking on the Peruvian Peasantry," *Pacific Viewpoint* 15 (September 1974): 89–110. See also Thomas R. Ford, *Man and Land in Peru* (Gainesville: University of Florida Press, 1955); Alvin Cohen, "Societal Structure, Agrarian Reform, and Economic Development in Peru," IAEA 18 (Summer 1964): 45–59; E. J. E. Hobsbawm, "A Case of Neo-Feudalism: La Convención, Peru," JLAS 1 (May 1969): 31–49; Delbert A. Fitchett, "Agricultural Land Tenure Arrangements on the Northern Coast of Peru," IAEA 20 (Summer 1966): 65–86; Antonio Díaz Martínez, "La antinomia andina: Latifundio-comunidad," *América Indígena* 29 (January 1969): 89–127; Mario C. Vázquez, *Hacienda, peonaje y servidumbre en los andes peruanos* (Lima: Editorial Estudios Andinos, 1961); and Henri Favre, Claude Collin Delavaud, and José Matos Mar, *La hacienda en el Perú* (Lima: Instituto de Estudios Peruanos, 1967).

Internal migration and urban squatter settlements are discussed in David A. Preston, "Rural Emigration in Andean America," *Human Organization* 28 (Winter 1969): 279–86; Donald Dyer, "Population of the Quechua Region of Peru," *Geographical Review* 52 (July 1962): 337–45; Frank M. Andrews and George W. Phillips, "The Squatters of Lima: Who They Are and What They Want," *Journal of Developing Areas* 4 (January 1970): 211–24; Henry Dietz, "Urban Squatter Settlements in Peru," *Journal of Inter-American Studies* 11 (July 1969): 353–70; David L. Bayer, "Urban Peru–Political Action as Sellout," *Trans-Action* 7 (November 1969): 36, 47–54; William P. Mangin, "Squatter Settlements," *Scientific American* 217 (October 1967): 21–29; José Matos Mar, "The 'Barriadas' of Lima: An Example of Integration into Urban Life," in Philip M. Hauser, ed., *Urbanization in Latin America* (New York: International Documents Service, 1961): 170–90; William P. Mangin, "Urbanization Case History in Peru," in W. P. Mangin, ed., *Peasants in Cities* (Boston: Houghton Mifflin, 1970): 47–54; John P. Robin and Frederick C. Terzo, *Urbanization in Peru* (New York: Ford Foundation, 1973); and José Matos Mar, *Urbanización y barriadas en América del Sur* (Lima: Instituto de Estudios Peruanos, 1968) which contains material on the shantytowns of Arequipa and Chimbote as well as those of Greater Lima.

The maldistribution of power, wealth, and the amenities of life is examined in Magli Sarfatti Larson and Arlene Eisen Bergman, *Social Stratification in Peru* (Berkeley: University of California Institute of International Studies, 1969); Eugene A. Brady, *The Distribution of Total Personal Income in Peru,* Iowa State International Studies in Economics, monograph no. 6 (Ames: IOWA-Peru Program, 1968); René Vandendries, "Income Distribution in Peru after World War II," *Jour-*

nal of Developing Areas 8 (April 1974): 421–36; Milton C. Taylor, "Taxation and Economic Development: A Case Study of Peru" IAEA 21 (Winter 1967): 43–54; Shane Hunt, "Distribution, Growth and Government Economic Behavior in Peru," in Gustav Ranis, ed., *Government and Economic Development* (New Haven, Conn.: Yale University Press, 1971); 375–416; Eugene A. Hammel, *Power in Ica* (Boston: Little, Brown & Co., 1969); José Matos Mar, "Consideraciones sobre la situación social del Perú," *América Latina* 7 (January–March 1964): 57–70; Carlos Malpica S.S., *Crónica del hambre en el Perú,* 2d ed. (Lima: F. Moncloa, 1970); and François Bourricaud, "Lima en la vida política peruana," *América Latina* 7 (October–December 1964): 89–96.

Peruvian education is discussed in Rolland G. Paulston, *Society, Schools and Progress in Peru* (Oxford, N.Y.: Pergamon Press, 1972); and Leopoldo Chiappo, "Estructura y fines de la universidad peruana," *Aportes,* no. 16 (April 1970): 56–90. Concerning the contemporary Catholic Church see Fredrick B. Pike, "The Modernized Church in Peru: Two Aspects," *Review of Politics* 26 (July 1964): 307–18; and Peruvian Bishops' Commission for Social Action, *Between Honesty and Hope: Documents from and about the Church in Latin America,* trans. John Drury (Maryknoll, N.Y.: Maryknoll Publications, 1970). Organized labor and related topics are treated in James L. Payne, *Labor and Politics in Peru* (New Haven, Conn.: Yale University Press, 1965); and David Chaplin, *The Peruvian Industrial Labor Force* (Princeton, N.J.: Princeton University Press, 1967).

General studies of Peruvian politics prior to 1968 include Carlos A. Astiz, *Pressure Groups and Power Elites in Peruvian Politics* (Ithaca, N.Y.: Cornell University Press, 1969); François Bourricaud, *Power and Society in Contemporary Peru,* trans. Paul Stevenson (New York: Praeger, 1970); James L. Payne, "Peru: The Politics of Structured Violence," *Journal of Politics* 27 (May 1965): 362–74; David Chaplin, "Peruvian Social Mobility: Revolutionary and Development Potential," *Journal of Inter-American Studies* 10 (October 1968): 547–70; David Chaplin, "Peru's Postponed Revolution," *World Politics* 20 (April 1968): 393–420; Terry L. McCoy, "Congress, the President, and Political Instability in Peru," in Weston H. Agor, ed., *Latin American Legislatures: Their Role and Influence* (New York: Praeger, 1971): 325–66; Rosendo A. Gómez, "Peru: The Politics of Military Guardianship," in Martin C. Needler, ed., *Political Systems of Latin America* (Princeton, N.J.: Van Nostrand, 1965): 291–316; Jack W. Hopkins, *The Government Executive of Modern Peru* (Gainesville: University of Florida Press, 1967); and Rudolph Gómez, *The Peruvian Administrative System* (Boulder: University of Colorado Bureau of Government Research and Service, 1969). Phillipe Spaey, *L'élite politique péruvienne* (Paris: Éditions Universitaires, 1972) is a fine quantitative analysis of Peru's political party leadership.

Works on the Peruvian "oligarchy" include Richard H. Stevens, *Wealth and Power in Peru* (Metuchen, N.J.: Scarecrow Press, 1970); François Bourricaud, "The Structure and Function of the Peruvian Oligarchy," *Studies in Comparative International Development* 2, no. 2 (1966): 17–36; Carlos Malpica S.S., *Los dueños del Perú*, 3d ed. (Lima Ediciones Ensayos Sociales, 1968); and José Matos Mar, ed., *La oligarquía en el Perú* (Lima: Francisco Moncloa Editores, 1969), a collection of provocative essays by François Bourricaud, Jorge Bravo Bresani, Henri Favre, and Jean Piel. Charles T. Goodsell, *American Corporations and Peruvian Politics* (Cambridge, Mass: Harvard University Press, 1974) is a judicious examination of United States investment in Peru and its influence on the political system. Contrast this with Claes Brundenius, "The Anatomy of Imperialism: The Case of the Multinational Mining Corporations in Peru," *Journal of Peace Research* 9 no. 3 (1972): 189–208; and Carlos Malpica S.S., *El mito de la ayuda exterior* (Lima: F. Moncloa, 1967), an influential Peruvian study of "economic imperialism." A good introduction to the literature of the dependency theory is C. Richard Bath and Dilmus D. James, "Dependency Analysis of Latin America: Some Criticisms, Some Suggestions," *Latin American Research Review* 11, no. 3 (1976): 3–54. General applications of this theory to Peru include Jean Piel, "Notas históricas sobre las estructuras de dominación interna y externa en la sociedad peruana," RMN 35 (1967–68): 188–210; and Julio Cotler, "The Mechanics of Internal Domination and Social Change in Peru," *Studies in Comparative International Development* 3, no. 12 (1967–68): 229–46.

A satisfactory, comprehensive history of Peru, tracing the nation's evolution from pre-Columbian times to the contemporary period, has yet to appear in any language. The point of departure for English readers is Fredrick B. Pike, *The Modern History of Peru* (New York: Praeger, 1967), which begins its treatment with the late colonial period. This well-written volume is especially valuable for intellectual history, but is marred by a strong anti-Aprista bias. Sir Robert Marett, *Peru* (New York: Praeger, 1969), is a shorter survey with a very brief discussion of the pre-Columbian and colonial periods. Luis Martin, *The Kingdom of the Sun: A Short History of Peru* (New York: Charles Scribner's Sons, 1974), concentrates on the colonial era. Its very short section on the twentieth century contains serious errors of fact. Sir Clements R. Markham's *History of Peru* (Chicago: C.H. Sergel and Co., 1892) is still useful for its colorful account of nineteenth-century politics.

All students of Peruvian history are indebted to Jorge Basadre, Peru's premier historian, whose more than 200 published works touch upon virtually every period of his nation's past. His encyclopedic *Historia de la república del Perú, 1822–1933,* 6th ed., rev., 17 vols. (Lima: Editorial Universitaria, 1970) is the basic reference for serious scholars.

Also important are Basadre's broad, interpretive essays: *La multitud, la ciudad y el campo en la historia del Perú* (Lima: Imprenta A. J. Rivas Berrio, 1929); *Perú, problema y posibilidad* (Lima: F. y E. Rosay, 1931); *Meditaciones sobre el destino histórico del Perú* (Lima: Ediciones Huascarán, 1947); "Notas sobre la experiencia histórica peruana," RH 19 (1952): 5–140; and *La promesa de la vida peruana y otros ensayos* (Lima: J. Mejía Baca, 1958). For a discussion of Basadre's work see Helen Delpar, "Las ideas históricas de Jorge Basadre," *Revista Chilena de Historia y Geografía*, no. 131 (1963): 225–48. Rubén Vargas Ugarte's *Historia general del Perú*, 10 vols. (Lima: Carlos Milla Batres, 1966–71) has a wealth of magnificent illustrations. The first six volumes examine the colonial period; the last four bring the narrative through the War of the Pacific.

Among the more specialized histories of the nation are Emilio Romero, *Historia económica del Perú*, 2d ed., 2 vols. (Lima: Editorial Universo, 1967); José Pareja Paz-Soldán, *Derecho constitucional peruano*, 3d ed. (Lima: Ediciones del Sol, 1963); Augusto Salazar Bondy, *Historia de las ideas en el Perú contemporáneo*, 2 vols. (Lima: Francisco Moncloa Editores, 1965); Luis Alberto Sánchez, *La literatura peruana*, 5 vols. (Lima: Ediciones Ediventas, 1965–66); Carlos Miró Quesada Laos, *Historia del periodismo peruano* (Lima: Librería Internacional del Perú, 1957); W. F. C. Purser, *Metal-Mining in Peru, Past and Present* (New York: Praeger, 1971); Carlos Dellepiane, *Historia militar del Perú*, 4th ed., 2 vols. (Lima: Imprenta del Ministerio de Guerra, 1943); and Henry F. Dobyns and Paul L. Doughty, *Peru: A Cultural History* (New York: Oxford University Press, 1976), a valuable contribution by two anthropologists which stresses the early period. Felipe de la Barra's *Objetivo: Palacio de gobierno* (Lima: Librería-Editorial J. Mejía Baca, 1967) briefly describes each of the successful military coups since independence. The evolution of Peru's political parties is traced in Carlos Miró Quesada Laos, *Autopsia de los partidos políticos* (Lima: Ediciones Páginas Peruanas, 1961). David P. Werlich, "The Conquest and Settlement of the Peruvian Montaña" (Ph.D. diss., University of Minnesota, 1968) surveys the history of Amazonian Peru.

🐚 Pre-Columbian Peru

EDWARD P. LANNING, *Peru before the Incas* (Englewood Cliffs, N.J.: Prentice-Hall, 1967) is a good introduction to Peruvian archaeology, although evidence of human settlement is placed some 10,000 years earlier by Richard S. MacNeish, "Early Man in the Andes," *Scientific American* 244 (April 1971): 36–46. A more detailed synthesis is Luis G. Lumbreras, *The Peoples and Cultures of Ancient Peru*, trans. B. J. Meggers (Washington, D.C.: Smithsonian Institution Press, 1974). Wendell C.

Bennett and Junius B. Bird, *Andean Culture History,* 2d ed. (London: Robert Hale, 1965) is still useful. John Alden Mason, *Ancient Civilizations of Peru,* rev. ed. (Harmondsworth, England: Penguin Books, 1968) remains the best one-volume treatment of Peru from the earliest times through the Inca Empire. Donald W. Lathrap, *The Upper Amazon* (New York: Praeger, 1970) examines the archaeology of the Montaña. The predecessors of the Incas on the north coast are discussed in John H. Rowe, "The Kingdom of Chimor," *Acta Americana* 6 (January–June 1948): 26–59; Elizabeth P. Benson, *The Mochica: A Culture of Peru* (New York: Praeger, 1972); and Victor Wolfgang Von Hagen, *The Desert Kingdoms of Peru* (Greenwich, Conn.: New York Graphic Society Publishers, 1965). Jorge E. Hardoy's *Pre-Columbian Cities,* rev. English ed. (New York: Walker and Company, 1973) devotes five chapters to Peru. Michael Edward Moseley, *The Maritime Foundations of Andean Civilization,* Cummings Archaeology Series (Menlo Park, Calif.: Cummings Publishing Co. 1975), advances an interesting hypothesis concerning the relationship between political organization and the development of irrigation.

John V. Murra, the outstanding ethnohistorian of ancient Peru, stresses the continuity of institutional development in "Social, Structural and Economic Themes in Andean Ethnohistory," *Anthropological Quarterly* 34, no. 2 (1961): 47–59. See also John V. Murra, "On Inca Political Structure," in Ronald Cohen and John Middleton, eds., *Comparative Political Systems* (Garden City, N.Y.: Natural History Press, 1967): 339–53; and John V. Murra, "Economic Organization of the Inca State" (Ph.D. diss., University of Chicago, 1956). "Inca Culture at the Time of the Spanish Conquest" is described by John H. Rowe in Julian H. Steward, ed., *Handbook of South American Indians,* Smithsonian Institution, Bureau of American Ethnology, Bulletin no. 143 (Washington D.C.: United States Government Printing Office, 1946), 2: 183–330. Burr C. Brundage, *Empire of the Incas* (Norman: University of Oklahoma Press, 1963) is a historian's very readable account of the rise and fall of the empire. Ann Kendall describes the *Everyday Life of the Incas* (London: B. T. Batsford, 1973). Louis A. Baudin's *A Socialist Empire: The Incas of Peru,* trans. Katherine Woods (Princeton, N.J.: Van Nostrand, 1961), first Published in 1928, is still valuable, especially for its bibliographic essay. Baudin's thesis is challenged by Alfred Métraux, "The Inca Empire: Despotism or Socialism," *Diogenes* 35 (Fall 1961): 78–98; and Métraux's general study of *The History of the Incas,* trans. George Ordish (New York: Pantheon Books, 1969). Sally F. Moore, *Power and Property in Inca Peru* (New York: Columbia University Press, 1958) also attacks the myth of "benevolent Inca socialism." Friedrich Katz, *The Ancient American Civilizations,* trans. K. Simpson (New York: Praeger, 1972) compares the political, economic, and social systems of the Andean area with those of pre-Columbian Mesoamerica.

See also Burr C. Brundage, *Two Earths, Two Heavens: An Essay Contrasting the Azetecs and Incas* (Albuquerque: University of New Mexico Press, 1975).

Many of the early descriptions of the Incas still can be read for information as well as pleasure. Pedro de Cieza de León was the greatest and most reliable of the Spanish chroniclers. *The Incas,* ed. V. W. Von Hagen, trans. Harriet de Onís (Norman: University of Oklahoma Press, 1959) is a compilation of Cieza's writings on that subject. The Jesuit Bernabé Cobo's *Historia del nuevo mundo,* ed. Francisco Mateos, 2 vols. (Madrid: Ediciones Atlas, 1956), although written in the early seventeenth century, remains a superior study of the Incas. Harold V. Livermore's translation of Garcilaso de la Vega's *The Royal Commentaries of the Incas and General History of Peru,* 2 vols. (Austin: University of Texas Press, 1965) is the best of several English-language editions of this classic. A good biography of Peru's first great mestizo is John G. Varner, *El Inca: The Life and Times of Garcilaso de la Vega* (Austin: University of Texas Press, 1968). A critical examination of these and other early works about the Incas is found in Harold Osborne, *Indians of the Andes, Aymarás and Quechuas* (Cambridge, Mass.: Harvard University Press, 1952).

Colonial Peru

WILLIAM H. PRESCOTT'S classic *History of the Conquest of Peru* (many editions since 1847) should be supplemented with John Hemming's *Conquest of the Incas* (New York: Harcourt Brace Jovanovich, 1970) a superb modern narrative. The capture of Atahualpa and the Spanish participants in that event are examined in James Lockhart, *The Men of Cajamarca: A Social and Biographical Study of the First Conquerors of Peru* (Austin: University of Texas Press, 1972). Concerning the Indian response to the Spanish invaders see Burr C. Brundage, *The Lords of Cuzco* (Norman: University of Oklahoma Press, 1967); and three articles by George Kubler: "The Behavior of Atahualpa, 1531–1533," HAHR 25 (November 1945): 413–27; "A Peruvian Chief of State: Manco Inca, 1515–1545," HAHR 24 (May 1944): 253–76; and "The Neo-Inca State, 1537–1572," HAHR 27 (May 1947): 189–203.

The drama of the conquest period is best conveyed by the early chroniclers. Still a teenager when he served as page to his cousin Francisco Pizarro, Pedro Pizarro wrote a vivid *Relation of the Discovery and Conquest of the Kindoms of Peru,* ed. and trans. P. A. Means (New York: Cortes Society, 1921). Pizarro's secretary Pedro Sancho also wrote *An Account of the Conquest of Peru,* ed. and trans. P. A. Means (New York: Cortes Society, 1917). After reaching Peru in 1544, treasury official Agustín Zárate interviewed many conquerors for his

History of the Discovery and Conquest of the Province of Peru, trans. J. M. Cohen (Harmondsworth, England: Penguin Books, 1968). The pioneer Peruvianist Sir Clements R. Markham translated Pedro de Cieza de León's excellent trilogy on the civil wars of the conquistadors for the Hakluyt Society. They are *The Civil Wars in Peru: The War of Las Salinas* (London, 1923); *The War of Quito* (London, 1913); and *The War of Chupas* (London, 1917). Raúl Porras Barrenechea, *Los cronistas del Perú, 1528–1650* (Lima: Sanmartí Impresores, 1962) is a masterful study of the chroniclers and their works.

On the demographic impact of the Spanish conquest upon the Inca Empire see Henry F. Dobyns, "An Outline of Andean Epidemic History to 1720," *Bulletin of the History of Medicine* 37 (November–December 1963): 493–515; C. T. Smith, "Depopulation of the Central Andes in the 16th Century," *Current Anthropology* 11 (October–December 1970): 453–64; and Alfred W. Crosby, "Conquistador y Pestilencia: The First New World Pandemic and the Fall of the Great Indian Empires," HAHR 47 (August 1967): 321–37. Compare the preceding studies with Daniel E. Shea, "A Defense of Small Population Estimates for the Central Andes in 1520," in William M. Denevan, ed. *The Native Population of the Americas in 1492* (Madison: University of Wisconsin Press, 1976): 157–80. The literature on this controversial topic is discussed in Henry F. Dobyns, "Estimating Aboriginal American Population: An Appraisal of Techniques With a New Hemispheric Estimate," *Current Anthropology* 7 (October 1966): 395–416.

John H. Rowe, "The Incas under Spanish Colonial Institutions," HAHR 37 (May 1957): 155–99, is a good introduction to that topic. Other general studies are George Kubler, "The Quechua in the Colonial World," in Julian H. Steward, ed., *Handbook of South American Indians,* Smithsonian Institution, Bureau of American Ethnology, Bulletin no. 143 (Washington, D.C.: United States Government Printing Office, 1946), 2: 331–410; Philip A. Means, *Fall of the Inca Empire and Spanish Rule in Peru, 1530–1780* (New York: Charles Scribner's Sons, 1932); and Karen W. Spalding's excellent "Indian Rural Society in Colonial Peru: The Example of Huarochirí" (Ph.D. diss., University of California, Berkeley, 1967). On Spanish exploitation of Indian labor consult Donald L. Wiedner, "Forced Labor in Colonial Peru," *The Americas* 16 (April 1960): 357–83; and Jorge Basadre, "El régimen de la mita," *Letras* 8 (1937): 325–64. The history of the *encomienda* is traced in Marvin Goldwert, "La lucha por la perpetuidad de las encomiendas en el Perú virreinal, 1550–1600," RH 22 (1955–56): 336–60, and RH, 23 (1957–58): 207–45.

The transfer of land from Indians to Spaniards and the evolution of new tenure systems is treated in Louis C. Faron, "From Encomienda to Hacienda in Chancay Valley, Peru, 1533–1600," *Ethnohistory* 13 (Summer–Fall 1966): 145–81; Robert G. Keith, *Conquest and Agrarian*

Change: The Emergence of the Hacienda System on the Peruvian Coast (Cambridge: Harvard University Press, 1976); Henry F. Dodyns, "The Struggle for Land in Peru: The Hacienda Vicos Case," *Ethnohistory* 13 (Summer–Fall 1966): 97–122; Karen W. Spalding, "Tratos mercantiles del corregidor de indios y la formación de la hacienda serrana en el Perú," *América Indígena* 30 (July 1970): 595–608; and Magnus Mörner, "En torno a la penetración mestiza en los pueblos de indios, las composiciones de tierras y los encomenderos en el Perú en el siglo XVII," RH 28 (1965): 210–20. Other economic matters involving Indians are examined in Joseph A. Gagliano, "The Popularization of Peruvian Coca," *Revista de Historia de América* 59 (January–June 1965): 164–79; and Karen Spalding,"*Kurakas* and Commerce: A Chapter in the Evolution of Andean Society," HAHR 53 (November 1973): 581–99.

The government of the Indians under the Spaniards is discussed in Charles C. Gibson, *The Inca Concept of Sovereignty and the Spanish Administration in Peru* (Austin: University of Texas Press, 1948); Guillermo Lohmann Villena, "El gobierno de los naturales en el Perú hasta la creación de los corregidores de indios, 1535–1565," *Estudios Americanos* 12, no. 61 (1956): 201–21; and Guillermo Lohmann Villena's outstanding *Corregidor de indios en el Perú bajo los austrias* (Madrid : Ediciones Cultura Hispánica, 1957). John H. Rowe, "El movimiento nacional Inca del siglo XVIII," *Revista Universitaria* [Cuzco] 43 (1954): 17–47 explores the background to the rebellion of Túpac Amaru II. The uprising itself is treated in Lillian E. Fisher, *The Last Inca Revolt, 1780–1783* (Norman: University of Oklahoma Press, 1966); P. A. Means, "The Rebellion of Tupac Amaru II, 1780–1781," HAHR 2 (February 1919): 1–25; John R. Fisher, "The Rebellion of Túpac Amaru, 1780," *History Today* 18 (August 1968): 562–69; and Oscar Cornblit, "Society and Mass Rebellion in Eighteenth-Century Peru and Bolivia," in Raymond Carr, ed., *St. Anthony's Papers. Number 22. Latin American Affairs* (London: Oxford University Press, 1970): 9–44.

James Lockhart, *Spanish Peru 1532–1560: A Colonial Society* (Madison: University of Wisconsin Press, 1968), is a fine social history of the early colony. Virgilio Roel, *Historia social y económica de la colonia* (Lima: Editorial Gráfica Labor, 1970) is a Marxist interpretation. Leon G. Campbell, "Racism Without Race: Ethnic Group Relations in Late Colonial Peru," in Harold E. Pagliaro, ed. *Racism in the Eighteenth Century* (Cleveland: Case Western University Press, 1973): 323–33 is a brief introduction to that topic. On the mestizo see Gabriel Escobar M., "El mestizaje en la región andina: El caso del Perú," *Revista de Indias* 24 (July–December 1964): 197–219; and Carlos Deustua Pimentel, "Algunos aspectos del mestizaje en el Perú durante el siglo XVIII," RH 28 (1965): 154–62; Blacks in Spanish Peru are discussed in Frederick P. Bowser, *The African Slave in Colonial Peru, 1524–1650* (Stanford: Stanford University Press, 1974); Luis Millones, "Gente negra en el

Perú: Esclavos y conquistadores," *América Indígena* 31 (July 1971): 593–624; and Leon G. Campbell, "Black Power in Colonial Peru: The 1779 Tax Rebellion of the Negro Militia of Lambayeque," *Phylon* 33 (Summer 1972): 140–52. Jean Descola, *Daily Life in Colonial Peru, 1720–1820,* trans. M. Heron (New York: Macmillan, 1968) is a popular account of Lima society. The flavor of the latter also can be gained from Robert Ryal Miller's translation of the classic *Chronicle of Colonial Lima: The Diary of Josephe and Francisco Mugaburu, 1640–1697* (Norman: University of Oklahoma Press, 1975).

The Colonial Catholic Church is examined in Fernando Armas Medina, *Cristianización del Perú, 1532–1600* (Seville: Universidad de Sevilla, Escuela de Estudios Hispano-Americanos, 1953); Rubén Vargas Ugarte, *Historia de la iglesia en el Perú,* 5 vols. (Burgos: Imprenta de Aldecoa, 1960–65); Brian R. Hamnett, "Church Wealth in Peru: Estates and Loans in the Archdiocese of Lima in the Seventeenth Century," *Jahrbuch Für Geschichte Von Staat, Wirtschaft und Gesellschaft Lateinamerikas* 10 (1972): 113–32; and three works by Antonine Tibesar: *Franciscan Beginnings in Colonial Peru* (Washington, D.C.: Academy of American Franciscan History, 1953); "The Alternativa: A Study in Spanish-Creole Relations in Seventeenth-Century Peru," *The Americas* 11 (January 1955): 229–83; and "The Peruvian Church at the Time of Independence in the Light of Vatican II," *The Americas* 26 (April 1970): 349–75, which also contains useful material about the first two decades of independence. The educational role of the Church is treated in Luis Martin, *The Intellectual Conquest of Peru: The Jesuit College of San Pablo, 1568–1767* (New York: Fordham University Press, 1968).

John Lynch provides a fine synthesis of the early development of the colonial economy in *Spain under the Habsburgs,* 2 vols. (New York: Oxford University Press, 1964–69), 2: 212–28. The mining industry is studied in Arthur P. Whitaker, *The Huancavelica Mercury Mine* (Cambridge, Mass.: Harvard University Press, 1941); David A. Brading and Harry E. Cross, "Colonial Silver Mining: Mexico and Peru," HAHR 52 (November 1972): 545–79; John Fisher, "Silver Production in the Viceroyalty of Peru, 1776–1824," HAHR 55 (February 1975): 25–43; and Gwendolin B. Cobb, "Supply and Transportation for the Potosí Mines, 1545–1640," HAHR 29 (February 1949): 25–45. The commerce of Peru with other American colonies and Spain is examined in Woodrow W. Borah, *Early Trade and Navigation between Mexico and Peru* (Berkeley: University of California Press, 1954); Juan Bromley y Seminario, "El Callao, puerto de Lima (años 1535 a 1637)," RH 26 (1962–63): 7–76 Demetrio Ramos, "Trigo chileno, navieros del Callao y hacendados entre la crisis agrícola del siglo XVII y la comercial de la primera mitad del XVIII," *Revista de Indias* 26 (July–December 1966): 209–321; L. A. Clayton, "Trade and Navigation in the Seventeenth-Century Viceroyalty of Peru," JLAS 7 (May 1975): 1–21;

A Guide to Further Study

and María E. Rodríquez Vicente, *El tribunal del Consulado de Lima en la primera mitad del siglo XVII* (Madrid: Ediciones Cultura Hispánica, 1960).

A classic introduction to colonial Latin American government is C. H. Haring, *The Spanish Empire in America* (New York: Oxford University Press, 1947). Newer interpretations can be found in Stanley J. Stein and Barbara H. Stein, *The Colonial Heritage of Latin America: Essays on Economic Dependence in Perspective* (New York: Oxford University Press, 1970); Richard M. Morse, "The Heritage of Latin America," in Louis Hartz, ed., *The Founding of New Societies* (New York: Harcourt, Brace & World, 1964): 123–77; and Charles Gibson, *Spain in America* (New York: Harper & Row, 1966). Arthur F. Zimmerman, *Francisco de Toledo, Fifth Viceroy of Peru, 1569–1581* (Caldwell, Idaho: Caxton Printers, 1938) is a biography of a key figure in the establishment of the colonial system in Peru. Colonial responsibility for military affairs is examined in Lawrence A. Clayton, "Local Initiative and Finance in Defense of the Viceroyalty of Peru: The Development of Self-Reliance," HAHR 54 (May 1974): 284–304. J. Preston Moore has published two volumes on municipal government: *The Cabildo in Peru under the Hapsburgs* (Durham, N.C.: Duke University Press, 1954); and *The Cabildo in Peru under the Bourbons* (Durham, N.C.: Duke University Press, 1966).

The Bourbon reforms and the dissension they caused are discussed in John R. Fisher, *Government and Society in Colonial Peru: The Intendant System, 1784–1814* (London: Athlone Press, 1970); John R. Fisher, "The Intendant System and the Cabildos of Peru, 1784–1810," HAHR 49 (August 1969): 430–53; Mark A. Burkholder, "From Creole to *Peninsular*: The Transformation of the Audiencia of Lima," HAHR 52 (August 1972); 395–415; and three articles by Leon G. Campbell: "A Creole Establishment: The Audiencia of Lima in the Later Eighteenth Century," HAHR 52 (February 1972); 1–25; "The Changing Racial and Administrative Structure of the Army of Peru Under the Later Bourbons," *The Americas* 32 (July 1975): 117–33; and "The Army of Peru and the Túpac Amaru Revolt," HAHR 56 (February 1976): 31–57. Arthur R. Steele, *Flowers for the King: The Expedition of Ruiz and Pavón and the Flora of Peru* (Durham, N.C.: Duke University Press, 1964) has a good discussion of the Enlightenment in Peru. The intellectual life of the late colonial period also is examined in Guillermo Lohmann Villena, "Espíritu crítico y reformismo en el Perú del siglo XVIII (notas para un ensayo)," MP, nos 474–75 (July–October, 1968): 434–46.

☙ The War of Independence to the War of the Pacific

THE BEST INTRODUCTION to the Latin American independence movements is John Lynch, *The Spanish-American Revolutions, 1808–*

1826 (New York: Norton, 1973) which has a fine section (chapter 5) about Peru. The literature concerning Peruvian independence is discussed in José A. de la Puente Candamo, "Historiografía de la independencia de Perú," *Revista de Historia de América,* no. 59 (January–June 1965): 280–93. On the origins of the independence movement see Perú, Comisión Nacional de Sesquicentenario de la Independencia del Perú, *La independencia nacional* (Lima: By the Commission, 1970), a collection of eight essays; Jorge Basadre, "Historia de la idea de 'patria' en la emancipación del Perú," MP 29 (August 1954): 644–83; John J. TePaske, "La crisis del siglo XVIII en el virreinato del Perú," in Bernardo García Martínez et al., *Historia y sociedad en el mundo de habla española* (Mexico, D.F.: El Colegio de México, 1970): 263–79; Aurelio Miró Quesada, "Consideraciones sobre el factor racial en la independencia del Perú," *Jahrbuch Für Geschichte Von Staat, Wirtschaft und Gesellschaft Lateinamerikas* 4 (1967): 557–65; Carlos Daniel Valcárcel, "Fidelismo y separatismo del Perú," *Revista de Historia de América*, nos. 37–38 (1954): 133–62; José A. de la Puente Candamo, "La idea de la comunidad peruana y el testimonio de los precursores," *Revista de la Universidad Católica del Perú* 15, no. 1 (1955): 43–72; César Pacheco Vélez, "La emancipación del Perú y la revolución burguesa del siglo XVIII," MP 35 (October 1954): 832–48; and César Pacheco Vélez, "El Perú ante el sesquicentenario de su independencia," MP, no. 476 (November–December 1968): 553–68.

The early independence movement under San Martín is treated in José A. de la Puente Candamo, *San Martín y el Perú* (Lima: Editorial Lumen, 1948); and three articles by Timothy E. Anna: "Economic Causes of San Martín's Failure in Lima," HAHR 54 (November 1974): 657–81; "The Peruvian Declaration of Independence: Freedom by Coercion," JLAS 7 (November 1975): 221–48; and "The Last Viceroys of New Spain and Peru: An Appraisal," *American Historical Review* 81 (February 1976): 38–65. J. C. J. Metford, *San Martín, The Liberator* (New York: Philosophical Library, 1950) is a brief biography. More detailed is Bartolomé Mitre, *The Emanciapation of South America,* ed. and trans. William Pilling (London: Chapman & Hall, 1893), a condensed translation of the classic, four-volume biography of San Martín. The period is studied through the experiences of San Martín's British aide in Robert A. Humphreys, *Liberation in South America, 1806–1827:* *The Career of James Paroissien* (London: University of London, 1952). Concerning the naval war and Lord Cochrane see Donald Worcester, *Sea Power and Chilean Independence* (Gainesville: University of Florida Press, 1962); James C. Carey, "Lord Cochrane: Critic of San Martín's Peruvian Campaign," *The Americas* 18 (January 1962): 340–51; and Edward B. Billingsley, *In Defense of Neutral Rights: The United States Navy and the Wars of Independence in Chile and Peru* (Chapel Hill, N.C.: University of North Carolina Press, 1967).

The controversial meeting of San Martín and Bolívar is discussed in William H. Gray, "Bolívar's Conquest of Guayaquil," HAHR 27 (November 1947): 603–22; Gerhard Masur, "The Conference of Guayaquil," HAHR 31 (May 1951): 189–229; and Vicente Lecuna, "Bolívar and San Martín at Guayaquil," HAHR 31 (August 1951): 369–93. The standard biography of the Venezuelan Liberator is Gerhard Masur, *Simón Bolívar* (Albuquerque: University of New Mexico Press, 1948). More succinct is John J. Johnson, *Simón Bolívar and Spanish American Independence, 1783–1830* (Princeton, N.J.: Van Nostrand, 1968). A lively account by the Liberator's chief aide is Daniel Florencio O'Leary, *Bolívar and the War of Independence,* ed. and trans. Robert F. McNerney, Jr. (Austin: University of Texas Press, 1970). Víctor Andrés Belaúnde, *Bolívar and the Political Thought of the Spanish American Revolution* (Baltimore: The Johns Hopkins Press, 1938) is an influential study by a noted Peruvian intellectual. For interesting descriptions of the independence period by contemporary diplomats see Charles K. Webster, ed., *Britain and the Independence of Latin America, 1812–1830: Selected Documents from the Foreign Office Archives,* 2 vols. (London: Oxford University Press, 1938), 1: 513–50; and William Ray Manning, ed., *Diplomatic Correspondence of the United States Concerning the Independence of the Latin American Nations,* 3 vols. (New York: Oxford University Press, 1925), 3: 1717–1848.

Jorge Basadre, *La iniciación de la república,* 2 vols. (Lima: F. y E. Rosay, 1929–30) contains thoughtful discussions of the political problems of the early republican period that are not found in his later general history. The personalities and politics of the first half century of independence are analyzed in three collections of essays by Jorge Guillermo Leguía: *Historia y biografía* (Santiago: Ediciones Ercilla, 1936); *Estudios históricos* (Santiago: Ediciones Ercilla, 1939); and *Hombres e ideas en el Perú* (Santiago: Ediciones Ercilla, 1941). Concerning the ideological struggles of the period see Raúl Ferrero Rebagliati, *El liberalismo peruano* (Lima: Tipografía Peruana, 1958); Fredrick B. Pike, "Heresy, Real and Alleged, in Peru: An Aspect of the Conservative-Liberal Struggle, 1830–1875," HAHR 47 (February 1967): 50–74; and Daniel Michael Gleason, "Ideological Cleavages in Early Republican Peru, 1821–1872" (Ph.D. diss., University of Notre Dame, 1974). On the religious issue read Francis M. Stanger, "Church and State in Peru," HAHR 7 (November 1927): 410–37; and Fredrick B. Pike, "Church and State in Peru and Chile Since 1840: A Study in Contrasts," *American Historical Review* 73 (October 1967): 30–50.

Several early nineteenth-century caudillos are discussed in N. Andrew N. Cleven, "Dictators Gamarra, Orbegoso, Salaverry, and Santa Cruz," in A. Curtis Wilgus, ed., *South American Dictators During the First Century of Independence* (Washington, D.C.: George Washington University Press, 1937): 289–333. On Santa Cruz and the Peru-Bolivia

Confederation consult Gustavo Navarro, "Ensayo sobre la Confederación Perú-Boliviana: El Crucismo," *Journal of Inter-American Studies* 10 (January 1968): 53–73; Lane C. Kendall, "Andrés Santa Cruz and the Peru-Bolivian Confederation," HAHR 16 (February 1936): 29–48; Robert W. Delaney, "General Miller and the Confederación Perú-Boliviana," *The Americas* 18 (January 1962): 213–42; and Raúl Serna Rivera, "Aspectos de la economía durante la Confederación Perú-Boliviana, 1836–1839," *Anuario de Estudios Americanos* 26 (1969): 611–39. Serviceable biographies of Peru's most important nineteenth-century leaders are Rubén Vargas Ugarte, *Ramón Castilla* (Buenos Aires: Imprenta López, 1962); Evaristo San Cristóval, *Manuel Pardo y Lavalle, su vida y su obra* (Lima: Editorial Gil, 1945); and Alberto Ulloa y Sotomayor, *Don Nicolás de Piérola: Una época de la historia del Perú* (Lima: Imprenta Santa María, 1949).

The state of the Peruvian economy at the beginning of the republic is described by British consul Charles M. Ricketts in R. A. Humphreys, ed., *British Consular Reports on the Trade and Politics of Latin America, 1824–1826,* Royal Historical Society Publications, 3d ser. 63 (London: Royal Historical Society, 1940): 114–58. The nation's foreign trade and its impact on the domestic economy is analyzed in Heraclio Bonilla, "La coyuntura comercial del siglo XIX en el Perú," RMN 35 (1967–68): 159–87. Ernesto Yepes del Castillo, *Perú 1820–1920: Un siglo de desarrollo capitalista* (Lima: Instituto de Estudios Peruanos, 1972) employs the dependency model. The best introduction to the economy of the guano era is Jonathan V. Levin, *The Export Economies: Their Patterns of Development in Historical Perspective* (Cambridge, Mass.: Harvard University Press, 1960): 27–123. Robert C. Murphy, *The Bird Islands of Peru* (New York: G. P. Putnam's Sons, 1925) describes the methods of exploiting the guano deposits. The manure trade and Britain's economic relations with Peru during the guano era are examined in four articles by W. M. Mathew: "Imperialism of Free Trade: Peru, 1820–1870," *Economic History Review,* 2d ser. 21 (December 1968): 562–79; "Peru and the British Guano Market, 1840–1870," *Economic History Review,* 2d ser. 23 (April 1970): 112–28; "The First Anglo-Peruvian Debt and Its Settlement, 1822–1849," JLAS 2 (May 1970): 81–98; and "Foreign Contractors and the Peruvian Government at the Outset of the Guano Trade," HAHR 52 (November 1972): 598–620. Also see Heraclio Bonilla, "Auguste Dreyfus y el monopolio del guano," RMN 39 (1973): 315–47. The nitrate industry and its nationalization are discussed in Robert G. Greenhill and Rory M. Miller, "The Peruvian Government and the Nitrate Trade, 1873–1879," JLAS 5 (May 1973): 107–31.

Peru's early financial institutions are investigated in Carlos Camprubí Alcázar, "Los bancos en el Perú en el siglo XIX," RH 21 (1954): 102–37. Italian naturalist Antonio Raimondi surveyed the country's natural resources and their exploitation in *El Perú,* 4 vols. (Lima: Imprenta del Estado, 1874–1902). A useful description of the mining industry with production statistics for the nineteenth century is Pedro Dávalos y Lisson, "La industria minera," *El Ateneo* 4, no. 19 (1901): 35–117. César Antonio Ugarte examines landholding and the government's agrarian policies in "La propiedad agraria en el Perú," MP 8 (June 1922): 891–907; and "La política agraria de la república," MP 10 (May 1923): 664–81. The Peruvian railroads and their builders are treated in Watt Stewart, *Henry Meiggs, Yankee Pizarro* (Durham, N.C.: Duke University Press, 1946); and Brian Fawcett, *Railways of the Andes* (London: George Allen & Unwin, 1963). On fiscal and monetary matters during the first century of independence read Charles Alfred McQueen, *Peruvian Public Finance,* United States Department of Commerce, Bureau of Foreign and Domestic Commerce, Trade Promotion Series, no. 30 (Washington, D.C.: United States Government Printing Office, 1926); and Carlos Capuñay Mimbela, "Historia del presupuesto nacional desde 1821 a 1899," *Revista de la Facultad de Ciencias Económicas,* no. 23 (April 1942): 67–116.

Concerning Peru's relations with its Latin American neighbors and the United States during the nineteenth century see Fernando Schwalb, "Apuntes históricos sobre la evolución de nuestra influencia internacional y diplomática en América," *Mar del Sur* 8 (November–December 1952): 68–84; Louis C. Nolan, "The Diplomatic and Commercial Relations of the United States and Peru, 1826–1875" (Ph.D. diss., Duke University, 1935); Louis C. Nolan, "Relations of the United States and Peru with Respect to Claims, 1822–1870," HAHR 17 (February 1937): 30–66; John P. Harrison, "Science and Politics: Origins and Objectives of Mid-Nineteenth Century Government Expeditions to Latin America," HAHR 35 (May 1955): 175–202; Percy A. Martin, "The Influence of the United States on the Opening of the Amazon to the World's Commerce," HAHR 1 (May 1918): 146–62; Gustave A. Nuermberger, "The Continental Treaties of 1856: An American Union 'Exclusive of the United States'," HAHR 20 (February 1940): 32–55; Robert W. Frazer, "The Role of the Lima Congress, 1864–1865, in the Development of Pan Americanism," HAHR 29 (August 1949): 319–48; Pedro Irigoyen, "El Gran Mariscal Castilla en el panorama de la vida internacional del Perú," *Revista del Instituto Libertador Ramón Castilla* 1 (December 1954): 182–98; and Oscar Barrenechea y Raygada, *Congresos y conferencias celebrados en Lima, 1847–1894* (Buenos Aires: Peuser, 1947). The war with Spain is described in William C. Davis, *The Last Conquistadores: The Spanish Intervention in Peru and Chile, 1863–1866* (Athens: University of Georgia Press, 1950); James W. Cortada, "Diplomatic Rivalry between Spain and the United States over Chile and Peru, 1864–1871," IAEA 27 (Spring 1974): 47–57; and Alberto Wagner de Reyna, *Las relaciones diplomáticas entre el Perú y Chile durante el conflicto con España (1864–1867)* (Lima: Ediciones del Sol, 1963).

Jorge Basadre discusses the changing structure of Peruvian society during the nineteenth century in "La aristocracia y las clases medias civiles en el Perú republicano," MP 44 (September–December 1963): 461–71. Also useful is his "Bosquejo sobre la clase militar en los primeros años de la república," MP 17 (March 1928): 181–99. Concerning slavery and its abolition see Héctor Centurión Vallejo, "Esclavitud y manumisión de negros en Trujillo," *Revista del Instituto Libertador Ramón Castilla* 5 (December 1959): 53–81. Important studies of the Indian and the "Indian problem" during the period are George Kubler, *The Indian Caste of Peru, 1795–1940: A Population Study Based Upon Tax Records and Census Reports,* Smithsonian Institution, Institute of Social Anthropology, Publication no. 14 (Washington, D.C.: United States Government Printing Office, 1952); Thomas M. Davies, Jr., "Indian Integration in Peru, 1820–1948: An Overview," *The Americas* 30 (October 1973): 184–208; and two fine articles by Jean Piel: "The Place of the Peasantry in the National Life of Peru in the Nineteenth Century," *Past and Present,* no. 46 (February 1970): 108–33; and "Rebeliones agrarias y supervivencias coloniales en el Perú del siglo XIX," RMN 39 (1973): 301–14.

Immigration to Peru in the nineteenth and early twentieth centuries is examined in Watt Stewart, *Chinese Bondage in Peru: A History of the Chinese Coolie in Peru, 1849–1874* (Durham, N.C.: Duke University Press, 1951); Janet Evelyn Worrall, "Italian Immigration to Peru, 1860–1914" (Ph.D. diss., University of Indiana, 1972); Mario C. Vázquez, "Immigration and *Mestizaje* in Nineteenth-Century Peru," in Magnus Mörner, ed., *Race and Class in Latin America* (New York: Columbia University Press, 1970): 73–95; Pedro Paz-Soldán y Unánue [Juan de Arona], *La inmigración en el Perú* (Lima: Imprenta del Universo de C. Prince, 1891); and Toraji Irie, "History of Japanese Migration to Peru," trans. William Himel, HAHR 31 (May 1951): 437–52; 31 (November 1951): 648–64; and 32 (February 1952): 73–82. Broader in scope is C. Harvey Gardiner, *The Japanese and Peru, 1873–1973* (Albuquerque: University of New Mexico Press, 1975). The story of Peruvian education during the first century of the republic is told in Felipe Barreda Laos, "Historia de la instrucción pública en el Perú independiente," in Argentina, Academia Nacional de la Historia, *IIº Congreso Internacional de Historia de América* (Buenos Aires: Peuser, 1938), 3:211–23.

Contemporary travel accounts of Peru during the first half century of independence often contain valuable information for the social and economic historian. The best travelogue is J. J. von Tschudi, *Travels in Peru (1838–1842),* trans. Thomasina Ross (London: D. Bogue, 1847). Other useful volumes, arranged in order of the period covered, are:

Basil Hall, *Extracts from a Journal Written on the Coasts of Chile, Peru and Mexico in the Years 1820, 1821, and 1822,* 2 vols. (Edinburgh: Archibald Constable, 1824); Charles Brand, *Journal of a Voyage to Peru* (London: H. Colburn, 1828); Richard J.. Cleveland, *Voyages and Commercial Enterprises of the Sons of New England,* 2d ed. (New York: B. Franklin, 1968); William S. W. Ruschenberger [An Officer of the United States Navy], *Three Years in the Pacific* (Philadelphia: Carey, Lea & Blanchard, 1834); Peter Campbell Scarlett, *South America and the Pacific,* 2 vols. (London: H. Colburn, 1838); Archibald Smith, *Peru as It Is,* 2 vols. (London: Richard Bentley, 1839); Philo White, *Philo White's Narrative of a Cruise in the Pacific,* ed. Charles L. Camp (Denver: Old West Publishing Co., 1965); Walter Colton, *Deck and Port* (New York: A. S. Barnes & Co., 1850); William L. Herndon and Lardner Gibbon, *Exploration of the Valley of the Amazon, Made under the Direction of the Navy Department,* 2 vols. (Washington, D.C.: R. Armstrong, 1854); S. S. Hill, *Travels in Peru and Mexico,* 2 vols. (London: Longman, Green Longman, and Roberts, 1860); H. Willis Baxley, *What I Saw on the West Coast of South America and North America, and at the Hawaiian Islands* (New York: D. Appleton & Co., 1865); Clements R. Markham, *Travels in Peru and India* (London: J. Murray, 1862); Frederick J. Stevenson, *A Traveller in the Sixties,* ed. Douglas Timins (London: Constable and Co., 1929); James Orton, *The Andes and the Amazon,* 3d ed., rev. (New York: Harper & Brothers, 1875); and Thomas J. Hutchinson, *Two Years in Peru,* 2 vols. (London: Sampson Low, Marston, Low, & Searle, 1873).

For a delightful account of Peru during the first half century of independence based on travel literature see Tom B. Jones, *South America Rediscovered* (Minneapolis: University of Minnesota Press, 1949). Several of the "traditions" of Ricardo Palma have been translated by Harriet de Onís as *The Knights of the Cape and Thirty-Seven Other Selections from the Tradiciones peruanas of Ricardo Palma* (New York: Alfred A. Knopf, 1945). Concerning Pancho Fierro and his work see Anna Pursche, "Scenes of Lima Attributed to Pancho Fierro," *Notes Hispanic* 4 (1944): 92–132; and José Flores Araoz, "Pancho Fierro, pintor mulato limeño," *Cultura Peruana* 5 (May 1945). This last item has forty-four unnumbered pages with scores of the artist's works reproduced in miniature.

◖ *The War of the Pacific to 1930*

WILLIAM J. DENNIS, *Tacna and Arica: An Account of the Chile-Peru Boundary Dispute and of the Arbitrations of the United States* (New Haven, Conn.: Yale University Press, 1931) is the most satisfactory general account of the War of the Pacific and the fifty-year diplomatic struggle that followed it. Robert N. Burr, *By Reason or Force: Chile and the Balancing of Power in South America, 1830–1903* (Berkeley: University of California Press, 1965) is an excellent study of the complex diplomacy before and after the war. Also useful is William S. Coker, "The War of the Ten Centavos: The Geographic, Economic, and Political Causes of the War of the Pacific," *Southern Quarterly* 7 (January 1969): 113–29. The struggle on the seas is treated in Donald E. Worcester, "Naval Strategy in the War of the Pacific," *Journal of Inter-American Studies* 5 (January 1963): 31–38; and Patrick Vaux, "Famous Sea Fight in Pan American Waters," *Pan American Union Bulletin* 54 (April 1922): 366–74, which describes the battle of Angamos. The story of the war's most famous ship is traced in David Woodward, *"Huascar*: Hi-Jacked Battleship," *History Today* 25 (January 1975): 48–54. Clements R. Markham, *The War Between Peru and Chile, 1879–1882* (London: Sampson Low, Marston, Searle, & Rivington, 1882) is highly partisan in favor of the Peruvians. Gonzalo Bulnes, *Chile and Peru: Causes of the War of 1879* (Santiago: Imprenta Universitaria, 1920) ably presents the Chilean position. William F. Sater, "Chile During the First Months of the War of the Pacific," *JLAS* 5 (May 1973): 133–58 discusses that nation's domestic problems during the period.

The involvement of North American and European interests in the conflict is examined in Herbert Millington, *American Diplomacy During the War of the Pacific* (New York: Columbia University Press, 1948); and V. G. Kiernan, "Foreign Interests in the War of the Pacific," *HAHR* 35 (February 1955): 14–36. The political struggles concerning the Treaty of Ancón are related in Daniel M. Gleason, "Peru under Miguel Iglesias, 1883–1885" (Master's thesis, Southern Illinois University at Carbondale, 1968). A great number of documents concerning the war and the diplomacy surrounding it were translated and presented to the president of the United States for his guidance in arbitrating the "question of the Pacific." See Chile, *Tacna-Arica Arbitration,* 4 vols. ([Washington, D.C.?]: n.p., [1923–24?]); and Peru, *Arbitration between Peru and Chile,* 4 vols. (Washington, D.C.: National Capital Press, 1923–24). A smaller but more accessible collection is William J. Dennis, *Documentary History of the Tacna-Arica Dispute,* University of Iowa Studies in the Social Sciences 8, no. 3 (Iowa City: University of Iowa, 1927).

A good overview of the postwar period is Jesús Chavarría, "La desaparición del Perú colonial (1870–1919)," *Aportes,* no. 23 (January 1972): 120–53. Concerning the intellectual disillusionment of the era read Jesús Chavarría, "The Intellectuals and the Crisis of Modern Peruvian Nationalism, 1870–1919," *HAHR* 50 (May 1970): 257–78; William R. Crawford, *A Century of Latin American Thought* (Cambridge, Mass.: Harvard University Press, 1961): 170–89; Leopoldo Zea, *The Latin American Mind,* trans. J. H. Abbott and L. Dunham

(Norman: University of Oklahoma Press, 1963): 179–97; and Eugenio Chang-Rodríguez, *La literatura política de González Prada, Mariátegui y Haya de la Torre* (Mexico, D.F.: Ediciones de Andrea, 1957). For the problems of the Indian and Indianism in the postwar decades see Mary Consuela Callagham, "Indianism in Peru, 1883–1939" (Ph.D. diss., University of Pennsylvania, 1951); Thomas M. Davies, Jr., *Indian Integration in Peru: A Half Century of Experience, 1900–1948* (Lincoln: University of Nebraska Press, 1974); François Chevalier, "Official *Indigenismo* in Peru in 1920: Origins, Significance, and Socioeconomic Scope," in Magnus Mörner, ed., *Race and Class in Latin America* (New York: Columbia University Press, 1970): 184–96; François Chevalier, "La expansión de la gran propiedad en Alto Perú en el siglo XX," *Comunidades* 3 (May–August 1968): 189–205; Jean Piel, "A propos d' un soulèvement rural péruvien au début du vingtième siècle: Tocroyoc (1921)," *Revue d'Histoire Moderne et Contemporaine* 14 (October–December 1967): 375–405; Moisés Poblete Troncoso, *Condiciones de vida y trabajo de la población indígena del Perú* (Geneva: Oficina Internacional del Trabajo, 1938); and Richard Collier, *The River that God Forgot* (New York: Dutton, 1968), which treats the Putumayo rubber scandals.

Thirty essays by leading authorities on education, military affairs, the economy, various industries and other activities are collected in José Pareja Paz-Soldán, ed., *Visión del Perú en el siglo XX,* 2 vols. (Lima: Ediciones Librería Studium, 1962–63). Enrique Chiriños Soto's admirably objective essay on political history after 1895, included in this collection, has been published separately as *El Perú frente a junio de 1962* (Lima: Ediciones del Sol, 1962); Manuel Fuentes Irurozgui, *Síntesis de la economía peruana* (Lima: Empresa Gráfica Sanmartí, 1950) is an economic history and useful compilation of statistics for the first half of the twentieth century. Informative general descriptions of Peru during the late nineteenth and early twentieth centuries include Richard M. Morse, "The Lima of Joaquín Capelo: A Latin American Archetype," *Journal of Contemporary History* 4 (November 1969): 95–110; Alexandro Garland, *Peru in 1906,* trans. G. R. Gepp (Lima: La Industria Printing Office, 1907); C. Reginald Enoch, *Peru* (London: T. E. Unwin, 1908); Marie Robinson Wright, *The Old and the New Peru* (Philadelphia: G. Barrie & Sons, 1908); Percy F. Martin, *Peru of the Twentieth Century* (New York: Longmans, Green & Co., 1911); and Francisco García Calderón, *Le Pérou contemporain* (Paris: Dujarric et Cie., 1907), an analysis by an important Peruvian intellectual.

On economic matters between the War of the Pacific and the Great Depression see Clarence F. Jones, "The Commercial Growth of Peru," *Economic Geography* 3 (January 1927): 23–49; G. M. Jones, "Ports of Peru," HAHR 2 (August 1919), 470–78; Jorge Basadre and Rómulo Ferrero, *Historia de la cámara de comercio de Lima* (Lima: Santiago Valverde, 1963); J. Fred Rippy, "The Dawn of Manufacturing in Peru," *Pacific Historical Review* 15 (June 1946): 147–57; Rory Miller, "The Making of the Grace Contract: British Bondholders and the Peruvian Government, 1885–1890," JLAS 8 (May 1976): 73–100; William E. Dunn, *Peru: A Commercial and Industrial Handbook,* United States Department of Commerce, Bureau of Foreign and Domestic Commerce, Trade Promotion series, no. 25 (Washington, D.C.: United States Government Printing Office, 1925); Leo S. Rowe, *Early Effects of the War upon the Finance, Commerce and Industry of Peru* (New York: Oxford University Press, 1920); Perú, Ministerio de Fomento, Dirección de Minas y Petróleo, *Síntesis de la minería peruana en el centenario de Ayacucho,* 2 vols. (Lima: Imprenta Torres Aguirre, 1924–27); Artidoro Alvarado Garrido, "Desarrollo de la industria del petróleo," MP 22 (January 1940): 27–43 and (February 1940): 94–108; Charles W. Sutton, "Agriculture and Irrigation in Peru," *Bulletin of the Pan American Union* 61 (July 1927): 642–48; and Howard L. Karno, "Julio César Arana, Frontier Cacique in Peru," in Robert Kerns and Ronald Dolkart, eds., *The Caciques: Oligarchical Politics in the Luso-Hispanic World* (Albuquerque: University of New Mexico Press, 1973): 89–98, a brief biography of Peru's principal rubber baron. A dependency analysis of the period is David Slater, "El capitalismo subdesarrollado y la organización del espacio: Perú: 1920–1940," *Revista Interamericana de Planificación* 9 (June 1975): 87–106.

Ricardo Martínez de la Torre, *Apuntes para una interpretación marxista de historia social del Perú,* 2d ed., 4 vols. (Lima: Impresa Editora Peruana, 1947–49) contains useful information on the early labor movement. For rural workers see Solomon Miller, "Hacienda to Plantation in Northern Peru: The Process of Proletarianization of a Tenant Farmer Society," in Julian H. Steward, ed., *Contemporary Change in Traditional Societies,* 3 vols. (Urbana: University of Illinois Press, 1967), 3: 135–225. University Reform and the early student movement are discussed in Gabriel del Mazo, ed., *La reforma universitaria,* 3d ed., 3 vols. (Lima: Universidad Nacional Mayor de San Marcos, 1967–68); Carlos Salazar Romero, "Cincuenta años de educación en el Perú (1918–1968)," MP, nos. 474–75 (July–October 1968): 462–78; Felipe Portocarrero, "El movimiento estudantil en el Perú," *Revista Mexicana de Sociología* 32 (July–August 1970): 1043–54; César Antonio Ugarte, "Aspectos de la reforma de la universidad," MP 17 (February 1928): 120–27; Julio C. Tello, "La reforma de la Universidad Mayor de San Marcos: De la universidad profesional a la universidad científica," MP 17 (February 1928): 128–38; and Pedro M. Olivera, "La reforma universitaria en el Perú," *Revista Chilena* 13, nos. 105–7 (January–March 1929): 118–50, 289–319.

Peruvian foreign relations during the first half of the twentieth century are treated in James C. Carey, *Peru and the United States,*

1900–1962 (Notre Dame, Ind.: University of Notre Dame Press, 1964); Dale William Peterson, "The Diplomatic and Commercial Relations Between the United States and Peru from 1883–1918" (Ph.D. diss., University of Minnesota, 1969); Gordon Ireland, *Boundaries, Possessions and Conflicts in South America* (Cambridge, Mass.: Harvard University Press, 1938); Frederic W. Ganzert, "The Boundary Controversy in the Upper Amazon Between Brazil, Bolivia and Peru, 1903–1909," HAHR 14 (November 1934): 427–49; Bryce Wood, *The United States and Latin American Wars, 1932–1942* (New York: Columbia University Press, 1966); Georg Maier, "The Boundary Dispute between Ecuador and Peru," *American Journal of International Law* 63 (January 1969): 28–46; David H. Zook, *Zarumilla-Marañón: The Ecuador-Peru Dispute* (New York: Bookman Associates, 1964); Ronald Bruce St. John, "The End of Innocence: Peruvian Foreign Policy and the United States, 1919–1942," JLAS 8 (November 1976): 325–44; Orazio Ciccarelli, "The Leticia Dispute, 1932–1934: A Reconsideration," *Southern Quarterly* 11 (July 1973): 277–96; and Edward N. Barnhart, "Japanese Internees from Peru," *Pacific Historical Review* 31 (May 1963): 169–78.

Relatively objective accounts of the Leguía regime are Howard Lawrence Karno, "Augusto B. Leguía: The Oligarchy and the Modernization of Peru, 1870–1930" (Ph.D. diss., University of California at Los Angeles, 1970); Graham H. Stuart, *The Governmental System of Peru* (Washington D.C.: Carnegie Institution, 1925); and Ernest Galarza, "Debts, Dictatorship and Revolution in Bolivia and Peru," *Foreign Policy Reports* 7 (May 13, 1931): 101–18. Laudatory biographies of the autocrat include René Hooper López, *Leguía: Ensayo biográfico* (Lima: Ediciones Peruanos, 1964), which emphasizes his career before the Oncenio; and Manuel E. Capuñay, *Leguía: Vida y obra del constructor del gran Perú* (Lima: Compañía de Impresiones y publicidad, 1952). Powerful indictments of the dictatorship are Abelardo Solís, *Once años* (Lima: Sanmartí y Cía., 1934); and Dora Mayer de Zulen, *El Oncenio de Leguía,* 2 vols. (Callao: n.p., 1932).

Jesús Chavarría, "José Carlos Mariátegui, Revolutionary Nationalist: The Origins and Crisis of Modern Peruvian Nationalism, 1870–1930" (Ph.D. diss., University of California at Los Angeles, 1967) is an outstanding study of the great Peruvian Marxist, his ideas, and political activities. Also useful are John M. Baines, *Revolution in Peru: Mariátegui and the Myth* (University: University of Alabama Press, 1972); and John M. Baines, "José Mariátegui and the Ideology of Revolution in Peru," *Rocky Mountain Social Science Journal* 7 (October 1970): 109–16. Jorge Basadre, in his youth a member of Mariátegui's circle, has written a fine introduction to Marjory Urquidi's translation of José Carlos's major work, *Seven Interpretive Essays on Peruvian Reality* (Austin: University of Texas Press, 1971). Catholic intellectual Víctor

Andrés Belaúnde answered Mariátegui's attack on the old order with *La realidad nacional,* 2d ed. (Lima: Ediciones "Mercurio Peruano," 1945).

❧ Peru, 1930–1968

A VAST BODY OF LITERATURE exists concerning APRA and its founder, Víctor Raúl Haya de la Torre. Peter F. Klarén, *Modernization, Dislocation, and Aprismo: Origins of the Peruvian Aprista Party, 1870–1932* (Austin: University of Texas Press, 1973) is an excellent study of the movement's leader and early history. Jeffrey L. Klaiber has contributed to the story of the party in two articles: "Religion and Revolution in Peru: 1920–1945," *The Americas* 31 (January 1975): 289–312; and "The Popular Universities and the Origins of Aprismo," HAHR 55 (November 1975): 693–715. High Aprista official and literary historian Luis Alberto Sánchez's *Haya de la Torre y el APRA* (Santiago: Editorial del Pacífico, 1955) is the best of the party's "court histories." However, this volume should be read with Sánchez's *Testimonio personal: Memorias de un Peruano del siglo XX,* 3 vols. (Lima: Ediciones Villasán, 1969) in which the author changes some of his earlier opinions, adds much new information, and gives life to the period through accounts of his own experiences. A less convincing "official history" is Felipe Cossío del Pomar, *Haya de la Torre, el indoamericano,* 2d ed. (Lima: Editorial Nueva Día, 1946). For brief biographies of more than a score of early party leaders see "Algunos datos biográficos de los presos apristas del Perú," *Claridad* [Buenos Aires] 17 (April 1938): 11 pp., and several other biographical sketches in the same unpaginated issue. Robert J. Alexander, *Prophets of the Revolution* (New York: Macmillan, 1962) devotes a highly laudatory chapter to Haya and his party. Eudocio Ravines, *The Yenan Way* (New York: Charles Scribner's Sons, 1951) has interesting material on the early years of APRA but should be used with caution. A one-time associate of Haya, Ravines later became a paid agent of Moscow, helped Mariátegui found the Peruvian Communist party, and then swung to the far right.

Robert E. McNicoll, "Intellectual Origins of Aprismo," HAHR 23 (August 1943): 424–40 traces the ideas of the movement back to Manuel González Prada. Long the standard work on APRA in English, Harry Kantor's *Ideology and Program of the Peruvian Aprista Movement* (Berkeley: University of California Press, 1953) is extremely favorable to the party, as is Alberto Baeza Flores, *Haya de la Torre, y la Revolución constructiva de las Américas* (Buenos Aires: Editorial Claridad, 1962). A good, brief analysis of Aprismo is found in Miguel Jorrín and John D. Martz, *Latin American Political Thought and Ideology* (Chapel Hill: University of North Carolina Press, 1970): 335–57. Thomas M.

Davies, Jr., "The *Indigenismo* of the Peruvian Aprista Party: A Rein-
terpretation," HAHR 51 (November 1971): 626–45, suggests that,
from the beginning, the party's "radical" program—especially its vaunt-
ed concern for the India—was largely campaign rhetoric. César A.
Guardia Mayorga, *Reconstruyendo el aprismo* (Arequipa: Tipografía
Acosta, 1945) is a Marxist critique of the party and its ideology. Víctor
Raúl Haya de la Torre, *Pensamiento político de Haya de la Torre,* 5 vols.
(Lima: Ediciones del Pueblo, 1961) is a convenient compendium of
Haya's major works. A fascinating interview with Haya is transcribed in
". . . Y después del mitin: Entrevista de seis horas," *Caretas* 21, no. 431
(March 3–12, 1971): 6–11 ff.; no. 432 (March 22–31, 1971): 16–21. A
most valuable contribution is Robert J. Alexander, ed. and trans.,
Aprismo: The Ideas and Doctrines of Víctor Raúl Haya de la Torre (Kent,
Ohio: Kent State University Press, 1973) which contains *El Antim-
perialismo y el APRA* in its entirety along with several of Haya's other
major statements. Alexander's annotations are very helpful.

Of the many works analyzing APRA as a political party the best are
Richard Lee Clinton, "APRA: An Appraisal," *Journal of Inter-American
Studies and World Affairs* 12 (April 1970): 280–97; and Liisa North,
"Orígenes y crecimiento del Partido Aprista y el cambio socioeco-
nómico en el Perú," *Desarrollo Económico* 38 (July–September 1970):
163–214. The latter is a preliminary version of North's "The Origins
and Development of the Peruvian Aprista Party" (Ph.D. diss., University of California at Berkeley, 1973). Fredrick B. Pike, "The Old and
the New APRA in Peru—Myth and Reality," IAEA 18 (Autumn
1964): 3–45, which initiated a trend toward revisionist studies of the
party in English, is a provocative though strained analysis. Another
caustic assessment, emphasizing the party's fascist overtones, is William
S. Stokes, "Democracy, Freedom, and Reform in Latin America," in
Fredrick B. Pike, ed., *Freedom and Reform in Latin America,* rev. ed.
(Notre Dame, Ind.: University of Notre Dame Press, 1967): 117–49.
The confusion of early observers concerning the nature of the party is
exhibited in Carleton Beals, "Aprismo: The Rise of Haya de la Torre,"
Foreign Affairs 13 (January 1935): 235–46. Party leader Carlos Manuel
Cox attempted to explain the differences between Aprismo, fascism,
and communism in "Nueva forma del estado," *Acción Social* [Santiago],
no. 36 (March 1935): 52–56. Grant Hilliker, *The Politics of Reform in
Peru: The Aprista and other Mass Parties of Latin America* (Baltimore:
The Johns Hopkins University Press, 1971) examines the party's
pragmatic politics since the 1940s. Useful studies in Spanish include
Alfredo Hernández Urbina, *Los partidos y la crisis del APRA* (Lima:
Ediciones Raíz, 1956); and José Raúl Cáceres, *El pasmo de una insurgen-
cia: ensayo de la realidad política peruana* (Lima: Editorial Perú, n.d.).

Orazio A. Ciccarelli, "The Sánchez Cerro Regimes in Peru, 1930–
1933" (Ph.D. diss., University of Florida, 1969) is a fine study of the

"Hero of Arequipa" and his troubled administrations. Orazio A. Ciccarelli explores one of the more controversial events of the twentieth century in *Militarism, Aprismo, and Violence in Peru: The Presidential Election of 1931,* State University of New York at Buffalo, Council on International Studies, Special Studies no. 45 (Buffalo: By the Council, 1973). Pedro Ugarteche, ed., *Sánchez Cerro: Papeles y recuerdos de un presidente del Perú* (Lima: Editorial Universitaria, 1969), vol. 1, contains documents concerning his career through 1930. Carlos Miró Quesada, *Sánchez Cerro y su tiempo* (Buenos Aires: Librería "El Ateneo," 1947) is sympathetic toward its subject, while Guillermo Thorndike, *El año de la barbarie: Perú 1932* (Lima: Editorial Nueva América, 1969) is a pro-Aprista interpretation of the period. Also useful for the struggles of the 1930s are Carleton Beals, *Fire on the Andes* (Philadelphia: J. B. Lippincott Company, 1934); and Rómulo Merino Arana, *Historia policial del Perú en la república* (Lima: Imprenta del Departamento de Prensa y Publicaciones de la Guardia Civil, 1966), containing much material on the civil guard's conflicts with the party. Some social and economic developments of the 1930s are discussed in Orazio A. Ciccarelli, "Sánchez Cerro and the Depression in Peru, 1930–1933," *Southern Quarterly* 9 (April 1971): 231–52; Carlos Camprubí Alcázar, "La depresión económica y los afanes peruanos (1931–1932)," *RH* 27 (1964): 221–59; and E. Rebagliati, "Compulsory Social Security in Peru," *Bulletin of the Pan American Union* 71 (November 1937): 827–34.

Concerning the Benavides regime see Genaro Arbaiza, "Benavides of Peru," *Current History* 48 (May 1938): 15–17; and Genaro Arbaiza "South America's No. 1 Tyranny," *Current History* 49 (October 1938): 26–29. Watt Stewart, "A Peruvian Election," *Social Science* 13 (October 1938): 319–25 discusses the strongman's rule as well as the ill-fated contest of 1936. Víctor Villanueva, "La revolución de Negus," *Caretas,* no. 488 (November 20–December 4, 1973): 24–28, describes an aborted Aprista plot to overthrow Benavides with Bolivian guns and Mexican money. Eduardo Sierralta Lorca, *El APRA y la sombra* (Mexico, D.F.: Editorial Tejada, 1957) is a semifictional work that conveys the flavor of the period and gives an unusual account of General Rodríguez's unsuccessful 1939 coup. Aprista Manuel Bedoya's *El General Bebevidas, monstruo de América* (Barcelona: Editorial Llamarada, 1939) is an outlandish parody of the regime.

The first Prado regime and the election of 1945 are examined in José M. Ramírez Gastón, *Política económica y financiera: Manuel Prado, sus gobiernos de 1939–45 y 1956–62* (Lima: Ediciones Litografía La Confianza, 1969); Carlos Miró Quesada Laos, *Pueblo en crisis* (Buenos Aires: Emecé Editores, 1946); H. B. Murkland, "Peru's Peaceful Revolution," *Current History* 9 (August 1945): 94–98; and Manuel Vázquez Díaz, "El triunfo del Aprismo en el Perú," *Cuadernos Americanos* 23 (September–October 1945): 55–67. José Luis Bustamante i Rivero defended his administration in *Tres años de la lucha por la democracia en el Perú* (Buenos Aires: Artes Gráficas Bartolomé U. Chiesino, 1949). APRA's actions during the Bustamante regime are denounced by Víctor Villanueva, *La tragedia de un pueblo y un partido: Páginas para la historia del APRA,* 2d ed. (Lima: Talleres Gráficos "Victory," 1956). An ex-Aprista and an organizer of the 1948 Callao mutiny, Villanueva's book was part of an outpouring of literature by disenchanted former Apristas attacking Haya and other party leaders. Two of the most hostile examples are Luis Eduardo Enríquez, *Haya de la Torre: La estafa política más grande de América* (Lima: Ediciones del Pacífico, 1951); and Alberto Hidalgo, *Por qué renuncié al APRA* (Lima: Imprenta "Leomir," [1954]). The economic policies of the period are discussed in Rolf Hayn, "Peruvian Exchange Controls, 1945–1948," IAEA 10 (Spring 1957): 47–70.

The Ochenio of Odría is surveyed in Tad Szulc, *Twilight of the Tyrants* (New York: Henry Holt and Co., 1959): 159–203. Also see Percy MacLean y Esteños, *Historia de una revolución* (Buenos Aires: Editorial E.A.P.A.L., 1953); Víctor Raúl Haya de la Torre, "My Five-Year Exile in My Own Country," *Life* 36 (May 3, 1954): 152–54 ff.; Fernando León de Vivero, *El tirano quedó atrás* (Mexico, D.F.: Editorial Cultura, 1951); John Davenport, "Why Peru Pulls Dollars," *Fortune* 54 (November 1956): 130–46 ff.; Alvin Cohen, "ECLA and the Economic Development of Peru," IAEA 17 (Summer 1963): 3–27; S. C. Tsiang, "An Experiment with a Flexible Exchange Rate System: The Case of Peru, 1950–1954," *International Monetary Fund, Staff Papers* 5 (February 1957): 449–76; and Rosemary Thorp, "Inflation and Orthodox Economic Policy in Peru," *Bulletin of the Oxford University Institute of Economics and Statistics* 29 (August 1967): 185–210.

Works examining the 1956 election and Manuel Prado's Convivencia government include M. Guillermo Ramírez y Berríos, *Grandezas y miserias de un proceso electoral en el Perú: Junio 17 de 1956* (Lima: Talleres Gráficos P. L. Villanueva, 1957); Luis Alberto Sánchez, "El actual proceso político peruano," *Cuadernos Americanos* 96 (November–December 1957): 29–48; W. Donald Beatty, "Peru's Growth toward Stability," *Current History* 40 (April 1961): 225–31; Rod Bunker, "Linkages and the Foreign Policy of Peru, 1958–1966," *Western Political Quarterly* 22 (June 1969): 280–97; and a series of articles by Richard W. Patch: "Setback for Democracy," AUFS-WC 5, no. 1 (1958); "Some Aspects of Peru's Economy," AUFS-WC 5, no. 3 (1958); "Fidelismo in Peruvian Universities," AUFS-WC 8, nos. 2–3 (1961); "Politics and the University," AUFS-WC 5, no. 5 (1958); and "Nixon in Peru," AUFS-WC 5, no. 4 (1958). The *Hispanic American Report,* a monthly digest of Latin American news, provided a wealth of information for the period from 1948 until it ceased publication in 1965.

The elections of 1962 and 1963 along with the intervening military regime are treated in Arnold Payne, *The Peruvian Coup D'Etat of 1962: The Overthrow of Manuel Prado,* Institute for the Comparative Study of Political Systems, Political Studies Series, no. 5 (Washington, D.C.: ICOPS, 1968), an excellent study; W. Obelson, *Funerales del APRA: El fraude electoral y fiscal* (Lima: Litografía Universo, 1962); Víctor Villanueva, *Un año bajo el sable* (Lima: Empresa Gráfica T. Scheuch, 1963); and the following reports by Richard W. Patch: "Peru Looks Forward to the Elections of 1962," AUFS-WC 8, no. 5 (1961); "The Peruvian Elections of 1962 and Their Annulment," AUFS-WC 9, no. 6 (1962); and "The Peruvian Elections of 1963," AUFS-WC 10, no. 1 (1963).

Fernando Belaúnde Terry presented his program for the nation's development in a 1959 book later revised and translated as *Peru's Own Conquest* (Lima: American Studies Press, 1965). The Belaúnde administration is discussed in James C. Carey, "Peru: Encouraging New Spirit," *Current History* 49 (December 1965): 321–27; Arnold Payne, "Peru: Latin America's Silent Revolution," IAEA 20 (Winter 1966): 69–78; Fredrick B. Pike, "Peru and the Quest for Reform by Compromise," IAEA 20 (Spring 1967): 23–38; J. Llosa Larrabure, " 'Cooperación Popular': A New Approach to Community Development in Peru," *International Labour Review* 94 (September 1966): 221–36; David E. Snyder, "The 'Carretera Marginal de la Selva': A Geographical Review and Appraisal," *Revista Geográfica,* no. 67 (December 1967): 87–99; and Daniel R. Kilty, *Planning for Development in Peru* (New York: Praeger, 1967).

The 1964 agrarian reform, peasant leagues, and guerrilla movements are treated in Richard W. Patch, "Peru's New President and Agrarian Reform," AUFS-WC 10, no. 2 (1963); and Richard W. Patch, "The Peruvian Agrarian Reform Bill: The Legislation of an Ideal," AUFS-WC 11, no. 3 (1964); James F. Petras and Robert LaPorte, Jr., *Cultivating Revolution: The United States and Agrarian Reform in Latin America* (New York: Random House, 1971): 33–123; Hugo Blanco, *Land or Death: The Peasant Struggle in Peru,* trans. Naomi Allen (New York: Pathfinder Press, 1972); Héctor Béjar, *Peru 1965: Notes on a Guerrilla Experience,* trans. William Rose (New York: Monthly Review Press, 1970); Richard Gott, *Guerrilla Movements in Latin America* (Garden City, N.Y.: Doubleday & Co., 1971):307–94; Hugo Neira, "Sindicalismo campesino en el Perú," *Aportes,* no. 18 (October 1970): 27–67; William F. Whyte, "Rural Peru: Peasants as Activists," *Trans-Action* 7 (November 1969): 37–47; E. J. Hobsbawm, "Peasant Land Occupations," *Past and Present,* no. 62 (February 1974): 120–52; and Howard Handelman, *Struggle in the Andes: Peasant Political Mobilization in Peru* (Austin: University of Texas Press, 1974). The literature on this subject is analyzed in Leon G. Campbell, "The Historiography of the Peruvian Guerrilla Movement, 1960–1965," *Latin American Research Review* 8 (Spring 1973): 45–70.

Concerning the IPC affair and Belaúnde's relations with the United States read Richard N. Goodwin, "Letter from Peru; Takeover of the International Petroleum Co.," *New Yorker* 45 (May 17, 1969): 41 ff.; Adalberto J. Pinelo, *The Multinational Corporation as a Force in Latin American Politics: A Case Study of the International Petroleum Company in Peru* (New York: Praeger, 1973); Augusto Zimmermann Zavala, *La historia secreta del petróleo* (Lima: Editorial Gráfica Labor, 1968); John Allen Peeler, "The Politics of the Alliance for Progress in Peru" (Ph.D. diss., University of North Carolina, 1968); and United States, Congress, Senate, Foreign Relations Committee, *United States Relations with Peru: Hearings before the Subcommittee on Western Hemisphere Affairs* (91st Cong., 1st sess., April 14–17, 1969). Vice-President Edgardo Seoane Corrales denounced Belaúnde's settlement with the IPC and other actions of his administration in *Ni tiranos ni caudillos: Cartas y hechos del proceso político, 62–68* (San Miguel: Editorial Italperú, 1968).

Discussions of the military coup that ousted Belaúnde include Robert J. Alexander, "Taming of Peru; Behind the Coup," *Commonweal* 89 (December 6, 1968): 340–43; François Bourricaud, "Los militares: Por qué y para qué?" *Aportes* 16 (April 1970): 13–55; François Bourricaud, "Perú: El círculo vicioso o militares y políticos," *Mundo Nuevo,* no. 31 (January 1969): 9–21; Julio Cotler, "Political Crisis and Military Populism in Peru," *Studies in Comparative International Development* 6 no. 5 (1970–71): 95–113; Omar Díaz de Arce, "Antecedentes del golpe militar peruano," *Cuadernos Americanos* 169 (March–April 1970): 7–24; José Zebedeo García, Jr., "The 1968 Velasco Coup in Peru: Causes and Policy Consequences" (Ph.D. diss., University of New Mexico, 1974); Guillermo Hoyos Osores, "Crisis de la democracia en el Perú: Causas de su quebranto y condiciones para su recuperación," *Cuadernos Americanos* 162 (January–February 1969): 7–31; Arnaldo Pedroso d' Horta, *Peru: Da oligarquia econômica à militar* (São Paulo: Editôra Perspectiva, 1971); and two articles by Manuel D'Ornellas Suárez: "La encrucijada peruana," *Mundo Nuevo,* no. 31 (January 1969): 4–8; and "Militares y oligarquía en el Perú," *Mundo Nuevo,* no. 43 (January 1970): 19–23. A semiofficial account of the coup is given in Augusto Zimmermann Zavala, *El Plan Inca: Objetivo, Revolución peruana* (Lima: Empresa Editora del Diario Oficial El Peruano, 1974).

The Peruvian Revolution, 1968–1976

MANY STUDIES concerning the Peruvian military and their reformist attitudes have appeared in recent years, including Liisa North, *Civil-Military Relations in Argentina, Chile, and Peru* (Berkeley: University of California Institute of International Studies, 1966); Stephen L. Rozman, "The Evolution of the Political Role of the Peruvian Military,"

Journal of Inter-American Studies and World Affairs 12 (October 1970): 539–64; Charles W. Johnson, "Perú: Los militares como un agente de cambio económico," *Revista Mexicana de Sociología* 34 (April–June 1972): 293–316; Richard Lee Clinton, "The Modernizing Military: The Case of Peru," IAEA 24 (Spring 1971): 43–66; Luis Valdéz Pallete, "Antecedentes de la nueva orientación de las fuerzas armadas en el Perú,"*Aportes,* no. 19 (January 1971): 163–81; Carlos A. Astiz and José Z. García, "The Peruvian Military: Achievement, Orientation, Training and Political Tendencies,"*Western Political Quarterly* 25 (December 1972): 667–85; James A. Osberg, "Centro de Altos Estudios Militares: Education for Change in the Peruvian Military, 1950–1973" (Ph.D. diss., Southern Illinois University at Carbondale, 1975); James Petras and Nelson Rimensnyder, "Los militares y la modernización del Perú," *Estudios Internacionales* 4 (April–June 1970): 90–123; Frederick M. Nunn, "Notes on the 'Junta Phenomenon' and the 'Military Regime' in Latin America with Special Reference to Peru, 1968–1972," *The Americas* 31 (January 1975): 237–51; three studies by Luigi R. Einaudi: "Revolution from Within? Military Rule in Peru since 1968,"*Studies in Comparative International Development* 8 (Spring 1973): 71–87; *The Peruvian Military: A Summary Political Analysis,* Research Paper RM-6048-RC (Santa Monica, Calif.: Rand Corporation, May 1969); *Peruvian Military Relations with the United States,* Research Paper P-4389 (Santa Monica, Calif.: Rand Corporation, June 1970); and two books by Víctor Villanueva: *¿Nueva mentalidad militar en el Perú?* (Buenos Aires: Editorial Replanteo, 1969); and *El CAEM y la revolución de la fuerza armada* (Lima: Instituto de Estudios Peruanos, 1972). This literature is analyzed in George Philip, "The Soldier as a Radical: The Peruvian Military Government, 1968–1975," JLAS 8 (May 1976): 29–51.

A perceptive general account of the Revolutionary Government of the Armed Forces is Abraham F. Lowenthal, "Peru's Ambiguous Revolution," *Foreign Affairs* 52 (July 1974): 799–817. A revised version of this article introduces Abraham F. Lowenthal, ed.,*Peruvian Experiment: Continuity and Change under Military Rule* (Princeton, N.J.: Princeton University Press, 1975), an outstanding collection of original essays. These will be cited separately below, along with certain items from David Chaplin, ed., *Peruvian Nationalism: A Corporatist Revolution* (New Brunswick, N.J.: Transaction Books, 1976), an anthology of older, previously published articles. Other useful surveys are Marvin Alisky, *Peruvian Political Perspective,* 2d ed. (Tempe: Arizona State University Center for Latin American Studies, 1975); E. J. Hobsbawm, "Peru: The Peculiar Revolution," *New York Review of Books* 17 (December 16, 1971): 29–36; James Petras and Nelson Rimensnyder, "What is Happening in Peru," *Monthly Review* 21 (February 1970): 15–28; Charles T. Goodsell, "That Confounding Revolution in Peru," *Current History* 68 (January 1975): 20–23; José Yglesias, "Report from

Peru: The Reformers in Brass Hats," *New York Times Magazine* (December 14, 1969): 58–59 ff.; Neiva Moreira, *Modelo peruano* (Buenos Aires: Editorial La Línea, 1974); Armando Ruiz de la Cruz, "La Revolución peruana," *Comercio Exterior* 24 (October 1974): 1029–37; and four articles in *Current History* by George W. Grayson, Jr.: "Peru's Military Government," 58 (February 1970): 65–72 ff.; "Peru's Military Populism," 60 (February 1971): 71–77 ff.; "Peru under the Generals," 62 (February 1972): 91–97 ff.; and "Peru's Revolutionary Government," 64 (February 1973): 61–65, 87.

Communist party leader Jorge del Prado supports the regime in "The Revolution Continues," *World Marxist Review* 16 (January 1973): 64–72, while independent Marxist Aníbal Quijano's *Nationalism and Capitalism in Peru: A Study in Neo-Imperialism,* trans. Helen R. Lane (New York: Monthly Review Press, 1971) expresses skepticism toward the government's intentions. Ian Lumsden, "Dependency, Revolution and Development in Latin America," *International Journal* 28 (Summer 1973): 525–51 compares the Peruvian revolution with those in Castro's Cuba and Allende's Chile. Alfredo Cánepa Sardón, *La Revolución Peruana (Ensayo polémico)* (Buenos Aires: Editorial Paracas, 1971) discusses the applicability of the "Peruvian model" to other countries, especially Argentina. Carlos Delgado, *El proceso revolucionario peruano: Testimonio de lucha* (Mexico, D.F.: Siglo Ventiun Editores, 1972) is a collection of short essays by a major theoretician of the revolution.

The political economy of the revolution is cogently analyzed in three works by E. V. K. Fitzgerald: *The State and Economic Development: Peru Since 1968* (Cambridge, England: Cambridge University Press, 1976); "The Political Economy of Peru, 1968–1975," *Development and Change* 7 (January 1976): 7–33; and "Peru: The Political Economy of an Intermediate Regime," JLAS 8 (May 1976): 53–71. Studies of the role of foreign investors after 1968 are Carlos Malpica S.S., "El capital extranjero en el modelo peruano," *Revista Interamericana de Planificación* 9 (June 1975): 74–86; Charles T. Goodsell, "The Multinational Corporation as Political Actor in a Changing Environment: Peru," IAEA 29 (Winter 1975): 3–22; Guy B. Meeker, "Fade-Out Joint Venture: Can It Work for Latin America?" IAEA 24 (Spring 1971): 25–42; and Shane Hunt, "Direct Foreign Investment in Peru: New Rules for an Old Game," in Lowenthal, ed., *Peruvian Experiment,* 302–49.

The Velasco administration's agrarian reform is examined in John Stephen Gitlitz, "Impressions of the Peruvian Agrarian Reform," *Journal of Inter-American Studies and World Affairs* 13 (July–October 1971): 456–74; Emilio Barrantes, "La nueva ley de reforma agraria del Perú," *América Indígena* 29 (October 1969): 1113–26; Hernando Aguirre Gamio, "El proceso de reforma agraria en el Perú," *Mundo Nuevo,* no.

43 (January 1970): 24–34; Edmundo Flores, "La reforma agraria del
Perú," *El Trimestre Económico* 37 (July–September 1970): 515–23;
Norman Long and David Winder, "From Peasant Community to Pro-
duction Co-operative: An Analysis of Recent Government Policy in
Peru," *Journal of Development Studies* 12 (October 1975): 75–94; David
Guillet, "Migration, Agrarian Reform and Structural Change in Rural
Peru," *Human Organization* 35 (Fall 1976): 295–302; Antonio García,
"Perú: Una reforma agraria radical," *Comercio Exterior* 20 (May 1970):
390–93; Antonio García, "La reforma agraria en el modelo peruano de
desarrollo," *El Trimestre Económico* 41 (April–June 1974): 439–57; and
Colin Harding, "Land Reform and Social Conflict in Peru," in Lowen-
thal, ed., *Peruvian Experiment,* 220–53.

 Industrial policy and the labor communities are discussed in
Donald W. Pearson, "The Comunidad Industrial: Peru's Experiment in
Worker Management," IAEA 27 (Summer 1973): 15–29; José Ab-
ramovitz, Vance R. Koven, and Abelardo L. Valdez, "The Peruvian
General Law of Industries," *Harvard International Law Journal* 12
(Spring 1971): 312–44; Luis Pásara and Jorge Santistevan, " 'Industrial
Communities' and Trade Unions in Peru: A Preliminary Analysis,"
International Labour Review 108 (August–September 1973): 127–42;
David K. Eiteman, "Wealth Versus Ownership Share under the Peru-
vian Industrial Law," *Michigan State University Business Topics* 20
(Spring 1972): 59–70; and Peter T. Knight, "New Forms of Economic
Organization in Peru: Toward Workers' Self-Management," in Low-
enthal, ed., *Peruvian Experiment,* 350–401. Two advisers to the Velasco
government have discussed the theories behind the social property
concept and worker participation in other enterprises. See Jaroslav
Vanek, *The Participatory Economy: An Evolutionary Hypothesis and a
Strategy for Development* (Ithaca, N.Y.: Cornell University Press, 1971);
and Branko Horvat, "Modelo institucional de la economía socialista
autogestionaria," *El Trimestre Económico* 41 (January–March, 1974):
3–26. The Social Property Law is examined in A. Covarrubias and J.
Vanek, "Self-Management in the Peruvian Law of Social Property,"
Administration and Society 7 (May 1975): 55–64; Edvard Jorgensen,
"The Peruvian Social Property Law," *Harvard International Law Journal* 16 (Winter 1975): 132–55; and Mark O. Dickerson, "Peru Insti-
tutes Social Property as Part of Its 'Revolutionary Transformation',"
IAEA 29 (Winter 1975): 3–22.

 The effectiveness of the government's reforms in raising the living
standard of the nation's poor is reported in Adolfo Figueroa, "El
impacto de las reformas actuales sobre la distribución de ingresos en el
Perú," *Revista Interamericana de Planificación* 7 (June 1973): 45–63; and
Richard Webb, "Government Policy and the Distribution of Income in
Peru, 1963–1973," in Lowenthal, ed., *Peruvian Experiment,* 79–127.
On economic planning read Robert E. Klitgaard, "Observations on the

Peruvian National Plan for Development, 1971–1975," IAEA 25 (Winter 1971): 3–22; Luis J. Paz Silva, "La política de precios en la planificación del desarrollo agrario del Perú," *Revista Interamericana de Planificación* 9 (June 1975): 16–35; and Willy Bezold, Jorge Cabrera, and Helan Jaworski, "La planificación participante y la planificación de base en el Perú," *Revista Interamericana de Planificación* 9 (June 1975): 5–15. The armed forces followed the innovative path advocated in William Foote Whyte, "Imitation or Innovation: Reflections on the Institutional Development of Peru," *Administrative Science Quarterly* 13 (December 1968): 370–85.

A useful collection of essays concerning relations between the United States and Peru during recent years is Daniel A. Sharp, ed., *U.S. Foreign Policy and Peru* (Austin: University of Texas Press, 1972). Especially valuable studies found in this volume are Charles T. Goodsell, "Diplomatic Protection of U.S. Business in Peru," 237–57; and David C. Loring, "The Fisheries Dispute," 57–118. Other works on the 200-mile limit controversy are Arthur D. Martinez, "The Politics of Territorial Waters: 12 Miles or 200?" *Studies in Comparative International Development* 7 (Summer 1973): 213–23; David C. Edmonds, "The 200 Miles Fishing Rights Controversy: Ecology or Higher Tariffs?" IAEA 26 (Spring 1973): 3–18; and Sergio Teitelboim, "Los países del Pacífico Sur y el mar territorial," *Estudios Internacionales* 4 (April–June 1970): 38–59. The dispute between the United States and Peru over compensation for the IPC is treated in H. Leslie Robinson, "The Hickenlooper Amendment and the IPC," *Pacific Historian* 14 (Spring 1970): 22–51; Richard S. Olson, "Economic Coercion in International Disputes: The United States and Peru in the IPC Expropriation Dispute of 1968–1971," *Journal of Developing Areas* 9 no. 3 (1975): 395–413; Jessica Pernitz Einhorn, *Expropriation Politics* (Lexington, Mass.: Lexington Press, 1974); and George M. Ingram, *Expropriation of U.S. Property in South America: Nationalization of Oil and Copper Companies in Peru, Bolivia and Chile* (New York: Praeger, 1974).

Additional works about the diplomacy of the revolution include Robert H. Swansbrough, "Peru's Diplomatic Offensive: Solidarity for Latin American Independence," in Ronald G. Hellman and H. Jon Rosenbloom, eds., *Latin America: The Search for a New International Role* (New York: Halsted Press, 1975): 115–30; Richard W. Dye, "Peru, the United States and Hemisphere Relations," IAEA 26 (Autumn 1972): 69–87; Marcel Niedergang, "Revolutionary Nationalism in Peru," *Foreign Affairs* 49 (April 1971): 454–63; and Dale V. Slaght, "The New Realities of Ecuadorian-Peruvian Relations: A Search for Causes," IAEA 27 (Autumn 1973): 3–14. Concerning the Andean Group see David Morawetz, *The Andean Group: A Case Study in Economic Integration Among Developing Countries* (Cambridge, Mass.: MIT Press, 1974); Kenneth A. Switzer, "The Andean Group: A Reappraisal," IAEA 26

(Spring 1973): 69–81; Edward S. Milenky, "From Integration to Developmental Nationalism: The Andean Group, 1965–1971," IAEA 25 (Winter 1971): 77–91; Edward S. Milenky, "Developmental Nationalism in Practice: The Problems and Progress of the Andean Group," IAEA 26 (Spring 1973): 49–68; and "The Andean Group: A Progress Report," *Bank of London and South America Review* 8 (May 1974): 251–58.

The military regime's policies toward education are examined in Robert S. Drysdale and Robert G. Myers, "Continuity and Change: Peruvian Education," in Lowenthal, ed., *Peruvian Experiment,* 254–301; and a four-part study by Norman Gall, "Peru's Educational Reform," AUFS-WC 21, nos. 3–6 (1974). The Velasco administration's approach to urban problems is treated in David Collier, *Squatters and Oligarchs: Authoritarian Rule and Policy Change in Peru* (Baltimore: The Johns Hopkins University Press, 1976); and David Collier, "Squatter Settlements and Policy Innovation in Peru," in Lowenthal, ed., *Peruvian Experiment,* 128–78. Richard W. Patch, "The Peruvian Earthquake of 1970," AUFS-WC 18, nos. 6–9 (1971) is a grim pictorial report on that disaster.

The Velasco government's programs for popular participation in the revolution are discussed in James M. Malloy, "Authoritarianism, Corporatism and Mobilization in Peru," *Review of Politics* 36 (January 1974): 52–84; James M. Malloy, "Peru before and after the Coup of 1968," *Journal of Inter-American Studies and World Affairs* 14 (November 1972): 437–54; David Scott Palmer, "Revolution from Above: Military Government and Popular Participation in Peru" (Ph.D. diss., Cornell University, 1973); Carlos Delgado, "Sobre algunos problemas de la participación en la Revolución Peruana," *Estudios Internacionales* 6 (January–March 1973); 24–43; David Scott Palmer and Kevin Jay Middlebrook, "Corporatist Participation under Military Rule in Peru," in Chaplin, ed., *Peruvian Nationalism,* 428–53; and three essays in Lowenthal, ed., *Peruvian Experiment:* Susan C. Bourque and David Scott Palmer, "Transforming the Rural Sector: Government Policy and Peasant Response," 179–219; Julio Cotler, "The New Model of Political Domination in Peru," 44–78; and Jane S. Jaquette, "Belaúnde and Velasco: On the Limits of Ideological Politics," 402–37.

The military regime's relations with organized labor are treated in Aníbal Quijano, "La coyuntura política y las tareas de la clase obrera en el Perú," *Investigación Económica* 32 (October–December 1973): 789–810; and Adrian DeWind, "From Peasants to Miners: The Background to Strikes in the Mines of Peru," *Science & Society* 39 (Spring 1975): 44–72. Church-state relations under the revolution are analyzed in G. W. Grayson, "The Church and Military in Peru: From Reaction to Revolution," in Donald Eugene Smith, ed., *Religion and Political*

Modernization (New Haven, Conn., Yale University Press, 1974): 303–24; and Carlos A. Astiz, "The Catholic Church in Latin American Politics: A Case Study of Peru," in David H. Pollock and Arch R. M. Ritter, eds., *Latin American Prospects for the 1970's: What Kinds of Revolutions?* (New York: Praeger, 1973): 131–48.

The internal politics of the military establishment are discussed in Jane S. Jacquette, "Revolution by Fiat: The Context of Policy Making in Peru," *Western Political Quarterly* 25 (December 1972): 648–66; and Guillermo Thorndike, *No, mi General* (Lima: Mosca Azul Editores, 1976). Juan Velasco Alvarado, *La Revolución peruana* (Buenos Aires: Editorial Universitaria, 1973) is a compilation of speeches made by the president from June 1969 to May 1972. H. H. A. Cooper, "Peru's 'New Look' Judiciary," *Judicature* 55 (April 1972): 334–37, reports on the judicial reform.

Other valuable sources of information on contemporary Peru include the *Andean Times* (formerly the *Peruvian Times and Andean Air Mail),* an English-language weekly published in Lima emphasizing economic news; *Oiga*, a weekly Peruvian news magazine from Lima; the topical, highly illustrated *Caretas,* published fortnightly in Lima; *Latin America,* a weekly report published in London stressing political analysis; the *Times of the Americas,* a weekly newspaper from Washington devoted to Latin America; *Facts on File,* a conveniently indexed, weekly digest of news drawn from the major newspapers of the world; and *Hispano Americano,* a Mexican weekly news magazine whose "América de Polo a Polo" section regularly contains reports from Peru.

INDEX

Abancay, 214

Abascal, José de, 59

Acción Popular (AP): and 1962 election, 269–72; and 1963 election, 279–80; and PDC alliance, 279, 280–81, 285, 288; split in, 286, 288, 296, 298, 342; and pact with APRA, 298; and the Revolutionary Government of the Armed Forces, 342, 343, 353–55, 356

Acción Popular Socialista, 342, 343

Agrarian reform: need for, 16–20, 251–52; and 1920 constitution, 154; and APRA, 184, 192–94, 240–41, 267, 283–85, 309–10, 311; and the UR, 194; and Manuel Prado, 262–63; and Belaúnde, 269, 283–85, 286, 308; and the *dictablanda*, 277, 278, 284; and the Revolutionary Government of the Armed Forces, 308–12, 319–20, 324, 327, 345, 347–48, 349, 365, 368, 372

Agricultural Bank, 158, 212, 214, 313, 343

Agriculture: described, 3, 6, 8, 16–20; Inca, 28–29, 33, 38; origins of, 29–31; colonial, 53, 55; early republican, 73; mid-nineteenth century, 99–100, 102; post–War of the Pacific, 119, 121, 124–26, 176; and World War I, 138, 141, 176; in the Oncenio, 159–60; in the 1930s, 211, 212, 214, 216; and Manuel

Prado, 229, 261; and Odría, 251–52; and Belaúnde, 287; and the Revolutionary Government of the Armed Forces, 309, 312–13, 358, 359. *See also* Agrarian reform; Cooperatives; Indigenous communities; Irrigation; Tenant farmers

Agriculture, National School of, 121, 158

Air Force: *See* Armed forces

Allende, Salvador, 336, 360

Almagro, Diego de, 40

Alpacas, 3, 29, 33

Amauta (periodical), 179–80, 185, 186, 187

Amautas (Inca wise men), 29

Amazon Basin. *See* Montaña

Amazon River, 6, 74–75, 89, 102, 122, 170, 172, 214

American Smelting and Refining Corporation, 251, 318

American Tunaboat Association, 333–34

Anarchists: and labor, 139–40, 165, 166, 179; and González Prada, 144, 145

Ancash, 314

Ancón, 94

Ancón, Treaty of, 118, 168

Andean Group, 337, 360

Andean Times, 357

Andes, Federation of the, 66, 70

Andes Mountains, 1–2

Index

National Coalition, 255
National Democratic League, 249
National Democratic party, 150
National Election Board, 130, 134, 151, 209–10, 230, 257, 270, 271, 272
National Exhibition Palace, 93
National Front, 209, 210
National Front of Democratic Youth, 256
National Industrial Society, 126, 343
National Liberation Army (ELN), 285–86
National Liberation Front, 271, 276
National Library, 117, 145, 240
National Planning Institute (INP), 278, 324,
National Social Property Commission, 321, 322, 365
National Society of Agriculture, 124, 152, 343
National Tourism Corporation, 240
National Union party, 145
NATO (North Atlantic Treaty Organization), 265
Nauta, 89
Navy. *See* Armed forces
Nazca, 100, 316
New Deal, 231, 267
New Fatherland, 150, 153, 161
New Laws, 43
Newspapers. *See* Press, freedom of the
Nicaragua, 90, 167–68, 185
Niño, El, 8, 317
Nitrates: mining of, described, 100–101; and the War of the Pacific, 107–9, 112, 115, 117, 118, 119
Nixon, Richard M.: Latin American tour of Vice-President, 264, 265; administration of President, and Peru, 330–31, 335, 337, 338, 350
Nixon, Richard M., Mrs., 337
Noriega, Zenón, 255
Núñez Vela, Blasco, 40, 43

Obrajes, 45, 53, 55
O'Donavan barracks, 197, 198
Odría, Manuel A.: early career of, 224, 239, 241, 245, 247–48; repressive rule of, 248–50, 254–55, 370; corruption of, 248, 257, 268, 278; 1950 election of, 249; economic policies of, 250–52, 261; public works of, 251, 252, 254, 259; and labor, 252–54; social-welfare programs of, 252–54; and education, 254; and the armed forces, 254, 255, 259; and the 1956 election, 255–58; and the 1962 election, 268–69, 271–73, 275; pact of, with Haya, 272, 279–80; and 1963 election, 279–80; death of, 342. *See also* APRA; UNO
Odría, María Delgado de, 253, 268, 281
O'Higgins, Bernardo, 60, 71
Oiga, 352–53, 355, 357
Oligarchy: Civilistas identified with, 128, 150, 194; and the armed forces, 147, 297, 303, 304, 344–45, 352, 372–73; and APRA, 184, 195
Onassis, Aristotle Socrates, 333
ONDEPJOV (National Organism for the Development of the Young Towns), 326–27
Opinion Libre, 357
Orbegoso, Luis de, 70
Organization of American States (OAS), 225, 265, 294, 336
Oro, El, 224
Osores, Arturo, 190, 191, 195

Pacasmayo, 94
Pachacuti, 34
Pacific Steam Navigation Company, 88, 99
Paita, 88, 94, 99
Palma, Ricardo, 104
Pamplona, 327, 343
Panama: colonial, 42, 52–53, 54; con-

Rizo Patrón, Luis, 218
Roads: Inca, 36; in the early republic,
    73, 74; and Castilla, 88, 89; and
    Leguía, 158, 213; and Benavides,
    213–14; and Manuel Prado, 224,
    228, 261; and Odría, 251, 252,
    254; and Belaúnde, 282–83
Rockefeller, Nelson, 335
Rodil, José Ramón, 65
Rodríguez, Antonio, 218
Roosevelt, Franklin D., 213, 267
Rosas, Juan Manuel de, 72
Royal Commentaries of the Incas (Gar-
    cilaso de la Vega), 48
Rubber, 6, 122–24, 152, 170, 226
Ruiz Eldridge, Alberto, 343
Ruschenberger, William, 100
Russell, Bertrand, 37

SAIS (Agricultural Societies of Social
    Interest), 311–12
Salaverry, 94
Salaverry, Felipe, 70–71
Salomón-Lozano Treaty, 170–73,
    194, 199, 202
Samánez Ocampo, David, 190–91,
    212
Sánchez, Luis Alberto, 238, 245–46
Sánchez Cerro, Luis M.: ousts Leguía,
    173, 187–88, 234; early career of,
    188–89; first administration of,
    189–90; and the 1931 election,
    190–91, 194–96; second adminis-
    tration of, 196–200; assassination
    of, 200–201, 202, 207, 211; eco-
    nomic policies of, 211–12; men-
    tioned, 220, 243, 304
Sandino, Augusto César, 185
San Juan, 229, 251
San Juan, battle of, 116
San Lorenzo Island, 173, 177
San Marcos University: founded, 50;
    growth of, 87, 145; and Leguía,
    133, 150, 152, 163–64, 165–66;
    and university reform, 145–47,
    149, 150, 151, 163, 176–77; and

Sánchez Cerro, 190, 197; and Be-
    navides, 203, 209, 217–18; and
    APRA, 236–37, 238; and Nixon,
    264. *See also* Universities
San Martín, José de, 60–63, 73, 88
San Román, Miguel, 90–91
Santa Corporation, 229
Santa Cruz, Andrés, 67, 69, 70–72
Santa River Valley, 94, 229
Santiago Conference (1856), 90
Saya y manto, 105
Selva. See Montaña
Seoane, Edgardo, 269, 286, 288, 296,
    343
Seoane, Juan, 197
Seoane, Manuel, 177, 197, 235, 269,
    272, 279, 281
*Seven Interpretive Essays on Peruvian
    Reality* (Mariátegui), 180
77 Group, 336
Sierra: region described, 1–4
Sima-Perú, 314
SINADI (National System of Infor-
    mation), 352
Sinamos (National System of Support
    to Social Mobilization): creation of,
    346–47; functions of, 347–49; and
    political unrest, 348–49; decline of,
    357, 361, 362
Slaves: pre-Columbian, 32, 36; in the
    colony, 49–50, 57; in revolutionary
    armies, 60, 73, 76, 83; in constitu-
    tions, 68, 86; in guano pits, 82; Cas-
    tilla frees, 84, 98, 104; Indian, in
    the rubber industry, 123, 161
Social Democratic party, 210
Socialists: *See* Peruvian Socialist party
Social Progressive Movement, 271,
    343
Social Property Enterprises (EPS):
    created, 321–23; criticized, 343,
    353; and unions, 344; and eco-
    nomic problems, 358; new policies
    concerning, 361, 362, 365, 367,
    371
Social Security system: participants